RACINE AND ENGLISH CLASSICISM

RACINE
and English Classicism

KATHERINE E. WHEATLEY

AUSTIN
UNIVERSITY OF TEXAS PRESS
1956

Copyright © 1956 by the University of Texas Press
Copyright © renewed 1984
First paperback printing 2014

All rights reserved
Printed in the United States of America

Requests for permission to reproduce material from this work
should be sent to:
  Permissions
  University of Texas Press
  P.O. Box 7819
  Austin, TX 78713-7819
  http://utpress.utexas.edu/index.php/rp-form

Library of Congress Catalog Number 56–7395

ISBN 978-1-4773-0700-7, paperback
ISBN 978-1-4773-0701-4, library e-book
ISBN 978-1-4773-0702-1, individual e-book

THIS BOOK IS DEDICATED

IN AFFECTION AND ADMIRATION TO

PROFESSOR ERNEST J. VILLAVASO

IF I HAVE LEARNED TO THINK CLEARLY, IT WAS HE

WHO TAUGHT ME TO, IN THOSE NOW REMOTE

DAYS OF MY UNDERGRADUATE WORK AT

THE UNIVERSITY OF TEXAS

PREFACE

THERE is no thorough study of adaptations and translations of Racine's tragedies made in England during the neo-classical period. Dorothea Canfield, in her *Corneille and Racine in England*, has studied adaptations of Racine and of the two Corneilles, but she is more concerned with the stage history of the plays than with their relationship to the originals. In the case of adaptations of Racine, she notes only the most superficial and obvious alterations in plot and characters, without any regard for the loss of what is peculiarly Racinian. As she views them, these adaptations are Racinian tragedies and classical pieces. Their failure in England she explains thus: "Most sincere effort was put forth during two centuries by various authors and with various methods, to give to the literary world of one nation the beauties of the literary world of the other.... It [the movement of imitation of the French in general] is a striking exemplification of the truth that national taste is a natural organic growth and that no efforts, however competent and strenuous, can radically change its inherent nature." This conclusion, in so far as it applies to Racine, is based on two unwarranted assumptions: first, that adapters and translators were competent; and second, that they made a sincere effort to give England the beauties of Racine.

F. Y. Eccles, in his brief essay *Racine in England*, comments in passing on the English adaptations. He contradicts much that Miss Canfield has said. He finds less to admire than she, and he looks upon the adapters as "romantic cobblers" endeavoring to adapt Racine to the taste of the English public rather than as classicists making a sincere effort to reveal the beauties of Racine to the English. One translation which Miss Canfield has commended for fidelity to the original and praised as English poetry Eccles considers contemptible English poetry and as far away from the original as a translation could possibly be. Neither Eccles nor Canfield has viewed the adaptations in historical perspective. Neither has studied the relation of the adaptations to English neo-classical theory of tragedy.

Racinian influence in England during the neo-classical period, a period when French influence was supposedly very strong, needs to be thoroughly investigated. The movement of imitation of Racine has considerable historical importance. Two of the adaptations are only slightly less important than *Cato* and *Irene* in the history of English classical tragedy. The reputation of Edmund Smith's *Phaedra and Hippolitus* (1707) endured to the end of the eighteenth century, and at the end of the century, when "regular" tragedy had fallen into disfavor, one critic names this play along with *Cato* and *Irene* as the highest achievement of the English in a form alien to their national genius. A second adaptation of Racine, Ambrose Philips's *The Distrest Mother*, was the most successful of all adaptations of French classical pieces. A third, Thomas Otway's *Titus and Berenice*, has attracted the attention of critics of the nineteenth and twentieth centuries because of the revival of interest in Otway. Canfield and Eccles, as well as others, have left the impression that Otway's piece is a fairly close, though abridged, translation of Racine's *Bérénice*. This estimate of the relationship of the two plays is generally accepted. Such a view lends support to the legend that Otway is the most Racinian of English tragic poets.

It is possible that English translations and adaptations of Racine made during the seventeenth and eighteenth centuries had some influence on English opinion of Racine long after the movement of imitation of Racine had come to an end. These were the only English versions of Racine until 1850. Before that date any Englishman who could not read French must of necessity have formed his opinion of Racine from a perusal of these versions. He would have had little reason to suspect that they were wretched travesties of Racine, for, almost without exception, English critics had proclaimed the superiority of the English plays to their originals. It would be impossible to prove that any judgment of Racine was based on these translations rather than on the originals; but such an assumption would explain the puzzling ineptitude of many remarks on Racine. We find English writers attributing to him characteristics that any reader would be hard put to it to find in his plays but which are to be found in English

PREFACE

adaptations. Hazlitt, for instance, makes the following comments: "The genius of Shakespeare is dramatic, that of Scott narrative or descriptive, that of Racine is didactic. He gives, as I conceive, the commonplaces of the human heart, but nothing or very little more. He enlarges on a set of obvious sentiments and well-known topics with a considerable elegance of language and copiousness of declamation, but there is scarcely one stroke of original genius nor anything like imagination in his writings. He strings together a number of moral reflections, and instead of reciting them himself, puts them into the mouths of his *dramatis personae*, who talk well about their own situations and the general relations of human life. Instead of laying bare the heart of the sufferer with all its bleeding wounds and palpitating fibres, he puts into his hand a commonplace book, and he reads us a lecture from this. This is not the essence of drama, whose object and privilege it is to give us the extreme and subtle workings of the human mind in individual circumstances, to make us sympathize with the sufferer, or feel as we should feel in his circumstances, not to tell the indifferent spectator what the indifferent spectator could just as well tell him."

To anyone familiar with Racine's tragedies this criticism is incredibly wide of the mark. Racine has all the qualities which Hazlitt denies him and none of the defects with which he is charged. It would be difficult, if not impossible, to find as many as half a dozen moralizing generalizations on familiar themes in all Racine's tragedies put together. The ineptitude of these remarks leads Eccles, who quotes Hazlitt's comments, to suspect that Hazlitt had never read through one whole act of one tragedy of Racine with or without a dictionary. I believe that Hazlitt did read at least one of the English adaptations of Racine. It is even possible to name the likely one. Charles Johnson's *The Victim* has all the characteristics that Hazlitt wrongly attributes to Racine. It is probable that Hazlitt read this adaptation of *Iphigénie* with an occasional glance at the original. He later comments on a scene in this play and attempts to quote a hemistich, in French. He misquotes it, a fact which suggests a very cursory reading.

I am not sure that the seventeenth- and eighteenth-century versions of Racine in English have ceased, even now, to influence English opinion. Racine's latest English biographer, Geoffrey Brereton, in his *Jean Racine*, published in London in 1951, cites two of them to support his contention that Racine is untranslatable.

RACINE AND ENGLISH CLASSICISM

For these reasons I have undertaken to determine the exact relation to the originals of English adaptations and translations of Racine which were produced on the English stage in the course of the seventeenth and eighteenth centuries. I have made detailed comparisons, with particular attention to the loss or the deliberate elimination of the peculiar essence of Racine. In addition to the adaptations for the stage, I have studied two translations of *Britannicus* intended for reading and purporting to present Racine exactly as he is to the English reading public. The distortion of Racine in these two translations should indicate what qualities eluded the English, since there can be no question here of deliberate alteration of Racinian tragedy to please English audiences.

I have traced the development of Aristotelian formalism in England in order to show, on the one hand, the relation of English theory of tragedy to French classical doctrine and, on the other, the relation of English adaptations to English neo-classical theory of tragedy.

In studying the relation of English translations and adaptations to the originals, I discovered that detailed comparisons had, for me at any rate, a value that I had not anticipated when I began the work. They threw into relief the art of Racine and illumined it as no other approach had. This illumination of Racine's art became for me the most valuable result of my study. I hope that it may serve in some measure to illumine Racinian tragedy for anyone who may read it, as making it has for me.

Permission has been granted by the *Romanic Review* to reproduce in slightly altered form articles that originally appeared in that publication. The articles have been incorporated in Chapters V and VI.

KATHERINE E. WHEATLEY

Austin, Texas
January 15, 1956

CONTENTS

Preface   vii

PART I
RACINE IMPROVED

I	John Crowne and Racine	3
II	Thomas Otway's *Titus and Berenice*	26
III	*The Mourning Bride*	57
IV	Abel Boyer's *Achilles*	82
V	Edmund Smith and Racine	93
VI	*Andromaque* as the "Distrest Mother"	118
VII	Charles Johnson's *The Victim*	139
VIII	*The Sultaness*	154
IX	*The Fatal Legacy*	184
X	Two Translations of *Britannicus*	192

PART II
RACINE AND ENGLISH CLASSICISM

XI	Neo-Classical Theory of Tragedy in England, 1674–1699	215
XII	English Judgments of Racine, 1675–1699	261
XIII	Racine and the Critics, 1700–1721	274
XIV	Summary and Conclusion	285

Index   341

« « I » »
RACINE IMPROVED

« « CHAPTER I » »

JOHN CROWNE AND RACINE

LESS AUSPICIOUS CIRCUMSTANCES could hardly be imagined than those which attended the introduction of Racinian tragedy to the English public. The greatest tragic poet of France ran afoul of the wounded vanity of a second-rate English playwright who had tried to exploit him. In the summer of 1674 an anonymous translation of *Andromaque* was presented at the Duke's Theatre and was coldly received.[1] The play was attributed to John Crowne, then at the beginning of his career as a dramatist. This *Andromache* was printed in 1675 with a prefatory epistle, signed J. C., in which Crowne disclaims the authorship. He says:

"This Play was Translated by a young Gentleman, who has a great esteem of all French Playes, and particularly of this; and thinking it pity the Town should lose so excellent a Divertisement for want of a Translation, bestow'd his pains upon it; and it happening to be in my hands in the long Vacation, a time when the Play-houses are willing to catch at any Reed to save themselves from Sinking, to do the House a kindness, and serve the Gentleman, who it seem'd, was desirous to see it on the Stage, I willingly perused it, but found neither the Play to answer the Gentlemans Commendation, nor his Genius in Verse very fortunate, and yet neither of e'm so contemptible as to be wholly slighted; but neither the Gentleman nor my self, having leisure enough to make those Emendations, which both the Play and the Verse needed; I begged leave of him to turn it into Prose; which I obtained, and so it is in the condition you see. If the Play be barren of Fancy, you must blame the Original Author. I am as much inclined to be civil to Strangers as any Man; but then they must be Strangers of Merit. I

[1] "We may fix the summer of 1674 as the date of the production of *Andromache*." (Arthur Franklin White, *John Crowne, His Life and Dramatic Works* [Cleveland, 1922], p. 75.)

would no more be at the pains to bestow Wit (if I had any) on a *French* Play, than I would be at the Cost to bestow Cloaths on every shabby *French-Man* that comes over; for neither of e'm would have qualities to deserve my Charity. Yet that I prejudice not the Book-Seller, I will do him and the Play this right to say, that this of *French* Playes, is far from being the worst. It is much esteemed in France, and here too, by some *English* who are admirers of the *French* Wit, and think this suffered much in the Translation, I cannot tell in what, except in not bestowing Verse upon it, which I thought it did not deserve; for otherwise there is all that is in the *French* Play *verbatim*, and something more, as may be seen in the last Act, where what is only dully recited in the *French* Play, is there represented; which is no small advantage: but to let those Gentlemen, whoever they are, enjoy the felicity of their opinions, I will make bold to affirm, the Play deserved a better liking than it found; and had it been Acted in the good well meaning times, when the *Cid Heraclius* and other *French* Playes met such applause, this would have passed very well; but since our Audiences have tasted so plentifully the firm *English* Wit, these thin *Regalio's* will not down. This I thought good to say, both for the Play, and also in my own behalf, to clear myself of the scandal of this poor Translation, wherewith I was slandered, in spite of what the Prologue and Epilogue affirmed on the Stage in publick, which I wrote in the Translators name, that if the Play met with any success, he might wholly take to himself a Reputation, of which I was not in the least ambitious."

The play is not entirely in prose as Crowne's remarks would lead us to believe. The scene in Act IV in which Hermione commands Orestes to murder Pyrrhus begins with a passage in prose interlarded with heroic couplets. This is followed by a dialogue which is a mixture of couplets and blank verse. From this point on there is no more prose.

Comments on the hybrid form of the play and on Crowne's preface comprise the bulk of the criticism which has been devoted to the first English adaptation of Racine. Dorothea Canfield thinks the preface "the most interesting part of the production, as it is full of side-lights on the way in which people of Crowne's standing regarded the great French dramatists."[2] Arthur Franklin White agrees and is even more

[2] *Corneille and Racine in England* (New York, Columbia University Press, 1904), p. 90.

sweeping in his inferences. He thinks that Crowne's preface "reveals the current English attitude towards French tragedy."[3] In view of the dearth of English critical comment on Racine, it is a temptation to make much of so unequivocal a judgment as Crowne's; but it seems to me a bit rash to assume that insolent contempt was the typical English attitude of the period towards all French tragedy.[4] The virulence of Crowne's strictures on Racine would incline one rather, it seems to me, to believe his statement that Racine's *Andromaque* was esteemed by "some *English* who are admirers of the *French* Wit, and think this suffered much in the Translation." Such criticism of Crowne, coming on the heels of the play's failure, might well account for the viciousness of his attack on Racine.

On the other hand, Crowne never showed a high regard for truth when he was on the defensive.[5] We might with justification ask: Did Crowne invent the young Racine enthusiast whose translation he tells us he polished up for the theatre during the dull season? Is the whole of the translation Crowne's work? If so, why did he write the first three acts in prose and the last two in verse? If Crowne really did make over into prose a verse translation which had been submitted to him, why didn't he complete the work? No one has questioned the veracity of Crowne's account of his part in the translation. It has been assumed that he did actually put into prose the verse translation of some unknown person.

Two conjectures have been offered in answer to the last question. White thinks Crowne may have retained the best of the "young Gentleman's" verse.[6] Miss Canfield attributes the vestiges of poetry to carelessness and indifference.[7] No one has attempted to answer the other questions. Nor has anyone made a careful comparison of the verse of the play with the portions in prose and with the original French. White

---

[3] White, *op. cit.*, p. 73.

[4] For Thomas Otway's attitude toward Racine, see below, Chap. II.

[5] White (*op. cit.*, p. 109) calls attention to Crowne's brazen denial of his obvious debt to Shakespeare in the prologue to his *Miseries of Civil War*.

[6] A satisfactory explanation of this unusual mixture of prose and couplets in the same play is not easy to find, but it may be that the couplet scenes represent those parts of the work of the "young Gentleman" which were not "so contemptible as to be wholly slighted." One might suggest, also, that the summer company demanded the play for production before Crowne had completed his prose rendering. (White, *op. cit.*, p. 76.)

[7] *Op. cit.*, p. 90.

calls the play a "reasonably literal but bald and uneven translation of the French play."[8] Miss Canfield says: "The superlative degree of badness which is attained at the beginning of this translation is kept up throughout."[9]

Miss Canfield's judgment would not be too severe if she had applied it to the prose portions only. The parts which are in verse are, it seems to me, immeasurably superior to the prose, and, as English translations of Racine go, decidedly not the worst. They will even stand comparison with the most successful of all English adaptations of Racine, Ambrose Philips's *The Distrest Mother*, a play which held the boards for a century, enjoyed a great reputation in its day, and has even called forth some praise in our own.[10] The "young Gentleman's" translation is throughout a more faithful rendering of Racine than Philips's and not a few passages are at least the equal of the corresponding passages in Philips's play by any standard. Here, for instance, is one passage in which both follow Racine closely. Hermione sends her confidante to tell Oreste that Pyrrhus must know that it is she, Hermione, who has commanded his death (vss. 1267–70):

> Va le trouver: dis-lui qu'il apprenne à l'ingrat
> Qu'on l'immole à ma haine, et non pas à l'Etat.
> Chère Cléone, cours: ma vengeance est perdue
> S'il ignore en mourant que c'est moi qui le tue.[11]

Crowne's "young Gentleman" renders the speech (p. 32):

> Run, find him!—Bid him tell the ungratefull man
> From whence, from whom it is he meets his fate,
> He's sacrificed to me, and not the state.
> The pleasure of Revenge all lost would be,
> If dying, he knows not he is slain by me.

Philips translates (p. 40):

> Oh, would *Orestes*, when he gives the Blow,

---

[8] *Op. cit.*, p. 75.
[9] *Op. cit.*, p. 92.
[10] Allardyce Nicoll says of Philips's *The Distrest Mother*: "The tragedy as a whole is a good one; the characters of Andromache and Pyrrhus are well drawn, making up for a certain stiffness in those of Hermione and Orestes." (*A History of Early Eighteenth Century Drama* [Cambridge, 1929], pp. 86–87.)
[11] References are to the Mesnard edition (Grands Ecrivains).

> Tell him he dyes my Victim!—haste *Cleone*;
> Charge him to say, *Hermione's* Resentments
> Not those of *Greece*, have sentenced him to Death.
> Haste my *Cleone*! My Revenge is lost,
> If *Pyrrhus* knows not that he dyes by me![12]

If economy and energy are qualities of style to be commended, it must be admitted that "he's sacrificed to me and not the state" is superior to "*Hermione's* Resentments,/ Not those of *Greece*, have sentenced him to Death." Certainly the sharpness and simplicity and the natural flow of the unknown translator's verse convey more effectively Hermione's fury than does Philips's tortuous word order.

Even when following Racine closely, Philips discards certain features of Racine's style which the unknown translator of the first *Andromache* imitates. The latter is apparently aware of the importance of verbs in Racine's swiftly flowing Alexandrines. Philips prefers adjectives and nouns. Hermione's anger at Oreste for demurring when she has commanded him to assassinate Pyrrhus, Racine expresses thus (vss. 1232-40):

> Ah! c'en est trop, Seigneur.
> Tant de raisonnements offensent ma colère.
> J'ai voulu vous donner les moyens de me plaire,
> Rendre Oreste content; mais enfin je vois bien
> Qu'il veut toujours se plaindre et ne mériter rien.
> Partez: allez ailleurs vanter votre constance,
> Et me laissez ici le soin de ma vengeance.
> De mes lâches bontés mon courage est confus.
> Et c'est trop en un jour essuyer de refus.

Philips translates this passage (p. 39):

> You but mock my rage!
> I was contriving how to make you happy.
> Think you to merit by your idle Sighs;
> And not attest your Love by one brave Action!
> Go! with your boasted Constancy! and leave
> *Hermione* to execute her own Revenge!
> I blush to think how my too easie Faith
> Has twice been baffled in one shameful Hour.

"Idle Sighs," "boasted Constancy," and "one brave Action" all replace

---

[12] References are to the first edition (London, 1712).

verbs, and Philips adds a superfluous adjective to his translation of
en un jour, which becomes "one shameful Hour." Note that the unknown translator retains the verbs (pp. 31–32):

> I hate so many reasonings—here I offer you
> Occasion to oblige and please me—
> But I perceive what to expect from you.
> You always would complain, but nothing do.
> Be gone, and boast your constancy elsewhere.
> Leave to my self the care of my revenge!
> I am ashamed I did descend to ask you.

While it cannot be said that the unknown translator's verse is everywhere the equal of Philips's, his translation certainly comes closer to rendering Racinian psychology. Take, for instance, Hermione's final denunciation of Oreste (vss. 1554–64):

> Qui t'amène en des lieux où l'on fuit ta présence?
> Voilà de ton amour le détestable fruit:
> Tu m'apportois, cruel, le malheur qui te suit.
> C'est toi dont l'ambassade, à tous les deux fatale,
> L'a fait pour son malheur pencher vers ma rivale.
> Nous le verrions encore nous partager ses soins;
> Il m'aimeroit peut-être, il le feindroit du moins.
> Adieu. Tu peux partir. Je demeure en Epire;
> Je renonce à la Grèce, à Sparte, à son empire,
> A toute ma famille; et c'est assez pour moi,
> Traître, qu'elle ait produit un monstre comme toi.

Philips translates this passage (p. 52):

> What had your rash, officious *Greeks*, dire Blood-Hounds,
> To do with my Revenge? What drew you hither,
> To bring on me the vengeful Woes that haunt you?
> Are these the Fruits of your detested Love?
> Your fatal Embassy, your hateful Presence,
> Drove *Pyrrhus* to my Rival; and destroys
> Both him and me.—He might have loved me still,
> Had you ne'er interposed. Avant! Be gone!
> And leave me in *Epirus*.—I renounce
> My Friends, my Country, *Greece*, and all Mankind:
> But chiefly I renounce Thee! Monster, Thee!

The unknown translator has (p. 44):

JOHN CROWNE AND RACINE

> Why camst thou hither, where we hate thy sight?
> See thy Loves cursed fruit!—I find too late,
> Thou camest to taint me with thy wretched fate.
> To shed the plagues that follow thee, on me,
> And all of us may curse thy Embassie.
> Be gone!—I here will stay, and I proclaim,
> I *Sparta, Greece*, and all my friends disclaim.
> Renounce my family, which curst must be,
> That such a Master [*sic*] has produc'd as thee.

Philips's thoughtless substitution of "all Mankind" for "toute ma famille" changes Hermione's revulsion of feeling towards Orestes into general misanthropy. If we assume, as I think we may, that "Master" is a misprint for "Monster," the unknown translator's lines come closer to adequate translation of the last terrible peripety in Racine's drama of the perfidy and cruelty of love. It can be said for his style that it has an evenness of texture that is lacking in Philips's. He does not try to whip up colloquial diction with such metaphors as Philips's "dire Blood-Hounds."

The unknown translator is, however, guilty of some heresies against Racine. The improvement of which Crowne boasts in his preface has often been commented on—the spectacle of the wedding ceremony and the assassination of Pyrrhus. I shall not dwell on this change except to say that it is effected without loss or alteration of Racine's dialogue.[13]

---

[13] Act V opens with Hermione's soliloquy. Claeone enters and Hermione questions her about the wedding procession and Orestes' intentions. The sound of trumpets and shouts is heard. The procession is moving toward the temple. Hermione, fearing that Orestes may disobey her, prepares to go to the temple to execute her vengeance herself, just as she does in Racine. But in Racine's tragedy she is interrupted by Orestes' entrance. He has already executed her orders. In the English version the scene shifts to the temple. We witness the ceremony. Pyrrhus crowns Andromache and proclaims Astyanax king of Troy. At this the Greeks rush upon him and kill him at the altar. They drag his body out of the temple by one door while Orestes starts for another with Andromache. As they are about to leave the temple, Hermione enters, poignard in hand. Andromache speaks Racine's lines (those of the earlier editions). There follows Hermione's denunciation of Orestes and her exit with Andromache, as in Racine. Orestes realizes the full horror of his deed; Pylades urges him to flee as they will be pursued by Pyrrhus's soldiers commanded by Andromache. Orestes wants to follow Hermione; but learns of her death when the Greek soldiers, retreating to the temple, carry in the bodies of Hermione and Pyrrhus. Orestes' madness sets in. The Greeks are attacked in the temple by Phoenix and Pyrrhus's guard; but escape to their ships taking Orestes with them. Andromache enters leading Astyanax and makes the closing speech.

RACINE AND ENGLISH CLASSICISM

Two other changes in the dénouement have gone unnoticed. They are slight but they seem to me to have some significance. The author introduces a touch of the macabre reminiscent of the ending of *Romeo and Juliet*. The bodies of Hermione and of Pyrrhus are brought in and Orestes' attack of madness comes on as he gazes at them. Racine's "L'un et l'autre en mourant je les veux regarder" (vs. 1623) becomes "In spite of e'm I'll sleep by e'm in death" (p. 47). The play does not end with Orestes' delirium as Racine's does. The translator anticipates Philips by having Andromache come back after the Greeks have fled with Orestes. As in Philips she speaks the final lines—but with a difference. The translator maintains here the tragic tone, while Philips contrives a semblance of a happy ending; his Andromache rejoices that Providence has found a way to rescue the innocent.[14]

There is one other significant change in this part of the play. The translator shares the English distaste for long speeches, a distaste which is more justifiable than the methods usually employed to remedy the supposed defect. This translator uses the aside to break up the long tirades in the Pyrrhus-Hermione scene. Pyrrhus's asides in this scene are particularly noteworthy, for he explains his motivation for the benefit of the audience. Hermione's famous ironical tirade is cut by two asides from Pyrrhus. First he says: "The Storm (as I desir'd) begins to rise," and later (p. 34):

---

[14] The final tirade of the first *Andromache* is entirely original with the translator:

> Ye Gods! what mysteries of fate are these,
> That I should here revenge my enemies?
> The fierce revenger of his death become,
> Who should have dyed upon my Husbands Tomb.
> Come Child from this unhappy place let's fly!
> But whither shall we leave our misery.
> Who to the unfortunate will kind appear,
> The wretched are unwelcome everywhere.
> On the wide Sea we rove where Tempests roar,
> And are forbid to Land on every shore.
> All the Estates of *Greece* are not asham'd,
> Gainst a poor Infant to have Wars proclaim'd.
> And all the help our wretched fate affords,
> Is but to fly from them to seek new Lords.

For a discussion of the last tirade of *The Distrest Mother*, see below, Chap. VI. For Samuel Richardson's severe but judicious comments on this ending, see below, Chap. VI.

JOHN CROWNE AND RACINE

> How pleasing to my ears these discords be,
> The jarring sounds increase my harmony.

When Hermione protests that she loves him, Pyrrhus tells the audience (p. 36):

> To pity I begin—
> But I'm afraid shall still pursue my sin.

Apparently Pyrrhus has come to Hermione in order to provoke her to anger and thus absolve himself from blame.

Despite these departures from Racine, I think it can be said that the last part of the first English translation of Racine is the work of someone who knew the French language thoroughly and who had a keener appreciation of Racinian psychology than most English translators. He had, too, some feeling for Racine's style. I should describe him as a man who had a fairly accurate conception of the essential characteristics of Racinian tragedy but who lacked the poetic gift to execute a wholly satisfactory English version.

If Crowne really changed into prose the first three acts of such a translation, he did Racine no favor. The prose is as stilted and verbose as the dialogue of a Victorian melodrama and wholly lacking in affective value. For instance, where Racine's Hermione says to Oreste (vss. 477-80):

> Le croirai-je, Seigneur, qu'un reste de tendresse
> Vous fasse ici chercher une triste princesse?
> Ou ne dois-je imputer qu'à votre seul devoir
> L'heureux empressement qui vous porte à me voir?

Crowne has:

Sir, may I believe any remains of your past friendship has suspended the publick cares wherewith Greece has laden you? or is it only to common respect and the duty of your imployment I must impute the honor of this visit? (p. 13)

But a careful examination of the prose translation shows that it was not based on an accurate verse translation such as we find in Acts IV and V. It is almost certainly translated directly from the original by someone whose knowledge of French was rudimentary. Many passages are obvious mistranslations of French. In a number Racine's meaning is entirely lost. Sometimes the English passage makes no sense at all but shows unmistakable traces of the original French, for all the world like the version of a sophomore of less than average intelligence. Any teacher of French will recognize at once this type of translation.

The turning point of the play, for instance, is completely garbled: In Racine, Andromaque has begged Hermione to intercede with Pyrrhus to dissuade him from surrendering Astyanax to the Greeks. Hermione has ironically suggested that she appeal directly to Pyrrhus (vss. 885-86):

> Vos yeux assez longtemps ont régné sur son âme.
> Faites-le prononcer: j'y souscrirai, madame.

Andromaque says to Céphise, her confidante (vs. 887):

> Quel mépris la cruelle attache à ses refus!

Whereupon Céphise urges her to act upon the advice that Hermione had offered ironically (vss. 888-90):

> Je croirois ses conseils, et je verrois Pyrrhus.
> Un regard confondroit Hermione et la Grèce . . .
> Mais lui-même il vous cherche.

This dialogue becomes in Crowne's version:

ANDROM. What contempt does she add to her refusal? [*sic*]
CEPH. Perhaps she may abate of this humour; I saw *Pyrrhus* and methought one regard mixt *Hermione* and *Greece*; but see, he comes in person to seek you. (p. 22)

After Pyrrhus's entrance Céphise continues to urge the despairing Andromaque to beg Pyrrhus himself not to yield Astyanax to the Greeks (vss. 895-96):

CÉPHISE
Qu'attendez-vous, rompez ce silence obstiné.

ANDROMAQUE
Il a promis mon fils.

CÉPHISE
Il ne l'a pas donné.

ANDROMAQUE
Non, non, j'ai beau pleurer, sa mort est résolue.

Crowne translates:

CEPH. What, Madam, do you wait for? force this obstinate Silence.[15]
ANDROM. He promised me my Son.
CEPH. But he has not performed his promise.
ANDROM. No, he has resolved his death. (p. 23)

If Crowne had been following an accurate verse translation, he might deliberately have altered Racine's meaning but he would hardly have written utter nonsense or the exact opposite of Racine's sense.[16]

The contrast between the accuracy of the verse translation and the gross inaccuracy of the prose suggests the following explanation of the genesis of the first English translation of Racine: John Crowne came by a fragment of a translation of *Andromaque*. An amateur of Racine, who knew French perfectly, had tried his hand at translating parts of *Andromaque*. He had got no further than experimentation with different verse forms. He had chosen to translate first the most highly dramatic scenes, those of Acts IV and V. He had started at the dénouement and had worked backwards, leaving only scattered couplets of

---

[15] In the 1668 edition, vs. 895 reads: "Qu'attendez-vous? *forcez* ce silence obstiné." Italics mine.

[16] It is sometimes difficult to distinguish deliberate alteration from mistranslation; but there are at least a score of mistranslations which are obviously the result of ignorance of the French language. Crowne cannot tell one tense from another; he cannot find the antecedent of a pronoun because the rule of agreement means nothing to him; he does not distinguish the relatives *qui* and *que*; he is baffled by pleonastic *ne*; common idioms are mysteries to him; he sometimes shows ignorance of the meaning of words where the syntax presents no difficulty. Here are a few examples (vss. 416, 420–21, 684, 695–96, 556; pp. 12, 17, 30, 18, 14):

> Ah! je l'ai trop aimé pour ne le point haïr.
> And yet I fear I have loved him too well, ever to hate him cordially.
>
> Cléone, avec horreur je m'en veux séparer
> Il n'y travaillera que trop bien, l'infidèle.
> With horrour I go to separate from him. It will be too much to his satisfaction. The unfaithful man endeavors that too much.
>
> Mon coeur court après elle et cherche à s'apaiser.
> I shall still seek to appease her.
>
> Ah! courez, et craignez que je ne vous rappelle.
> . . . run, and do not fear, I shall recall you.
>
> Que de pleurs vont couler!
> De quel nom sa douleur me va-t-elle appeler!
> Let her weep and call me by what name she please.
>
> Cruelle, c'est donc moi qui vous méprise ici?
> . . . it is me whom you thus contemn.

translation of the first part of Act IV.[17] The manuscript of this unfinished experiment having found its way into Crowne's hands, Crowne decided to utilize it for the theatre during the dull season. He therefore undertook to translate into prose directly from the French the remainder of Racine's tragedy, even filling in with prose the gaps which the original translator had left in Act IV.[18] It seems likely that the young Racine enthusiast is no fiction but that he brought Crowne only a fragment of translation. Crowne preferred not to admit entire responsibility for the prose translation and accordingly pretended that he had done over into prose an unsatisfactory verse translation of the whole of Racine's tragedy. The fact that it did not occur to him to disclaim all responsibility is evidence that he had some part in the translation. As he did try to make a literal translation, he might well have been sincere in his assertion that the English translation contains "all that is in the *French* play *verbatim*." People are seldom aware of the extent of their ignorance of a foreign language until they have learned more about it than Crowne knew about the French language when he made this assertion.

[17] Eight years before the presentation of Crowne's *Andromache*, Saint-Évremond had written to Corneille: "M. Waller, un des plus beaux esprits du siècle, attend toujours vos pièces nouvelles, et ne manque pas d'en traduire un acte ou deux en vers anglois pour sa satisfaction particulière." (G. Lanson, *Choix de lettres du XVII⁰ siècle*, pp. 453–54.) It is not unreasonable to suppose that there were still English gentlemen who liked to try their hand at translating fragments of French plays as Waller had done; and that it was one of these fragmentary translations that Crowne used for his *Andromache*.

[18] In the scene where prose and verse are mixed, there is the same contrast between the accuracy of the verse and the inaccuracy of the prose (vss. 1173–78, p. 30):

      HERMIONE
    Hé quoi? votre haine chancelle?
  Ah! courez, et craignez que je ne vous rappelle.
  N'alléguez point des droits que je veux oublier;
  Et ce n'est pas à vous à le justifier.

      ORESTE
  Moi, je l'excuserois? Ah! vos bontés, Madame,
  Ont gravé trop avant ses crimes dans mon âme.

HERM. What! does your hate languish? run, and do not fear, I shall recall you, regard not you the rights which I forget.
  I have resolved revenge, and he shall dye,
  'Tis not for you his deeds to justifie.
OREST. I justifie him: Your bounties too [*sic*] him have long since engraven his crimes in my Soul.

JOHN CROWNE AND RACINE

While ignorance of French plays an important part in the unfortunate alterations of Racine's tragedy, some changes have been made deliberately in the prose portions. These changes are significant because they follow patterns which will recur not only in the later translation of *Andromaque* but in translations of others of Racine's tragedies. Crowne cuts Orestes' long speeches in the exposition with brief remarks from Pylades. He makes Pylades a sort of nodder who now and then asks a polite question or makes a comment to show he is listening. For instance:

> OREST. It seems confused murmurs fill all *Greece*, and *Pyrrhus* on every side is threatened, they complaining that he, forgetting both his alliance and promise, protects and educates in his Court, the young publick Enemy of Greece.
> PYLAD. *Astyanax*, the unfortunate Infant, Son of Hector?
> OREST. The same. (p. 3)

Nothing is accomplished by this method except to call attention to the English aversion to long speeches.

Misunderstanding of French and insensitiveness to the emotional implications of Racine's dialogue combine to eliminate all drama from several scenes. Excision, mistranslation, and deliberate alteration destroy the dramatic clash between Pyrrhus and Andromache in their first meeting. The transformation is effected chiefly by omitting or altering every line in which Andromache goads Pyrrhus to fury by implying that he is persecuting her with deliberate cruelty. In Racine, when Andromaque enters, Pyrrhus foolishly betrays his delight at the thought that she may be seeking him (vss. 258–59):

> Me cherchiez-vous, madame?
> Un espoir si charmant me seroit-il permis?

He is rewarded with (vss. 260–62, italics mine):

> Je passois jusqu'aux lieux où l'on garde mon fils.
> *Puisqu'une fois le jour vous souffrez que je voie*
> Le seul bien qui me reste et d'Hector et de Troie.

Crowne omits the verse in italics.

Stung by this rebuff and the insinuation of unnecessary cruelty directed at her, Racine's Pyrrhus hints at a greater threat to Andromaque's happiness, a threat coming from the Greeks. Andromaque's reply carries another bitter thrust at Pyrrhus (vss. 266–67):

> Et quelle est cette peur dont leur coeur est frappé,
> Seigneur? *Quelque Troyen vous est-il échappé?*

This is entirely lost in Crowne's "Why, sir, what new anger does possess 'em?"

Pyrrhus explains that the Greeks fear Hector's heir. Andromaque replies (vss. 279–82, italics mine):

> Hélas! on ne craint point qu'il venge un jour son père;
> On craint qu'il n'essuyât les larmes de sa mère.
> Il m'auroit tenu lieu d'un père et d'un époux;
> Mais il me faut tout perdre, *et toujours par vos coups.*

The last two verses are lost in Crowne's translation: "Is it I that make him criminal? It is through him that they seek to wound me; the pretence is against him, but the hate to me" (p. 9). These thrusts of Andromaque exasperate Pyrrhus, and finally bring forth his threat (vss. 365–72, italics mine):

> Oui, mes voeux ont trop loin poussé leur violence
> Pour ne plus s'arrêter que dans l'indifférence;
> *Songez-y bien: il faut désormais que mon coeur,*
> *S'il n'aime avec transport, haïsse avec fureur.*
> Je n'épargnerai rien dans ma juste colère:
> Le fils me répondra des mépris de la mère;
> La Grèce le demande; et je ne prétends pas
> Mettre toujours ma gloire à sauver des ingrats.

The verses in italics have no equivalent in Crowne and the last verse is mistranslated and weakened by the unaccountable intrusion of the word "perhaps," thus: "I perhaps shall not expose my glory to save the ingrateful" (p. 10). Andromaque accepts his harsh decree but not without another bitter thrust at him (vss. 373, 377–80, italics mine):

> Hélas! il mourra donc! (vs. 373)
> . . . .
> Je prolongeois pour lui ma vie et ma misère;
> Mais enfin sur ses pas j'irai revoir son père.
> Ainsi tous trois, seigneur, *par vos soins réunis,*
> Nous vous . . .

Again Crowne omits Andromache's barb for Pyrrhus. He translates: "And with him I shall go visit his Father, from whose Heroick shade I have been long absent in life with much impatience." (pp. 10–11)

When Crowne omits from this scene "il faut désormais que mon coeur,/ S'il n'aime avec transport, haïsse avec fureur," we suspect that he may not quite understand the equivalence of love and hate which gives rise to the peripeties of Racine's tragedy. This suspicion is confirmed in Hermione's first scene. Her confidante advises her to see Oreste and prepare to leave Epirus. She is a little skeptical of Hermione's professed hatred for Pyrrhus, and she reveals her skepticism in her question: "Ne m'avez-vous pas dit que vous le haïssiez?" (vs. 412). It is to this skepticism that Hermione reacts, and her protestations are all the more violent because she herself does not know whether she loves or hates Pyrrhus (vss. 413–16):

> Si je le hais, Cléone! Il y va de ma gloire,
> Après tant de bontés dont il perd la mémoire.
> Lui qui me fut si cher, et qui m'a pu trahir!
> Ah! je l'ai trop aimé pour ne le point haïr.

Cléone then tries to force her to a decision: "Fuyez-le donc, madame." Hermione temporizes with Cléone and with herself (vss. 418–21):

> Ah! laisse à ma fureur le temps de croître encore!
> Contre mon ennemi laisse-moi m'assurer;
> Cléone, avec horreur je m'en veux séparer.
> Il n'y travaillera que trop bien, l'infidèle.

She is trying to hide both from Cléone and from herself her real motive in wishing to remain in Epirus, the hope that Pyrrhus may return to her. Cléone relentlessly unmasks her motive: "Il vous auroit déplu s'il pouvoit vous déplaire" (vs. 426). And Hermione admits: "Je crains de me connaître en l'état où je suis." (vs. 428)

Crowne eliminates the skepticism in the confidante's question, which he translates: "You have confessed to me you hate him." To this Hermione replies with the following calm self-analysis: "I know not *Claeone*, if I may trust my heart or no. My sense of glory, and his base ingratitude, stir me violently. He that was so dear to me, thus to betray me! And yet I fear I have loved him too well, ever to hate him cordially" (p. 12). Here two essential characteristics of the Racinian psychology of love are lost, the tendency to self-deception and the kinship of love and hate. And with them goes all the drama of the scene in the original, as well as the foreshadowing of the catastrophe.

We could scarcely expect Crowne to appreciate the affective values of Racine's style when he obviously knew so little French that he frequently missed the meaning of Racine's lines. But there is one feature of Racine's style which he rejects so systematically that one suspects distaste for it. It should be noted, for later translators also reject it. This is the use of questions, in colloquial diction, to convey a speaker's emotion. For instance, the force of Oreste's ironic reproach to Hermione is weakened by the loss of Racine's questions (vss. 555–60):

> Poursuivez! il est beau de m'insulter ainsi:
> Cruelle, c'est donc moi qui vous méprise ici?
> Vos yeux n'ont pas assez éprouvé ma constance?
> Je suis donc un témoin de leur peu de puissance?
> Je les ai méprisés? Ah! qu'ils voudroient bien voir
> Mon rival comme moi mépriser leur pouvoir!

Crowne has:

Pursue! Pursue!—You do well to insult over me thus cruel!—it is me whom you thus contemn, who have not given proofs enough of my constancy. I am a witness indeed of the little power of your beauty, which I have always despised. Ah! that for your own satisfaction my rival contemned it in the manner that I do. (p. 14)

Hermione's impatience at having her joyous effusions interrupted by her disconsolate rival is cast by Racine in the form of two questions (vss. 857–58):

> Dieux! ne puis-je à ma joie abandonner mon âme?
> Sortons! que lui dirois-je?

Crowne translates: "Gods! I cannot forsake my joy to entertain her. Let us go. I have nothing to say to her." (p. 22)[19]

Lovers of Racine may find a grain of comfort in the fact that Crowne's bumptiousness did not deprive them of a more than passable

---

[19] Philips rejects the same device of Racine's rhetoric of passion:

> Dieux! ne puis-je à ma joie abandonner mon âme?
> Sortons. Que lui dirois-je?

becomes (p. 28):

> I would indulge the Gladness of my Heart.
> Let us retire: Her Grief is out of Season.

He omits Oreste's ironical speech.

For further discussion of the loss of irony, the distaste for interrogation in Philips's translation, and the rejection of interrogation in other translations of Racine, see below, Chap. VI.

translation of the whole of *Andromaque,* for it is likely that he preserved all the work of the young gentleman who so admired Racine's tragedy. But Crowne's claim that his version of *Andromache* contains all that is in the original verbatim is the most wryly ironical of many ironical circumstances attending Racine's fortunes in England.

Despite his low opinion of Racine, Crowne again tried to exploit the French dramatist, in *The Destruction of Jerusalem,* Part II, which was produced in 1677, some time after Otway's *Titus and Berenice.* When he published his play (1677), he denied any debt to Racine and referred contemptuously to Otway's imitation of *Bérénice*:

> ... Some persons accused me of stealing the parts of Titus and Berenice from the French play written by Mr. Racine on the same subject; but a gentleman having lately translated that play, and exposed it to public view on the stage, has saved me that labour, and vindicated me better than I can my self. I wou'd not be asham'd to borrow, if my occasion compell'd me, from any rich author: But all foreign coin must be melted down, and receive a new stamp, if not an addition of metal, before it will pass current in England, and be judged sterling: That borrowing or stealing from Mr. Racine could not have supplied my occasions; but I am not so necessitous yet, nor have lived so prodigally on my small stock of poetry to be put so soon to those miserable shifts.[20]

Crowne's imitation of scenes from *Bérénice* is not close enough, verbally, to offer any evidence that might either support or refute my theory of his part in the translation of *Andromaque.* But the use he made of material from *Bérénice* serves to show what kind of emendation Racine's plays needed in his opinion. The scenes from *Bérénice* are scattered through the play. The scene shifts back and forth between Jerusalem and the Roman camp outside the city, where Berenice, the Jewish queen, awaits the outcome of the siege. Titus is wavering between his love for Berenice and his "gloire," as in Racine. The scenes in the Roman camp are concerned with the parting of Titus and Berenice and are all suggested by scenes from Racine's play. The parallelism will be obvious from the following summary: Tiberias, commander of the Roman army under Titus, urges Titus to dismiss Berenice. Titus tries to tell Berenice they must part but cannot bring himself to utter the words and leaves her abruptly to avoid her questions. An

---

[20] *The Dramatic Works of John Crowne,* with Prefatory Memoir and Notes, ed. James Maidment and W. H. Logan (London, 1873), II, 238.

ally of Titus's declares his love and Berenice rejects him. After this declaration it occurs to her that Titus's evasiveness and coldness may be due to jealousy. A friend of Titus's delivers the message of banishment to Berenice. She refuses to believe him. Titus himself confirms the message. Berenice threatens suicide but finally gives Titus up for the sake of his honor. In addition to this similarity in the action, there are verbal echoes scattered here and there throughout these scenes.

Crowne displays a perverse ingenuity in destroying the qualities and exaggerating the defects of Racine's tragedy. Having followed Racine rather closely in the first interview between Titus and Berenice, i.e., Titus's unsuccessful attempt to tell Berenice of his decision, Crowne adds a scene in which the very same thing happens all over again—Titus tries to tell Berenice, cannot bring himself to so so, and leaves abruptly to avoid her questions. The action is not advanced at all by this scene. It is a completely superfluous repetition of the first scene.

Racine's Antiochus has been criticized as a useless character not sufficiently involved in the main action to warrant the introduction of the rôle. Crowne introduces two more rivals for his Titus and parcels out the rôle of Antiochus among them. In addition to Antiochus, Monobazus and Malchus love the Queen. The three of them do little more in the Titus-Berenice sequences than hover around in the background confiding to the audience in asides their love for the Queen. As a sample of Crowne's style and his portrayal of the passion of love, one of these asides is well worth quoting. Antiochus confides to the audience (p. 362):

> I must to the fair Queen before I go,
> My thirsty Soul does more intemprate grow:
> That hot elixir I must hourly taste,
> Which I'm assur'd will burn me at the last.

Of the three suitors, only Monobazus declares his love. The scene of the declaration is purely episodic, serving no purpose in the action. He declares his love merely to "ease his soul." He says (p. 365):

> Till now in humble duty I supprest
> The tor'ing (?) secret till it burnt my breast.
> My bosom could have fire retain'd,
> It would have less my scorching vitals pain'd.

In this scene of Monobazus' declaration—which follows the two scenes

JOHN CROWNE AND RACINE

in which Titus tries to tell Berenice of his decision and fails—Crowne includes Berenice's false explanation of Titus's coldness. She says, in an aside (p. 366):

> And oh! good Heav'n! What starts into my thought?
> I've found what has this change in Titus wrought;
> I've been too lavish in this stranger's praise,
> That, that did this disorder in him raise.

Turning to Monobazus, she says (p. 366):

> Sir, you have ruin'd me, have friendship shewn,
> To make my fate as wretched as your own:
> To save my life have you your sword employ'd,
> And all the comforts of that life destroy'd.

Both psychologically and dramatically this is a far cry from Racine's use of the same idea. Racine's Bérénice, instead of being in despair at this explanation of Titus's conduct, finds in it evidence of his love for her: "Si Titus est jaloux, Titus est amoureux." With this line Racine ends Act II of his tragedy. The thought is the culmination of a sort of deliberation of Bérénice's. She is shocked and bewildered by Titus's coldness and his sudden departure. She searches in her mind for an explanation. Antiochus having declared his love earlier in the play (Act I) she wonders if Titus has not some hint of this rivalry. That would explain all. Titus is jealous. And if he is jealous, it means that he loves her still. The act ends with Bérénice as unprepared as ever for the shock of Titus's repudiation of his promises. If in the interval between the acts she questions her comforting explanation of the warning signs of a change in Titus, we are prepared for the self-deception with which she rejects Antiochus' report of Titus's decision. As far as I can see, the incident as Crowne uses it has no consequences. It is a detached episode and appears superfluous, whereas in Racine it serves to build up the tension which reaches its climax in the scene where Titus himself tells Bérénice they must part.

Crowne's talent for discarding essentials is nowhere better illustrated than in the scene where Berenice learns from a third person that she must give Titus up. In Racine it is Antiochus who delivers Titus's message. Titus has asked his friend to break the news to Bérénice and to comfort her, without knowing, of course, that Antiochus himself loves the Queen and has been rejected by her. At the moment when Antiochus thought all hope gone, he has heard the news that all along he had been hoping for: Titus will not marry Bérénice. But has he really any reason to rejoice? He shrinks from wounding Bérénice and he realizes that her pain will be all the more acute if she hears the terrible news from the lips of her rejected suitor. Antiochus says to his confidant:

> Et ne la crois-tu pas assez infortunée
> D'apprendre à quel mépris Titus l'a condamnée,
> Sans lui donner encor le déplaisir fatal
> D'apprendre ce mépris par son propre rival?
> Encor un coup, fuyons; et par cette nouvelle
> N'allons point nous charger d'une haine immortelle.

But at this moment Bérénice enters. She is obviously looking for Titus. Her disappointment at finding Antiochus instead stings him into protesting that he would not be there if Titus himself had not detained him. Without realizing what he is doing he aggravates Bérénice's anxiety to such a pitch that she threatens him with her hatred unless he will tell her why Titus detained him and what Titus said concerning her (Antiochus has let it slip that their conversation had been about her). He is then forced to give her Titus's message. Bérénice cannot believe it. It must be some sort of trick. Antiochus protests indignantly at her doubt of him and she turns on him with a perfidious and unjust accusation, which nevertheless has enough truth in it to make it doubly painful to him. She says: "Vous le souhaitez trop pour me persuader." She commands him never to appear in her presence again, and turns to leave the stage. Before she exits, however, she has a flash of insight into her own motivation. She says to her confidante: "Hélas! pour me tromper je fais ce que je puis." (vs. 918)

In Crowne's adaptation of this scene, Titus's message is delivered by Tiberias, who corresponds to Racine's Paulin. Tiberias is the voice of duty as Paulin is in Racine. Fearing that Titus's resolution may weaken, Tiberias actually offers to deliver the message. To him Berenice is merely an obstacle to Titus's glorious career. He asks nothing better than to be of some assistance in removing the obstacle. He loses no time in informing Berenice that she must part from Titus and he does so in the presence of the trio of suitors who hover around her. Berenice is stunned but it is not she who accuses Tiberias of lying. The chivalrous Antiochus comes to her defense with "All this is falsehood and the Queen's betray'd." Monobazus begs Berenice's leave to avenge her. But she orders him from her presence and he leaves, saying that he will go to his death in battle. Berenice then repeats Antiochus' accusation, challenging Tiberias to prove his assertion and threatening to have his head if he has lied. He meets the challenge by asserting that Titus himself will confirm his message and he leaves to bring Titus to the Queen. Only a love of the heroic combined with a lack of psychological perception and dramatic sense could account for the changes which Crowne has made in this scene. He has weakened the emotional tension by transferring Titus's message to a character who is indifferent to Berenice and not involved in the main action. He has destroyed Racine's concentration by distributing the dialogue among five characters. By having Antiochus instead of Berenice accuse Tiberias of lying, he has substituted heroics for Racinian psychology.

Bits of Racine's dialogue float dismally in the stream of Crowne's rhetoric. It is of some significance that he comes closest to Racine where the dialogue of the original has no psychological subtlety, no nuances of emotion. For instance, Crowne imitates the end of the first Titus-Berenice scene (p. 333):

> TIT. My heart did never greater passion feel.—
> But—
> BER. Finish, sir!
> TIT. Alas!—
> BER. Speak, speak my doom!—
> TIT. Some god assist me now—the Empire—Rome—
> Sound to th' assault, I'll to my squadron straight.
> My soul's opprest, I can no more relate.

Here is the corresponding dialogue in Racine (vss. 621-24):

> TITUS
> Non, Madame, Jamais, puisqu'il faut vous parler,
> Mon coeur de plus de feux ne se sentit brûler.
> Mais . . .
> BÉRÉNICE
> Achevez.
> TITUS
> Hélas!
> BÉRÉNICE
> Parlez.
> TITUS
> Rome . . . l'Empire . . .

RACINE AND ENGLISH CLASSICISM

BÉRÉNICE
Hé bien?

TITUS
Sortons, Paulin; je ne lui puis rien dire.

When Racinian psychology is the least bit subtle, Crowne goes off into vague paraphrase. This tendency is illustrated in the same scene. Racine says (vss. 585-94):

TITUS
N'en doutez point, Madame; et j'atteste les dieux
Que toujours Bérénice est présente à mes yeux.
L'absence ni le temps, je vous le jure encore,
Ne vous peuvent ravir ce coeur qui vous adore.

BÉRÉNICE
Hé quoi! vous me jurez une éternelle ardeur,
Et vous me la jurez avec cette froideur?
Pourquoi même du ciel attester la puissance?
Faut-il par des serments vaincre ma défiance?
Mon coeur ne prétend point, Seigneur, vous démentir,
Et je vous en croirai sur un simple soupir.

Crowne has (p. 332):

TIT. Ah, madam! all the gods can witness bear,
Queen Berenice is always present there [in his heart.]
Nor time nor absence ever shall deface
That image love once in my heart did place.
BER. Why, sir, do you invoke the gods for this:
Does Titus need a friend to Berenice?
All they can witness will superfluous be;
Titus is Heav'n and all the gods to me.

Titus's exaggerated assurances and his cold manner spring from his guilty conscience. Racine's Bérénice senses this and her misgivings grow. Her reply is not an assurance of her love; she expresses her alarm that Titus should think hyperbolic protestations necessary, and should pronounce them with unconvincing coolness. By omitting the reference to Titus's cold manner and the line, "Et je vous en croirai sur un simple soupir," Crowne has changed completely the emotional implications of Berenice's lines. As far as I can make out the meaning of Crowne's lines, his Berenice replies to Titus's exaggerated protestations of his love for her with equally exaggerated protestations of her love for him, as though he had shown doubts of her love.

In every scene of the Titus-Berenice sub-plot of his play Crowne has used some material from Racine. But he has used it with complete disregard for its function or its meaning in Racine nor does he weld it together into a continuous dramatic action. By transferring parts of Antiochus' rôle and of Berenice's to other characters and by adding two superfluous characters, he has destroyed continuity and coherence; he has considerably reduced emotional tension and has eliminated altogether Racinian psychology.

« « CHAPTER II » »

THOMAS OTWAY'S
TITUS AND BERENICE

IN OTWAY'S PREFACE to his brilliantly successful *Don Carlos* (1676) we find the following reference to Racine:

I dare not presume to take to myself what a great many, and those (I am sure) of good Judgment too, have been so kind to afford me, (viz.) That it [*Don Carlos*] is the best Heroick Play that has been writen of late, for, I thank Heaven, I am yet not so vain, but this I may modestly boast of, which the Author of the *French Bernice* has done before me, in his Preface to that Play, that it never fail'd to draw Tears from the Eyes of the Auditors.[1]

This is Otway's only mention of Racine. Of his attitude towards the French tragic poet we know only that, like Racine, he counted a tragedy successful if it moved the audience to tears. When, the next year, he imitated Racine's *Bérénice* in his *Titus and Berenice*, he made no acknowledgment of a debt to Racine. He did, however, choose as his epigraph the following verses from Petronius:

> Grandis Oratio non est turgida,
> Sed naturali pulchritudine exsurgit.

From this epigraph we may infer that he was attracted by the simplicity of Racine's style.

Otway alters the structure of Racine's tragedy. He compresses Racine's five acts into three. He makes some changes in the order of the incidents; he expands considerably one scene, changing the motivation of the characters. He adds a scene of his own and introduces several incidents of his own invention in his third act. A summary of the action of the two plays will indicate Otway's method of condensation and his departures from Racine.

---

[1] *The Complete Works of Thomas Otway*, ed. Montague Summers (Bloomsbury, 1926), I, 76. All references are to this edition, which reproduces the text of the first edition.

THOMAS OTWAY'S *TITUS AND BERENICE*

The subject of Racine's tragedy is the parting of Titus and Bérénice: "Titus reginam Berenicen, cui etiam nuptias pollicitus ferebatur, statim ab urbe dimisit invitus invitam" (Suetonius, as quoted by Racine in his preface). The scene is at Rome. The three principal characters are Titus, Bérénice (the Jewish queen whom Titus loves and who has been in Rome since Titus's conquest of Jerusalem), and Antiochus, "roi de Comagène" (who has been Titus's ally in his conquest of Jerusalem). Antiochus had been a suitor of Bérénice before Titus invaded her country and won her love. Rejected by Bérénice he has followed her to Rome, and has remained at the court, the cherished friend of Titus and Bérénice, who do not suspect that he still loves Bérénice. Racine's play opens at the moment when the official mourning for Vespasian has come to an end, the moment when Bérénice is expecting to be made Empress. Antiochus has heard the rumor of Bérénice's imminent marriage, which will put an end to the hope that has kept him in Rome, the hope that circumstances would arise to separate Titus and Bérénice and that she would turn to him. He asks for an interview with Bérénice, declares his love and bids her good-bye. Bérénice's confidante regrets that Bérénice has consented to his departure. Titus has not yet spoken. She has misgivings. But Bérénice is still confident.

Act II. Titus reveals to his confidant, Paulin, his decision to send Bérénice away, despite his love for her and his grief at the thought of the separation. Paulin encourages him, reminding him of Rome's hatred of foreign queens. Bérénice interrupts this conversation. Titus cannot find the courage to tell her his decision. He breaks off the interview by leaving abruptly and without explanation. Bérénice's anxiety is acute; but she interprets Titus's strange conduct as the effect of jealousy of Antiochus. This thought restores her confidence.

Act III. Titus asks Antiochus to inform Bérénice of his decision. Antiochus begins to hope again but shrinks from delivering Titus's message to Bérénice. Bérénice enters, seeking Titus, and forces the reluctant Antiochus to reveal Titus's decision. She accuses him of lying out of jealousy and orders him never to appear in her presence again, but leaves shaken by what he has told her. Antiochus is torn between indignation at her accusation and solicitude for the grief-stricken Bérénice.

Act IV. Bérénice feverishly awaits Titus, who is coming in response to a message from her. Her confidante persuades her to retire for a

27

moment to arrange her disheveled hair. Titus enters, sends Paulin to tell Bérénice he is coming, and reveals in a soliloquy that he is resolved to tell Bérénice himself that they must part. Bérénice re-enters and, on learning that Titus wishes her to leave Rome, she reproaches him for the tragic irony of her situation: he has waited to tell her until the very moment when there is no obstacle to their marriage but his own will. She believes he no longer loves her. She leaves threatening suicide. Titus's resolution is shaken. Antiochus enters to plead with Titus to save the despairing Bérénice from taking her own life. Titus's counselors urge him to go at once to the Senate which is impatiently awaiting him. He yields but promises to see Bérénice on his return.

Act. V. Antiochus learns that Bérénice has planned to leave Rome at once without seeing Titus, to whom she has written a farewell letter. For a moment he hopes again, but his hope vanishes when Titus returns on his way to Bérénice's suite, and apparently more in love than ever. Antiochus exits, hinting that he too will kill himself. Titus and Bérénice enter. He is begging her to delay her departure. He has forced her to give him her farewell letter. He reads it and learns that she has planned suicide. Titus tells her that he cannot give up the throne but there is a solution for him—a solution worthy of a Roman: he will take his own life. At this moment Antiochus enters and, thinking that Titus and Bérénice are reconciled, confesses to Titus that he has been his rival, and reveals his own resolution to end his life. Bérénice is now convinced of Titus's deep love for her. She will leave Rome believing in his love. She begs Titus and Antiochus to follow her example of renunciation and resignation. The play ends with Antiochus' "Hélas!"

Otway's Act I is made up of material from Racine's first two acts: Antiochus' soliloquy is omitted (Racine, Act I, Scene 2); but bits of it are introduced into the conversation between Antiochus and his confidant, Arsaces. This scene is much shorter than the corresponding one in Racine; but, even so, much of the dialogue has no equivalent in Racine. Antiochus' declaration is cut drastically, as are the long political discussions in the conversation between Titus and his confidant, Paulinus. The Titus-Berenice dialogue is left almost intact.

Act II corresponds to Act III of Racine. Otway has cut out almost entirely the dialogue between Antiochus and his confidant, Arsaces; so that this act consists of two scenes, Titus-Antiochus and Berenice-

Antiochus. In the first of these two scenes, Otway makes his first important shift in the order of events: Antiochus confesses to Titus that he loves Berenice, a confession which Racine had placed in the dénouement of his tragedy. This confession does not deter Titus from asking Antiochus to convey his message of banishment to Berenice. After Titus's exit Antiochus is expressing to his confidant his reluctance to deliver the message, when Berenice enters. Berenice forces him to tell her what Titus has said, accuses him of lying out of jealousy, and leaves Antiochus indignant and firmly resolved to depart from Rome at once.

Act III of Otway is composed of material from Racine's Acts IV and V with additions and changes. Early in this act Otway makes another shift in the order of the scenes. Antiochus' first entrance is placed before instead of after Titus tells Berenice they must part. Antiochus reproaches Titus for the distress he has caused Berenice. Titus then tells him that he has resolved to tell Berenice himself that she must leave Rome. In this speech to Antiochus Otway reproduces the lines of Titus's soliloquy in Racine (Act IV, Scene 4). The dialogue between Titus and Berenice which follows is a free translation of the corresponding dialogue in Racine with some of the speeches cut or omitted altogether. After this scene, Otway departs from Racine's guidance. There is so much more of Otway than of Racine in the action and the dialogue from now on that a more detailed analysis is necessary. Titus, yielding to Paulinus' entreaties, decides to send word to the Senate that Berenice will leave Rome the next day. He is resolved not to see Berenice again and he sends her a letter of farewell. Antiochus enters with attendants to take formal leave of Titus. Titus tells Antiochus he has broken with Berenice. At this moment Titus sees her approaching and leaves to avoid her ("Oh! Heav'n, she's entring, from her Charms let's fly" [p. 174]). Berenice kneels to Antiochus and asks forgiveness for her unjust accusation. She tells him she is leaving Rome. He begs her to stay (p. 175):

> No rather here continue and be great,
> Whilst I lie ever hopeless at your feet.

She is firm in her resolution to depart. Antiochus begs her to accept his love. When she rejects him, he flings himself at her feet in despair. Seeing the Emperor approaching, Berenice urges Antiochus to rise and leave with her. Titus enters ("Spite of my self I wander this way still,"

says he, by way of explanation of his unexpected entrance [p. 176]).
He detains Berenice, and apparently Antiochus, too, remains. Titus
reproaches Berenice for shunning him and pleads with her not to leave
him—ever. She hands him the tablets on which he has written his farewell to her. He reads and finds there her farewell letter to him, in
which she tells him she will kill herself, or so it appears, for he says
(p. 177):

> Your cruel resolution I descry;
> To be reveng'd of me you seek to dye.

Titus kneels to Berenice to beg her to believe he loves her. She accuses
him of having brought her to Rome merely to adorn his triumph. At
this Titus rises and attempts to stab himself. Berenice springs to intercept the blow and begs him to strike her heart instead, her heart that
is all his own. Titus falls to his knees and tells her he will renounce the
Empire for her sake (p. 178):

> Thus at your Feet a happy prostrate laid,
> I'm much more blest than if the world I sway'd.

Berenice, convinced now that he loves her, tells him she will voluntarily
exile herself. Titus falls on Antiochus' neck and begs him to go with
Berenice and never to forsake her. Antiochus says to his confidant
(p. 179):

> *Arsaces!* on thy bosome let me lie,
> Whilst I but take one last dear look, and die.

Berenice admonishes Antiochus to live and, with her and Titus, set an
example of "a most tender, though unhappy Love" (an echo of Racine,
this). At her departure Titus in a thundering tirade swears he will
take vengeance on Rome for his unhappiness by practicing the cruel
tyranny Rome has taught him.

In Otway's version condensation is effected by cutting drastically or
omitting altogether protagonist-confidant scenes. The structure of
Racine's tragedy is further altered by displaced scenes: Antiochus' confession to Titus is placed in the middle of Otway's play instead of at
the end, and Antiochus' entrance in Act IV of Racine (Act III of Otway) comes before instead of after Titus dismisses Berenice. In his
last act, Otway introduces a scene of his own invention (Antiochus'
second declaration) and several incidents not found in Racine: Titus's

farewell letter to Berenice, Titus's actual attempt at suicide (he had merely resolved on suicide in Racine), Berenice's interception of the blow, Titus's sudden decision to abdicate, and finally his metamorphosis into a cruel tyrant.

The incidents which Otway has introduced into his dénouement are obviously intended to make his last act more dramatic according to his conception of the dramatic: movement and surprise. One of these changes, Titus's attempt to stab himself, does afford more physical action than was in Racine without destroying the motivation. Berenice is convinced of Titus's love by an act rather than by the sincerity of his grief ("J'ai vu couler vos larmes"). By Berenice's interception of the blow Otway tries to motivate Titus's offer to abdicate. Here he is less successful. Titus's willingness to abdicate and to an even greater degree his resolution to conquer the world and tyrannize over Rome are peripeties introduced at the sacrifice of Racine's motivation and of plausibility.

The displacement of Antiochus' confession to Titus,[2] Titus's offer to abdicate,[3] and his metamorphosis at the end[4] have all been mentioned by modern critics who have commented on the two plays. No one has commended these changes; but, except for this adverse criticism—and it is mild—Otway's *Titus and Berenice* has received more favorable comment in our own day than any of the other English adaptations of Racine. It is easy to understand why this particular adaptation has attracted the attention of critics and scholars. The name of Thomas Otway is an important one in the history of English drama. Otway was Dryden's most formidable rival in the seventeenth century. All during the eighteenth century he was considered, next to Shakespeare, the greatest tragic poet of England. His reputation rested largely on *The Orphan* and *Venice Preserved*. In the eighteenth century *Titus and Berenice* seems to have been unknown. But naturally the play has received some notice in our own day not only from students of Anglo-French relations in the classical period but from critics interested primarily in English drama. Of the modern critics of Otway's *Titus and Berenice*, only the Frenchman, Louis Charlanne, has no praise for

---

[2] See below, n. 8.
[3] Dorothea Canfield, *Corneille and Racine in England* (New York, Columbia University Press, 1904), pp. 99-100.
[4] F. Y. Eccles, *Racine in England* (Oxford, The Clarendon Press, 1922), p. 4.

Otway's play.⁵ Of the foreign critics only F. Y. Eccles implies that Otway's version is inferior to the original and even Eccles thinks that some of the spirit of Racine has passed over into Otway's play and he considers it superior to other adaptations of Racine's tragedies.⁶ Several critics are quite positive that Otway's play is superior to Racine's. Unfortunately this criticism is not sufficiently particularized to be very revealing.⁷

Racinophile that I am, I prefer Racine's tragedy to Otway's. But I am not concerned with the relative value of the two as works of art. It is my purpose to try to define the differences between the two plays and to illustrate these differences by copious citations so as to give as clear an idea as possible of the contrast between them. I get the impression

---

⁵ See below, n. 8.

⁶ *Op. cit.*, p. 6. See also below, n. 8.

⁷ In the introduction to his edition of Otway's *Works*, Montague Summers has the following comments on *Titus and Berenice*: "Notwithstanding occasional infelicities . . . *Titus and Berenice* attains a very high level. There are some passages of tender beauty, which owe not entirely all their charm and all their loveliness to Racine. It has been well said that 'In spite of its very considerable variations from the original *Titus and Berenice* may, perhaps, claim to be the most satisfactory attempt at transplanting French tragedy to the English stage. It almost attains the ideal of translation.' This is very high but not unmerited praise. We have only to compare Otway's work with that extraordinarily wooden translation of *Andromaque*, which if it were not perpetrated by Crowne himself, he at any rate midwived into the world, to recognize Otway's genius." (*Op. cit.*, I, lix.)

I have the impression that Dorothea Canfield prefers Otway's play to Racine's. Some of her remarks contradict others. She makes some equivocal statements. Sifting her critique for unequivocal statements, I have culled the following: "Antiochus he [Otway] makes at once more prominent and more completely admirable. He intensifies the sad nobility of the man and makes him a very touching and dignified figure." (*Op. cit.*, p. 97.) She says of his Berenice: "As for his treatment of Berenice, Otway has done the impossible. Racine had already written of her in his most artful and ardent vein, and it would seem out of the question for another poet to convey a still more tender feeling for her misfortunes. But the English poet's peculiar gift for expressing at once sorrow and passion enables him to give a new and thrilling pathos to his heroine. The final scene of leave-taking between the two lovers is, if one dare to say it, more moving even than the original." (*Loc. cit.*) She cites one verse of Otway's which she considers superior to the original: "The rendering of 'Mon coeur de plus de feux ne se sentit brûler' by 'My heart . . . Was ne'er more full of love nor half so like to break' is a distinct improvement, and instances are not rare where the simplicity and feeling of Otway are heard in phrases not in the original." (*Loc. cit.*) This is the only one which she cites. The rest of Miss Canfield's critique is a confusing jumble of contradictory assertions.

from critical comment that Otway's play is a translation and a rather close translation, though greatly abridged, of Racine's *Bérénice*. Those critics who mention a loss of Racinian psychology attribute the loss to excisions and say nothing of Otway's interpolations. They leave the impression that what Otway has retained of Racine's play is very close to the original.[8] I do not agree. Otway condenses Racine's tragedy by making drastic excisions in the protagonist-confidant scenes. Very little is left except the protagonist-protagonist scenes. In these scenes there are some excisions but there are many interpolations. Otway shortens the scene of Antiochus' declaration but near the end of the play he introduces a second declaration scene, entirely original. He shortens the Titus-Bérénice scenes, but still makes some interpolations. He lengthens considerably the Titus-Antiochus scene (*Bérénice*, Act III, Scene 1), yet retains very little of Racine's dialogue. He also expands the second Bérénice-Antiochus scene.

In these protagonist-protagonist scenes Otway paraphrases freely some of Racine's lines and occasionally translates them; but interpolations not even suggested by anything in Racine often alter the effect and the significance of the original. The most striking result of Otway's interpolations is a transformation of the character of Antiochus. In addition to this change, interpolations together with excisions impair greatly what might be called the "psychological drama" of these scenes.

[8] Several critics who have compared the two plays note the loss of Racinian psychology but attribute this loss to abridgment, implying that what is left of Racine is translated or paraphrased rather closely: ". . . imitation servile, traduction littérale, parfois, de l'oeuvre de Racine. De cinq actes, cependant, la pièce était réduite à trois et les discours perdaient par là toute l'ampleur, toute la psychologie raciniennes. . . . Ce résumé, en vers rimés, de l'oeuvre de Racine. . . ." (Louis Charlanne, *L'Influence Française en Angleterre au XVIIe Siècle* [Paris, 1906], p. 376.)

"We are unprepared for the final tirade in which Titus threatens to avenge his private wound by becoming a tyrant of his people. Throughout, the logic of passion is merely obscured by merciless excisions. With all this, the English play is a translation, and in many parts a close one, and it is not true that nothing of Racine's spirit has passed into the verse of Otway." (Eccles, *op. cit.*, pp. 4–5.)

"Every speech of Otway's is based to a greater or less degree on the French, and many of them are translated line for line; nevertheless, there is not a passage which is not English." (Canfield, *op. cit.*, pp. 93–94.)

"It is useless to analyse a play which owes so little to its English garb." (Edmund Gosse, "Thomas Otway," *Seventeenth Century Studies* [London, 1885], p. 283.)

According to Professor Daniel Mornet, Racine's Antiochus is a survival of a *précieux* type to which Professor Mornet gives the name of *mourant*. Racine's Antiochus is, says he, "le 'mourant' que l'on peut dire classique."⁹ He describes the "mourants" of *précieux* poetry as "toujours prêts à mourir de mille morts, et par métaphore, pour les beaux yeux d'une cruelle."¹⁰ The qualifying adjective *classique* implies that Racine tones down the style and motivates more naturally the conventional attitudes of the victims of tyrannic love in *précieux* poetry. Racine's Antiochus *is* wholly preoccupied with his love for Bérénice. He alternately hopes and despairs in the manner of the *mourant*, but more convincingly than the typical *mourant* since he deludes himself quite naturally with the hope that if any obstacle should arise to the marriage of Titus and Bérénice, Bérénice will turn to him. He sighs, but he never announces that any particular sigh is likely to be his last. He is never at the point of death from his mistress's cruelty only to be revived by her pity. Antiochus' chivalrous conduct towards Bérénice springs from delicacy, tenderness, and sympathetic imagination, and not from obedience to a code. In my opinion, Racine's Antiochus comes no closer to the *mourant* type than certain romantic poets of the nineteenth century. His madrigals bear more resemblance to certain romantic lyrics (particularly Lamartine's) than to the *précieux* madrigals of Racine's day.

If Racine's Antiochus is "le 'mourant' que l'on peut dire classique," it would be understatement to say that Otway's Antiochus is "le mourant" without any qualifications. He might be described as "le mourant le plus mourant de tous les mourants." Otway eliminates the qualities that make Racine's Antiochus atypical: the delicacy, the tenderness, the sympathetic imagination. He obeys all the rules of the *précieux* madrigal. One French poet lists his themes: "Il se plaint de la cruauté de sa maîtresse"; "Il s'applaudit de son amour, malgré les rigueurs de sa maîtresse"; "Que les rigueurs de sa maîtresse n'épuiseront pas sa constance," etc. These themes might serve as heads for a discussion of the rôle of Otway's Antiochus if all the conventions which Otway has introduced into the rôle could be included under them. But, in addition to the themes of "la poésie mourante," Otway introduces the *courtois* code, and two other traditional themes, the conflict of love and "gloire" and the conflict of a code of love with a code of friendship.

⁹ *Histoire de la Littérature Française Classique* (Paris, 1947), p. 147.
¹⁰ *Ibid.*, p. 133.

THOMAS OTWAY'S *TITUS AND BERENICE*

As early as the opening scene of the play, Otway's Antiochus is the perfect *mourant*. When his confidant suggests that he cultivate indifference to the indifferent Berenice, he protests in hyperbole his faithful love (pp. 151-52):

> *Arsaces*, how false Measures dost thou take!
> Remove the *Poles* and bid the *Sun* go back;
> Invert all Natures Orders, Fates Decrees;
> Then bid me hate the Charming *Berenice*.

To the confidant's admonition to court Berenice haughtily as she is proud, Antiochus protests that Berenice's pity is the only reward he expects for his fidelity (p. 152):

> *Arsaces*, No; she's gentle as a Dove,
> Her Eyes are Tyrants, but her Soul's all Love.[11]
> And owes so little for the Vowes I've made,
> That if she pity me, I'm more than paid.

There is nothing at all in Racine's dialogue that could have suggested the first speech which I have quoted. Possibly one line of Racine's suggested the pity motif of the second speech. If so, the difference is great and very significant. Racine's line occurs in a soliloquy which Otway has cut out. Antiochus has heard the rumor that Bérénice will that day be made empress of Rome. If the rumor is true, he can no longer hope that Titus will give Bérénice up and that she will turn to him, Antiochus. He has decided to leave Rome if he finds that the report is true. He must see Bérénice. Shall he tell her that he still loves her? At this, the most inopportune moment, he is impelled to tell her. Without realizing it, he is clinging, against all reason, to the hope that has kept him in Rome for five years. Will Bérénice be offended if he declares his love? He persuades himself that no harm can possibly come of it: "Au lieu de s'offenser, elle pourra me plaindre" (vs. 47). This is the specious reasoning by which he justifies his irrational impulse to speak to Bérénice of his love. This is the only mention that Racine's Antiochus ever makes of pity. Otway has replaced characteristic Racinian psychology with a typical *précieux* sentiment.

Otway needed no suggestion from Racine to compose madrigals on

---

[11] The eyes as tyrants recall the earlier and more *précieux* Racine of *Alexandre* (vss. 895-96):

> Mais, hélas! que vos yeux, ces aimables tyrans,
> Ont produit sur mon coeur des effets différents!

the theme of pity. Later in his play, in a scene that is entirely of his own invention (Antiochus' second declaration), when Berenice refuses to listen to Antiochus' profession of love, Antiochus flings himself at her feet, crying (p. 175):

> O stay, since of the Victory you're secure;
> Pity the pains and anguish I endure,
> In Wounds, which you and none but you can cure.
> Look back, whilst at your feet my self I cast,
> And think the sigh that's coming is the last.

To make Antiochus the perfect *mourant*, Otway has to introduce still one more theme: complaints of his mistress's cruelty. Otway begins early in the play to introduce into the rôle of his Antiochus these conventional plaints, expressed in *précieux* clichés. Furthermore he gives the impression of being bent upon introducing the theme at any cost. In the first instance, Antiochus' plaint is not even faintly justified by anything that Berenice has done or said. The effect is the more shocking because the plaint is in the form of an aside, a technical gaucherie universally condemned by French critics but favored by English dramatists. When Berenice appears in answer to Antiochus' request to speak to her (we are back now in Act I), delighted at last to escape from obsequious courtiers and to talk quietly with Titus's dear friend and hers, Antiochus is impatient to know whether or not Titus will that day marry Berenice. He asks Berenice to confirm the rumor. She replies that she has not seen Titus and that she has been puzzled by his avoidance of her, but that she believes he will soon come to tell her that she will that day become his empress. To this Racine's Antiochus replies: "Et je viens donc vous dire un éternel adieu." Here is the corresponding *réplique* in Otway (p. 153):

> How she insults and triumphs in my ill!
> Sh'as with long practice learnt to smile and kill.
> Oh, *Berenice*, Eternally Farewell.

In the same scene, when Berenice urges him to remain in Rome, Otway's Antiochus accuses her of wishing to keep him there in order to enjoy the sight of his despair. In a later scene, Otway embroiders the theme of the lady's cruelty (p. 167):

> Oh *Berenice*! remorseless cruel Fair!
> Born only for my torment and despair.

THOMAS OTWAY'S *TITUS AND BERENICE*

> Was it for this so faithfully I serv'd?
> Is this the recompence I have deserv'd?
> I, who for you did all Ambition wave,
> And left a Kingdom to become your Slave!
> Curse on my Fate![12]

Into this madrigal Otway has introduced another conventional sentiment, this time a motif from the *roman courtois* and the *tragédie galante*. His Antiochus, in addition to being the *mourant*, is the *héros de roman*. He has renounced a kingdom, his "gloire," his ambition to become love's slave. In another speech he obeys the *courtois* code. When Racine's Bérénice is desperately trying to force Antiochus to explain the mystery of Titus's evasiveness and coldness, she finally resorts to threats: "Quoi? vous craignez si peu de me désobéir?" (vs. 881). Antiochus replies: "Je n'ai qu'à vous parler pour me faire haïr" (vs. 882). Otway expands these two lines in the following dialogue (p. 165):

> BER. You told me once, *Antiochus,* you lov'd;
> But sure 'twas only that you might betray;
> Or else you would more fear to disobey.
> ANT. I disobey you! ask my life, and try
> How gloriously I for your sake can dye.

This is a curious distortion of the motivation in Racine. The only connection between the two passages is the one word *désobéir*. From Racine's dialogue we get the impression that Bérénice is driven to use the word by her now almost unbearable anxiety in the face of Antiochus' stubborn refusal to end her agonizing doubts and fears by telling her what Titus plans to do. Antiochus demurs because he cannot bear to deliver the painful message. He dreads the effect that it will inevitably have. Bérénice's pain and humiliation will cause irrational hate of him, Antiochus. If the haughtiness implicit in the word *désobéir* springs from anything but her morbid emotional state, it is from Bérénice's consciousness of her position as the future empress. Certainly she is not

---

[12] This plaint has some justification. Berenice has accused Antiochus of lying out of jealousy. These lines are an interpolation of Otway's. Racine's Antiochus refers to Bérénice as "cruelle" only once (vss. 947–48):

> Allons; et de si loin évitons la cruelle,
> Que de longtemps, Arsace, on ne nous parle d'elle.

These lines are in the scene immediately following Bérénice's unjust accusation. They are not addressed to Bérénice.

commanding complete submission to her will *as proof of Antiochus' love*. That is exactly what Otway's Berenice does. And his Antiochus protests at the implication that he does not know how the *parfait amant* should act. Berenice has accused him of infringing the *courtois* code. I do not know whether there was any immediate source for these lines of Otway's but they remind one of the prototypes of *courtois* lovers, Chrétien's Lancelot and Guenièvre.

The Titus-Antiochus scene of Otway's Act II is based on Racine's Act III, Scene 1, a scene in which Titus, not knowing that Antiochus loves Bérénice, asks him to tell Bérénice that she must leave Rome. In Racine there are 103 verses in this scene. The corresponding scene in Otway has 156. Otway has omitted much of Racine's dialogue and replaced it with dialogue that bears not the slightest resemblance to Racine's. In this scene Antiochus is still the perfect *mourant* and the perfect *héros de roman*. In addition he is the perfect friend and his code of friendship conflicts with his love. In order to introduce the love-friendship conflict,[18] Otway places here the confession that Racine's Antiochus makes in the dénouement. Antiochus makes his confession in a banal melodramatic metaphor (p. 162):

> When first you thought your self of me possest,
> You took a very Serpent to your brest.[14]

Titus does not at first grasp Antiochus' meaning. When Antiochus makes it clear, there ensues a contest of generosity. Titus says (p. 162):

> A braver Rival I'd not wish to find,
> Than him that dares be just, and tell his mind.

[18] In introducing a contest of generosity between the emperor and his friend, in putting great emphasis on the love-friendship struggle, Otway was incorporating into Racine's play a theme that had been used by Roger Boyle, Earl of Orrery. It has been suggested that Orrery revived a theme that had been popular in Elizabethan, Jacobean, and Caroline drama. (See L. J. Mills, "The Friendship Theme in Orrery's Plays," *Publications of the Modern Language Association*, LIII, No. 3 [1928], 795-806.) Quite probably he was inspired by earlier English drama. It should be noted, however, that Corneille made much of the theme of the friendship of two brothers rivals for a throne and for the love of a princess in his *Rodogune*. But, whether the theme as used by Otway came from Orrery or from Corneille, it certainly did not come from Racine.

[14] Compare the words of the same confession in Racine, Act V, Scene 7 (vss. 1441-42):

> Mais le pourriez-vous croire, en ce moment fatal,
> Qu'un ami si fidèle étoit votre rival?

THOMAS OTWAY'S *TITUS AND BERENICE*

> So far's Resentment from my heart remov'd,
> That *Berenice* is by my friend belov'd,
> That I, *Antiochus*, the thing extol,
> For she was made to be ador'd by all:
> And happy he that shall possess her.

Antiochus replies (p. 162):

> True;
> But 'tis fit none should be so blest but you.
> And *Berenice* for none could be design'd,
> But him that's the Delight of all Mankind.
> 'Tis for this cause to *Syria* I repair;
> For when you're blest, no envy should be near.

Despite Antiochus' confession, Titus asks him to bear the message of banishment to Berenice, justifying this gratuitous cruelty to Berenice—a cruelty of which he is, for that matter, entirely unaware—with lofty and implausible sentiments (p. 163):

> None but a King, my Rival, and my friend,
> Is fit to speak the torments of my mind.
> In my behalf you *Berenice* must see.[15]

Like Racine's Antiochus, Otway's Antiochus misunderstands. Thinking that Titus wishes him to announce to Berenice that she will be made empress, he protests (p. 163):

> Is that an office, *Titus*, fit for me?
> Is't not enough her Cruelties I bear,
> But you must too solicite my despair?

This plaint, characteristic of Otway's Antiochus, replaces the words of Racine's tender Antiochus, words which dramatic irony make sharp as a sword-thrust to Titus (vss. 704–707):

> Ah! parlez-lui, Seigneur. La reine vous adore.
> Pourquoi vous dérober vous-même en ce moment
> Le plaisir de lui faire un aveu si charmant?
> Elle l'attend, Seigneur, avec impatience.

Titus makes his meaning clear: He intends to break with Berenice. Racine's Antiochus reacts to the shock of this news, which brings a

[15] Edgar Schumacher thinks that Otway intended by this act of Titus's to make the situation more heroic than in Racine; but he doubts if the psychological truth of the play is improved thereby. (*Thomas Otway* [Bern, 1924], p. 64.)

renewal of his hope, with: "Qu'entends-je? O ciel!" Otway's Antiochus expresses incredulity in a *précieux* cliché:

> It cannot be: No Slave that wears her Chains,
> Upon so easie terms his Freedom gains.¹⁶

Despite Berenice's cruelty, Antiochus will allow no one to wrong her with impunity, not even the Emperor. When Titus tells him he plans to send Berenice away, Antiochus says (pp. 163-64):

> Now if my heart was to Revenge alli'd,
> How might I triumph in her falling Pride!
> To see her Cruelties to me repaid,
> And with them all her tortur'd soul upbraid.
> But, *Titus*, I'm more just, and rather mov'd,
> That ev'n, Sir, you dare wrong the thing I've lov'd.¹⁷

Otway's play does not end, as Racine's does, with a sigh from Antiochus ("Hélas!"); but the last word of Otway's Antiochus is, quite

---

¹⁶ Racine's *Bérénice* is not free from the jargon of gallantry; and it must be admitted that this is, to modern ears, a serious blemish. The lines

> Madame, il vous souvient que mon coeur en ces lieux
> Reçut le premier trait qui partit de vos yeux

are a discordant note in the sad and beautiful melody of Antiochus' declaration. And we could wish that Bérénice had chosen other words for her parting speech to Antiochus than: "Portez loin de mes yeux vos soupirs et vos fers." The word "fers" here and in the other line in which it occurs in the sense of "enslavement" may be said to be a dead metaphor. It is not to Otway's credit that he revived the image by elaborating it. Racine's use of the jargon of gallantry must have been inconspicuous in his day. Otway's use of it suggests that he considered it the proper language of strong emotion.

¹⁷ These lines may have been suggested by a speech of Racine's Antiochus in the second of his scenes with Bérénice. She is angry at Antiochus' refusal to tell her what Titus has said about her in his conversation with Antiochus. Antiochus says (vss. 861-68):

> Suspendez votre ressentiment.
> D'autres, loin de se taire en ce même moment,
> Triompheroient peut-être, et pleins de confiance,
> Céderoient avec joie à votre impatience;
> Mais, moi, toujours tremblant; moi, vous le savez bien,
> A qui votre repos est plus cher que le mien,
> Pour ne le point troubler, j'aime mieux vous déplaire,
> Et crains votre douleur plus que votre colère.

Otway has replaced the tenderness of Racine's Antiochus with assertive obedience to a code.

fittingly, the word *die*. He falls on the bosom of his confidant, saying (p. 179):

> *Arsaces!* on thy bosome let me lie,
> Whilst I but take one last dear look, and die.

The conventional *précieux* sentiments of Otway's Antiochus are the more artificial and incongruous because they are unmotivated. Otway introduces them on the slightest pretext—in asides, if necessary—and leaves them *en l'air*, so to speak, since he does not change his Berenice to fit the pattern. Berenice is not guilty of the willful and capricious cruelty of which Antiochus complains. Nor does she exercise any of the prerogatives of a Guenièvre. It is not at her command that Antiochus has sacrificed his "gloire," his ambition, to become her slave. She does not demand the fidelity and the abject obedience which he gratuitously professes, except in the dialogue, which I have discussed, from the scene in which Antiochus delivers Titus's message of banishment. In this scene, with baffling inconsistency, Otway makes his Berenice first a coquette and then a Guenièvre.

When Racine's *Bérénice* first appeared, a hostile critic referred to it as nothing but "un tissu galant de madrigaux et d'élégies." What would such a critic have thought of the rôle of Antiochus in Otway's *Titus and Berenice*? What English critics of Otway's own time thought of his play we do not know. Particularly arresting, however, is modern criticism of Otway's Antiochus. Three German critics and one American have noted that Otway's conception of the character of Antiochus is quite different from Racine's. One German critic dismisses Racine's Antiochus with the one contemptuous epithet, "Seladon" (Céladon), and proceeds to describe Otway's Antiochus as more warm-blooded and manly. These critics assert that Otway's Antiochus is more admirable, more dignified, more sad and noble, more forceful, livelier—and more natural—than Racine's.[18] Racine has been repeatedly criti-

---

[18] Otway's Antiochus has inspired more admiration than ever Racine's did either at home or abroad. He has been particularly admired by German scholars. Reinhard Mosen says: "... ist unter seiner hand Antiochus aus einem unglücklichen liebhaber und seladon ein heissblütiger, kräftiger mensch geworden." ("Ueber Thomas Otway's leben und werke," *Englische Studien*, I [1877], 444.)

Schumacher (*op. cit.*, p. 65) notes with approval this comment of Mosen and illustrates the greater manliness and vehemence of Otway's Antiochus: "Mosen hebt hervor, dass Antiochus in Otways Darstellung männlicher und leidenschaftlicher geworden ist. Bei Racine antwortet er z.B. auf die Kunde, dass Berenice

cized for the "gallantry" of his young heroes and for the "jargon of gallantry." I am not prepared to give statistics, but it would hardly be an exaggeration to say that there is as much of the jargon of gallantry

---

am selben Tag noch Roms Kaiserin sein werde, mit einem blossen 'hélas' (demselben Ausruf, mit dem er die Tragödie dann beschliesst); Otways Antiochus fährt auf:

> "What do I hear? Confusion on thy tongue!
> To tell me this, why was thy speech so long?
> Why didst thou not ruin with more speed afford?
> Thou mightst have spoke, and kill'd me in a word."

Otway's Antiochus finds his greatest admirer in Dr. Joseph Spies, author of a monograph on the two plays. This is a sophomoric little essay written in barbarous English and consisting largely of summaries of the two plays and comparisons of corresponding characters. It would be otiose to quote Dr. Spies, if it were not for the fact that he admires in Otway's Antiochus the very traits which make him a conventional and precious characterization and yet he finds him more "natural" than Racine's Antiochus. He says: "How does Antiochus appear in Otway? This character is painted more lively and, as it seems to me, more natural than in Racine. A very great importance is attributed to the deep and true love of Antiochus. For it is impossible to prejudice him against Berenice, though his confident Arsaces clearly shows that Berenice in her present dignity looks down upon him with pride and even contempt. [This is an error on Dr. Spies's part.] But all endeavors in this respect are frustrated by his love:

> "Remove the Poles and bid the Sun go back;
> Invert all Natures Orders, Fates Decrees,
> Then bid me hate the charming Berenice,

he answers and would be happy, if she would but pity him. In order not to afflict her, he will rather die than make her acquainted with the hard resolution of Titus:

> "Ask my Life and try
> How gloriously I for your Sake can die.

"How great is his affliction and despair he is put in by the distrust and wrath of Berenice! He curses his fate, and will learn to forget, to hate and scorn her. . . .

"It remains to mention his relation to Titus. Otway has described it in a manner that, I must confess, the dramatic interest is raised to a higher degree than in Racine. Titus had made him his confidant and reveals to him all the secrets of his heart. Antiochus, however, considering his being a rival of the emperor, does not think himself worth his intimate friendship and will, at all events, depart from Rome, that no envy may be near the happy marriage of Titus and Berenice. By confessing to Titus, even at their first meeting, to be his rival, it must be almost impossible for him to remain any longer at Rome, to see Berenice in Titus behalf, and disinterestedly make her acquainted with the message of Titus." (*Otway's Titus and Berenice and Racine's Bérénice, a Parallel* [Wetzlar, 1891], p. 10.)

For Dorothea Canfield's opinion of Otway's Antiochus, see above, n. 7.

as well as of gallant sentiments in the one rôle of Otway's Antiochus as in all the rôles of Racine's young lovers put together in all the plays from *Andromaque* to *Phèdre*. Yet there are no references to gallantry or the jargon of gallantry in these comparisons of the two plays. Let him who can, explain the anomaly.

The loss of Racinian psychology in Otway's adaptation is due to some extent to his excisions in protagonist-confidant scenes. But it seems to me that excisions and more especially interpolations in protagonist-protagonist scenes are far more deadly to Racinian psychology. In other words, it is not abridgment alone that is responsible for the loss of Racinian psychology. In these scenes, the psychology is the drama. The flux of emotion in the minds of the characters is the action. The speakers react to a word, a gesture, a facial expression. The swift interplay of emotion sweeps the characters along against their will. At the end of the scene we find their *état d'âme* quite different from what it was at the beginning. The tension has mounted. Otway's excisions and his interpolations obscure this flux of emotion. His interpolations break the emotional current and retard dramatic movement.

The scene in which Antiochus announces Titus's decision to Bérénice is a good example of the effect of Otway's interpolations on Racine's psychological drama:

Titus has asked Antiochus to tell Bérénice that she must leave Rome. (Racine's Titus does not know that Antiochus loves Bérénice; Otway's Titus does.) Antiochus has decided not to deliver the message which would be the more painful and humiliating to Bérénice if conveyed by Titus's unsuccessful rival—who has just been reprimanded for speaking to her of his love when she is about to marry the Emperor. Antiochus shrinks from causing Bérénice pain and fears to incur her hatred. At this moment Bérénice appears. She is in a state of morbid anxiety. She is unable to bear any longer the *attente douloureuse* to which she has been subjected by Titus's avoidance of her. She must know at once why Titus has been acting so strangely. She has come to find him and beg for an explanation. And at the moment when she expects at last to end the unendurable agony of her doubts and fears, she finds, not Titus, but Antiochus. Her words express her surprise, and not very flatteringly to Antiochus: "Hé quoi, Seigneur! Vous n'êtes point parti?" (vs. 850). To the sensitive Antiochus, her disappointment is all too evident in her face. He is stung by it (vss. 851–52):

> Madame, je vois bien que vous êtes déçue
> Et que c'étoit César que cherchoit votre vue.

He cannot help defending himself against the implication that he is lingering unnecessarily at Rome. He adds (vss. 853-56):

> Mais n'accusez que lui, si malgré mes adieux
> De ma présence encor j'importune vos yeux.
> Peut-être en ce moment je serois dans Ostie,
> S'il ne m'eût de sa cour défendu la sortie.

Bérénice is too preoccupied with Titus's strange conduct towards her to be concerned with Antiochus. His defense of himself means only one thing to her: Titus is not avoiding everybody as he is avoiding her. He is seeking Antiochus' company. In defending himself, Antiochus has merely aggravated Bérénice's anxiety. She says: "Il vous cherche vous seul. Il nous évite tous" (vs. 857). She cannot yet bring herself to say that he is avoiding her alone. Antiochus sees her distress and tries to comfort her: "Il ne m'a retenu que pour parler de vous" (vs. 858). Far from comforting her this makes her anxiety acute: "De moi, Prince!" Antiochus replies simply: "Oui, Madame." So Titus will not speak *to* her but he speaks to others *about* her. What can this mean? Now Bérénice must find out what Titus has said: "Et qu'a-t-il pu vous dire?" (vs. 859). At this point Antiochus realizes that he has been brought dangerously near to revealing Titus's decision. He must not do so. Anyone else could more fittingly deliver the painful message. Antiochus says: "Mille autres mieux que moi pourront vous en instruire" (vs. 860). That is all he says. Bérénice replies, Quoi, Seigneur." Seeing that she is angry, Antiochus interrupts to protest against her anger. She should know him well enough, he tells her, to realize he is motivated only by consideration of her. Her peace of mind is dearer to him than his own (vss. 866-67):

> Pour ne le [votre repos] point troubler, j'aime
>   mieux vous déplaire,
> Et crains votre douleur plus que votre colère.

And so he has revealed that what Titus has said of her will be painful to her! The distraught Bérénice confesses her desperate anxiety and begs him to end her agony of suspense. How ironical that Antiochus should think that his silence can preserve her peace of mind! When Antiochus still demurs, she resorts to threats. She commands him to tell her what Titus has said. Finally she insists that if he does not he will incur her undying hatred. Antiochus delivers the message of banishment. Bérénice is stunned by the blow. She cannot believe it. She turns to her confidante in bewilderment. She gropes for an explanation that will enable her to reject the truth. She murmurs to her confidante that this must be some trap to cause misunderstanding between her and Titus. She must see Titus. She starts to leave. But Antiochus is indignant at her insinuations. He stops her with the protest: "Quoi? vous pourriez ici me regarder . . ." (vs. 913). Bérénice interrupts him with the accusation: "Vous le souhaitez trop pour me persuader" (vs. 915). Then she commands him never to see her again (vss. 915-16):

> Non, je ne vous crois point. Mais quoi qu'il en
> puisse être
> Pour jamais à mes yeux gardez-vous de paraître.

Antiochus is silent in the face of the perfidious accusation and the cruel command. Bérénice is unable to bear his presence any longer. She turns to leave and as she leaves, she says to her confidante: "Hélas! pour me tromper je fais ce que je puis" (vs. 918). She has recognized the fact that her accusation of Antiochus sprang from the necessity to hide from herself a truth that was too painful to bear. This is characteristic Racinian psychology. His personages deceive themselves. They unconsciously invent pretexts to believe what they want to believe. But they have pathetic flashes of insight into their motives.

There are 65 lines in this scene in *Bérénice*. Many of the speeches consist of one verse, some of a hemistich, some of three syllables only. Bérénice's first speech creates a tension between herself and Antiochus against which they are both powerless. What follows is like a chain reaction of emotions which neither she nor Antiochus can check.

The corresponding scene in Otway has 100 lines. Otway leaves very few of the short *répliques* as he found them in Racine. He adds one or two or several verses. His interpolations destroy the effect of a swift interplay of emotions where they do not obscure hopelessly the emotional implications of Racine's dialogue. Otway begins by destroying the tension created by the first two speeches:

> BÉRÉNICE
> Hé quoi, Seigneur! vous n'êtes point parti?

> ANTIOCHUS
> Madame, je vois bien que vous êtes déçue
> Et que c'étoit César que cherchoit votre vue.
> Mais n'accusez que lui, si malgré mes adieux
> De ma présence encor j'importune vos yeux.
> Peut-être en ce moment je serois dans Ostie,
> S'il ne m'eût de sa cour deféndu la sortie.

Otway translates Bérénice's line: "My Lord, I see you are not gone."[19] Then his Berenice adds (coyly?): "Perhaps 'tis me alone that you would shun." What did Otway imagine to be Berenice's *état d'âme* at this moment? I cannot even guess. But she is calm and collected enough to play the coquette with Antiochus. And how does she speak her first line? Does she involuntarily betray unpleasant surprise as Racine's Bérénice does? Or does she speak the line in such a manner as to convey the idea that she is glad to find Antiochus still in Rome, though she had feared that he had already left? Obviously this is what she does, for Antiochus so interprets the line. Here is his reply (p. 165):

> You came not here Antiochus to find,
> The visit to another was design'd;
> *Caesar.*

Antiochus accuses her of insincerity, of pretending to be looking for him. He does not react to disappointment betrayed by her expression or an involuntary gesture. Antiochus himself is cool and collected enough to reprove her for coquetry. Later, Bérénice asks Antiochus what Titus has said of her: "Et qu'a-t-il pu vous dire?" In Otway this hemistich becomes (p. 165):

> Of me, my Lord! Forbear this courtly art,
> Y'are brave, and should not mock an easie heart.
> In my distress what pleasure could you see?
> Alas! or what could *Titus* say of me?

Read out of its context this speech has a certain pathos. In the context it retards the movement and we lose the impression of desperate anxiety and impatience on Berenice's part.

With Antiochus' answer to this question, Otway begins to depart altogether from Racine. It is at this point that Racine's Antiochus realizes that he has come dangerously near to making the revelation

[19] In the early editions of Racine's play, the line was: "Enfin, Seigneur, vous n'êtes point parti."

that he had resolved not to make. He is certainly not the person to give Bérénice the painful message. It would be more fitting and less painful to both of them if anyone else delivered it. Antiochus says: "Mille autres mieux que moi pourront vous en instruire." Otway translates this line with the following unintelligible line: "Better a thousand times than I can tell." It is impossible to determine whether Otway missed the meaning of Racine's line or deliberately altered it. He gives the line some semblance of meaning by adding seven lines of his own. Here is the whole passage (p. 165):

> BER. Alas! or what could Titus say of me?
> ANT. Better a thousand times than I can tell.
> So firm a passion in his heart does dwell,
> When you are nam'd he's from himself transform'd,
> And ev'ry way betrays how much he's charm'd.
> Love in his Face does like a Tyrant rise,
> And Majesty's no longer in his Eyes.

As in Racine, when Berenice finally orders Antiochus to tell her what Titus had said or incur her hatred, Antiochus tells her. Otway alters the dialogue in which Bérénice accuses Antiochus of lying out of jealousy, with a serious loss of Racinian psychology. As Bérénice starts to go in search of Titus to have the truth from his own lips since she cannot accept Antiochus' account, Antiochus protests: "Quoi? vous pourriez ici me regarder . . ." (vs. 913). Bérénice interrupts him with (vss. 914-18):

> Vous le souhaitez trop pour me persuader.
> Non, je ne vous crois point. Mais, quoi qu'il
>   en puisse être,
> Pour jamais à mes yeux gardez-vous de paraître.
>   (A Phénice.)
> Ne m'abandonne pas dans l'état où je suis.
> Hélas! pour me tromper je fais ce que je puis.

In Otway, Antiochus' indignant "Quoi? vous pourriez ici me regarder . . ." (vs. 913) is replaced by the unintelligible statement "Too well you may behold him here" (p. 167). Berenice's "Vous le souhaitez trop pour me persuader" (vs. 914) takes the form of a stycomythic echo of Antiochus' unintelligible line (p. 167):

> ANT. Too well you may behold him here.
> BER. Too well you wish it to perswade it; No;

Otway is not content to leave Berenice's accusation in the form of one passionate outcry springing almost involuntarily from her pain and her humiliation like an instinctive blow struck at Antiochus to prevent him from wounding her more deeply. He spins it out into five lines of deliberate vituperation (p. 167):

> ANT. Too well you may behold him here.
> BER. Too well you wish it to perswade it; No;
> In this your base degenerate Soul you show;
> When you no other stratagem could find
> T'abuse my heart, you would betray your friend.
> How e're he prove, Know I your sight abhor,
> And from this minute never see me more.

She does not leave the stage here as she does in Racine. Her accusation calls forth a torrent of characteristic plaints from Antiochus (p. 167):

> Oh *Berenice*! remorseless cruel Fair!
> Born only for my torment and despair.
> Was it for this so faithfully I serv'd?
> Is this the recompence I have deserv'd?
> I, who for you did all Ambition wave,
> And left a Kingdom to become your Slave!
> Curse on my Fate!

Berenice quite deliberately repeats her accusation (p. 167):

> If e're my Heart you priz'd,
> You never had this cruelty devis'd;
> Never to work my Torment, been thus bold,
> And so Triumphantly the story told.
> Away, *Phaenicia*; no more I'le hear him speak.
> [*Ex. Ber. and Phae.*]

All this sounds not at all like an unconscious pretext on Berenice's part to reject an unbearably painful truth. She is entirely given over to her anger at Antiochus and believes firmly that Antiochus has lied to her. Otway of course omits Bérénice's recognition of her motivation. He drops the line: "Hélas! pour me tromper je fais ce que je puis."

There is little of Racine left in this scene. It bears some resemblance to a scene of *dépit amoureux* from a courtly romance. Otway may have deliberately rejected Racinian psychology. I believe, however, that he altered the emotional implications of Racine's dialogue because he did not perceive them. He is apparently insensitive to what might be called

THOMAS OTWAY'S *TITUS AND BERENICE*

the psychological obligato to Racine's lines. This impression is strengthened by alterations which he makes in other scenes. A bit of dialogue from the first Bérénice-Antiochus scene (Antiochus' declaration at the beginning of the play) will serve to show how vague is Otway's notion of what is going on in the minds of Racine's personages. Here are the two passages (vss. 259-78):

> BÉRÉNICE
> Seigneur, je n'ai pas cru que, dans une journée
> Qui doit avec César unir ma destinée,
> Il fût quelque mortel qui pût impunément
> Se venir à mes yeux déclarer mon amant.
> Mais de mon amitié mon silence est un gage:
> J'oublie, en sa faveur, un discours qui m'outrage.
> Je n'en ai point troublé le cours injurieux;
> Je fais plus: à regret je reçois vos adieux.
> Le ciel sait qu'au milieu des honneurs qu'il m'envoie
> Je n'attendois que vous pour témoin de ma joie.
> Avec tout l'univers j'honorois vos vertus.
> Titus vous chérissoit, vous admiriez Titus.
> Cent fois je me suis fait une douceur extrême
> D'entretenir Titus dans un autre lui-même.
> ANTIOCHUS
> Et c'est ce que je fuis. J'évite, mais trop tard,
> Ces cruels entretiens où je n'ai point de part.
> Je fuis Titus: je fuis ce nom qui m'inquiète,
> Ce nom qu'à tous moments votre bouche répète.
> Que vous dirois-je enfin? Je fuis des yeux distraits
> Qui, me voyant toujours, ne me voyoient jamais.

Otway has (p. 154):

> BER. Though it could never enter in my mind,
>   Since Caesar's Fortunes must with mine be join'd,
>   That any Mortal durst so hardy prove
>   T'invade his Right, and talk to me of Love:
>   I bear th'unpleasing Narrative of yours,
>   And Friendship, what my Honour shuns, endures.
>   Nay more; your parting I with trouble hear,
>   For you, next him, are to my Soul most dear.
> ANT. In justice to my Memory and Fame,
>   I fly from *Titus* that unlucky Name.
>   A name, which ev'ry Moment you repeat,
>   Whilst my poor heart lies bleeding at your feet.

Racine's Bérénice, with the self-absorption and the unconscious cruelty of a woman in love, evokes the memory, pleasant to her, but painful to Antiochus, of conversations in which Titus, though absent, occupied all Bérénice's thoughts and Titus's name was constantly on her lips. The repetition now of Titus's name, the unbearably painful reminder that his rôle has been merely that of proxy for Titus, precipitate Antiochus' outburst. Bérénice does not intend to wound him, but calculated cruelty could not have chosen more painful words than:

> *Titus* vous chérissoit, vous admiriez *Titus*.
> Cent fois je me suis fait une douceur extrême
> D'entretenir *Titus* dans un autre lui-même.

Otway replaces these lines with: "For you next him are to my Soul most dear." Berenice says nothing to call up the memory of her conversations with Antiochus; she does not mention the name Titus. Otway chooses this moment to introduce the "gloire" motif and then proceeds to translate bits of Antiochus' impassioned protest against the constant repetition of Titus's name. He reproduces the explosion after omitting the spark that set it off and after delaying it by introducing the reference to "Memory and Fame." And to Antiochus' description of the suffering caused him by Bérénice's absent eyes, dreamy with thoughts of Titus:

> "Je fuis des yeux distraits
> Qui, me voyant toujours, ne me voyoient jamais,"

he prefers a banal metaphor ludicrously elaborated: "Whilst my poor Heart lies bleeding at your Feet."[20]

In the Titus-Berenice scenes, Otway comes somewhat closer to Racine than in the scenes between Berenice and Antiochus. In the Titus-Berenice interview of Racine's Act IV, Otway makes excisions and interpola-

---

[20] By this substitution Otway avoids one *précieux* trick of style only to fall into a worse one. The play on *voir* is perhaps precious; but the preciosity is redeemed by the precision of the psychological notation and the image evoked. Otway's substitute is an elaboration of a banal metaphor hardly less ludicrous than Mascarille's heart "écorché de la tête aux pieds." Titus also expresses his suffering in such a metaphor: "My Heart bleeds now; I feel the Drops run down" (p. 170). The same metaphor occurs once in Racine's play, but it is not prolonged. Titus (explaining to Paulin how difficult it has been to come to the decision to send Bérénice away) says (vss. 453-54):

> Crois qu'il m'en a coûté, pour vaincre tant d'amour,
> Des combats dont mon coeur *saignera* plus d'un jour.

tions as he did in the Berenice-Antiochus scenes. But here his interpolations do not alter the characters and their relationship to each other. They are merely unnecessary padding of the short *répliques*. Excision causes the greatest damage. Otway cuts out entirely the speech in which Bérénice reproaches Titus for the irony of her situation: When there were obstacles to their marriage, he professed constancy; now that there are none, he tells her they must part. This, more than anything, causes Bérénice to doubt that he loves her. He also cuts out the speech of Titus which calls forth these reproaches from Bérénice, the one ending with the verse: "Car enfin, ma princesse, il faut nous séparer" (vs. 1060) and Titus's reply to Bérénice's reproaches ending with the verse: "Mais il ne s'agit plus de vivre, il faut régner" (vs. 1102). These two verses he manages to bring into Titus's very first speech by tacking on at the end the following priggish pronouncement (p. 170):

> For dearest *Berenice* we must part.
> And now I would not a dispute maintain,
> Whether I lov'd [*sic*], but whether I must Reign.

Most of the dialogue of this scene I should call paraphrase. Otway's rendering of important first and last lines of Racine's dialogue is particularly vague and unsatisfactory. For instance, the first two verses of Titus's first speech read (vss. 1045-46):

> N'accablez point, Madame, un prince malheureux,
> Il ne faut point ici nous attendrir tous deux.

Otway renders these verses thus (p. 170):

> O! stop the deluge, which so fiercely flows:
> This is no Time t'allay each others woes.

If this is not paraphrase, it deserves an unkinder name—mistranslation. The same thing can be said of other verses in this scene. For instance, Bérénice's line, "Pourquoi m'enviez-vous l'air que vous respirez?" (vs. 1129) becomes in Otway's version: "Or why d'ye envy me the air I breath?" (p. 170). Where now are the famous tenderness, pathos, and poignancy of Otway? What could have impelled him to rob Racine's line of those very qualities by a mere change of subject?

Otway comes closest to Racine in the first Titus-Berenice interview (Act II, Scene 4, in Racine). It is from this scene that Miss Canfield quotes parallel passages to show how accurately and how successfully

Otway can translate Racine. It is from this scene too that she takes the one line which she uses to illustrate her statement that "instances are not rare where the simplicity and feeling of Otway are heard in phrases not in the original."[21] It is from this scene that Eccles chooses his one example of felicitous translation.[22] I agree that the line which Miss Canfield quotes is superior to the original and that the one which Eccles quotes is a felicitous rendering of Racine's line. There is in this scene, however, a loss of a dramatic quality which is characteristically Racinian. Racine's personages usually suspect that words are spoken to hide feelings. They search for the fleeting shades of emotion in a face, an involuntary gesture, a tone that will reveal the truth which words are intended to conceal. Racine's Bérénice is alarmed rather than reassured by Titus's protestations of his great love for her. They are unnecessary, and he has spoken them with alarming coldness. A sigh would have convinced her. She says (vss. 593-94):

> Mon coeur ne prétend point, Seigneur, vous démentir,
> Et je vous en croirai sur un simple soupir.

Otway translates (p. 159):

> In you I trust, would onely for you live,
> And what you say, I ever must believe.

It seems to me that Otway's Berenice has said almost the opposite of what Racine's Bérénice has said. The loss of Racinian psychology here is slight and does not seriously affect the dramatic quality of the scene. But it is the same kind of loss that we find in the Berenice-Antiochus scenes, where it affects the drama more seriously.

Otway makes changes in the structure of Racine's play which have little importance as departures from Racine since they destroy nothing peculiarly Racinian. They have a certain interest, however. They show the ineffectual efforts of an early English classicist to use the technique of French classical tragedy. When he departs from Racine's guidance, Otway has difficulty with the principle of continuity of action and with *liaison des scènes*. He displaces one entrance, that of Antiochus at the end of Racine's Act IV. This one displaced entrance brings several technical gaucheries in its wake. Otway brings Antiochus on the stage *before* instead of *after* Titus has dismissed Berenice and she has left

[21] See above, n. 7.
[22] *Op. cit.*, p. 5.

threatening suicide. Otway's Antiochus enters at the moment when Titus is expecting to see Berenice. We are unprepared for this entrance, for at the end of Otway's Act II we think we have seen the last of Antiochus.[23] Otway motivates the entrance awkwardly. By way of explaining his unexpected return, Antiochus says to Arsaces:

> I said I'd never see her face again;
> But come and find my boastings all were vain.

On entering, he finds Titus, who tells him that he is on his way to see Berenice to tell her that they must part. Whereupon Antiochus speaks the words which Racine's Antiochus had used under quite different circumstances, i.e., after Bérénice had left the stage in despair and threatening suicide, after Titus has told her they must part. Otway's Antiochus says: "What have you done, Sir? *Berenice* will die, . . ." He then describes Berenice's despair in Racine's words (before she reaches despair). Presumably Antiochus exits before Berenice enters but there is nothing in the lines to indicate that he does. After Titus's interview

---

[23] At the end of Act III, Racine's Antiochus is preparing to leave Rome at once. He tells himself that, thanks to Bérénice's unjust treatment of him, he will leave indifferent to her. But he hesitates because of his solicitude for the unhappy Bérénice (vss. 944-52):

> Non, je la quitte, Arsace.
> Je sens qu'à sa douleur je pourrois compatir:
> Ma gloire, mon repos, tout m'excite à partir.
> Allons; et de si loin évitons la cruelle,
> Que de longtemps, Arsace, on ne nous parle d'elle.
> Toutefois il nous reste encore assez de jour:
> Je vais dans mon palais attendre ton retour.
> Va voir si sa douleur ne l'a point trop saisie.
> Cours; et partons du moins assurés de sa vie.

These lines, which close Racine's Act III, hint that Antiochus' tenderness, his sympathetic imagination, will bring him back to Bérénice before he sails away. They prepare the audience for his return to Titus's palace in the next act, for his visit (off-stage) to the despairing Bérénice, and for his entrance at the end of Act IV to beg Titus to save Bérénice from suicide, an entrance which contributes to the tension of the last scene of Act IV.

Otway's Antiochus betrays no sympathy for Berenice at the end of Act II (Act III in Racine). His decision to leave Rome seems definitive, untroubled by any solicitude for Berenice (p. 167):

> She left me cruelly, and let her go;
> My honour and Repose command it too:
> For ever to my eyes a stranger be,
> Till I have learn't to scorn as well as she.

with Berenice, Paulinus enters and announces that the tribunes and the senate are impatiently demanding that Titus dismiss Berenice. Titus instructs Paulinus to tell them that Berenice will leave Rome the next day. He has decided, definitively it seems, that he will not see Berenice before her departure. He sends her a letter of farewell. Then, in a soliloquy, he meditates:

> Would I had never known what 'tis to live,
> Or a new Being to my self could give;
> Some monstrous and unheard of Shape now find,
> As Savage and as Barbarous as my Mind.

According to French classical doctrine, Otway has at this point ended his play. But no. In comes Antiochus, this time to take formal leave of Titus. Almost immediately they see Berenice approaching. Titus exits, saying: "Oh! Heav'n! she's entring, from her Charms let's fly." This is a rather naïve use of the *liaison de fuite*; but it is subtlety itself compared with Titus's last entrance. Titus's exit leaves the stage free for the scene of Antiochus' second declaration—all Otway's own. After Berenice has rejected Antiochus, Otway has to bring Titus back for the dénouement. Just at the right moment, back comes Titus, saying:

> Spite of my self I wander this way still.
> Why would you, *Berenice*, my presence shun?

Compared with the style of later adaptations of Racine, that of Otway appears to have something of Racine's simplicity. And yet Otway does show a distaste for Racinian dialogue when it takes the form of very short speeches in simple language and with the tone of everyday speech. I have already noted several instances of the expansion of such speeches in Otway. His aversion for them is very marked in the scene with which he opens his third act, which corresponds to Scene 2 of Racine's fourth act. Bérénice has heard from Antiochus that Titus wishes her to leave Rome. She had tried to persuade herself that Antiochus is lying. Titus must tell her himself that he has repudiated all his promises. She has sent her confidante to beg Titus to come to her. At last the confidante returns to end Bérénice's *attente douloureuse*. Before the confidante can speak, Bérénice questions her:

> Chère Phénice, hé bien! as-tu vu l'Empereur?
> Qu'a-t-il dit? Viendra-t-il?

Phénice tries to answer her questions:

> Oui, je l'ai vu, Madame,
> Et j'ai peint à ses yeux le trouble de votre âme.
> J'ai vu couler des pleurs qu'il vouloit retenir.

To the distraught Bérénice these well-meant reassurances are unendurable temporizing. She breaks in with the question: "Vient-il?" And at last Phénice gives her the answer: "N'en doutez point, Madame, il va venir." Bérénice's repetition of the all-important question tersely and directly seems not only natural but inevitable under the circumstances. Yet it is the simple question, "Vient-il?" dictated by Bérénice's anxiety and impatience, which Otway avoids. Here is the corresponding dialogue in Otway's play (p. 168):

> BER. *Phaenice*, Well, my *Titus* hast thou seen?
> What will he come and make me live again?
> PHAE. Madam, the Emperor I alone did find;
> And saw in his the trouble of your mind;
> I saw the tears he would have hid, run down.
> BER. But was he not asham'd they shou'd be shown?
> Lookt he not as he thought his Love disgrace?
> And was not all the Emperor in his face?
> PHAE. Doubt it not, Madame, he will soon be here.

So determined is Otway to eliminate the offending "Vient-il?" that he is oblivious of the fact that he makes the confidante answer the question which is no longer there. Rhetoric, awkward inversion, and an unaccountable twisting of the meaning of one line ("Et j'ai peint à ses yeux le trouble de votre âme"—"And saw in his the trouble of your mind") complete the transformation of Racine's realistic dialogue. Here Otway obviously avoids simple language which expresses emotion as it is expressed in everyday speech. I have already noted two features of Otway's style which are part of his characterization of Antiochus: he frequently indulges in hyperbole and he uses the jargon of gallantry more lavishly and more obtrusively than Racine. Two other tricks of style make Otway's verse less swift and flowing than Racine's. He is fond of pairs of adjectives, one of which is usually superfluous, such as: "unsteady, anxious mind," "remorseless, cruel Fair," "fond, obedient Fool," "base, degenerate Soul"; and the reader frequently has to pick his way slowly through awkward and ambiguous word order, as in the following verses (pp. 162, 164, 165):

> So far's Resentment from my heart remov'd,
> That *Berenice* is by my friend belov'd,
> That I, *Antiochus*, the thing extol.
>
> That ev'n, Sir, you dare wrong the thing I've lov'd.
>
> And Friendship, what my Honour shuns, endures.
>
> How gloriously I for your sake can dye.

Otway writes in a more simple style than other adapters of Racine, with the exception of Ambrose Philips. But when Racine's simplicity and economy make his style most dramatic, Otway rejects Racinian simplicity and economy in favor of verbose grandiloquence. He has conventionalized the character of Antiochus both in sentiments and in language. He has in one scene made of his Berenice a coquette and a Guenièvre, really the "cruel Fair" which Antiochus calls her on several occasions. Of all Racine's protagonist-protagonist scenes, only one is left intact. In all the others thoughtless excisions and incongruous interpolations obscure the interplay of emotions in the minds of the characters which constitutes the drama. Whether Otway's *Titus and Berenice* be called a translation or an adaptation of Racine's *Bérénice*, it could give an English reader or spectator only a very faint idea of the original.

« « CHAPTER III » »

THE MOURNING BRIDE

VARIOUS sources have been suggested for Congreve's *The Mourning Bride*,[1] not the least important of them being Racine's *Bajazet*. The fact is that *The Mourning Bride* is reminiscent of several earlier plays but no one influence is dominant enough to justify the assertion that any one of these plays is the chief source. Congreve's contemporary, Charles Gildon, mentioned several possible sources. He thought that Congreve had *Bajazet* in mind "when he formed his Design."[2] In 1904 Professor J. P. Wickersham Crawford devoted a short article to a repetition of Gildon's remark, going into greater detail in describing the resemblance between the plot of *The Mourning Bride* and that of *Bajazet*. Crawford thought that he was the first to point out Racine's influence in Congreve's play.[3] He thinks this influence of some im-

---

[1] William Congreve's *The Mourning Bride* was first produced on February 27 (or 28), 1697. See D. Crane Taylor, *William Congreve* (London, 1931), p. 98, and John C. Hodges, *William Congreve the Man* (New York, 1941), p. 58. It was first published on March 15. Soon afterwards Congreve revised the play and put out a second edition. All my references are to *The Complete Works of William Congreve*, ed. Montague Summers (Soho, The Nonesuch Press, 1923). This edition reproduces the text of the first edition.

[2] Gildon mentions the romance of *Cleopatra* and calls attention to Zara's resemblance to Nourmahal in *Aureng Zebe* and Almeria in *The Indian Emperor*. Then he says: "I know some will have the whole Play a kind of a Copy of that; but I confess I cannot discover likeness enough to justify that Opinion; unless it be Zara's coming to the Prison to *Osmin* as *Almeria* does to Cortez. I believe our Poet had the *Bajazet* of *Racine* in view, when he formed his Design, at least there is as much Ground for this as the Former Opinion." (*Lives and Characters of the English Dramatic Poets* [London, 1699].) (Gildon's continuation of Langbaine.)

[3] "On the Relation of Congreve's *Mourning Bride* to Racine's *Bajazet*," *Modern Language Notes*, XIX (1904), 193-94. At the time when Professor Crawford wrote, Gildon's suggestion had long since been forgotten or was ignored by

portance. He says: "Congreve added many details to Racine's story, and changed it, but stripping *The Mourning Bride* of these unessential elements, I think the basis of the two plays is the same."[4] On the other hand, F. Y. Eccles states without any qualifications that nothing in *The Mourning Bride* recalls Racine.[5] This contradiction may be attributed to different views of what is essential in a play. If the outline of a story is the important thing, then Crawford's statement is accurate. If, on the other hand, *mise en oeuvre* is the essential, Eccles comes nearer the truth.

I lean to Eccles's point of view. Indeed Racine's influence on *The Mourning Bride* is so slight as hardly to justify the inclusion of the play in this study. And yet the play seems to me to be important in a study of Racine's influence in England for the following reasons: using Racine's *Bajazet* as a *point de départ*, Congreve has constructed a tragedy that is antithetical in every respect to the Racinian genre; his play was a sensational success at a moment when Aristotelian formalism was still dominant in the criticism of advocates of the rules; it was the only play inspired by Racine which was written during Rymer's ascendancy (unless it is assumed that Rymer was already a force in English criticism when Otway adapted *Bérénice*); the most detailed contemporary critique describes it as a "regular" tragedy and finds in its success evidence of classical taste in the English public;[6] the popularity

---

editors and critics. Crawford quotes Edmund Gosse and A. W. Ward as saying that the plot, so far as is known, is Congreve's own invention (p. 193). When Montague Summers prepared his edition in 1923 he in turn ignored both Gildon and Crawford. He says: "The somewhat intricate plot of *The Mourning Bride* would seem to be original, and the resemblances offered by this play are of quite a general character. Thus the situation between Zara, Osmyn, and Almeria is not unlike that of Zempoalla, Montezuma, and Orazia, in Howard and Dryden's *The Indian Queen*, produced at the Theatre Royal, January, 1663-4. It is, perhaps, yet more vaguely reminiscent of the Almeria, Cortez, and Cydaria episodes (especially IV, 4, 'A Prison') in *The Indian Emperor*, Theatre Royal, 1665. Zara is of the same stock, undoubtedly, as Lyndaraxa and the Empress Nourmahal; and Congreve, moreover, may have taken a hint for her circumstances from Almeyda, 'a Captive Queen of *Barbary*.'" He then quotes from Davies (*Dramatic Miscellanies*, III, p. 348) to the effect that Congreve was well read in the Greek dramatists, and that the interview between Osmyn and Almeria in Act II is reminiscent of the scene in Sophocles's *Electra* where Orestes reveals his identity to his sister. (*The Complete Works of William Congreve*, II, 175.)

[4] Crawford, *op. cit.*, p. 194.
[5] *Racine in England* (Oxford, The Clarendon Press, 1922), p. 19.
[6] The critique by Sir Richard Blackmore is quoted later in this chapter.

of the play endured throughout the eighteenth century;[7] modern criticism still ranks it as the best tragedy of its age, i.e., the age between Otway and Rowe and Addison.[8]

A brief summary of the plot of *The Mourning Bride*, such as Crawford includes in his article, would make the resemblance to Racine's *Bajazet* seem much greater than it is. I can see no way to bring out the enormous differences in the dramatic technique and in the appeal that the two plays have for an audience except to analyze Congreve's play in great detail. A performance of *The Mourning Bride* must have made the spectator's blood run cold and his hair stand on end. I hope that my summary will give a faint idea of the thrill that audiences must have experienced; and, what is more important, that it will help to define the nature of the play's appeal.

Act I. scene: *Granada, a room of state in the palace of King Manuel.* "The Curtain rises slowly to soft Musick, discovers Almeria in Mourning, Leonora waiting in Mourning."

Almeria, daughter of Manuel, King of Granada, mourns for the death of Anselmo, the old king of Valentia, mortal enemy of her father. Anselmo has died in prison in Granada. In her grief Almeria wishes for death and calls on the name of Alphonso, son of Anselmo, apostrophizing him as "My Love, my Lord, my Husband." Leonora, her confidante, is startled at these words and Almeria realizes too late that she has inadvertently revealed her secret. ("What have I done? My Grief has hurried me beyond all Thought.") She then explains to Leonora that she was once a captive in Valentia of this same Anselmo who has just died, her father's enemy, that Anselmo was kind to her and wished her to marry Alphonso, his son. But Manuel marched on Valentia. Alphonso, to protect the Queen, his mother, and Almeria from Manuel's cruelty should Valentia fall to him, had taken them on board a ship. At the news of the fall of Valentia to Manuel's armies, the ship set sail. Almeria and Alphonso were married on board ship. The ship was wrecked off the coast of Africa and Alphonso was drowned. Almeria has worn mourning garb since her husband's death but has told her father that she wears it to fulfill a vow made in gratitude for her escape from death.

Now, as she mourns for Anselmo and for Alphonso, she makes another solemn vow (p. 189):

[7] See below, n. 15. [8] Taylor, *op. cit.*, p. 95.

> If ever I do yield or give consent,
> By any Action, Word or Thought, to wed
> Another Lord; may then just Heav'n, show'r down
> Unheard of Curses on me.

At this moment Gonsalez, favorite of King Manuel, enters and announces (in an epic description) that Manuel is returning victorious from a battle with Moorish invaders. A symphony of warlike music strikes up and Manuel enters attended by officers and followed by prisoners in fetters and guards who range themselves around the stage. Manuel rebukes his daughter for wearing mourning on a day of rejoicing. He then tells her he has chosen for her husband Garcia, son of Gonsalez. She faints. When she is revived, she asks leave to retire. Garcia conducts her to the door. Alonzo, an officer ("Creature to Gonsalez") announces the approach of Zara, captive Moorish queen, attended by the captain of the Moorish horse, Osmyn by name. Osmyn's great valor has attracted the attention of Manuel and Garcia. Manuel questions Garcia about him and Garcia says (p. 194):

> I would oblige him, but he shuns my Kindness;
> And with a haughty Mien, and stern Civility,
> Dumbly declines all Offers: If he speaks
> 'Tis scarce above a word; as he were born
> Alone to do, and did disdain to talk.

Manuel suspects that Zara is in love with Osmyn. (He himself loves Zara.)

The taciturn and mysterious Osmyn and the beauteous Zara are now led in, conducted by Perez, captain of Manuel's Guard, and attended by Selim and several mutes and eunuchs. Osmyn and Zara are in fetters. Manuel orders the fetters removed. There ensues the following dialogue between Manuel and Osmyn (p. 195):

> KING.   Whence comes it, Valiant *Osmyn*, that a Man
>   So great in Arms, as thou art said to be,
>   So ill can brook Captivity,
>   The common Chance of War?
> OSMYN.   Because Captivity has robb'd me of a just Revenge.
> KING.   I understand not that.
> OSMYN.   I would not have you.
> ZARA.   That gallant *Moor*, in Battle lost a Friend,
>   What more than Life he lov'd; and the Regret,
>   Of not revenging on his Foes, that Loss,

THE MOURNING BRIDE

     Has caus'd this Melancholy and Despair.
 KING. She does excuse him; 'tis as I expected. (To
     Gonsalez.)

Manuel asks the name of Osmyn's friend, is told it is Heli, and sends Garcia to search among the prisoners to see if Heli has survived. The act ends with the King's madrigal to Zara's eyes (p. 196):

> But late I find that War is but her [Fortune's] Sport;
> In Love the Goddess keeps her awful Court!
> Fickle in Fields, unsteadily she flies,
> But Rules with settled Sway in Zara's Eyes.

ACT II. *The scene represents the ile of a temple.* Enter Garcia, Heli, and Perez. Among the prisoners Garcia has found Heli, the friend whom Osmyn thinks dead. They are searching for Osmyn, who, they have been told, has come to the temple. Perez sees Osmyn at a distance. Osmyn has seen the three men and he moves away to avoid them. Heli then asks to be allowed to follow him alone. (He fears that Osmyn's melancholy and his pride may drive him to some act of violence.) After Heli leaves, Garcia tells Perez that the King has instructed him to spy on Zara and Osmyn as he suspects them of being lovers. Perez says there is no doubt:

> To me 'twas long since plain,
> And every Look of his and hers confess it.

Hearing footsteps they leave.

Enter Almeria and Leonora. Almeria, in despair at the thought of marrying Garcia, is on her way to Anselmo's tomb. Leonora thinks she hears the sound of voices. Almeria says (pp. 197–98):

> No, all is hush'd, and still as Death—'Tis dreadful!
> How rev'rend is the Face of this tall Pile,
> Whose ancient Pillars rear their Marble Heads,
> To bear aloft its arch'd and pond'rous Roof,
> By its own Weight made stedfast and immoveable,
> Looking Tranquility. It strikes an Awe
> And Terror on my aking Sight; the Tombs
> And Monumental Caves of Death look Cold,
> And shoot a Chilness to my trembling Heart.
> Give me thy Hand, and speak to me: nay, speak,

And let me hear thy Voice;
My own affrights me with its Echo's.[9]

Leonora urges her to turn back but Almeria wishes to go on. She says (p. 198):

> Lead me o'er Bones and Skulls and mouldring Earth
> Of Humane Bodies; for I'll mix with them,
> Or wind me in the Shroud of some pale Coarse
> Yet green in Earth, rather than be the Bride
> Of *Garcia*'s more detested Bed.

(Cf. *Romeo and Juliet*, Act IV, Scene 2.) They move on.

"The scene opening discovers a Place of Tombs. One Monument fronting the View, greater than the rest."

Re-enter Almeria and Leonora. They find the marble door of Anselmo's tomb standing open. Almeria says (pp. 198-99):

> Sure 'tis the friendly Yawn of Death for me;
> And that dumb Mouth, significant in Show,
> Invites me to the Bed where I alone
> Shall rest; shews me the Grave, where Nature wearied,
> And long oppres'd with Woes and bending Cares,
> May lay the Burden down, and sink in Slumbers
> Of eternal Peace. Death, grim Death, will fold
> Me, in his leaden Arms, and press me close
> To his cold clayie Breast: My Father then
> Will cease his Tyranny; and Garcia too
> Will fly my pale Deformity with loathing.
> My Soul enlarg'd from its vile Bonds, will mount,
> And range the starry Orbs, and Milky Ways,
> Of that refulgent World, where I shall swim
> In liquid Light, and float on Seas of Bliss
> To my *Alphonso*'s Soul. O Joy too great!

---

[9] This is the passage which Dr. Johnson admired so extravagantly. A modern biographer of Congreve makes some illuminating remarks concerning it. Having commented on the Senecan fustian in this play and others of the period, he notes that occasionally we find "clear serene passages of rare beauty and loveliness that are the supreme achievements of English drama." He continues: "It was a passage of this kind that kept alive the fame of *The Mourning Bride* long after its prevailing fustian had relegated it to the dusty shelves. This one flare of great poetry became celebrated through the encomium of Dr. Johnson, who said: 'If I were required to select from the whole mass of English Poetry the most poetical paragraph, I know not what I could prefer to an exclamation in *The Mourning Bride*.'" (Taylor, *op. cit.*, p. 96.)

THE MOURNING BRIDE

> O Extasie of Thought! Help me, *Anselmo*;
> Help me, *Alphonso*; take me, reach thy Hand:
> To thee, to thee I call, to thee, *Alphonso*:
> O *Alphonso*.

As she calls out to Alphonso in heaven, a figure ascends from the tomb, crying (p. 199):

> Who calls that wretched thing, that was *Alphonso*?
> Whence is that Voice, whose Shrilness, from the Grave,
> And growing to his dead Father's Shrowd, roots up
>   *Alphonso*?

Thinking she sees the ghost of Alphonso, Almeria cries (p. 199):

> Mercy and Providence! O speak to it,
> Speak to it quickly, quickly. . . .

(Cf. *Hamlet*, Act I, Scene 1.) The figure comes forward. It is Osmyn, who is, in effect, Alphonso. He too thinks he sees a ghost, for he had thought Almeria dead. He catches her as she falls in a faint, and discovers that she is alive. He faints.

Heli enters and finds their prostrate senseless forms. He revives them. Explanations follow—some hundred lines—before Heli's presence is noticed by the reunited pair. Then there is a second recognition. Heli is Antonio, Alphonso's bosom friend, whom he had thought dead. More explanations. Then Heli warns Osmyn that Zara is approaching (p. 203):

> You must be quick, for Love will lend her Wings.

Almeria asks the meaning of this and Osmyn replies (p. 203):

> She's the Reverse of thee; she's my Unhappiness.
> Harbour no Thought that may disturb thy Peace.

Almeria has no further misgivings. She leaves so as not to arouse Zara's suspicions. Enter Zara. We learn how Osmyn was rescued after the shipwreck. Zara found him lying unconscious on the shore. She describes the scene (p. 205):

> Kneeling on Earth, I loos'd my Hair,
> And with it dry'd thy wat'ry Cheeks; chafing
> Thy Temples, till reviving Blood arose,
> And like the Morn vermillion'd o'er thy Face.
> O Heav'n! how did my Heart rejoice and ake,

> When I beheld the Day-break of thy Eyes,
> And felt the Balm of thy respiring Lips!

After a long account of her rescue of Osmyn and her machinations to protect him, Zara tells him that Manuel loves her and that she can make use of her power over him to free Osmyn, if Osmyn will return her love (p. 206):

> We may be free; the Conqueror is mine;
> In Chains unseen, I hold him by the Heart,
> And can unwind, or strain him as I please.
> Give me thy Love, I'll give thee Liberty.

Osmyn refuses. Zara flies into a rage and berates him. She is sure he loves her but she thinks he is afraid to be a rival to the King.

The King enters just as Zara says, "The King's thy Rival." The King has overheard. He asks who dares to be his rival. Zara accuses Osmyn of daring to make love to her (cf. Seneca's Phaedra). The King orders him tortured and thrown into prison.

ACT III. *A prison.* Osmyn alone; then Heli. Through Almeria, Heli has gained admittance. He brings three messages: (1) Almeria will visit Osmyn in prison at midnight. (2) There is a mutiny brewing among Manuel's troops and the Valentians are arming for revolt against Manuel's rule. (3) Zara still loves Osmyn and her love can be used to set him free if he will conceal his aversion for her (cf. *Bajazet*, Act II, Scene 5, and vss. 1011-12). Heli exits. Enter Zara, veiled. Osmyn, thinking it is Almeria, says (p. 211):

> What Brightness breaks upon me, thus thro' Shades,
> And promises a Day to this dark Dwelling!
> Is it my Love?—

(Cf. *Romeo and Juliet*, Act II, Scene 2.) Zara says (p. 211):

> O that thy Heart, had taught
> Thy Tongue that Saying.

She lifts her veil and Osmyn starts, saying (p. 211):

> Zara! I'm betrayed
> By my Surprise.

Neither his surprise nor his words, which Zara has heard, cause her to suspect she has a rival. She says (p. 211):

THE MOURNING BRIDE

> What, does my Face displease thee?
> That having seen it, thou do'st turn thy Eyes
> Away, as from Deformity and Horrour.
> If so, this sable Curtain shall again
> Be drawn, and I will stand before thee seeing,
> And unseen. Is it my Love? ask again
> That Question, speak again in that soft Voice,
> And look again with Wishes in thy Eyes.

She then begs his forgiveness for having had him thrown into prison, and promises to contrive to free him before morning. She leaves him, saying (p. 212):

> But as
> The present Form of our Engagements rests,
> Thou hast the Wrong, 'till I redeem thee hence;
> That done, I leave thy Justice to return
> My Love. Adieu.

Osmyn says (p. 213):

> This Woman has a Soul
> Of God-like Mould, intrepid and commanding,
> And challenges, in spight of me, my best
> Esteem; to this she's fair, few more can boast
> Of personal Charms, or with less Vanity
> Might hope to captivate the Hearts of Kings.
> But she has Passions which out-strip the Wind,
> And tear her Virtues up, as Tempests root
> The Sea. I fear when she shall know the Truth,
> Some swift and dire event of her blind Rage
> Will make all fatal.

Enter Almeria. A long scene follows in which Osmyn and Almeria express their despair over Almeria's impending marriage to Garcia. Two bits from Almeria's speeches will suffice to illustrate the style (pp. 214, 216):

> Am I the bosom Snake,
> That sucks thy warm Life-Blood, and gnaws thy Heart?
> . . . .
> O, I am struck; thy Words are Bolts of Ice,
> Which shot into my Breast, now melt and chill me.
> I chatter, shake, and faint with thrilling Fears.

Enter Zara. She has the King's signet ring as token of her power, and is prepared to free Osmyn. But she sees him leading Almeria to the door and realizes that Almeria is her rival (p. 217):

> Trembling and weeping as he leads her forth!
> Confusion in his Face, and Grief in hers!

(Cf. *Bajazet*, Act III, Scene 7, and vs. 1069.) This discovery causes her to countermand her orders for Osmyn's release and to instruct the prison guards to keep close watch on him, not even permitting Almeria to visit him. The act ends with Zara's threat (p. 218):

> Yes, thou shalt know, spite of thy past Distress,
> And all those Ills which thou so long hast mourn'd;
> Heav'n has no Rage, like Love to Hatred turn'd,
> Nor Hell a Fury, like a Woman scorn'd.

ACT IV. SCENE: *A room of state*. We learn what Zara has done to carry out her vague threat at the end of the preceding act. She has accused Osmyn of collusion with Manuel's mutinous troops. Selim, her servant, reports the subsequent course of events. Manuel has signed a warrant for the public execution of Osmyn. Heli has fled to join the revolt. Zara now repents of her accusation. She cannot bear the thought of Osmyn's death. She commands Selim to devise a scheme to save him. He does so and Zara decides to act on his suggestion. She will tell the King that a public execution would be too great a risk. It would afford an opportunity for Osmyn's fellow conspirators to rescue him. She herself will have him put to death secretly. She will have her mutes strangle him. To avoid miscarriage of these plans the King must forbid access to the prison to everyone but Zara herself and her mutes.

Enter the King, Gonsalez, Garcia, Perez. Gonsalez reports to the King a rumor that Alphonso is alive and leading the uprising in Valentia. Zara now suspects that Osmyn is Alphonso but pursues her plan to save him. In urging the King to allow no one access to Osmyn's prison, she insists that Almeria be forbidden to see Osmyn. She reports to Manuel that Almeria has already visited Osmyn in his prison. This and Zara's vacillating attitude towards Osmyn arouse Gonsalez' suspicions. He suspects that jealousy is her motive in keeping Almeria from visiting Osmyn and that she, Zara, is planning Osmyn's release rather than his death. But the King, on hearing that Almeria has visited the prison, suspects his daughter of conspiring against him. Gonsalez suggests that the King tell Almeria that Osmyn has been condemned to death so as to watch her reaction (cf. *Bajazet*, Act III, Scene 8).

Enter Almeria. The King accuses her of helping his enemies. Then he tells her that Osmyn will be tortured and put to death. Almeria thinks Gonsalez has discovered her secret and revealed it to the King. She denounces him and thus inadvertently reveals Osmyn's identity and her marriage to him. The King thinks she has gone mad and exits after giving her maids instructions to watch her carefully. Only Gonsalez hears her final revelation: that Osmyn is Alphonso. Almeria's ravings are characteristic of the style of Congreve's dialogue (p. 227):

> Was it the doleful Bell, toling for Death?
> Or dying Groans from my *Alphonso*'s Breast?
> See, see, look yonder! where a grizled, pale,
> And ghastly Head, glares by, all smear'd with Blood,
> Gasping as it would speak; and after it,
> Behold a damp, dead Hand has dropp'd a Dagger:
> I'll catch it—hark! a Voice cries Murder! 'tis
> My Father's Voice; hollow it sounds, and from
> The Tomb it calls——I'll follow it, for there
> I shall again behold my dear Alphonso.

(Cf. *Macbeth*, Act II, Scenes 1, 2.) After this delirious (prophetic) vision Almeria exits with her attendants, leaving Gonsalez to lay plans for removing the obstacle to his son's marriage to Almeria. He instructs Alonzo to procure for him the garb of one of Zara's mutes. Alonzo exits and Gonsalez informs the audience that he will murder Osmyn-Alphonso and marry Garcia to his widow. Thus Garcia will inherit the crown as his father had planned.

ACT V. SCENE: *A room of state*. Enter the King, Perez, and Alonzo. The King spies one of Zara's mutes trying to slip out of the palace. He orders Alonzo to seize him. Alonzo kills the mute and finds on him a letter from Zara to Osmyn revealing her plans to free him. A reference to Manuel's guards seems to implicate Perez in the conspiracy. The King accuses him of being a traitor and strikes him. Nevertheless he entrusts a vital mission to him. He orders him to stab Osmyn in his cell, to dim the lights in the cell and to bring him Osmyn's robe. He plans to disguise himself as Osmyn and wait in the cell for the arrival of the perfidious Zara. He sees Zara approaching and exits to avoid her.

Enter Zara and Selim. Zara is troubled by the failure of her messenger to return. Then she sees Manuel as he strides away. His angry look indicates that he has discovered her plot. Osmyn is lost. She will die with him. She orders Selim to prepare two bowls of poison.

The scene shifts to the prison. Enter Gonsalez, "disguis'd like a Mute, with a Dagger." He exits in the direction of Osmyn's cell.

Enter Garcia and Alonzo.

Re-enter Gonsalez, "bloody."

Garcia announces that the rebel army has entered the city and that Perez has freed Osmyn, now identified as Alphonso, and fled with him to join the rebels. Gonsalez insists that Osmyn is dead for he has killed him. He confidently sends Garcia to look at the body lying in Osmyn's cell and see for himself. Garcia goes and returns distracted, for in Osmyn's cell lies a body weltering in blood and clad in Osmyn's robe but it is the body of the King. When Gonsalez realizes he has killed the King he falls prostrate before Garcia and begs him to run him through with his sword. This is his moral recognition scene (p. 234):

> O my Son, from the blind Dotage
> Of a Father's Fondness these Ills arose;
> For thee I've been ambitious, base, and bloody;
> For thee I've plung'd into this Sea of Sin,
> Stemming the Tide, with one weak Hand, and bearing
> With the other, the Crown, to wreath thy Brow,
> Whose Weight has sunk me 'ere I reach'd the Shore.

Garcia says, "Fatal Ambition!" Shouts are heard. The rebel army is marching on the palace. Garcia thinks that the news of the King's death would complete the demoralization of the defenders. Alonzo says he has a plan for concealing the King's death from the soldiers. He does not reveal his plan but is given permission to execute it. He exits and returns to report: he has severed the head from the King's body, muffled the head in the mute's costume (which Gonsalez had worn) and left it in a dim corner. The "bloody and undistinguishable" trunk (still clad in Osmyn's robe) he has left in view so that the Guards will mistake the body for Osmyn's. Exeunt Gonsalez, Garcia, Alonzo.

Enter Zara, followed by Selim and two mutes, bearing the bowls of poison. Zara speaks (p. 235):

> Silence and Solitude are ev'ry where!
> Thro' all the Gloomy Ways, and Iron Doors
> That hither lead, nor Humane Face nor Voice

THE MOURNING BRIDE

> Is seen, or heard. A dreadful Din was wont
> To grate the Sense, when entred here; from Groans
> And Howls of Slaves condemn'd, from Clink of Chains,
> And Crash of rusty Bars and creeking Hinges.

She sends the mutes to warn Osmyn. They return "looking affrighted." Zara questions them. For answer they "go to the Scene which opens and shews the Body." Zara rants (p. 236):

> Ha! prostrate! bloody! headless! O——start Eyes,
> Split Heart, burst ev'ry Vein, at this dire Object!
> At once dissolve and flow; meet Blood with Blood;
> Dash your encountering Streams with mutual Violence,
> 'Till Surges roll and foaming Billows rise,
> And curl their Crimson Heads, to kiss the Clouds!

Enter Selim. Zara curses him because his plan to save Osmyn has miscarried. She stabs him. It seems that he has discovered that Osmyn is still alive but dies one word before the revelation that would have saved Zara. He says (p. 236):

> Drink not the Poyson—for *Alphonso* is—

(Cf. *Rodogune*, vs. 1647.) "As thou art now," says Zara. She drinks the poison from one of the bowls and dies. The mutes kneel and mourn over her body.

Enter Almeria and Leonora. They find first the body of Selim, then that of Zara, the two mutes bending over it. Leonora is the first to see the third body lying upstage. She tries to prevent Almeria from looking at it; but, even before she looks, Almeria knows what she will see. She thinks that the mutes have murdered both Zara and Osmyn. She accuses them and tells them to kill her too. They shake their heads and point to the poison bowl on the floor. She finds it empty. The mutes point to the other cup—the one Zara had intended for Osmyn. Almeria prepares to drink the poison; but before touching it she will give Osmyn a farewell kiss. She moves upstage towards the body—and finds it headless. The shock causes her to drop the bowl of poison just as the victorious Osmyn enters. Almeria faints. When she is revived, the lovers rejoice at this second reunion after Osmyn's second resurrection. Osmyn closes the play by speaking the moral, addressed to Garcia (p. 240):

O *Garcia*,
Whose Virtue has renounc'd thy Father's Crimes,
Seest thou, how just the Hand of Heav'n has been?
Let us that thro' our Innocence survive,
Still in the Paths of Honour persevere,
And not from past or present Ills Despair:
For Blessings ever wait on virtuous Deeds;
And tho' a late, a sure Reward succeeds.

The action of *Bajazet* may be summarized more briefly: The scene is at Constantinople in the Sultan's seraglio. The Sultan Amurat is besieging Babylon. At Constantinople he has left his Sultaness, Roxane, to rule in his stead. He has thrown his young brother Bajazet into prison and has actually sent to Constantinople an agent with orders to strangle Bajazet. But Bajazet has been saved by the vizir Acomat. Acomat, who has fallen into disfavor with Amurat and has been relieved of his command in the army, who knows that if the Sultan returns victorious he himself will have to flee for his life, has planned a coup d'état to set Bajazet on the throne. He has ordered Amurat's messenger to be thrown into the sea. He has arranged for Roxane to see Bajazet. She has fallen in love with the young prisoner. With Roxane's help Acomat is planning a revolution that will make Bajazet sultan. The young princess Atalide, cousin of Bajazet, has been Roxane's confidante and has brought her messages of love from Bajazet. Acomat plans to marry Atalide in order to fortify his position against the fickle favor of sultans. But Acomat does not know that Atalide and Bajazet love each other and that Atalide has conveyed Bajazet's (false) messages of love to Roxane in order to save Bajazet's life.

Act I. The moment is ripe for the coup d'état that will place Bajazet on the throne. Roxane will not give the final word until she is convinced that Bajazet loves her, as Atalide has assured her he does (in order to rescue him from prison and to save him from death). Roxane has misgivings: she has interviewed Bajazet in secret and has seen no evidence in his manner of the ardent love which Atalide has described. She plans to put him to the test. He must be brought before her without being forewarned of her intentions. She will then demand that he marry her. More certainly than rejection or acceptance of her demand, his facial expression on hearing this unexpected stipulation will reveal his real feelings towards her.

THE MOURNING BRIDE

Act II. Roxane demands that Bajazet prove his love by marrying her. Bajazet demurs. According to Ottoman tradition the sultan does not marry. (Amurat has made Roxane his sultaness but he has not married her.) Roxane reminds him that his life depends on her protection of him. She can at any moment carry out Amurat's order for his execution. When he still refuses to marry her, she orders his arrest. She cancels all plans for a revolution and tells Acomat that she recognizes the authority of Amurat. But she does not throw Bajazet into prison; she leaves him free to converse with Acomat and later with Atalide, a fact which Acomat interprets as a hopeful sign of her uncertainty.

The Machiavellian Acomat urges Bajazet to promise marriage to Roxane and after he is sultan to break his promise. Atalide begs him for her sake to placate Roxane, to say anything to save his life. Bajazet yields to her entreaties.

Act III. Atalide awaits news of the outcome of Bajazet's second interview with Roxane. Her confidante and Acomat bring word that Bajazet has made his peace with Roxane. Acomat has watched the interview from a distance and describes it as the reconciliation of two people whose love for each other was obvious from their manner. Atalide begins to doubt Bajazet's love for her. She cannot bear the thought of Bajazet's marriage to Roxane. She plans suicide.

Bajazet enters and the jealous Atalide hints that she will kill herself and reproaches him for having been more ardent than necessary. (She has accepted Acomat's account as a faithful one, probably because it gives her some justification for her jealousy.) Bajazet tries to explain: Roxane interpreted his request to see her as a change of heart. So eager was she to believe he loved her that he did not need to say anything. Bajazet sees from Atalide's expression that she is not convinced. Indignantly he threatens to tell Roxane the truth and take the consequences.

Enter Roxane. When she speaks of their plans to Bajazet, he answers coldly, turns on his heel and leaves. Roxane questions Atalide. Her suspicions are aggravated by the very eagerness with which Atalide assures her that Bajazet still loves her. She orders Atalide to leave. She reflects on what she has seen. She remembers Atalide's face and Bajazet's when she came upon them talking together: "Bajazet interdit! Atalide étonnée!" Does Bajazet love Atalide? Has she (Roxane) planned to betray Amurat only to help the fortunes of a rival?

Roxane's reflections are interrupted by the entrance of Zatime, her confidante. Zatime brings the news that Amurat has sent a second messenger, the most faithful and ruthless of his slaves, the African Orcan. Roxane is certain that Orcan has come to see that Bajazet is murdered. Shall she protect him or obey the Sultan? Before deciding, she must know whether or not Bajazet loves Atalide. She plans to trap Atalide. She will use the Sultan's message to frighten her into a confession. "Couronnons l'amant, ou perdons le perfide."

Act IV. In order to watch Atalide's reaction, Roxane tells her that the Sultan has commanded her to put Bajazet to death. She will obey him. Atalide faints. She has betrayed herself. But, thinks Roxane, this proves only that Atalide loves Bajazet. Does *he* love *her*? At this point she cannot bring herself to pursue her inquiry further. She will go on with her plans to make Bajazet sultan. "Je veux tout ignorer."

But she is confronted with the proof of Bajazet's love for Atalide, a letter found on Atalide in which Bajazet protested that he loved only Atalide. Roxane sends orders to her mutes to prepare to strangle Bajazet. Zatime warns her that Amurat is more to be feared than Bajazet. But her warning goes unheeded. Roxane can think of nothing but Bajazet's perfidy and the deception that he and Atalide have practiced upon her.

Enter Acomat. Roxane tells him of her discovery. He offers to punish Bajazet. She forbids him, saying:

> Je veux voir son désordre et jouir de sa honte.
> Je perdrois ma vengeance en la rendant si prompte.

Acomat is not deceived by this pretext. There is still hope. He says to Osmin, his lieutenant:

> Malgré son déspoir,
> Roxane l'aime encore, Osmin, et le va voir.

Act V. Atalide has discovered the theft of Bajazet's letter. Roxane must know the truth now. What has she done? Is Bajazet already dead?

Enter Roxane. She curtly orders Atalide to leave. Atalide stammers a reply. Roxane tells her to be silent and puts her under arrest. Roxane then explains to Zatime that preparations have been made for the murder of Bajazet. Orcan and the mutes are stationed outside the room. She has sent for Bajazet. She will give him one more chance. She can save him by keeping him with her. If he leaves the room the mutes have orders to strangle him. Bajazet enters, unaware of the trap that has been set for him. Roxane offers him a chance to live and reign. He must come with her and watch Atalide die. Bajazet pleads for Atalide. Roxane listens in silence. When Bajazet appeals to Roxane's love for him in order to save her rival, Roxane speaks the one word, "Sortez." Bajazet leaves.

Zatime brings word that Acomat and his followers have seized the palace. It is not known whether he has betrayed Roxane or is acting in her interests. Roxane rushes out to confront Acomat.

Atalide questions Zatime. Where is Bajazet? What has happened to him? The woman refuses to answer.

Enter Acomat searching for Bajazet.

Enter Zaïre, confidante to Atalide. She announces that Orcan has just assassinated Roxane. Atalide thinks Bajazet has been saved.

Enter Osmin. He reveals that Roxane's mutes had strangled Bajazet before Orcan assassinated Roxane. Atalide realizes that her jealousy has caused Bajazet's death. She kills herself.

It is obvious from these summaries that the plots of the two plays have something in common. In both a woman (Roxane-Zara) who wields great power because of a sovereign's love for her (Amurat-Manuel) is herself in love with a prisoner (Bajazet-Osmyn) of this sovereign's. The prisoner may gain his freedom by returning her love but jeopardizes his life if he rejects it. Incensed at his indifference, she threatens his life but cannot bring herself to carry out her threats. The prisoner (Bajazet-Osmyn) loves a princess (Atalide-Almeria) but must conceal his love from Roxane-Zara in order to preserve his life.

Congreve uses frequently one characteristic Racinian device. Like Racine's characters in *Bajazet*, the characters of *The Mourning Bride* have something to conceal from one another. They try to penetrate the secrets of others by watching for the involuntary gesture or the fleeting shade of facial expression that betrays. They believe, like Racine's personages, that facial expression is a surer index to truth than words (Perez says: "And every Look of his and hers confess it"). Three times in Congreve's play perception of facial expression is important in the plot. Zara discovers from their facial expression as they part that Osmyn and Almeria love each other. (She sees Almeria "Trembling and weep-

ing as he leads her forth/Confusion in his face and Grief in hers!")
The King discovers his daughter's relation to Osmyn by watching her
reaction as he tells her Osmyn has been condemned to death. In the
scene where this scheme is carried out, however, there is no resemblance
to the corresponding scene in *Bajazet*. Zara realizes from the King's
angry look that he has discovered her plot to save Osmyn. She asks for
no further proof and resolves to die with Osmyn.

Of these three scenes the first two were suggested by scenes in *Bajazet* (Act III, Scenes 5, 8). The third is Congreve's invention. It is
characteristic that in this third case, Zara, instead of noting the King's
expression briefly and simply, gives a hyperbolic description of it:

> Ha! 'twas
> The King that parted hence; frowning he went;
> His Eyes like Meteors roll'd, then darted down
> Their red and angry Beams; as if his Sight
> Would like the raging Dog-Star, scortch the Earth,
> And kindle Ruine in its Course.

Compare Racine's method at a crucial moment like this one. Bajazet
tries to explain to Atalide that the reconciliation with Roxane was
effected without any protestations of love from him. He watches her face
as he explains and he sees that she is not convinced (vss. 1003-1004):

> Je vois enfin, je vois qu'en ce même moment
> Tout ce que je vous dis vous touche faiblement.

In Congreve the device is often little more than a pretext for description or a melodramatic episode which is introduced apparently for its
own sake and has no effect on the course of the action (see the summary of Act III above).

The only similarity between the two plays lies in the use of this device,
in the relation of Bajazet-Osmyn and Atalide-Almeria to Roxane-Zara
and Amurat-Manuel, and in Zara's vacillations, with the difference here
that Roxane uses threats to command Bajazet's love and Zara punishes
Osmyn for his indifference only to repent afterwards and try to undo
the harm she has done. Zara actually endangers Osmyn's life twice,
rescues him once and tries to rescue him a second time. Roxane threatens Bajazet but continues to protect him, until she no longer has any
doubt of his perfidy and circumstances force her to come to a decision.

The Osmyn-Almeria-Zara triangle is different from the Bajazet-

Atalide-Roxane relationship. Indeed Almeria's situation is not at all that of Atalide. She is not jealous of Osmyn, while Atalide's unreasonable jealousy causes Bajazet's death, and the realization that she has destroyed him leads to her own suicide. By eliminating jealousy in Almeria, Congreve has eliminated the tragic from his play. His Almeria is merely pathetic. Her situation is that of Juliet. Secretly married to the son of her father's greatest enemy, she is commanded by her father to marry the man of his choice and prefers death to marriage with another. Almeria becomes an example of noble constancy in love and of oppressed innocence.

Having eliminated all that was tragic from the material which he took from Racine, Congreve proceeded to change a psychological drama to one of intrigue. One editor of Racine's tragedy describes the action thus:

C'est peu de dire que toute l'action réside dans ces passions forcénées réagissant les unes sur les autres. Il faut voir que la chaîne, l'engrenage, est de douleur. Nul, dans cet enfer, ne peut faire un geste, prononcer une parole, qui n'inflige souffrance, qui ne supplicie. Et c'est peu de dire que l'angoisse grandit de scène en scène, c'est la misère de la créature humaine qui, plus elle souffre, et plus elle frappe cruellement; si bien qu'à la fin, il est naturel que tout le monde meure et nous laisse dans la pitié et dans l'horreur.[10]

For the clash of violent emotions and the inevitable progress towards despair and death, Congreve substitutes the plot-spinning of the wicked and brings about his dénouement through the entanglement and the consequent miscarriage of the plots of these evil personages. The appeal for the audience is one of suspense. The effects are carefully prepared. At the end of the first scene of Act V, the spectator knows that the King has sent Perez to kill Osmyn and that the King plans to disguise himself as Osmyn, and to wait in Osmyn's dimly lighted cell for the coming of Zara. We are given no hint as yet that Perez will betray the King and free Osmyn. We know that Zara is aware that the King has discovered her plan to free Osmyn and that she plans to take a bowl of poison to his cell and to die with him. We know too that Gonsalez plans to disguise himself as a mute and murder Osmyn in his cell. We do not know which one of the plotters will reach Osmyn first. In order to hide the sequence of events from the audience, Congreve shifts the

[10] J. E. Morel, *Bajazet* (Classiques Larousse), *Notice*, p. 10.

scene to the prison, at a spot *outside* the room where Osmyn is imprisoned, in order to veil the events that will take place there. We are first shown Gonsalez disguised as a mute and going in the direction of Osmyn's cell. (Who is in Osmyn's cell?) Re-enter Gonsalez, bloody. He has killed someone. Whom? Garcia reveals the rumor of Perez's betrayal of the King and his flight with Osmyn, now identified as Alphonso. But Gonsalez is certain that Osmyn lies dead in his cell. He himself has dispatched him. Garcia discovers the horrible miscarriage of his father's plot. Two of the wicked have met their just deserts—the King and Gonsalez. What of the third, Zara? And what of the innocent Almeria?

Enter Zara followed by her mutes, who carry the poison bowls. She does not know that Manuel is dead and Osmyn free. She finds the headless body. Selim rushes in to tell her all. She stabs him. He almost succeeds in saving her. One more word and she will know the truth. But his dying gasp comes before he can utter that word. The mistaken identity of the headless corpse becomes the instrument of her death.

Enter Almeria. (What will be the effect on her of the sight of Osmyn-Alphonso's dead body? *We* know of course that Alphonso is alive and marching on the palace with the rebel army. (Will he arrive in time to save her from a fatal mistake?) The pantomime with the mutes delays the fatal moment. (How near is Alphonso?) Almeria picks up a poison bowl!—and finds it empty (Blessed delay!). She finds the full cup. She prepares to drink. (Will Alphonso never come?) She decides to give Alphonso a farewell kiss—*before* the poison touches her lips. (Happy thought.) She moves towards the body lying upstage. Headless! She lets fall the poison cup. The spectacle of the headless corpse has saved innocence from death for a moment longer, just long enough for the hero to reach her side and, happily reunited with his bride, to point out that Heaven watches over the innocent and the virtuous, and punishes the wicked. An irreverent critic might remark that Heaven shows a penchant for near misses in the punishment of the guilty and hair-breadth escapes in the rescue of the innocent.

To the effects of surprise and suspense is added the appeal to the senses. The first curtain rises slowly to the sound of soft music—to heighten the distress of the mourning bride. The King enters to the sound of warlike music and the scene is played against a background of armed guards and files of prisoners in chains. The setting in Act II contributes a macabre atmosphere reinforced by descriptions of the settings spoken by the personages. The macabre atmosphere envelops the last scene too.

Since Congreve substitutes material for psychological events—for the reaction of one personage to another and the crescendo of emotions that constitute the drama in Racine—his dialogue is almost everywhere static. His characters react to events and comment on them. The style is bombastic and highly figurative. Love scenes are done in *précieux* hyperbole and conceits (Zara beholds the "day-break" of Osmyn's eyes; she holds the King in "chains unseen" and can "unwind or strain him" as she pleases; to Osmyn, Almeria's presence is a brightness that breaks upon him and promises a Day to his dark dwelling). Scenes of horror are done in Senecan hyperbole.

In all essentials Congreve's play is antithetical to the Racinian genre. It is a "pièce à trucs," a melodrama with the appeal of a Grand Guignol thriller. Yet the most detailed contemporary criticism of it indicates that it was looked upon as a classical tragedy. Sir Richard Blackmore says:

The Fable, as far as I can judge at first sight, is a very artful and masterly Contrivance; the characters are well chosen, and well delineated; that of Zara is admirable. The Passions are well touched, and skillfully wrought up. The Diction proper, clear, beautiful, noble, and diversified agreeably to the Variety of the Subject. Vice, as it ought to be, is punished; and oppressed Innocence at last rewarded. Nature appears happily imitated, except for one or two doubtful Instances, through the whole piece, in which there are no immodest Images or Expressions; no wild unnatural Rants, but, some few exceptions being allowed, all Things are chaste and decent. This Tragedy, as I said before, has mightily obtained, and that without the unnatural and foolish mixture of Farce and Buffoonery; without so much as a Song or Dance, to make it more agreeable. By this it appears, that as a sufficient Genius can recommend itself, and furnish out abundant Matter of Pleasure and Admiration, without the paultry Helps above named; so likewise, that the taste of the Nation is not so depraved, but that a regular and chaste Play will not only be forgiven but highly applauded.[11]

---

[11] Preface to *King Arthur* (1697), as quoted by Taylor, *op. cit.*, p. 95. After quoting this critique, Taylor says: "We might agree with all this criticism except for the remark that the drama has 'no wild unnatural rants.'" Later (p. 96) he quotes Dr. Johnson's high praise of a poetical passage from Act II but fails to mention Johnson's very cogent criticism of the play. See below, n. 15.

This criticism is quoted by Charles Gildon[12] and echoed by others.[13]

After Aristotelian formalism had lost some of its prestige, Addison still considered *The Mourning Bride* a "noble tragedy," and that at the very moment when he was attacking the theory of tragedy that demanded the rescue of the innocent as the only "regular" dénouement, at the very moment too when he was satirizing the use of spectacle and accessories to heighten the appeal of tragedy.[14] The reputation and the popularity of *The Mourning Bride* endured throughout the period when adaptations of Racine were in vogue.[15]

Despite the antithesis to Racinian tragedy presented by *The Mourning Bride*, it is possible to understand how it could have been looked upon as classical by Congreve's contemporaries. The only thing in his play—in addition to verbal reminiscences of Shakespeare—that is incontrovertibly native and traditional is the taste for the macabre, present in Shakespeare (*Romeo and Juliet*, Act IV, Scene 2, and Act V, Scene

---

[12] *Op. cit.*, p. 23.
[13] See below, Chap. XI.
[14] *Spectator*, Nos. 40, 42, 44.
[15] The popularity of *The Mourning Bride* in the theatre continued unabated until after the end of the century (see Montague Summers's theatrical history of the play in his edition of Congreve, II, 176–77).

In the second half of the century, however, critics were not so kind to it as Addison and Blackmore had been. Horace Walpole said: "Theatric genius turned to tuneful nonsense in *The Mourning Bride*." (Postscript to *The Mysterious Mother* [1768], p. 10.) With wit and perspicuity Dr. Johnson pointed out its defects and defined its appeal. He said: "In this play, of which, when he afterwards revised it, he reduced the versification to greater regularity, there is more bustle than sentiment; the plot is busy and intricate and the events take hold on the attention, but, except in a very few passages, we are rather amused with noise and perplexed with stratagem than entertained with any true delineation of natural characters. This, however, was received with more benevolence than any other of his works, and still continues to be acted and applauded." (*The Lives of the English Poets*, ed. George Birkbeck Hill [Oxford, 1905], II, 218–19.) (Johnson is using the word "amuse" in the sense of "to capture the attention." I believe he means to imply that the appeal of the play is not a legitimate esthetic one.) Modern criticism has done Dr. Johnson an injustice by quoting his extravagant praise of one passage from the play and failing to record his astute judgment of it as a play. Despite these adverse criticisms *The Mourning Bride* was not without enthusiastic admirers among the critics of the second half of the eighteenth century. Henry Home, Lord Kames, for instance, esteemed it more highly than any English tragedy since Shakespeare. Or, to put it more accurately, it was the only English tragedy outside those of Shakespeare for which he had any admiration at all and his admiration for it was very great (*The Elements of Criticism*).

THE MOURNING BRIDE

3) and accentuated in Ford and Webster. Whether the word "chaste," as Blackmore uses it, has a moral or an esthetic sense, Congreve's play is chaste as compared with the licentiousness of Restoration drama and the horrors of such plays as Ravenscroft's *Titus Andronicus*. Carefully plotted, closely knit intrigue (without sub-plot) we certainly do not find in heroic plays or in Shakespeare. Congreve's plot might be looked upon as conforming to Aristotelian emphasis on plot in tragedy. It is obvious too that Congreve intended to introduce Aristotelian discovery and peripeteia into his plot. The recognition scene of Act II is actually reminiscent of the recognition of Orestes by Electra in the *Electra* of Sophocles.[16] But there is an important difference between the two recognition scenes. In Sophocles the appeal to the audience is that of dramatic irony; in Congreve, surprise. In the *Electra* the spectator knows Orestes' identity; Electra does not. In Congreve, Osmyn's identity is very carefully concealed from the spectator. Prior to the discovery scene, we know Osmyn only as a Moor who fought valiantly in Zara's armies. Just before the recognition scene Perez says he is certain that Osmyn and Zara are in love with each other (this to ensure the surprise of Osmyn's real identity, and his relationship to Almeria.) We are not told why Osmyn has come to the temple. We do not know that he has gone down into Anselmo's vault. When he rises from the tomb, the spectator might well mistake him for a ghost, as Almeria does. Even this illusion, however, has an analogue in classical antiquity. In the *Aeneid*, Aeneas in his wanderings has come to the port of Buthrotum. Leaving his ships in the harbor and walking inland, he comes upon Andromache, as she lays offerings on Hector's tomb. Andromache, who thinks Aeneas dead, mistakes him for a ghost and asks (Bk. III, vss. 306-12):

> Vivisne? Aut, si lux alma recessit,
> Hector ubi est?

Almeria's attitude towards ghosts, however, is English and reminiscent of *Hamlet* ("Speak to it!").

Thus Congreve gives discovery a melodramatic turn. Even more melodramatic is his use of peripeteia. He himself calls attention to his use of peripeteia and reveals his conception of it. Alphonso says to Almeria (p. 239, italics mine):

[16] See above, n. 3.

RACINE AND ENGLISH CLASSICISM

> Thy Father fell, *where he design'd my Death.*
> *Gonsalez* and *Alonzo,* both of Wounds
> Expiring, have with their last Breath confess'd
> The *just Decrees of Heav'n, in turning on*
> *Themselves, their own most bloody Purposes.*

Such a conception of peripeteia Congreve might easily have found in French interpreters of Aristotle, notably La Mesnardière.[17]

Apostles of French criticism in England might have found justification of their approval of *The Mourning Bride* in French theory of tragedy. They might too have found a precedent for some of Congreve's accessories and melodramatic tricks in French drama of the seventeenth century. Today we look upon Racine as the essence of classicism; complicated plot, elaborate scenic effects, melodramatic accessories and tricks are un-Racinian, ergo, not classical. This was not the attitude of Racine's contemporaries.[18] The English classicists were more inter-

[17] See below, Chap. XI.

[18] In France the purely psychological action of *Bérénice*, for instance, struck some of Racine's contemporaries as "irregular" (Racine's Preface). No one (except Racine) questioned the "regularity" of Corneille's complicated intrigue. As Professor Daniel Mornet has remarked, Corneille was considered by some more "regular" than Racine. (*Histoire de la littérature française classique* [Paris, 1947], p. 242.)

We need look no further than Corneille for the use in tragedy of disguised identity, poison cups, suspense (*Héraclius, Rodogune*). However, I know of nothing quite comparable to Congreve's macabre variant of the mistaken identity motif, the headless body with its fatally misleading costume. But see Shakespeare, *Cymbeline,* Act IV, Scene 3.

Racine reveals his attitude towards spectacular scenic effects in his preface to *Esther.* He says: "On peut dire que l'unité de lieu est observée dans cette pièce, en ce que toute l'action se passe dans le palais d'Assuérus. Cependant, comme on vouloit rendre ce divertissement plus *agréable à des enfants,* en jetant quelque *variété* dans les *décorations,* cela a été cause que je n'ai pas gardé cette unité avec la même rigueur que j'ai fait autrefois dans mes tragédies." (Italics mine.) Today elaborate scenic effects strike us as contrary to the spirit of classical tragedy. "C'est tricherie de surprendre les yeux au lieu de captiver l'âme." (Lanson, *Histoire de la littérature française,* p. 649.) It is true that tragic poets in France during the classical generation (1660–85) did not indulge in lavish scenic effects. But in opera scenic effects were exploited to the fullest. It is true too that, while French tragedy was tending towards simplicity of setting, the English were reveling in sensational scenic effects. But French classical doctrine did not condemn spectacular scenic effects. D'Aubignac is particularly concerned with the problem of achieving varied scenic effects without violating strict unity of place. Here is an ingenious example of "une belle Décoration" achieved without violating unity of place: the stage represents an abandoned palace on the seashore. It

THE MOURNING BRIDE

ested in French criticism than in Racine's practice. English playwrights often chose other models than Racine. I do not think that the sensational success of *The Mourning Bride* can be looked upon as a revolt against subservience to French dogma or a vindication of native drama. But it does show quite plainly that English classicism was developing along lines that would hinder rather than favor a just appreciation of Racine in England or imitations that might preserve the essence of Racinian tragedy.

Of all Racine's tragedies, *Iphigénie* comes closest to the pattern of *The Mourning Bride*. An adapter had only to eliminate the characteristics of Racine's Eriphile which made her pitiable and tragic and to show the dénouement in action, and the pattern was followed perfectly: music, spectacle, the discovery of disguised identity which rescued oppressed innocence and turned the machinations of the wicked back upon themselves. These possibilities in *Iphigénie* were soon to be exploited in England.

---

is first shown in ruins and inhabited by peasants. A prince is shipwrecked near the palace. He decorates the palace with rich tapestries, chandeliers, paintings, etc. Then, the palace is destroyed by fire; the sea appears in the background and the poet is at liberty to show a naval battle taking place. (*La Pratique du théâtre*, ed. Pierre Martino [Paris, 1927], p. 102.) According to Louis Charlanne, English *mise en scène* was an importation from France for which D'Avenant was responsible. (*L'Influence Française en Angleterre au XVIIe Siècle* [Paris, 1906], pp. 290–93.) However un-Racinian and unclassical Congreve's use of elaborate setting may seem to us, there was no reason for English classicists to object to it. Nor is there any reason to look upon it as a native tradition and peculiar to the English. As Charlanne has pointed out (*loc. cit.*), Shadwell and Steele later deplored the English taste for elaborate *mise en scène* imported from a "neighboring nation," and advocated a return to the simplicity of Shakespeare. And before 1697, the date of *The Mourning Bride*, Racine himself had set the example of music and spectacle in *Athalie*, which had been published but had not been performed in public.

81

« « CHAPTER IV » »

ABEL BOYER'S *ACHILLES*

IN 1699, two years after the first presentation of Congreve's very successful *The Mourning Bride*, Racine's *Iphigénie* was adapted for the English stage by the Huguenot refugee Abel Boyer. Boyer gave his adaptation the title *Achilles, or Iphigenia in Aulis*.[1] Boyer is the first adapter of Racine to acknowledge his source and praise the author. He says in his preface:

"Monsieur Racine manag'd his Subject with a great deal of Mastery: His Expressions are free and lofty; his Sentiments noble and virtuous, his Passions moving and natural; his turns well-manag'd and surprizing. The success answer'd his extraordinary Performance; *Iphigenia*, at her first Appearance on the French Stage, drew Tears, and commanded Admiration both from the Court and the City, for many Months successively, and set Monsieur Racine above the Level of all French tragic Writers.

"The great success of Racine's Iphigenia, and the Encouragement I received from some Persons of a just Discernment made me venture to make her appear upon an English Theatre; now whether she has gain'd or lost any Thing by her new Dress, I leave to the Judicious to determine. All I can say in her Favor, is, That her numbers are easy and flowing; and that she speaks English like a genteel well-bred Lady, and not like an affected, pedantick Would-be-Wit. But in this I must owe my self oblig'd to my honour'd and ingenious Friend Mr. Cheek, to whom I owe some of the smoothest lines. I wish he had a greater

---

[1] Boyer's *Achilles* was published in 1700. In 1714, when Charles Johnson's adaptation of *Iphigénie*, entitled *The Victim*, proved more successful than Boyer's had been, the latter put out a second edition of his play under the same title as Johnson's and with a preface in which he accused Johnson of plagiarism. My references are to the first edition.

share in the whole Play, for then I am sure the Town would have lik'd it a great deal better."

The success of Racine's *Iphigénie* in France may have had something to do with Boyer's choice of this play; but he doubtless had other reasons. Of all Racine's tragedies *Iphigénie* lends itself most easily to alteration in the direction of operatic melodrama, a type which had enjoyed such great success in the case of *The Mourning Bride*. The most drastic changes which Boyer makes are designed to add music and spectacle to Racine's classical piece. As the curtain rises on Act IV, Eriphile and Doris are discovered sitting on a "green bank." Eriphile sings a song "set by Mr. Purcell." The theme is jealousy. The song ended, Doris questions Eriphile, as in Racine, and the rest of the act is a fairly close translation. The catastrophe is completely altered, so as to afford both music and spectacle. Taking suggestions from the account given by Ulysse in Racine, Boyer shows the whole dénouement in action. Clytemnestra exits and "while a symphony is playing an Altar is raised near the Sea-Shore." Enter King Agamemnon, *weeping*, Menelaus, Nestor, Ulysses, Arcas, etc. Calchas, Iphigenia, *between two Priests*, Eriphile, Doris. A chorus of priests sings an invocation to Diana. After the chorus, as Iphigenia "is leading to be Sacrific'd, the Sun is Eclips'd; Shrieks in the Air; Subterranean Groans and Howlings; Thunder." Particularly noteworthy are the "subterranean groans and howlings." No ghost rises, however. Calchas speaks and his words are not from Racine:

> What mean these Horrours!
> The Sun withdraws his beamy Light; the Air
> Is filled with hideous Shrieks, and gloomy Hell
> Sends up fierce Groans and Subterranean Cries.
> Almighty Jove himself, with threatening Thunder,
> Declares his Wrath; all Nature is in Pain.

Enter Achilles and his followers, determined to stop the sacrifice. Calchas says to Achilles:

> My Lord, contain your Passion; I bid you, hold.
> The Gods themselves are angry. They must first be heard.

Another clap of thunder. Calchas goes behind the altar to consult the oracle and then returns with a "wild, staring Look, trembling Hands." ("L'oeil farouche, l'air sombre et le poil hérissé." Racine, vs. 1744.) He explains that the oracle demands the death of another Iphigenia, points to Eriphile and says:

> There she stands. 'Tis she
> The Gods demand.

Eriphile snatches the knife from him and speaks lines resembling those which Ulysse quotes in Racine. She says:

> Butcher, avaunt! Let not thy impious Hands
> Profane that Blood from which thou says't I sprang.

From this point on, Boyer's lines are entirely his own. Eriphile dies with Achilles' name on her lips:

> Now, Doris, tho' the Angry Goddess bids me die,
> I fall a Victim to a greater Power
> Almighty Love now strikes the fatal Blow,
> Achilles—Dear—Achilles.

Iphigenia says, "Unhappy Maid!" There is thunder and lightning. "The Altar is lighted, the flat scene opens, and discovers a Heaven at a distance; Diana, in a Machine, crosses the Stage; the Priests worship as she passes."

Agamemnon now bestows Iphigenia's hand on Achilles. The winds roar and shoutings are heard. Achilles rejoices:

> Oh! Transports of Delight! Oh! Rapturous Bliss,
> My Love is crown'd; The Winds begin to roar,
> And fill our spreading Sails; To Troy, to Troy,
> To Victory and Fame!

Calchas speaks the moral of the piece:

> Let After-Ages learn from this Great Day,
> To reverence the Gods' supreme Decrees:
> For they are just, and ever recompense,
> True Piety, and spotless Innocence.[2]

Aside from these changes in Act V, Boyer's play follows Racine's rather closely. Except for one or two unimportant interpolations, he adds only the verses necessary to cut long tirades in the accepted Eng-

---

[2] Compare Racine's ending. After hearing Ulysse's account of Iphigénie's rescue and Eriphile's death, Clytemnestre says (vss. 1795-96):

> Par quel prix, quel encens, ô ciel, puis-je jamais
> Récompenser Achille, et payer tes bienfaits?

lish fashion. He does not strain his ingenuity to do so. In the exposition all these interpolations are questions; in the rest of the play, exclamations. Here are a few samples: "Oh! dutiful Respect! Oh! wondrous Love!" "Oh! cruel hopeless Love!" "Oh! she'll unman me with her tender Words!" "Oh! cruel Honour! Unfortunate Alliance!"

The characters are unchanged, with the exception of Eriphile. Boyer makes her less complex and conveys none of the morbid intensity of the most tragic figure in Racine's play. Boyer's Eriphile is little more than a conventional victim of unrequited love. Boyer effects the change in the character by being inappropriately explicit and also inappropriately vague. The result is a shift of emphasis. Racine's Eriphile believes that the gods have singled her out to vent on her a mysterious and perverse hatred. They have deprived her of her parents in her infancy and of the only friend who knew the secret of her parentage. An oracle has warned her that if she discovers the secret of her birth she will die. As the culminating irony of their persecution the gods have caused her to fall in love with the instrument of their persecution, the ruthless Achilles, who has destroyed her home and slaughtered her friends, among them the man who knew the identity of her parents. She knows only that she is of royal birth and she has pride of race. Her love for Achilles she looks upon as a madness unworthy of the nobility of soul that should be her birthright. But she cannot resist this unnatural love. The fact that it is unrequited adds to her humiliation, as does also the fact that jealousy has robbed her of the generosity that her noble birth should give her: instead of gratitude towards her benefactress she has only hatred for her rival. Boyer eliminates none of the springs of Eriphile's melancholy and vindictiveness. He merely shifts the emphasis.

Racine's Eriphile reveals her feeling of persecution thus (vss. 485-86):

> Le ciel s'est fait, sans doute, une joie inhumaine
> A rassembler sur moi tous les traits de sa haine.

Boyer translates:

> 'Tis unrelenting Heaven's Decree,
> Still to pursue me with immortal Hatred,
> And crush my tender Heart with Cares of Love.

Boyer's explicitness amounts to mistranslation. "Cares of Love" suggests only the suffering of unrequited love, while Racine's Eriphile was thinking at the same time of all the circumstances that made her hopeless passion ironical and cruel and of love as the last in a long series of misfortunes sent upon her by a malevolent deity.

Racine's Eriphile comes to Aulis in the hope that her mere presence may involve Iphigénie and Achille in her own unhappy destiny (vss. 516-20):

> Une secrète voix m'ordonna de partir,
> Me dit qu'offrant ici ma présence importune,
> Peut-être j'y pourrois porter mon infortune;
> Que peut-être, approchant ces amants trop heureux,
> Quelqu'un de mes malheurs se répandroit sur eux.

Here is Boyer's version of these lines:

> A secret Voice
> Bid me attend my Guardian——
> Presaging that I might leave on this Shore,
> All my Misfortunes, and like a Libation,
> Pour them upon the Heads of these blest Lovers.

By rendering "porter" with "leave" and by introducing an inept simile, "like a Libation," Boyer eliminates the insane malignity of Eriphile's lines.

With all her malignity, Racine's Eriphile is more pitiable than Boyer's, pitiable chiefly because of her suffering. It is not without self-reproach that she admits her impulse to destroy Iphigénie's happiness (vss. 503-508):

> Iphigénie en vain s'offre à me protéger
> Et me tend une main prompte à me soulager:
> *Triste effet des fureurs dont je suis tourmentée!*
> Je n'accepte la main qu'elle m'a présentée
> Que pour m'armer contre elle, et sans me découvrir,
> Traverser son bonheur *que je ne puis souffrir.*

By altering the phrases which I have italicized Boyer eliminates the self-reproach and loses the effect of reluctant surrender to an impulsion:

> Kind *Iphigenia* offers me Protection,
> But all in vain, *since my tormenting Furies*
> Bid me lay hold of my Protectress's Hand
> Only to crush a Rival, and unseen
> Disturb the Joys *which cause my Sufferings.*

ABEL BOYER'S *ACHILLES*

Boyer retains the aristocratic pride of Racine's Eriphile in her last speech before her death, but to Racine's lines he adds:

> Now Doris tho' the Angry Goddess bids me die,
> I fall a Victim to a greater Power.
> Almighty Love now strikes the fatal Blow,
> Achilles—Dear—Achilles.

Racine's Eriphile considers her mad passion for her enemy and captor degrading and unworthy of her (vss. 526-28):

> Dans la nuit du tombeau j'enfermerai ma honte,
> Sans chercher des parents si longtemps ignorés,
> Et que ma folle amour a trop déshonorés.

Boyer's translation leaves the impression that Eriphile's shame springs merely from love unrequited:

> A speedy Death will end my Miseries;
> And without wasting time in fruitless Search
> After my unknown Parentage, the Grave
> Will hide my Love and Shame.

Everywhere except in the lines I have quoted Boyer conveys Racine's meaning. But he makes no attempt to imitate Racine's style. The devices by which Racine suggests the emotion from which the words spring Boyer discards systematically, with the result that dramatic dialogue is often transformed into declamation and almost never conveys emotion with the sharpness and intensity of Racine's lines. As I have already noted, a characteristic device of Racine's is to cast simple diction in the form of questions, thus informing with emotion the most natural and unadorned style. Boyer does not discard interrogation as a rhetorical device; but he does, in many instances, change a question to a statement or give it an oratorical form where in Racine it was sharp and sudden, giving the effect of a spontaneous outburst. For instance, when Agamemnon tries to persuade Achille to abandon the Trojan expedition, Achille's indignant protest takes the form of two characteristic questions (vss. 245-46):

> Moi, je m'arrêterois à de vaines menaces?
> Et je fuirois l'honneur qui m'attend sur vos traces?

Boyer combines these questions in an oratorical period:

> Besides, think you, my Lord, those frivolous Threats

> Will 'ere deter Achilles from pursuing
> Honour and Glory under your Command?

In the scene where Iphigénie accuses Eriphile of being the cause of Achille's supposed defection, ironical probing takes the form of pointed questions (vss. 662–66):

> Vous m'entendez assez, si vous voulez m'entendre.
> Le sort injurieux me ravit un époux;
> *Madame, à mon malheur m'abandonnerez-vous?*
> Vous ne pouviez sans moi demeurer à Mycène,
> *Me verra-t-on sans vous partir avec la Reine?*

Boyer indicates in the stage directions that these words are spoken in an ironical tone and proceeds to eliminate one question and make the other less pointed:

> Nay, Madam, too, too well
> You know its meaning—yet, if barbarous Fate
> Robs me of a Husband, *sure you'll be more kind*
> *Than to abandon me in my Misfortune.*
> Tha'd been a Torment for you to have staid
> At *Mycene* without me. *Shall the Queen*
> *Now leave you here alone?*

Later in this scene, when Iphigénie has accused Eriphile of being in love with Achille and reproaches her for her perfidy, Boyer translates the reproach but alters the question in which Iphigénie's bitterness reaches its climax (vss. 695–700):

> Je vous pardonne, hélas! des voeux intéressés,
> Et la perte d'un coeur que vous me ravissez.
> Mais que, sans m'avertir du piège qu'on me dresse,
> Vous me laissiez chercher jusqu'au fond de la Grèce
> L'ingrat qui ne m'attend que pour m'abandonner,
> Perfide, cet affront se peut-il pardonner?

Boyer has:

> The Robbing me of him I could forgive,
> But to be brought to this detested Shore
> To meet th'ungrateful Man who now forsakes me,
> And grace the triumph of a treacherous Friend,
> This, this is an abuse I cannot bear!

Apparently Boyer's stylistic changes spring from a desire to "elevate the tone" of Racine's tragedy. His favorite device for achieving his purpose is the use of epithet. His indulgence in epithet is so immoderate as to be ludicrous. Where Racine uses a noun, Boyer adds an adjective. "Ma colère" becomes "my boiling Passion"; "mille vertus" becomes "a thousand blooming Virtues." If Racine uses one adjective, Boyer adds a second which is often a synonym of the first. "Ma foible puissance" becomes "my unsettled feeble Power"; "vos superbes secours" becomes "your haughty, proud Assistance."

Boyer introduces his epithets everywhere. Often he changes Racine's lines so as to use adjective-noun combinations where they were not used at all in Racine. As I have said before, Racine's lines often fall into the rhythms and tones which emotion imposes on natural speech. Whether or not the line has the stress patterns and the intonation of natural speech, the words which convey the emotion are in high relief; they are in stressed position and no extraneous ideas or images are present to weaken their force. Boyer's intrusive epithets and his eternal adjective-noun combinations blur the focus of Racine's lines. For instance, Iphigénie cuts short Eriphile's hypocritical protestations ("Moi, j'aimerois, Madame, un vainqueur furieux?" etc., vss. 675 ff.) by repeating her accusations: "Oui, vous l'aimez, perfide!" (vs. 678). Boyer translates: "Traytress, yes, you love the fierce Destroyer." His epithet and noun, as complement of the verb love, rob the verb of the stress it had in Racine's line. The line is no longer a spontaneous outburst.

Racine's Eriphile describes her childhood (vss. 424-26):

> Remise dès l'enfance en des bras étrangers,
> Je reçus et je vois le jour que je respire,
> Sans que père ni mère ait daigné me sourire.

Racine gives the explanation of the situation in the first line; the period rises to a climax of pathos in the last line. Boyer seems more concerned with explanation than with pathos. Note the loss of pathos by the intrusion of the explanatory adjective in the last line:

> Whilst from my Infancy expos'd to Dangers,
> My *unknown* Parents never Smil'd on me.

Boyer's usual method is to use epithets for every noun and these epithets have the effect of introducing comment or description which destroys the drama of Racine's dialogue. Any scene, picked at random, would offer a number of examples. Three will suffice to illustrate the method. When Clytemnestre asks Achille to protect Iphigénie while she goes to confront Agamemnon, she says (vss. 943-46):

> Seigneur, daignez m'attendre, et ne la point quitter.
> A mon perfide époux je cours me présenter.
> Il ne soutiendra point la fureur qui m'anime.
> Il faudra que Calchas cherche une autre victime.

Then to Iphigénie (vss. 947-48):

> Ou, si je ne vous puis dérober à leurs coups;
> Ma fille, ils pourront bien m'immoler avant vous.

Boyer translates:

> My Lord, I beg you, stay 'till I return.
> I fly to meet my cruel, treacherous Husband,
> And with just Rage oppose his wild Design.
> I'll force the Priest to seek another Victim;
> Or should my best Efforts prove vain, to ward
> The fatal Blow, I'll die with my dear Daughter.

Racine permits himself one epithet, *perfide*. In six lines Boyer adds *cruel, just, wild, fatal*, and *dear*. The effect is to introduce comment on the situation that is hardly natural under the circumstances. Clytemnestra takes time to say that her anger is justified, that Agamemnon's plan is mad, and that she loves her daughter. And instead of addressing her last words to the daughter she loves so deeply, she addresses them to Achilles or perhaps to nobody in particular merely because a noun with an epithet is more to Boyer's taste than a pronoun.

At the end of Act I Agamemnon begs Ulysse for time to make sure Clytemnestre will not witness the sacrifice (vss. 392-94):

> Allez. Mais cependant faites taire Calchas;
> Et m'aidant à cacher ce funeste mystère,
> Laissez-moi de l'autel écarter une mère.

Boyer inappropriately introduces comment and a visual image:

> Yet engage the Priest
> To Silence for a while. Let me at least
> Be guiltless for one Moment: Let me hide
> From Clytemnestra my black barbarous Arts;
> And spare her tender Heart the cruel Sight
> Of a dear Daughter bleeding on an Altar.

ABEL BOYER'S *ACHILLES*

The dialogue (vss. 1649-52):

> IPHIGÉNIE (to her mother)
> Allez: Laissez aux Grecs achever leur ouvrage,
> Et quittez pour jamais un malheureux rivage,
> Du bûcher qui m'attend trop voisin de ces lieux,
> La flamme de trop près viendroit frapper vos yeux.

becomes offensively explicit in Boyer's translation:

> Fly from the Sight of those devouring Flames,
> Which would oppress your tender Heart with Grief
> While they consume your guiltless Daughter.

To use an eighteenth-century verb in a sense somewhat different from the usual one, Boyer has Englished Racine's tragedy—and with a vengeance. Brunetière mentions, among the qualities of Racinian tragedy which the French esteem most, the "négligence apparente, mais étudiée, du style dont le contour sinueux imite, en quelque sorte, ce qu'il y a de plus caché dans les mouvements de la passion."[3] It is just this quality of Racine's style which Boyer sacrifices to a preconceived notion of what poetic diction should be, and a peculiarly English conception of poetic diction at that.[4] Commenting on the characteristics of Racine's tragedies mentioned by Brunetière, Louis Charlanne says: "Les Anglais ne pouvaient ni voir ni sentir ces qualités."[5] But Boyer was a Frenchman. How can we account for his refusal to imitate the essential qualities of Racine's style? I cannot believe that it would be impossible to imitate them in English. The magic of Racine's poetry might be inevitably lost, but his dramatic effects could be preserved. The abortive effort of the first translator of *Andromaque* demonstrated the possibility. Perhaps Boyer quite cynically imitated certain English *procédés*. Perhaps Thomas Cheek's collaboration was largely responsible for the style of Boyer's adaptation.

A contemporary document gives an account of the composition of Boyer's *Achilles* which suggests that Cheek's collaboration was more active than the reference in Boyer's preface would indicate. In the anonymous *A Comparison between the Two Stages*, we find the following comments:

[3] Ferdinand Brunetière, *Manuel de l'Histoire de la Littérature française* [Paris, 1898], p. 193.
[4] See Chap. XI, n. 53, and Chap. XIII.
[5] *L'Influence Française en Angleterre au XVIIe Siècle*, p. 479.

Critick. This Forreign Author, having a plaguy deal of spite in him, Clubs with an honest Gentleman to write a Tragedy on the same Subject [*i.e.* the same subject as John Dennis's *Iphigenia*]: I don't say the Story was the same, because indeed they are directly contrary: Why, so were the Stages, *Ergo*, so should the Plays be. This Amphibious Author, half *English*, half *French*, looks over his own *French Dictionary*, and finds *Madam Iphigenia* very much degraded in t'other Play; she scorn'd to escape from the Sacrifice; she was an errant Termagant, and wou'd dye when she was in the Humour; and why a dickins shou'd Mr. *Dennis* use her so very barbarously as to give her Life: No, I'll prove it to his Face and the World's, that *Madam Iphigenia* dy'd in *Aulis* and all the Town shall know it; besides, his Poetry is stark naught, and I'll make it appear by comparing it with mine, and you shall see how Mr. C—— and I will mawl him: So he falls to't, and being a little cripled in the first Act, he makes a Crutch of his Friend, and so as the Proverb runs—Mr. C——*helps a lame D——— over the Stile.*[6]

Later Boyer and Cheek are referred to as "this new Fletcher and Beaumont."[7] However, the unknown critic's obvious ignorance of the play would make his statements about the author suspect.

Despite the efforts of Boyer or Boyer and Cheek to emend Racine's tragedy to suit English taste, the play was a failure. It was acted at Drury Lane shortly after Dennis's *Iphigenia* had opened at Lincoln's-Inn-Fields. Boyer tells us in the preface that the public having been bored with Dennis's play did not risk being bored a second time by a play which, as they thought, dealt with the same subject. Dryden, in a letter dated December 14, 1699, makes the following remark concerning the two plays: "Both the 'Iphigenias' have been play'd with bad success; and both being acted one against the other in the same week, clash'd together, like two rotten ships which could not endure the shock, and sunk to rights."[8]

[6] *A Comparison between the Two Stages*, ed. Staring B. Wells (Princeton, 1942), p. 24.
[7] *Loc. cit.*
[8] *Works*, ed. Scott-Saintsbury (Edinburgh, 1883), XVIII, 170.

« « CHAPTER V » »

EDMUND SMITH AND RACINE

In the *Muses Mercury; or, Monthly Miscellany* for the month of March, 1707, there appeared the following notice:

Mr. Smith's *Phaedra and Hippolitus* will be play'd about the middle of April; and tho that Gentleman's Friends have perhaps done him Justice only, in the kind Things they have said of his Tragedy; yet the raising the Expectation of the Audience so much, before 'tis acted, is very dangerous. If the Play answers, it will be a Service to the Drama, as well as to the Author. We don't hear of any other Play of Note that will be represented this Season; and cannot hope for many more the next, unless the Poets are encourag'd a little, as well as the Singers, Dancers, &c. (p. 76)

Phaedra and Hippolitus was duly produced with the great Elizabeth Barry as Phaedra and Betterton as Theseus.[1] Ismena was played by Mrs. Oldfield. Despite this excellent cast, the misgivings of the *Muses* critic proved to be justified. The audience did not like the play. Later, however, it became fairly popular as an acting play and very popular as reading. The critics liked it from the first. In 1711 Addison still resented the cold reception of what he apparently considered a masterpiece.[2] In 1712 an anonymous elegy praises the play:

> *Hippolitus*, elate, declares thy Praise,
> In loud Acclaim, among the Shades below,
> His joyful Sentiments expresses, vaunts
> His happy State, first introduc'd by You

[1] Advertisements in the *Daily Courant* indicate that Monday, April 21, 1707, was the date of the première. The play had four performances. It was probably published in June, 1707. The *Daily Courant* for Tuesday, May 13, 1707, announces that it will be published the following week; but there is no further announcement until June 20. On that date the play is advertised as being published that day.

[2] *The Spectator*, No. 18 (March 21, 1711). See below, Chap. XIII.

On *British* Theatre: not Philip's Son
More pleas'd, when at Pelide's Tomb he stood
Greedy of Glory, nor with the Universe
Content; had he obtained his darling Wish
And Sire *Maeonides* his mighty Feats
Of Arms, in never-dying Verse recorded.
Thus shall he live, be thus deliver'd down
To After-Time, drawn to the Life, he seems
Himself, nor his own Native Dress becomes
Him more; *Euripides, Seneca, Racine,*
Nor boast superior Merit: *Greece, Latium, Gaul,*
Confess thy up-grown Genius, over-peering,
And Ostentatious share the second Honors.[3]

Oldisworth's "character of Mr. Smith," which was prefixed to the 1719 edition of Smith's *Works*, is in the same strain of unreserved eulogy:

His *Phaedra* is a consummate tragedy and the success of it was as great as the most sanguine expectations of his friends could promise or foresee. The number of nights, and the common method of filling the house, are not always the surest marks of judging what encouragement a play meets with; but the generosity of all the persons of a refined taste about town was remarkable on this occasion; and it must not be forgotten how zealously Mr. Addison espoused his interest, with all the elegant judgement and diffusive good-nature for which that accomplished gentleman and author is so justly valued by mankind. But as to *Phaedra*, she has certainly made a finer figure under Mr. Smith's conduct, upon the English stage, than either Rome or Athens; and if she excels the Greek and Latin *Phaedra*, I need not say she surpasses the French one, though embellished with whatever regular beauties and moving softness Racine himself could give her.[4]

Dr. Johnson says that Oldisworth's "character" of Smith is given "with all the partiality of friendship."[5] Dr. Johnson himself has reservations in his criticism of Smith's play. He considers it poor as an acting play, the mythological fable being unconvincing, the manners too foreign to English manners, and the diction "too luxuriant and splendid for dialogue." Yet he is willing to grant that "it is a scholar's play, such as may please the reader rather than the spectator; the work of a

[3] *On the Death of Mr. Edmund Smith, Late Student of Christ-Church, Oxon., A Poem in Miltonic Verse* (London, 1712), pp. 3-4.
[4] Quoted by Dr. Johnson in his "Life of Smith," *Lives of the English Poets*, ed. George Birkbeck Hill (Oxford, 1905), II, 7-8.
[5] *Ibid.*, p. 1.

vigorous and elegant mind, accustomed to please itself with its own conceptions, but of little acquaintance with the course of life."[6]

George Sewell referred to Smith's play as an "incomparable tragedy."[7]

As late as 1752, one critic at least is still willing to give the play unqualified praise. In the prefatory essay of an anonymous poem appears the statement: "The *Distressed Mother* and the *Briton* of Philips, and the *Phaedra and Hippolitus* of Smith, are Tragedys which will pass through all Ages with the Approbation of Men of Taste and Judgement; for they approach nearer to that classical Purity, which gives the Stamp of Immortality, than any other of our English Tragedys."[8]

Near the end of the eighteenth century, after the classical pattern had lost favor, one critic mentions *Cato, Irene*, and *Phaedra and Hippolitus* as "regular" tragedies of some value.[9]

There can be little doubt that Smith's play was held in high esteem by neo-classicists of the eighteenth century. It is surprising that so execrable a play should have called forth such fulsome praise. But even more surprising is the fact that, if eulogists of the play mention Racine at all, they do so only in order to proclaim the superiority of Smith's *Phaedra* to Racine's. Except for the condescending sentence which ends the paragraph quoted from Oldisworth's character, I have found no hint of a debt to Racine in any of these panegyrics. Matthew Prior's epilogue mentions Euripides as the source of Smith's play.

In the nineteenth century, after the reputation of the play has waned, there is a tendency to absolve Euripides and Seneca from blame and lay the faults of Smith's play at Racine's door. Genest attributes several of Phaedra's speeches to Euripides and says that the use of Hippolitus' sword to prove his guilt comes from Seneca. He objects to the character

---

[6] *Ibid.*, p. 16.

[7] "The Life of Mr. John Philips," in John Philips, *Works* (London, 1720), pp. viii–ix.

[8] *The Tryal of Hercules, an Ode on Glory, Virtue, and Pleasure* (London, 1752), p. 3.

[9] "Many of our modern tragedies, it must be acknowledged, are regular and faultless performances; some of them are not only free from material defects, but possess a considerable share of real excellence; for instance, Cato, Irene, and Phaedra and Hippolitus. The diction of these plays is lofty and poetical without being inflated; the sentiments just and noble, the plots regularly conducted, the characters skilfully diversified, and the unities strictly preserved." (W. Belsham, *Essays Philosophical and Moral, Historical and Literary* [London: G. G. and J. Robinson, 1799], p. 471.)

of Hippolitus (which he says is modeled on Racine's Hippolyte) as violating the rule that a playwright should not depart from tradition in the portrayal of historical or legendary characters. He then continues: "Dr. Johnson calls this a scholar's play; but how can this be said with propriety of a play in which the author has followed Racine rather than Euripides or Seneca?" It is not clear whether he is referring merely to the character of Hippolitus or finds other evidence of imitation of Racine.[10] In his article on Smith in the *Dictionary of National Biography*, Sidney Lee calls the *Phaedra and Hippolitus* "an artificial and bombastic effort modelled on Racine's *Phèdre* rather than on Seneca's *Hippolitus*." I infer that Lee blames Racine rather than Seneca for Smith's inflated style.

In recent studies Racine is given more credit and less blame. Dorothea Canfield says: "In a consideration of the play itself it is a little hard to tell how much comes from Smith's Latin and Greek sources, and how much directly from the French; but a careful comparison of his text with that of Euripides, Seneca, and Racine inclines one to think that a great deal more comes from Racine than is usually granted." Specifically, she quotes four speeches from Phaedra's first scene and shows that they come from Racine's *Phèdre* rather than from Euripides' *Hippolytus*. The fact that Hippolitus is represented as being in love she says "can be referred to nothing but an imitation of Racine."[11]

F. Y. Eccles says: "This tragedy is only in part a paraphrase of *Phèdre*. Smith went directly to Euripides and to Seneca for a great part of his material; apart from a number of particular passages, he got from Racine the idea of Hippolitus in love."[12]

Allardyce Nicoll says Smith's play is "taken mostly from Racine's *Phèdre*. He devotes a short paragraph in his *History of Early Eighteenth Century Drama* to Smith's play. He says: "Here we have an example of the classicised heroic play. Taken from Racine, it has about it all the atmosphere of the older type." As evidence that material taken from Racine is altered in the direction of the heroic play, he says that Hippolitus and Ismena are the familiar hero and heroine.[13]

[10] John Genest, *Some Account of the English Stage* (London, 1832), II, 370–71.
[11] Dorothea Canfield, *Corneille and Racine in England* (New York, Columbia University Press, 1904), pp. 131–33.
[12] F. Y. Eccles, *Racine in England* (Oxford, The Clarendon Press, 1922), p. 9.
[13] Cambridge, 1929, pp. 72, 80.

EDMUND SMITH AND RACINE

No one since John Dennis has, I believe, mentioned *Bajazet* as a source.[14]

The action of Smith's play is as follows:

ACT I. The scene is in Crete. The play opens with a conversation between Cratander, Captain of the Guards, and Lycon, Minister of State. We learn that Phaedra, the Queen, is mysteriously ill and that Theseus, King of Crete, is absent, making war on the enemies of Crete. Lycon thinks that Theseus's absence cannot be the cause of Phaedra's melancholy since she does not love Theseus. Lycon fears that, if the Queen should die, Hippolitus, whom he hates, will mount the throne. (We learn later that Lycon himself aspires to the throne.) Lycon intends to destroy Hippolitus, whether the Queen lives or dies. Ismena, captive princess, daughter of Theseus's enemy Pallas, enters and asks Lycon to find out the cause of the Queen's illness. Ismena is apparently lady-in-waiting to Phaedra and has been watching over her. Phaedra enters. Lycon persuades her to confess her secret. She admits her love for Hippolitus. Ismena hears the confession and we learn, from an aside, that she is in love with Hippolitus. A messenger enters and announces that Theseus is dead. Lycon urges Phaedra to woo Hippolitus. In a soliloquy that closes the act, we learn that Lycon expects Hippolitus to repulse Phaedra and that he, Lycon, hopes to profit by Phaedra's anger in order to imprison Hippolitus.

ACT II. Phaedra declares her love to Hippolitus, in Lycon's presence and with Lycon's help, as it is he who tells Hippolitus that the Queen loves him. He rejects her with horror and indignation. Phaedra exits, threatening to destroy herself and Hippolitus. Lycon puts Hippolitus under guard, accusing him of fomenting rebellion against the throne. Ismena enters and begs Hippolitus to placate the Queen in order to save his life. He finally consents to give the Queen hope. Lycon enters and tells Ismena that Hippolitus and the Queen are reconciled. He thinks they will marry. Ismena begins to doubt Hippolitus' love for her. She thinks that so guileless a youth could not have feigned love for Phaedra. His love for Phaedra must be sincere. When Hippolitus returns from his interview with the Queen, she reproaches him. Hippolitus reassures her and urges her to flee with him. She consents.

---

[14] Dennis does not share the enthusiasm of his fellow-classicists for Smith's play. See below, Chap. XIII.

Act III. Hippolitus and Ismena are captured and brought before Phaedra. Phaedra upbraids Hippolitus and Ismena for their deception, threatening to have Ismena killed before Hippolitus' eyes. Hippolitus begs Phaedra to spare Ismena and punish him; Ismena protests that it was she who urged Hippolitus to deceive Phaedra. Ismena accuses Lycon of conspiring against Hippolitus. Phaedra is moved at the thought of the danger to Hippolitus and begs him to accept the crown and her love. Hippolitus rejects her and she seizes his sword to kill herself. Lycon enters and snatches the sword away from her. He announces that Theseus is alive and is approaching. Phaedra flees from the sight of Theseus. Hippolitus asks his father's permission to leave Crete.

Act IV. Phaedra has tried to kill herself but has been prevented by her attendants. Lycon urges her to spare her son the shame of her suicide. He advises her to forget Hippolitus and respond to Theseus's love. She fears that Hippolitus will betray her. Lycon encourages this fear and suggests that Phaedra accuse Hippolitus of attempting to violate her. Theseus enters and Phaedra gives Lycon permission to make the accusation. Lycon accuses Hippolitus to Theseus, offering the sword as proof. Theseus confronts Hippolitus and refuses to believe either Hippolitus' or Ismena's protestations. He orders Hippolitus to kill himself with the guilty sword and commands Cratander to see that his orders are carried out.

Act V. Phaedra accuses Lycon of having driven her to crime, taking advantage of her emotional confusion. Theseus enters. A messenger announces that Theseus's orders have been carried out and that Hippolitus is dead. Phaedra, who says she has taken poison, confesses, then stabs herself and dies. Theseus orders that Lycon be punished by torture and death. Ismena is about to stab herself when Hippolitus enters. He has outwitted and killed Cratander and escaped.

Act I. In the scene of Phaedra's confession of her love for Hippolitus, Smith is obviously following Racine rather than Euripides. He echoes passages from Racine which have no parallel in Euripides.[15]

[15] His Phaedra, like Racine's, describes her first meeting with Hippolitus and her attempts to free herself from obsessive thoughts of him. Among other parallel passages we find the following (p. 9, vss. 285-88):

PHAEDRA: If to the Gods I pray'd, the very Vows

Where Racine paraphrases Euripides, Smith's lines are so close to Racine's as to leave no doubt that Racine rather than Euripides was his model.[16]

ACT II. The scene of Phaedra's declaration of her love to Hippolitus is based on Racine and on Seneca. Phaedra's lines contain many echoes of Racine, while those of Hippolitus are reminiscent of Seneca. At the end of this scene, Smith begins to introduce material from Racine's *Bajazet*. The scene of the declaration does not end in Smith's version as it ended in *Phèdre*. Rejected by Hippolitus, Smith's Phaedra threatens him in the manner of Roxane. He is placed under arrest by Lycon's order. So, at the end of the declaration scene, we find Smith's Hippolitus in the situation of Racine's Bajazet after his first interview with Roxane. The rest of Act II is based on Racine's *Bajazet*, scenes in which Ismena persuades Hippolitus to feign love for Phaedra in order to save his life, then, when her plan succeeds, doubts Hippolitus' fidelity. There is striking verbal similarity (pp. 18–20, vss. 787–88, 792, 761–62, 867, 917–18):

                      I made to Heaven, were by my erring Tongue
                      Spoke to Hippolitus.
PHÈDRE: Quand ma bouche imploroit le nom de la Déesse,
                      J'adorois Hippolyte; et le voyant sans cesse,
                      Même au pied des autels que je faisois fumer,
                      J'offrois tout à ce dieu que je n'osois nommer.

(Page references are to the first edition of Smith's play, published by Bernard Lintott, London, without date. See note 1 above. Verse references are to the verse numbers of the Mesnard edition of Racine.)

[16] We find such verbal echoes of Racine as the following (p. 4, vs. 161; p. 4, vs. 168; p. 6, vss. 226–28; p. 6, vss. 257–58):

PHAEDRA: All, all conspire to make your Queen unhappy.
PHÈDRE: Tout m'afflige et me nuit, et conspire à me nuire.

ISMENA: And hate the Light you sought.
OENONE: Vous haïssez le jour que vous veniez chercher?

PHAEDRA: And let me die to save the black Confession.
LYCON: Die then, but not alone; old faithful Lycon
            Shall be a Victim to your cruel Silence.
PHÈDRE: Je meurs pour ne point faire un aveu si funeste.
OENONE: Mourez donc, et gardez un silence inhumain;
            Mais pour fermer vos yeux cherchez une autre main.

PHAEDRA: And since the cruel God of Love requires it,
            I fall the last, and most undone of all.
PHÈDRE: Puisque Vénus le veut, de ce sang déplorable
            Je péris la dernière et la plus misérable.

Ismena:	Say what Occasion, Chance, or Heav'n inspires
	. . . .
	Say, to preserve your Life, say any thing.
Atalide:	Ah! daignez sur ce choix ne me point consulter.
	L'occasion, le ciel pourra vous les dicter.
	. . . .
	Dites . . . tout ce qu'il faut, Seigneur, pour vous sauver.
Ismena:	Come on, I'll lead you on to Phaedra;
	I'll tell her all the Secrets of our Love.
Atalide:	Venez, cruel, venez; je vais vous y conduire;
	Et de tous nos secrets c'est moi qui veux l'instruire.
Ismena:	Does he then wed the Queen?
Lycon:	At least I think so.
Atalide:	L'épouse-t-il enfin?
Acomat:	Madame, je le croi.
Ismena:	Perhaps new Graces darted from her Eyes,
	Perhaps soft Pity charm'd his yielding Soul.
Atalide:	Peut-être en la voyant, plus sensible pour elle,
	Il a vu dans ses yeux quelque grâce nouvelle.

The self-deception of jealousy in Ismena (now become Atalide) is very Racinian because Smith translates or paraphrases many of Racine's lines. But we soon see that he has introduced these scenes from *Bajazet* merely to motivate an episode of his own invention. Hippolitus succeeds in allaying Ismena's jealousy—once and for all—and persuades her to flee with him.

Act III of Smith's play is based on *Phèdre* and on *Bajazet*. When Phaedra learns that Hippolitus, who has professed to love her, has eloped with Ismena, she echoes Phèdre's tirade of jealousy ("O douleur non encore éprouvée"). When Hippolitus and Ismena are captured and brought before the enraged Phaedra, Smith introduces incidents from two scenes of *Bajazet*. Phaedra now becomes Roxane. She threatens to have Ismena killed and to force Hippolitus to watch her die (*Bajazet*, Act V, Scene 4). Ismena offers to die to save Hippolitus (*Bajazet*, Act V, Scene 6). Hippolitus takes the blame for the deception of Phaedra and pleads for Ismena's life (*Bajazet*, Act V, Scene 4).[17] At this point

[17] In these scenes Smith's Phaedra becomes Roxane. F. C. Green sees in Smith's delineation of the character of Phaedra reminiscences of *Venus and Adonis*, and of the two Cleopatras, Shakespeare's and Dryden's. To me, Smith's

Ismena accuses Lycon of plotting Hippolitus' death. Phaedra relents. Hippolitus pities her. Encouraged by his pity, Phaedra begs for his love and offers him empire (as Racine's Phèdre had planned to do). The rest of the scene is made up of incidents from *Phèdre*. Rejected by Hippolitus, Phaedra seizes his sword to stab herself. Lycon enters and snatches away the sword. He announces that Theseus is alive and is approaching.

In Act IV, Smith follows *Phèdre* in outline and there are passages which are plainly taken from Racine; but much of this act is original with Smith, notably the long scene in which Lycon convinces Theseus of Hippolitus' guilt.

Act V is almost entirely original with Smith. There are, however, verbal echoes of both Racine and Seneca. The scene of Phaedra's death, though it contains more verbal reminiscences of Racine than of Seneca, is Senecan not Racinian in tone. When Lycon describes Theseus's terrible rage at Hippolitus, Phaedra has a vision of Hippolitus' death. She is more preoccupied with Hippolitus' physical beauty than her own guilt:

> See his rich Blood in Purple Torrents flows,
> And Nature sallies in unbidden Groans;
> Now mortal Pangs distort his lovely Form,
> His Rosie Beauties fade, his Starry Eyes
> Now darkling swim, and fix their closing Beams.

When a messenger enters and announces that Hippolitus is dead, Phaedra confesses her guilt to Theseus, says she has taken poison (echoing Racine's lines here), and addresses to the supposedly dead Hippolitus the following apostrophe from Seneca:

> Thee I pursue, (oh great ill-fated Youth!)
> Pursue thee still, but now with chast Desires;
> Thee thro' the dismal waste of gloomy Death;
> Thee thro' th'glimm'ring Dawn and purer Day,
> Thro' all th' *Elysian* Plains.

She then goes into a delirium, mistakes Theseus for Lycon, tries to stab him, then stabs herself and dies.

It is evident that Racine's two plays, *Phèdre* and *Bajazet*, are the

---

Phaedra seems largely the result of an unhappy combination of the imperious, amoral, elemental Roxane and Phèdre, self-critical, conscience-stricken, chaste of soul. Cf. F. C. Green, *Minuet* (London, 1935), p. 132.

most important sources of Smith's *Phaedra and Hippolitus*. Smith knew Seneca's *Phaedra* and made a few borrowings from it. But only in the scene of the declaration does Seneca compete with Racine. It is possible that Smith knew Euripides' *Hippolytus*;[18] but, of Euripides' play, he imitates only scenes that Racine has imitated, and comparison of passages imitated shows that he is following Racine rather than Euripides in these scenes. Except for a few echoes of Seneca, when Smith departs from Racine's *Phèdre*, it is either to imitate *Bajazet*[19] or to substitute scenes of his own invention.

In view of the reputation which Smith's play enjoyed among English classicists, Smith's changes—additions and excisions—assume as much importance as his borrowings from Racine, since they must, to a certain extent, reflect the taste of his contemporaries. They should throw some light on the English ideal of classical tragedy of the eighteenth century. What Smith rejected of his Racinian sources and what he chose to change should indicate some differences between English classicism and the French classicism of Racine's generation.

In creating his version of the story of Phaedra's love for Hippolytus, Racine discards little of the legend and adds little.[20] Racine's originality

[18] Smith's Hippolitus, like Euripides' hero, takes an oath not to reveal Phaedra's secret. In Euripides the oath is a solemn religious vow; in Smith's play, Hippolitus swears on his sword.

[19] Smith hay have known Pradon's *Phèdre et Hippolyte*. There is one point of resemblance between Smith's play and Pradon's which could not have come from *Phèdre* or from *Bajazet*. Theseus explains, in Smith as in Pradon, that he himself spread the rumor of his own death in order to elude his enemies. (This device could have been suggested by Racine's *Mithridate*.) All other points of resemblance between Smith's *Phaedra and Hippolitus* and Pradon's play may be traced to Racine's *Bajazet*, a common source of the two plays. In all three plays a ruler, away at war, has left the woman he loves to rule in his stead. This woman ruler, in love with a young kinsman of the absent ruler, has the power of life and death over the young man and the princess whom he loves and who loves him. In all three her young rival is in her confidence. In all three she threatens, when she discovers that her confidante is her successful rival, to have her killed before her lover's eyes. In all three the young man pleads for mercy for his beloved and asks to be killed in her stead. In all three the young girl doubts for a while her lover's constancy. Verbal reminiscences of *Bajazet* in Smith's play leave no doubt as to which play is his source. There is no such verbal similarity between Smith's play and Pradon's as between Smith's play and *Bajazet*.

[20] His chief additions are: (1) Hippolytus is in love (an innovation first made by earlier French dramatists); (2) Hippolytus' beloved is Aricie, daughter of

lies in his imaginative use of motifs from the legend to make his Phaedra a more noble and a more pitiable tragic figure, and in the precision with which he traces the psychological steps by which Phaedra's love for her stepson drives her to deceit and guile, despite an innate honesty, and to violence and crime, despite her gentleness. Each step toward degradation and catastrophe is a mad impulse acted upon at a moment when her reason is assailed by violent emotion. Racine discards the gnomic and didactic elements in Euripides and Seneca to build a psychological drama around the character of Phaedra.

We first see Phèdre in a trance-like despair, obsessed by the thought of Hippolyte and spent with her struggle to free herself from her loathsome passion. Oenone, her old nurse, persuades her to reveal her secret. She confesses her love for Hippolyte. She recounts her struggles to free herself. She has banished Hippolyte but is haunted by thoughts of him. Filled with self-loathing, Phèdre wants to escape in death while she is still without guilt except in her own conscience. Then comes the false news of Theseus's death and of an uprising in Athens against Phèdre and her son, with one faction pressing Aricie's claim to the throne. To the blindly devoted and less high-minded Oenone, but not to Phèdre, Theseus's death transforms Phèdre's unholy passion into a blameless love. Oenone urges Phèdre to ask for Hippolyte's aid in support of her son's claim to the Athenian throne. Phèdre, with Oenone's encouragement, deludes herself into thinking she must seek an interview with Hippolyte for her son's sake. Face to face with Hippolyte, she cannot help revealing her love. Rejected, she begs for understanding (vss. 693-97):

> Que dis-je? Cet aveu que je te viens de faire,
> Cet aveu si honteux, le crois-tu volontaire?
> Tremblante pour un fils que je n'osois trahir,

Pallas, Theseus's defeated enemy and rival for the throne of Athens; (3) instead of a mere rumor that Theseus is in Hades, his death is definitely announced, though this report later proves to be false; (4) with the false news of Theseus's death comes news that two factions in Athens are opposing the claim to the throne of Theseus's son by Phaedra, the one supporting Hippolytus, the other, Aricie; (5) instead of having Phaedra herself accuse Hippolytus of attempted rape, Racine has a servant do so, with Phaedra's consent; (6) Phaedra is the daughter of that Minos who judges the dead in Hades. Of these additions, Smith discards only the uprising to place Aricie on the throne. Smith's Hippolytus, like Racine's, is in love with a daughter of Pallas, but Smith gives her the name of Aricie's confidante, Ismène (Ismena).

> Je te venois prier de ne le point haïr.
> Foibles projets d'un cœur trop plein de ce qu'il aime!

Hippolyte makes his horror and contempt all too evident. Phèdre is left to brood in memory over his harshness and her shame. The news comes that her young son by Theseus has been made king of Athens. She again deludes herself, this time with the hope that Hippolyte can be tempted by power, and wishes to offer him the regency. Oenone now sees the hopelessness of Phèdre's love and tries to check the course of her self-deception. Oenone protests that Hippolyte hates all women. (The Hippolytus of Seneca and of Euripides hated women; Racine's Hippolyte has the reputation of being a woman-hater.) This fact comforts Phèdre. She need fear no rival: "Je ne me verrai point préférer de rivale"[21] (vs. 790). Phèdre sends Oenone to plead again with Hippolyte and she herself offers a prayer to Venus.

Oenone announces that Thésée has returned. She suggests that Phèdre accuse Hippolyte of having tried to assault her. At first Phèdre refuses. Oenone insists that Thésée will merely exile Hippolyte. Thésée appears with Hippolyte. Phèdre thinks she reads in Hippolyte's eyes his intention of betraying her to Thésée. In a spasm of fear, she tells Oenone to do what she can to save her. Oenone has accused Hippolyte and offered his sword as proof. Thésée confronts Hippolyte with this proof of his guilt. Hippolyte denies Phèdre's charge and confesses his love for Aricie. Thésée thinks this confession a subterfuge, exiles Hippolyte and asks Neptune to destroy him. Phèdre, fearing for Hippolyte, goes to Thésée to plead for him, perhaps even to confess her guilt. Thésée reveals Hippolyte's professed love for Aricie. While Thésée had thought Hippolyte's confession a subterfuge, Phèdre realizes that Hippolyte has told the truth. The shock of the discovery, the more violent because she has clung to the desperate comfort that she will never have a rival, completely usurps Phèdre's mind. When she can again think rationally, it is too late to save Hippolyte. His horses, frightened by a sea monster, have wrecked his chariot and he has been killed. Now not even in death can Phèdre escape. In Heaven and Hell her illustrious ancestors await her (vss. 1276–78):

---

[21] This line is a translation of Seneca (243), but it takes on a dramatic irony that it did not have in Seneca, since Racine's Hippolyte is in love and the audience is acquainted with the fact when Phèdre speaks this line. (References to Seneca are to the verse numbers of the Loeb edition.)

EDMUND SMITH AND RACINE

> Le ciel, tout l'univers est plein de mes aïeux.
> Où me cacher? Fuyons dans la nuit infernale.
> Mais que dis-je? mon père y tient l'urne fatale.

She takes poison, confesses, and dies.

Racine stresses the Senecan motif of Venus's hatred for the descendants of Apollo and her implacable persecution of them with unnatural love. Phèdre considers herself the victim of Venus's wrath. She is horrified at her passion for her stepson and struggles against it. She has built a temple to Venus to placate her. She suffers the more intensely because she has a Christian nostalgia for innocence and an aristocratic pride of race, a feeling of *noblesse oblige*, which she has betrayed by her shameful love. She is the granddaughter of Apollo. The sun in Racine's play becomes the symbol of the purity for which Phèdre longs and a reproach to her for having been unworthy of her illustrious birth.[22] On her first entrance, she addresses the sun (vss. 169-72):

> Noble et brillant auteur d'une triste famille,
> Toi, dont ma mère osoit se vanter d'être fille,
> Qui peut-être rougis du trouble où tu me vois,
> Soleil, je te viens voir pour la dernière fois.

On learning of Hippolyte's love for Aricie, she bursts into a tirade of threats of vengeance on Aricie. And then (vss. 1273-75):

> Misérable! et je vis? et je soutiens la vue
> De ce sacré soleil dont je suis descendue?
> J'ai pour aïeul le père et la maître des Dieux.

Her last words are (vss. 1641-44):

> Déjà je ne vois plus qu'à travers un nuage
> Et le ciel et l'époux que ma présence outrage;
> Et la mort, à mes yeux dérobant la clarté,
> Rend au jour, qu'ils souilloient, toute sa pureté.

Smith discards much of the legend which Racine had used so imaginatively. He is at pains to eliminate the motif of Venus's hatred for Phaedra's family. Racine's lines (vss. 249-50):

---

[22] This motif is suggested by Seneca. After Phaedra's declaration Hippolytus says: "tuque, sidereum caput, radiate Titan, tu nefas stirpis tuae speculare?" (677-79). But here Hippolytus, not Phaedra herself, has the feeling that she has disgraced her illustrious family.

> O haine de Vénus! O fatale colère!
> Dans quels égarements l'amour jeta ma mère!

become (p. 16):

> O cruel Venus!
> How fatal Love has been to all our Race!

Ariadne is mentioned but not Pasiphae. While paraphrasing Phèdre's description of her love, he omits references to the curse of Venus.[23] Like Phèdre, his Phaedra offers a prayer to Venus. It is a free paraphrase of Phèdre's prayer but informed with quite a different emotion. As Lycon goes to tell Hippolitus that the Queen wishes to see him, Phaedra, resolved to declare her love, prays to Venus (p. 11):

> And thou, O Venus, aid a suppliant Queen,
> That owns thy Triumphs, and adores thy Pow'r;
> O spare thy Captives, and subdue thy Foes.
> On this cold Scythian let thy Pow'r be known.
> And in a Lover's Cause assert thy own.

Smith's Phaedra prays to the goddess of love to help her win Hippolitus. Humiliated and at bay, after Hippolyte has rejected her, Racine's Phèdre begs a truce from her enemy (vss. 813–23):

> O toi qui vois la honte où je suis descendue,
> Implacable Vénus, suis-je assez confondue!
> Tu ne saurois plus loin pousser ta cruauté.
> Ton triomphe est parfait; tous tes traits ont porté.
> Cruelle, si tu veux une gloire nouvelle,
> Attaque un ennemi qui te soit plus rebelle.
> Hippolyte te fuit; et bravant ton courroux,
> Jamais à tes autels n'a fléchi les genoux;
> Ton nom semble offenser ses superbes oreilles:
> Déesse, venge-toi; nos causes sont pareilles.
> Qu'il aime. . . .

Smith's Phaedra is also the granddaughter of the sun, but Smith discards the Racinian symbolism.[24] Smith omits Phèdre's apostrophe to

---

[23] He omits such lines as (vss. 277–78):

> Je reconnus Vénus et ses feux redoutables,
> D'un sang qu'elle poursuit tourments inévitables.

[24] Phaedra's descent from the sun is referred to in Lycon's description of her beauty (p. 24):

> How her Eyes sparkle! how their radiant Beams

the sun in her first scene, although he is following Racine closely in this scene. Phèdre's horror at her criminal rage against Aricie, Smith paraphrases, substituting Minos for the sun (p. 30):

HIPPOLITUS: And can you doom her Death? can Minos Daughter
Condemn the Virtue which her Soul admires?
Are not you Phaedra? once the boast of Fame,
Shame of our Sex, and Pattern of your own.
PHAEDRA: Am I that Phaedra? No.—Another Soul
Informs my alter'd Frame. Cou'd else Ismena
Provoke my Hatred, yet deserve my Love?
Aid me, ye Gods, support my sinking Glory,
Restore my Reason, and confirm my Virtue.

These words of Phaedra's are as near as Smith's heroine comes to the feeling of *noblesse oblige* of Racine's Phèdre. Smith's Phaedra has no sense of sin and no self-loathing, and no nostalgia for innocence. The struggle in Phaedra's soul is between her passion for Hippolitus and (p. 9):

All the ambitious Thirst of Fame and Empire,
And all the honest Pride of conscious Virtue.

Instead of aristocratic pride we have lip-service to conventional morality (p. 9):

Yes, I wou'd die, Heaven knows, this very moment,
Rather than wrong my Lord, my Husband Theseus.

Smith not only discards the Racinian motifs; he changes the legend drastically. His Phaedra is young and beautiful.[25] A widow with one

---

Confess their shining Ancestor the Sun!

Compare Seneca (vss. 379–80):

et qui ferebant signa Phoebeae facis
oculi nihil gentile nec patrium micant.

Phaedra apostrophizes the sun along with all her ancestors, to inspire her to vengeance on Hippolitus (p. 29):

Now all the Spirits of my Godlike Race
Enflame my Soul and urge me on to Vengeance.
Arsamnes, Minos, Jove, th' avenging Sun
Inspire my Fury and require my Justice.

[25] Cratander refers to her as "one so gay, so beautiful and young" (p. 1). She is of the same age as Hippolitus (p. 2):

son, she has married Theseus out of gratitude for services to Crete in order to reward him with the crown. Theseus is not the inconstant seducer of the legend. But he is very old.[26]

Thus the "roman de la femme de trente ans" (Lemaître) is transformed into the stock comic situation of the doting old husband and the young wife in love with a man of her own age. Phaedra has been a wife to Theseus in name only.[27] This fact apparently saves her from any feeling of guilt in wooing Hippolitus after Theseus's supposed death. After her declaration of love to Hippolitus, when he upbraids her, she replies (p. 14):

> Alas, my Lord! believe me not so vile,
> No by thy Goddess, by the chaste Diana,
> None but my first, my much lov'd Lord Arsamnes
> Was e're receiv'd in these unhappy Arms.
> No! for the Love of thee, of those dear Charms,
> Which now I see are doom'd to be my Ruin,
> I still deny'd my Lord, my Husband Theseus,
> The chaste, the modest Joys of spotless Marriage.[28]

CRATANDER: Why did she wed old Theseus? While his Son,
　　　　　　The brave Hippolitus, with equal Youth,
　　　　　　And equal Beauty might have fill'd her Arms.

[26] Smith avoids all references to Theseus's philandering. Note the substitution of Theseus's age for his infidelities in the following parallel passages (vss. 634–40, pp. 13–14):

PHÈDRE: Oui, Prince, je languis, je brûle pour Thésée.
　　　　　Je l'aime, non point tel que l'ont vu les enfers,
　　　　　Volage adorateur de mille objets divers,
　　　　　Qui va du dieu des morts déshonorer la couche;
　　　　　Mais fidèle, mais fier, et même un peu farouche,
　　　　　Charmant, jeune, traînant tous les coeurs après soi,
　　　　　Tel qu'on dépeint nos Dieux, ou tel que je vous voi.

PHAEDRA: Love him, indeed! dote, languish, dye for him,
　　　　　　Forsake my Food, my Sleep, all Joyes for Theseus,
　　　　　　(But not that Hoary venerable Theseus,)
　　　　　　But Theseus, as he was, when mantling Blood,
　　　　　　Glow'd in his lovely Cheeks; when his bright Eyes
　　　　　　Sparkl'd with youthful Fires; when ev'ry Grace
　　　　　　Shone in the Father, which now crowns the Son;
　　　　　　When Theseus was Hippolitus.

[27] Compare (p. 10):

　　　And bless'd be Heav'n that steel'd my stubborn Heart,
　　　That made me shun the bridal Bed of Theseus,
　　　And give him Empire, but refuse him Love.

[28] These lines replace Racine's (vss. 670–78):

EDMUND SMITH AND RACINE

Smith transforms the disinterested and blindly devoted nurse of the legend into a plot-spinning villain, Lycon, kinsman of Phaedra, who aspires to the throne of Crete and encourages Phaedra in her love for Hippolitus in order to destroy Hippolitus, his enemy and rival for the crown. Lycon speaks many of Oenone's lines but his devotion to Phaedra is feigned. His motives are revealed in Iago-like soliloquies and asides. At the end of the first act, he urges Phaedra to (pp. 10–11):

> ... forget the wrinkled Theseus
> And take the youthful Hero to your Arms.
> . . . .
> Then rouze your Soul, and muster all your Charms,
> Sooth his ambitious Mind with Thirst of Empire,
> And all his tender Thoughts with soft Allurements.

Phaedra is not too reluctant. Her only fear is that Hippolitus will reject her. After Phaedra's exit in this scene, Lycon explains his intentions (p. 11):

> If she proposes Love, why then as surely
> His haughty Soul refuses it with Scorn.
> Say I confine him, if she dies he's safe;
> And if she lives I'll work her raging Mind.
> A Woman scorn'd with Ease I'll work to Vengeance;
> With humble, fawning, wise, obsequious Arts
> I'll rule the Whirl and Transport of her Soul.

Lycon does indeed "rule the whirl and transport" of Phaedra's soul. Where Phèdre's own imagination drives her to catastrophe, Lycon's wiles ensnare Smith's Phaedra. This shift is apparent in the scene leading up to Phaedra's consent to the false accusation of Hippolitus. In Racine's play it is Phèdre herself who first thinks of the burden of shame that her children will have to bear if she commits suicide. In Smith's play Lycon reminds Phaedra of her son. In Racine's play, the

---

> Ah! cruel, tu m'as trop entendue.
> Je t'en ai dit assez pour te tirer d'erreur.
> Hé bien! connois donc Phèdre et toute sa fureur.
> J'aime. Ne pense pas qu'au moment que je t'aime,
> Innocente à mes yeux, je m'approuve moi-même,
> Ni que du fol amour qui trouble ma raison
> Ma lâche complaisance ait nourri le poison.
> Objet infortuné des vengeances célestes,
> Je m'abhorre encor plus que tu ne me détestes.

sight of Hippolyte and what Phèdre imagines she reads in his eyes motivate Phèdre's consent to the false accusation of Hippolyte (vss. 909-12):

> Ah! je vois Hippolyte;
> Dans ses yeux insolents je vois ma perte écrite.
> Fais ce que tu voudras, je m'abandonne à toi.
> Dans le trouble où je suis, je ne puis rien pour moi.

In Smith's play Lycon conjures up a frightening picture of Hippolitus' triumph with bait for Phaedra's jealousy guilefully insinuated (p. 36):

> Then the fierce Scythian—Now methinks I see
> His fiery Eyes with sullen Pleasures glow,
> Survey your Tortures, and insult your Pangs;
> I see him, smiling on the pleas'd Ismena,
> Point out with Scorn the once proud Tyrant Phaedra.

After Phaedra's second plea for Hippolitus' love in Smith's play, Lycon snatches Hippolitus' sword away from Phaedra and says to the audience, "This will do service yet." He puts the sword to good use when he denounces Hippolitus to Theseus. This accusation, which does not take place on the stage in Racine's play, furnishes a long scene in Smith's play. Lycon displays the sword in order to overcome Theseus's skepticism. Sure of persuading Theseus that Hippolitus is guilty, Lycon gloats in an aside (p. 43):

> What easie Tools are these blunt honest Heroes,
> Who with keen Hunger gorge the naked Hook,
> Prevent the Bate the Statesman's Art prepares,
> And post to Ruin.—Go, believing Fool,
> Go act thy far fam'd Justice on thy Son,
> Next on thy self, and both make way for Lycon.[29]

When Phaedra turns upon Lycon, he does not, like Oenone, commit suicide. He has planned to escape with his fortune. Like Acomat, in

---

[29] Smith follows Racine in not having Phaedra herself make the accusation; but, by having the highborn Lycon do so instead of a servant, Smith violates the rule of decorum which Racine was following when he transferred the accusation from Phèdre to Oenone. Cf. Racine's preface: "J'ai cru que la calomnie avait quelque chose de trop bas et de trop noir pour la mettre dans la bouche d'une princesse qui a d'ailleurs des sentiments si nobles et si vertueux. Cette bassesse m'a paru plus convenable à une nourrice, qui pouvoit avoir des inclinations plus serviles, et qui néanmoins n'entreprend cette fausse accusation que pour sauver la vie et l'honneur de sa maîtresse."

EDMUND SMITH AND RACINE

Bajazet, he has a ship in readiness (p. 34). But, at Theseus's command, he is arrested. Brought before Theseus, he pleads for his life (p. 59):

> Oh chain me! whip me! let me be the Scorn
> Of sordid Rabbles, and insulting Crowds,
> Give me but Life, and make that Life most wretched.

But Theseus orders (p. 59):

> Drag him to all the Torments Earth can furnish,
> Let him be wrackt and gancht, impal'd alive;
> Then let the mangl'd Monster, fixt on high,
> Grin o'er the shouting Crowd, and glut their Vengeance.

At first sight of Hippolitus, Phaedra is seized with a passion quite as violent as Phèdre's, and she describes her experience somewhat less delicately than Phèdre (vss. 272-77):

> PHÈDRE: Athènes me montra mon superbe ennemi.
> Je le vis, je rougis, je pâlis à sa vue;
> Un trouble s'éleva dans mon âme éperdue;
> Mes yeux ne voyoient plus, je ne pouvois parler;
> Je sentis tout mon corps et transir et brûler.
> Je reconnus Vénus et ses feux redoutables.

Smith translates (p. 7):

> PHAEDRA: ... for that unhappy Hour
> In which the Priests join'd Theseus's Hand to mine,
> Shew'd the young Scythian to my dazled Eyes.
> Gods! how I shook! what boiling Heat inflam'd
> My panting Breast! how from the Touch of Theseus
> My slack Hand dropt, and all the idle Pomp,
> Priests, Altars, Victims swam before my Sight!
> The God of Love, ev'n the whole God possest me.

But Smith interpolates a long account of how Hippolitus has saved Phaedra from a wild boar and of his solicitous visits to her afterwards (p. 8). Thus to *l'amour-passion* is added *l'amour-reconnaissance*.

Smith's contributions to the legend, a young and beautiful Phaedra married to a wholly admirable but aged Theseus, a white marriage, a touch of the sentimental in Phaedra's love for Hippolitus, a "cool, deliberate villain" whose motive is political ambition, and a melodramatic use of the motif of Hippolitus' sword, have so robbed the play of tragic inevitability that his final contribution, a happy ending, seems quite appropriate. Hippolitus outwits Cratander and returns, just in time to save Ismena from suicide. As she "offers to stab herself," Hippolitus enters and cries (pp. 62-63):

> O forbear Ismena!
> Forbear, chast Maid, to wound thy tender Bosom.

Hippolitus and Ismena indulge in a Cornelian duet of rejoicing: Ismena says, "O killing Joy!" "Oh Extasie of Bliss!" responds Hippolitus. Hippolitus informs the audience that "Unguarded Vertue human Arts defies," and the curtain falls.

This happy ending resembles that of *The Mourning Bride*. In both plays the young heroine is about to commit suicide when the hero, supposedly dead, rushes in to stay her hand. Congreve's dénouement has suspense by reason of the fact that the spectators know that the hero is alive but are not sure that he will arrive in time to save the heroine. The resurrection of Hippolitus comes as a complete surprise to the spectator as well as to the heroine.

If anything further was needed to save the audience from the devastating effect of the tragic emotions, it was furnished by the salacious burlesque epilogue spoken by Ismena. She tells the audience:

> Well! Phaedra liv'd as chastly as she cou'd,
> For she was Father Jove's own Flesh and Blood;
> Her aukward Love, indeed, was odly fated,
> She and her Poly were too near related;
> And yet that Scruple had been laid aside,
> If honest Theseus had but fairly dy'd:
> But when he came, what needed he to know,
> But that all Matters stood in Statu quo:
> There was no harm, you see, or grant there were,
> She might want Conduct, but He wanted Care.
> 'Twas in a Husband little less than rude,
> Upon his Wife's Retirement to intrude:
> He shou'd have sent a Night or two before,
> That he wou'd come exact at such an Hour;
> Then he had turn'd all Tragedy to Jest,
> Found ev'ry thing contribute to his Rest;
> The Picquet Friend dismiss'd, the Coast all clear,
> And Spouse alone, impatient for her Dear.[30]

[30] Dr. Johnson thinks Prior "happily facetious" in this epilogue. (*Op. cit.*, II, p. 204.)

EDMUND SMITH AND RACINE

In addition to these changes in the fable, Smith has made excisions and interpolations in material taken from Racine which reveal tastes and a concept of tragedy quite different from Racine's. There is a loss of dramatic intensity as a result of displacement of scenes and the interpolation of lyric interludes. For instance, Phèdre discovers Hippolyte's love for Aricie only after Thésée has exiled Hippolyte. She has come to plead for Hippolyte. She learns from Thésée of Hippolyte's love for Aricie. The shock is so great that Phèdre, completely possessed by her mad jealousy, does not speak for Hippolyte and he goes to his death. Smith places Phaedra's discovery of Hippolitus' love for Ismena much earlier in the play, before Theseus's return. The discovery is followed by the tirade of jealousy echoing Phèdre's, as shown above. But here Phaedra's jealousy serves no dramatic purpose. The tirade becomes static poetry.

By displacing Phèdre's discovery that she has a rival, Smith has destroyed the whole structure of Racine's tragedy. The discovery in *Phèdre* is the fourth act climax characteristic of Racine. It is here that the action veers definitely towards catastrophe and the dénouement begins. Racine has built up the shock of this discovery. His Hippolyte has the reputation of hating all women. Phèdre finds her only consolation in the thought that she will never have a rival. The audience is prepared for the discovery. We have known from the beginning that Hippolyte loves Aricie. This knowledge on the part of the spectator gives dramatic irony to Phèdre's prayer to Venus and to her refusal to heed Oenone's warning that Hippolyte will scorn her as he scorns all women. The discovery brings about an ironic reversal of Phèdre's magnanimous intention. She has come to Thésée in order to save Hippolyte by confessing her guilt. The discovery that Hippolyte loves Aricie leaves her with the desire to destroy both Hippolyte and Aricie. This mad impulse is followed by a scene of spiritual realization: Phèdre's recognition of the evil in herself. She sees that the magnanimity that should be her heritage has for a moment been obliterated by a savage instinct. In that moment, in her own eyes, she has forfeited the right to live. By displacing the discovery, Smith has rejected Racine's tragic plot.

In declaring his love to Aricie, Hippolyte says (vss. 547-52):

> Moi-même, pour tout fruit de mes soins superflus,
> Maintenant je me cherche et ne me trouve plus,

> Mon arc, mes javelots, mon char, tout m'importune;
> Je ne me souviens plus des leçons de Neptune;
> Mes seuls gémissements font retentir les bois,
> Et mes coursiers oisifs ont oublié ma voix.

Smith expands these lines into a lyric piece which Hippolitus speaks at the end of Act II, after Ismena has consented to elope with him (pp. 23-24):

> Come let's away, and like another Jason
> I'll bear my beauteous Conquest thro' the Seas:
> A greater Treasure and a nobler Prize
> Than he from Colchos bore. Sleep, sleep in Peace
> Ye Monsters of the Woods, on Ida's top
> Securely roam; no more my early Horn
> Shall wake the lazy Day. Transporting Love
> Reigns in my Heart, and makes me all its own:
> So when bright Venus yielded up her Charms,
> The blest Adonis languisht in her Arms;
> His idle Horn on fragrant Mirtles hung,
> His Arrows scatter'd, and his Bow unstrung:
> Obscure in Coverts lye his dreaming Hounds,
> And bay the fancy'd Boar with feeble Sounds.
> For nobler Sports he quits the Savage Fields,
> And all the Heroe to the Lover yields.[81]

Excisions in scenes from Racine paraphrased or translated by Smith show Smith to be recalcitrant to the psychological realism which is the distinguishing characteristic of French classical literature. For instance, Smith imitates very closely Phèdre's description of her meeting with Hippolyte and how thoughts of him obsessed her. But for Phèdre's lines (vss. 289-90):

> Je l'évitois partour. O comble de misère!
> Mes yeux le retrouvoient dans les traits de son père[82]

---

[81] In all likelihood Racine and his contemporaries would have condemned such static poetry as "languissant."

[82] These lines may have suggested a later speech of Phaedra's. In Act IV of Smith's play, when after Theseus's return, Lycon urges Phaedra to forget Hippolitus and "wooe him [Theseus] with your Eyes," Phaedra replies (p. 35):

> Impossible! What wooe him with these Eyes
> Still wet with Tears that flow'd?—But not for Theseus?
> . . . .
> Touch, Love, Caress him! while my wand'ring Fancy

Smith substitutes (p. 9):

> I sent him, drove him from my longing sight:
> In vain I drove him, for his Tyrant Form
> Reign'd in my Heart, and dwelt before my Eyes.

Persuaded by Oenone that she must placate Hippolyte and ask his protection for her son, Phèdre sends word to Hippolyte that she wishes to speak to him. On seeing Hippolyte, she says (vss. 581–82):

> Le voici. Vers mon cœur tout mon sang se retire.
> J'oublie, en le voyant, ce que je viens lui dire.

Smith prefers (p. 12):

> But see he comes, the lovely Tyrant comes,
> He rushes on me like a Blaze of Light,
> I cannot bear the Transport of his Presence,
> But sink oppress'd with Woe.

After learning of Hippolyte's love for Aricie, Phèdre says (vss. 1236–40):

> Hélas! ils se voyoient avec pleine licence.
> Le ciel de leurs soupirs approuvoit l'innocence;
> Ils suivoient sans remords leur penchant amoureux;
> Tous les jours se levoient clairs et sereins pour eux.

Smith translates (p. 26):

> Alas! they hid it not, the well pleas'd Sun
> With all his Beams survey'd their guiltless Flame;
> Glad Zephyrs wafted their untainted Sighs,
> And Ida eccho'd their endearing Accents.

The emphasis is shifted from Phèdre's agony. The nostalgia for innocence is gone. Instead we have the conceit of nature's approval of the innocent.

Phèdre misinterprets the expression in Hippolyte's eyes when he appears with Thésée (vss. 909–10):

> Ah! je vois Hippolyte;
> Dans ses yeux insolents je vois ma perte écrite.

> On other Objects strays? a lewd Adultress
> In the chast Bed? and in the Father's Arms.
> (Oh horrid Thought! oh execrable Incest!)
> Ev'n in the Father's Arms embrace the Son?

This misinterpretation precipitates a panic fear which causes Phèdre to yield to Oenone's suggestion that she be allowed to accuse Hippolyte. Smith omits this line from his adaptation of this scene. Instead of fear it is anger and desire for vengeance incited by Lycon that drive his Phaedra to accept Lycon's offer to accuse Hippolitus.

Smith eliminates the self-deception of passion as a tragic force. Racine's Phèdre, before the scene of the declaration, persuades herself that her motive in seeking an interview with Hippolyte is to ask his protection for her son. Smith, while imitating Racine rather closely in this scene, omits all self-delusion. His Phaedra prays to Venus for success in winning Hippolitus. In the scene of the declaration, he omits Phèdre's speech (vss. 693-97):

> Que dis-je? Cet aveu que je te viens de faire,
> Cet aveu si honteux, le crois-tu volontaire?
> Tremblante pour un fils que je n'osois trahir,
> Je te venois prier de ne le point haïr.
> Foibles projets d'un coeur trop plein de ce qu'il aime!

Smith's Phaedra justifies herself by protesting that she has shunned the marriage bed of Theseus. The scene following the declaration, in which Oenone tries to persuade Phèdre to abandon hope and in which Phèdre continues to delude herself—this time with the idea that Hippolyte is ambitious and can be tempted by the throne—Smith omits altogether. Since it is to Lycon's interest and is part of his plot to encourage Phaedra's pursuit of Hippolitus, Smith could not use this scene. Throughout Smith's play Phèdre's self-deception as a tragic force is replaced by the machinations of the villain, Lycon.

Sometimes it is difficult to say whether Smith's changes are due to an incomprehension of psychological realism or a distaste for simplicity of style. In his efforts to inflate and embellish the style of his play Smith sacrifices psychological precision, as shown in passages quoted above. Smith has a pronounced taste for visual imagery, though his metaphors and similes are so banal or so forced that they give the impression of a deliberate *procédé* laboriously followed rather than that of a mind accustomed to think in images. Sometimes there is an elaboration of the metaphor in one word of Racine and usually in the direction of a visual image. For instance, Racine has (vss. 214-16):

> Réparez promptement votre force abattue,

EDMUND SMITH AND RACINE

> Tandis que de vos jours, prêts à se consumer
> Le flambeau dure encore et peut se rallumer.

Smith translates (p. 15):

> Feed with new Oil the wasting Lamp of Life,
> That winks and trembles, now, just now expiring.

Smith's style is embellished with many Homeric similes which recall Seneca, such as (p. 15):

> Shame, Rage, Confusion tear
> And drive me on to act unheard-of Crimes,
> To murther thee, my self, and all that know it.
> As when Convulsions cleave the lab'ring Earth,
> Before the dismal Yawn appears, the Ground
> Trembles and heaves, the nodding Houses crash.

Smith's changes in material taken from Racine show a trend away from the tragic towards the melodramatic and away from the dramatic towards the lyric and the static. His excisions show him to be unimpressed by Racine's psychological realism. His interpolation of metaphors and Homeric similes suggests that he did not find the simplicity of Racine's style to his taste. His play, to use Faguet's term, is a *mélodrame-opéra*. It is patchwork of borrowings from Racine's *Phèdre* and *Bajazet* robbed of all that is essentially Racinian.

« « CHAPTER VI » »

ANDROMAQUE AS THE "DISTREST MOTHER"

FIVE YEARS after the first presentation of *Phaedra and Hippolitus*, English classicists offered their patronage to Ambrose Philips's *The Distrest Mother*,[1] perhaps the most successful adaptation of a French tragedy ever produced on the English stage.[2] In later years these two adaptations of Racine were referred to as timeless examples of "classical purity,"[3] but the plays contrast sharply in the authors' approach to their Racinian models. Smith's play is a debased and romanticized version of Racine's *Phèdre* with extensive interpolations from *Bajazet*. The style is turgid and bombastic. The many liberties which Smith took with his originals have made his play a lurid melodrama. Neither Smith nor his admirers admitted any debt to Racine. His panegyrists go so far as to assert the superiority of his play to Euripides' *Hippolytus* and Seneca's *Phaedra*. Racine is beneath their notice. Philips, on the other hand, announces that he has taken Racine as his model and pays the French poet a handsome compliment. He says: "I have had the Advantage to Copy after a very great Master, whose Writings are deservedly admired in all Parts of *Europe*, and whose Excellencies are too well known to the Men of Letters in this Nation, to stand in need of any farther Discovery of them here."[4]

He had no pretensions to originality and makes no claims to superiority. His attitude is reverent and humble.

---

[1] First presented in March, 1711/12.

[2] This is the opinion of Dorothea Canfield (*Corneille and Racine in England* [New York, Columbia University Press, 1904], p. 140). Allardyce Nicoll's list of productions of *The Distrest Mother* supports this opinion. See *History of Early Eighteenth Century Drama* (Cambridge, 1929), p. 348.

[3] *The Tryal of Hercules, An Ode on Glory, Virtue, and Pleasure* (London, 1752), p. 3.

[4] Preface to *The Distrest Mother* (London, 1712).

ANDROMAQUE AS THE "DISTREST MOTHER"

The great success of Philips's play and the author's attitude toward his model suggest that there existed an ardent cult of Racine in England at the time of the first production of this play. It is important, then, to establish the exact relationship of *The Distrest Mother* to *Andromaque* in order to determine how close an admiring and humble English adapter has been able to come to the spirit of Racine and in order to evaluate eighteenth-century criticism of the play as an index of the English attitude towards Racine. Both Dorothea Canfield and F. Y. Eccles have noted certain changes which Philips makes and commented briefly on them.[5] But a more detailed comparison is necessary to bring out the significance of the adaptation and the criticism of it with respect to Racine's reputation in England.

Philips's preface shows that he looked upon Racine as an exemplar of simplicity of style and his own play as an experiment in the language of tragedy:

In all the Works of Genius and Invention, whether in Verse or Prose, there are in general but two Manners of Style; the one simple, natural, and easie; the other swelling, forced, and unnatural. An injudicious Affectation of Sublimity is what has betrayed a great many Authors into the latter; not considering that real Greatness in Writing, as well as in Manners, consists in an unaffected Simplicity. The true Sublime does not lie in strained Metaphors and the Pomp of Words; but rises out of noble Sentiments and strong Images of Nature; which will always appear the more conspicuous, when the Language does not swell to hide and overshadow them.... These are the Considerations, that have induced me to write this Tragedy in a Style

---

[5] Miss Canfield notes with approval that Philips has shortened "long declamatory" speeches. This she considers the most serious change introduced by Philips. She notes also the change in the ending, the reappearance of Andromache at the end, her grief for the death of Pyrrhus, which Canfield considers "inconsistent but spectacular," and the moralizing sextet with which the play ends. (*Op. cit.*, pp. 162-63.)
Eccles says: "In general I would say that Philips follows his author scene by scene, and most often speech by speech, is commendably anxious to let nothing drop, and sometimes shows himself skilfully concise; but that his whole tendency is to be explicit where Racine was reserved and that this result is obtained chiefly by a deplorable prodigality of epithet, but also by the systematic addition of moralizing tirades at the end of every act." He does not discuss these tirades further. He notes that Philips dared to deprive his audience of a bloody scene and abstained from scenic effects until near the end. He notes that Philips prolongs the delirium of Orestes and that Andromache is brought back on the stage at the end. (*Racine in England* [Oxford, The Clarendon Press, 1922], pp. 12-13.)

very different from what has been usually practised amongst us in Poems of this Nature.[6]

A second aim which Philips has in mind but does not state is revealed in certain significant interpolations which he introduces into his paraphrase of Racine's second preface:

> In order to bring about this beautiful Incident [Andromache's distress for her son by Hector], so necessary to *heighten in Andromache the Character of a tender Mother, an affectionate Wife, and a Widow full of Veneration for the Memory of her deceased Husband*; the Life of Astyanax is indeed prolonged beyond the Term fixed to it by the general Consent of the Ancient Authors. [Italics mine.]

As Faguet has pointed out, Racine's *Andromaque* is "une tragédie qui contient un mélodrame."[7] Philips doubtless saw the play as a drama of innocence persecuted and bourgeois virtue glorified. Hence his choice of this particular tragedy as his model. And he was not content with the germ of melodrama which he found in Racine's tragedy. He felt impelled to heighten the melodrama. Rather apologetically he admits having made some changes:

> If I have been able to keep up to the Beauties of Monsieur *de Racine* in my Attempt, and to do him no Prejudice in the Liberties I have taken frequently to vary from so great a Poet, I shall have no reason to be dissatisfied with the Labour it has cost me to bring the compleatest of his Works upon the English Stage.

Since Philips indicates that he regarded his tragedy chiefly as an essay in simplicity of style with Racine as guide, a careful analysis of the style of *The Distrest Mother* as compared with that of *Andromaque* should be our first consideration. Philips's remarks on simplicity of

---

[6] In this passage Philips is echoing, indeed almost quoting, Addison. In the *Spectator*, No. 39 (April 14, 1711), Addison remarks that in English tragedy the thoughts are often obscured by the "sounding phrases, hard metaphors, and forced expressions in which they are clothed." He considers Shakespeare often "very faulty in this particular." "For my own part," says he, "I prefer a noble sentiment that is depressed with homely language, infinitely before a vulgar one that is blown up with all the sound and energy of expression." An anonymous pamphlet attacking *The Distrest Mother* points out the inconsistency of the neoclassicists who praised Smith's *Phaedra and Hippolitus* for sublimity of style and are now praising Philips's play for "humility of language." (*A Modest Survey of that Celebrated Tragedy, "The Distrest Mother"* [London, 1712], p. 5.)

[7] *Propos de théâtre*, 2d Series, p. 73.

language in his preface do not augur success. They indicate that he had noticed the absence of simile and elaborate metaphor in Racine. But an imitator could hardly capture the peculiar quality of his style merely by abstaining from the use of metaphor and simile. On the positive side, Philips's idea of style forebodes incomprehension of Racine, for no close student of the French poet could think that his style is characterized by "sublimity" rising out of "noble sentiments." And, indeed, an examination of Philips's play shows that everywhere Racine's economy and evocativeness escape his imitator.

Two important characteristics of Philips's style have been noted and commented upon by students of Racine's fortunes in England. Dorothea Canfield approves of the shortening of Racine's long, "declamatory" speeches, which she considers the most serious change introduced by Philips, and F. Y. Eccles notes the "deplorable prodigality of epithet" in Philips's play (see above, note 5). The shortening of long speeches might seem at first glance a commendable process of condensation. But on closer study it is seen to be not at all a pruning of superfluous rhetoric but, rather, indiscriminate excisions. Occasionally some of the essence of Racine is lost. For instance, in the scene between Pyrrhus and Hermione, the latter notices Pyrrhus's abstracted look and says (vss. 1375-79):

>   ... Perfide, je le voi,
> Tu comptes les moments que tu perds avec moi!
> Ton coeur impatient de revoir ta Troyenne,
> Ne souffre qu'à regret qu'un autre t'entretienne.
> Tu lui parles du coeur, tu la cherches des yeux.[8]

These lines Philips omits. This omission is significant when you consider that in Racine's psychological drama, in scenes of great tension, the characters scan each other's faces in their desire to penetrate beyond words to secret thoughts. They interpret or misinterpret a tone of voice, a change of facial expression, a movement of the eyes; and their interpretation of the involuntary gesture often precipitates a critical turn in the action. At the beginning of this scene, Hermione, seeing Pyrrhus approaching, hopes that he may be returning to her and sends to tell Oreste not to attempt to assassinate Pyrrhus until Oreste has talked to her again. At the end of the scene, Pyrrhus's absent look

[8] References are to the Mesnard edition.

redoubles her fury and seals his doom. Philips has omitted something characteristic and essential.

Excision is not the only method which Philips employs to shorten the long speeches. He often cuts a tirade with a short speech from the interlocutor. These interruptions, sometimes inept, usually go unheeded by the person addressed. For instance, Andromaque admonishes Pyrrhus (vss. 297-310):

> Seigneur, que faites-vous, et que dira la Grèce?
> Faut-il qu'un si grand coeur montre tant de foiblesse?
> Voulez-vous qu'un dessein si beau, si généreux
> Passe pour le transport d'un esprit amoureux?
> Captive, toujours triste, importune à moi-même,
> Pouvez-vous souhaiter qu'Andromaque vous aime?
> Quels charmes ont pour vous des yeux infortunés,
> Qu'à des pleurs éternels vous avez condamnés?
> Non, non, d'un ennemi respecter la misère,
> Sauver des malheureux, rendre un fils à sa mère,
> De cent peuples pour lui combattre la rigueur,
> Sans me faire payer son salut de mon coeur,
> Malgré moi, s'il le faut, lui donner un asile:
> Seigneur, voilà des soins dignes du fils d'Achille.

Philips translates (p. 11):

ANDROMACHE: Consider, Sir, how this will sound in Greece!
How can so great a Soul betray such Weakness?
Let not Men say, so generous a Design
Was but the Transport of a Heart in Love.
PYRRHUS: Your Charms will justifie me to the World.
ANDROMACHE: How can Andromache, a Captive Queen,
O'er-whelm'd with Grief, a Burden to her self,
Harbour a Thought of Love? Alas! what Charms
Have these unhappy Eyes, by you condemn'd
To weep for ever?—Talk of it no more.—
To reverence the Misfortunes of a Foe,
To succour the Distrest; to give the Son
To an afflicted Mother; to repel
Confederate Nations, leagued against his Life;
Unbribed by Love, unterrify'd by Threats,
To pity, to protect him: These are Cares,
These are Exploits worthy Achilles' Son[9]

[9] References are to the first edition (London, 1712).

ANDROMAQUE AS THE "DISTREST MOTHER"

Apparently Philips is merely following a mechanical system of preventing any one character from speaking more than twenty-odd lines without interruption. Dilution and diffusion rather than condensation characterize Philips's translation throughout. Prodigality of epithet is only one aspect of this process. Two examples will suffice to show how a lavish use of banal adjectives dilutes Racine's concentrated style (vss. 9–12, pp. 1–2):

> PYLADE: J'en rends grâces au ciel, qui m'arrêtant sans cesse
> Sembloit m'avoir fermé le chemin de la Grèce,
> Depuis le jour fatal que la fureur des eaux
> Presque aux yeux de l'Epire écarta nos vaisseaux.
>
> PYLADES: Blest be the Powers, who barr'd my Way to Greece
> And kept me here! e'er since th' unhappy Day,
> When warring Winds (Epirus in full View)
> Sundered our Barks on the loud, stormy Main.
>
> ORESTE: Enfin, quand Ménélas disposa de sa fille
> En faveur de Pyrrhus, vengeur de sa famille. . . .
>
> ORESTES: And when at last the hoary King, her Father,
> Great Menelaus gave away his Daughter,
> His lovely Daughter, to this happy Pyrrhus. . . .

It is perhaps this predilection for adjectives which prevents Philips from seeing the importance of verbs in the density and swiftness of Racine's style. Oreste's famous lines (vss. 491–92):

> J'ai mendié la mort chez des peuples cruels
> Qui n'apaisoient leurs dieux que du sang des mortels,

become in Philips's translation (p. 17):

> . . . Through stormy Seas,
> And savage Climes, in a whole Year of Absence,
> I courted Dangers, and I long'd for Death.

Racine's metaphor "J'ai mendié la mort" is vivid and highly charged with emotion. "I courted Dangers" is a banal and inappropriate metaphor. "I long'd for Death" is padding. Racine's method is to illumine with a sudden flash the innermost thoughts and feelings of his characters. These revelations are unpremeditated, sometimes even involuntary, and therefore must be expressed in the most concentrated and evocative language. In such passages Philips is likely to use twice as many words and say only half as much as Racine. There is a striking example in the same scene from which Philips has omitted Hermione's characteristic lines (quoted above, beginning "Perfide, je le voi"). Pyrrhus has come to inform Hermione of his approaching marriage to Andromaque. Up to this point he has apparently thought that he could find happiness in a marriage to which Andromaque had consented only because of his threats and bribes. Suddenly he reveals his recognition of his wretched plight (vss. 1295-98):

> Je vous reçus en reine et jusques à ce jour
> J'ai cru que mes serments me tiendroient lieu d'amour.
> Mais cet amour l'emporte, et par un coup funeste
> Andromaque m'arrache un coeur qu'elle déteste.

Philips translates (p. 40):

> I sent Ambassadours to call you hither;
> Receiv'd you as my Queen; and hoped my Oaths,
> So oft renew'd, might ripen into Love.
> The Gods can witness, Madam, how I fought
> Against Andromache's too fatal Charms!
> And still I wish I had the Power to leave
> This Trojan Beauty and be just to you.

Philips's four lines, "The Gods can witness," etc., are in the one word "arrache." Pyrrhus's bewildered agony, expressed in the hemistich "un coeur qu'elle déteste," is entirely lost in Philips's translation.

Philips has little taste for interrogation, perhaps Racine's favorite figure of speech.[10] Interrogation in Racine is often a vehicle for irony. Whether through distaste for interrogation or for irony itself, Philips either eliminates irony from his translation or makes it heavy and awkward. This tendency is strikingly illustrated in Philips's translation of the famous tirade which the French call the "couplet d'ironie." Here, in the original, the irony becomes most biting in the verses (1313-14):

---

[10] "On peut dire de l'interrogation qu'elle est sa figure favorite. Toute interrogation sans doute n'est pas une figure. Mais elle en devient une, ou en prend un faux air quand c'est la passion qui questionne. . . . Dans tous les cas, que l'interrogation soit stratégie . . . ou pure expression de curiosité . . . ou explosion de la fureur, elle est, comme disaient les anciens, *un geste du discours*, dont elle accroît la force; ajoutons qu'elle est le geste le mieux approprié à ce drame de violence et de tragique incertitude." (G. Le Bidois, *De l'Action dans la tragédie de Racine* [Paris, 1900], pp. 317-18.)

ANDROMAQUE AS THE "DISTREST MOTHER"

> Est-il juste, après tout, qu'un conquérant s'abaisse
> Sous la servile loi de garder sa promesse?

Philips paraphrases these lines (p. 41):

> A Hero should be bold; above all Laws:
> Be bravely false; and laugh at solemn Ties.
> To be perfidious shews a daring Mind:
> And you have nobly triumphed o'er a Maid![11]

Philips, unlike Racine, is inordinately fond of exclamation. Exclamations often play variations on a theme in Racine with a loss of psychological precision. For instance, Racine's Hermione, abandoned by Pyrrhus, turns to Oreste. Hoping to win back his love, which she thinks she may have lost, she says:

> Enfin qui vous a dit que, malgré mon devoir,
> Je n'ai pas quelquefois souhaité de vous voir?

The melancholy, paranoid Oreste, for an instant, but for an instant only, is beside himself with joy. But he is immediately skeptical again (vss. 527–32):

> Souhaité de me voir! Ah! divine princesse . . .
> Mais, de grâce, est-ce à moi que ce discours s'adresse?
> Ouvrez vos yeux: songez qu'Oreste est devant vous,
> Oreste, si longtemps l'objet de leur courroux.

Philips translates (p. 18):

> Wished to see Orestes!
> Oh Joy! Oh Extasie! My Soul's entranc'd!
> Oh charming Princess!—Oh transcendent Maid!
> My utmost Wish!—Thus, thus let me express

---

[11] Instances of the elimination of irony, whether expressed in interrogation or not, occur frequently. For instance (vss. 267–68, p. 10; vss. 680–82, p. 22; italics mine):

> ANDROMAQUE: Et quelle est cette peur dont leur coeur est frappé,
> Seigneur? *Quelque Troyen vous est-il échappé?*
> ANDROMACHE: Alas! What Threats? What can alarm the Greeks?
> *There are no Trojans left.*
> PHOENIX: Allez, Seigneur, vous jeter à ses pieds.
> Allez, en lui jurant que votre âme l'adore,
> A de nouveaux mépris l'encourager encore.
> PHOENIX: O, go not, sir!—There's Ruin in her Eyes!
> You do not know your Strength: You'll fall before her,
> Adore her Beauty, and revive her Scorn.

RACINE AND ENGLISH CLASSICISM

> My boundless Thanks!—I never was unhappy.—
> Am I Orestes?

Racine's Oreste cannot forget for long that he is persecuted by an unjust destiny. Much of this is lost in the rant of Philips's translation. For, despite his avowed purpose of imitating Racine's simple and natural style, Philips cannot resist bombast and hyperbole; and apparently he is insensitive to the complex emotions that electrify Racine's simple words. A striking example of the difference in style and the loss of psychological subtlety occurs in the scene between Pylades and Orestes, when Orestes resolves to abduct Hermione (vss. 752-64):

> PYLADE: Au lieu de l'enlever, fuyez-la pour jamais.
> Quoi? Votre amour se veut charger d'une furie
> Qui vous détestera, qui toute votre vie,
> Regrettant un hymen tout prêt à s'achever,
> Voudra . . .
> ORESTE: C'est pour cela que je veux l'enlever.
> Tout lui riroit, Pylade; et moi, pour mon partage,
> Je n'emporterois donc qu'une inutile rage?
> J'irois loin d'elle encor tâcher de l'oublier?
> Non, non, à mes tourments je veux l'associer.
> C'est trop gémir tout seul. Je suis las qu'on me plaigne:
> Je prétends qu'à mon tour l'inhumaine me craigne,
> Et que ses yeux cruels, à pleurer condamnés,
> Me rendent tous les noms que je leur ai donnés.

Philips's translation is (p. 25):

> PYLADES: Think not to force her hence;
> But fly from her destructive Charms.
> Her Soul is linked to Pyrrhus: Were she yours,
> She would reproach you still, and still regret
> Her disappointed Nuptials.—
> ORESTES: Talk no more!
> I cannot hear the Thought! She must be mine!
> Did Pyrrhus carry Thunder in his Hand,
> I'd stand the Bolt, and challenge all his Fury,
> Ere I resigned Hermione.—By Force
> I'll snatch her hence, and bear her to my Ships!
> Have we forgot her Mother Helen's Rape?[12]

[12] From this scene Philips omits altogether Oreste's characteristic lines (vss. 772-78):

> Mon innocence enfin commence à me peser.

ANDROMAQUE AS THE "DISTREST MOTHER"

Orestes' rôle is one epileptic outburst after another and there is little left of Racine's "homme fatal." But the bombast is not due to Philips's different conception of this character. Instances of gratuitous inflation occur in other rôles.[18]

In the scenes mentioned above and in others where Racine is followed most closely, Philips's method is first to simplify the emotion of Racine's character, to reduce it to the elemental, then to inflate the language in which the now elemental emotion is expressed. Although the adaptation is close enough to Racine to preserve some of the drama of the original, there is a tendency to transform what Lanson calls "des vibrations dramatiques" into "des effusions lyriques." In the scenes which Philips adds, there is a complete reversion to traditional English style; and all the added scenes are apparently intended to perform one function in the structure of the play: they make Andromache much more the central figure of the play than she had been in Racine's tragedy.

Philips's most radical changes occur at the end of each act. In the first three acts he merely adds a moralizing tirade. To Acts IV and V he adds fairly long scenes with the spotlight on Andromache. In Racine's tragedy Andromaque speaks the final lines of one act only. In Philips's play she has the curtain speech of all except one act. These curtain speeches give Philips a chance to indulge his taste for static poetry and to introduce simile, from which he had the fortitude to

---

> Je ne sais de tout temps quelle injuste puissance
> Laisse le crime en paix et poursuit l'innocence.
> De quelque part sur moi que je tourne les yeux,
> Je ne vois que malheurs qui condamnent les Dieux.
> Méritons leurs courroux, justifions leur haine,
> Et que le fruit du crime en précède la peine.

[18] Compare the following originals and their translations (vss. 343-44, p. 12; vs. 1021, p. 33; vs. 1374, p. 42):

Pyrrhus:	Et le puis-je, Madame? Ah! que vous me gênez! Comment lui rendre un coeur que vous me retenez?
Pyrrhus:	Why do you mock me thus? You know I cannot. You know my Heart is yours; My Soul hangs on you: You take up every Wish: My waking Thoughts, And nightly Dreams are all employ'd on you.
Andromaque:	Chère épouse, dit-il en essuyant mes larmes.
Andromache:	My Wife, my dear Andromache, said he, (Heaving with stifled Sighs to see me weep).
Hermione:	Vous ne répondez point?
Hermione:	See, if the barbarous Prince vouchsafes an Answer.

abstain in the scenes where he followed Racine. But, what is most significant, these added scenes betray an insensitiveness to Racine's dramatic effects and an incomprehension of his psychological action. For instance, at the end of Act II, Pyrrhus, incensed at Andromache's indifference to him, has resolved to give Astyanax up to the Greeks and to marry Hermione. Scene 5, in Racine and in Philips, is a conversation between Pyrrhus and Phoenix in which the former boasts of his triumph over himself and unconsciously reveals that he is still obsessed with the thought of Andromache. Phoenix knows how unstable his decision is likely to be and urges him to act at once, to give up Astyanax and to see Hermione. In Racine, Pyrrhus realizes that Phoenix is right and that he must act quickly before he weakens. He interrupts Phoenix to say: "Faisons tout ce que j'ai promis." (vs. 708)

This is the end of the act. Philips follows Racine up to this point. But his Pyrrhus remains on the stage to describe his emancipation as though it were indeed an emancipation (p. 23):

> 'Tis with a secret Pleasure I look back
> And see the many Dangers I have pass'd.
> The Merchant thus, in dreadful Tempests tost,
> Thrown by the Waves on some unlook'd for Coast,
> Oft turns, and sees, with a delighted Eye,
> 'Midst Rocks and Shelves the broken Billows fly!
> And while the outrageous Winds the Deep deform,
> Smiles on the Tumult and enjoys the Storm.[14]

Racine ends his acts with short, sharp, portentous speeches. In Philips's play foreshadowing and suspense are gone; Racine's psychological drama remains just beyond his imitator's comprehension and Racine's lesson in simplicity of style cannot banish altogether from an English play descriptive passages in figurative style.

In Act IV Philips makes more extensive changes and additions. Pyrrhus has told Hermione of his plan to marry Andromaque. Hermione exits with the threatening words (vss. 1385–86):

---

[14] Despite his condemnation of traditional English style in tragedy, Addison seems to have approved of ending an act with such a lyric piece. Speaking of the use of rhyme, he says: "I would not, however, debar the poet from concluding his tragedy, or, if he pleases, every act of it, with two or three couplets, which may have the same effect as an air in the Italian opera after a long recitativo, and give the actor a graceful exit." (*Spectator*, No. 39.)

ANDROMAQUE AS THE "DISTREST MOTHER"

> Porte aux pieds des autels ce coeur qui m'abandonne;
> Va, cours. Mais crains encore d'y trouver Hermione.

Phoenix, alarmed, warns Pyrrhus of his danger. But Pyrrhus will not listen: "Andromaque m'attend. Phoenix, garde son fils." (vs. 1392)

Here Act IV of Racine's play ends. Philips adds a scene between Andromache and Cephisa. Some of this scene is taken from Act IV, Scene 1 of *Andromaque*,[15] but much is Philips's own. Andromache appears in her royal bridal robes and blazing with jewels. She reveals to Cephisa her plan to kill herself after the ceremony. A certain nostalgia for ghosts and the macabre is evident in her lines (pp. 44-45):

> Thou mays't remember, for thou oft hast heard me
> Relate the dreadful Vision, which I saw
> When first I landed Captive in Epirus.
> That very Night, as in a Dream I lay,
> A ghastly Figure, full of gaping Wounds,
> His Eyes a-glare, his Hair all stiff with Blood,
> Full in my Sight thrice shook his Head and groaned.
> I soon discern'd my slaughter'd Hector's Shade;
> But, oh, how chang'd! Ye Gods, how much unlike
> The living Hector!—Loud he bid me fly!
> Fly from Achilles' Son! Then sternly frowned
> And disappeared.[16]

The final tirade of this act brings in the characteristic simile (p. 47):

ANDROMACHE: No more! Thy Tears, Cephisa, will betray me.
            Assume a cheerful Look: But still remember—
            (Flourish within).
            Hark, how the Trumpet, with its sprightly Notes,
            Proclaims the appointed Hour and calls us hence!
            Hector, I come, once more a Queen, to join thee!
            Thus the gay Victim, with fresh Garlands crown'd,
            Pleased with the sacred Fife's enlivening Sound,
            Through gazing Crowds, in solemn State proceeds
            And drest in fatal Pomp, magnificently bleeds.

---

[15] This is the last scene in which Andromaque appears in all the editions of Racine's tragedy except those of 1668 and 1673.

[16] Senecan influence probably accounts for these lines. In the *Troades* Andromache has a vision of Hector who appears to her in her sleep to bid her hide Astyanax when the Greeks are plotting to kill him. Seneca's apparition also is unlike the living Hector. His hair is matted (but not stiff with blood). He shakes his head (but not three times). (Loeb ed., I, 161.)

In Act V Philips brings Andromache back for the final curtain. She appears after the delirium of Orestes and after the Greeks have fled. She hurls imprecations at the departed Greeks. Then, when the corpse of Pyrrhus is borne along by his soldiers, off stage presumably, she says:

> Ill fated Prince! Too negligent of Life!
> And too unwary of the faithless Greeks!
> Cut off in the fresh ripening Prime of Manhood,
> Even in the Pride of Life; thy Triumphs new
> And all thy Glories in full Blossom round thee!
> The very Trojans would bewail thy Fate.

Cephisa says:

> Alas! then will your Sorrows never end!

Andromache answers (p. 56):

> Oh! never—While I live, my Tears
> Will never cease; for I was born to grieve.

Although the words are not the same, it is difficult to believe that Andromache's grief for Pyrrhus was not suggested by a scene in the 1668 and 1673 texts of *Andromaque*, a scene which was suppressed in later editions.[17] Racine's Andromaque is brought in as Oreste's captive. She expresses her grief for Pyrrhus thus:

> Je ne m'attendois pas que le ciel en colère
> Pût, sans perdre mon fils, accroître ma misère,
> Et gardât à mes yeux quelque spectacle encor
> Qui fît couler mes pleurs pour un autre qu'Hector.

The first two speeches of Philips's heroine are apparently suggested by this scene in the early version of Racine's tragedy. The third speech of Andromache is suggested by a *récit* which occurs in Racine's play after Hermione has berated Oreste for Pyrrhus's death and has left the stage (together with Andromaque in the earlier version). Pylade reports (vss. 1589-90):

> Andromaque elle-même, à Pyrrhus si rebelle,
> Lui rend tous les devoirs d'une veuve fidèle . . .

Philips indulges his taste for descriptive poetry in the following lines which Andromache herself speaks (p. 56):

[17] See Mesnard edition of Racine, II, 119, notes 1, 2.

ANDROMAQUE AS THE "DISTREST MOTHER"

> Give present Orders for the Funeral Pomps:
> Let him be robed in all his Regal State;
> Place round him every shining mark of Honour;
> And let the Pile, that Consecrates his Ashes,
> Rise like his Fame, and blaze above the Clouds.

At this point Philips faces the problem of finding a happy ending if he can. A trumpet sounds off stage. Cephisa says (p. 57):

> That Sound proclaims the Arrival of the Prince:
> The Guards conduct him from the Citadel.

Andromache forgets all about Pyrrhus and indulges in an effusion of mother love and optimistic moralizing (p. 57):

> With open Arms I'll meet him!—Oh, Cephisa!
> A springing Joy, mixt with a soft concern,
> A Pleasure, which no Language can Express,
> An Extasie, that Mothers only feel,
> Plays round my Heart, and brightens up my Sorrow,
> Like Gleams of Sun-shine in a louring Skie.
> Though plunged in Ills, and exercised in Care,
> Yet never let the noble Mind despair.
> When prest by Dangers, and beset with Foes,
> The Gods their timely Succour interpose;
> And when our Vertue sinks, o'erwhelmed with Grief,
> By unforeseen Expedients bring Releif.[18]

If Racine was as well known and as much admired among British men of letters as Philips affirms that he was (see Preface quoted above), it might be expected that at least one voice would be raised in protest against the bad taste of Philips's emendations; or, failing that, at least a critique noting the differences. There was one violent attack against the play but the anonymous author was far from being a champion

[18] Having seen a performance of *Andromaque* designed to have a popular appeal, Emile Faguet pointed out that *mise en scène* and orchestral flourishes had pushed Racine's tragedy in the direction of melodrama. Then he facetiously suggested "une indiscrétion de plus": "D'autant que le trône est resté au fond de la scène, faites, après les 'fureurs d'Oreste,' reparaître Andromaque, venant du fond par la gauche, la couronne en tête, accompagnée d'un peuple sympathique. Et qu'elle monte sur le trône et que Céphise par la droite lui apporte son enfant et qu'Andromaque le prenne sur ses genoux et l'embrasse, avec sensibilité. La toile tombe. A vous, Diderot! Je suis sûr que vous auriez approuvé ce petit supplément au dénouement." Philips had anticipated Faguet by nearly two hundred years. (*Propos de théâtre*, 2d Series, p. 73.)

of Racine. He explains his motives thus: "Neither Pique nor Malice drew my Pen on this Subject; but an honest and hearty Warmth for the Honour of our British Poetry in Discouragement of all French Importations of this kind, unless better refined and cleared from their original Dross and Rubbish."[19]

In his prologue to Philips's play, Richard Steele, without mentioning Racine's name, indicates that the play is an imitation of a very successful French tragedy and that Philips has been concerned chiefly with writing a "regular" tragedy, because he recognizes his own "feeble force":

> Our Author does his feeble Force confess,
> . . . .
> Your Treat with study'd Decency he serves:
> Not only Rules of Time and Place preserves,
> But strives to keep his Characters intire,
> With French Correctness and with British Fire.

In his very enthusiastic review of the play, which he had heard read before the stage performance, Steele reveals the fact that the tragedy appealed to him chiefly as a drama of sensibility:

We have seldom had any female distress on the stage which did not, upon cool imagination, appear to flow from the weakness rather than the misfortune of the person represented; . . . the character which gives name to the play, is one who has behaved herself with heroic virtue in the most important circumstances of a female life, those of a wife, a widow, and a mother. . . . Domestic virtues concern all the world, and there is no one who is not interested that Andromache should be an imitable character.[20]

Although one is hardly justified in taking Sir Roger de Coverley's comments as serious dramatic criticism, it is apparent that Addison was interested in Philips's play as illustrating two features of classicism that preoccupied him at the moment, simplicity of style and the banishment of scenes of bloodshed from the stage. There is no evidence of any interest in Racine.[21]

In *St. James's Journal* (April 20, 1723) a critic who signs himself "Dorimant" gives us the reasons why English tragedy is superior to foreign tragedy, especially the French:

---

[19] *A Modest Survey of that Celebrated Tragedy, "The Distrest Mother"* (London, 1712 [anonymous]), Postscript.
[20] *Spectator*, No. 290.
[21] See Canfield, *op. cit.*, pp. 152–54, and below, Chap. XII.

ANDROMAQUE AS THE "DISTREST MOTHER"

The English, in this Species of Writing, undoubtedly excel all their Neighbors; they have a Force of Thought, as well as of Style and Expression, which is no more to be described, than imitated: The latter indeed is in a good measure owing to the Strength and Manliness of our Language, but the Former is born with us; the true Poetick Spirit, that noble Enthusiasm, which distinguishes the Works of our Countrymen from the jejune and insipid, tho' possibly more correct Compositions of Foreigners. And therefore there are few Translations of ours, from the French especially, which do not exceed the originals: We give them Life and Spirit; the want of which makes them languish and tasteless in the Reading, in spite of all the Care and Correctness in their Composition. I shall produce only two instances: The first is the *Distres'd Mother* of *Mr. Philips*, and the other the new Tragedy, called the *Fatal Legacy*. . . .[22]

By far the most detailed and in a sense the most judicious criticism of *The Distrest Mother* comes from the pen of the novelist, Samuel Richardson. It occurs in the second part of *Pamela*. Richardson's heroine, now in her exalted condition as the wife of her would-be seducer, writes from London to give her sister-in-law her impressions of London entertainment. As an example of the kind of tragedy which Londoners enjoy, she chooses *The Distrest Mother*.[23]

English classicists such as Addison and Philips himself may be said to have approved of Racine without appreciating him. Richardson, on the other hand, appreciated Racine without approving of him. He does not profess to be familiar with the original of *The Distrest Mother* and he supposes that the play is a faithful translation from the French. Pamela says:

> The play I first saw was the tragedy of *The Distressed Mother* and a great many beautiful things I think there are in it: But half of it is a tempestuous, cruel, ungoverned rant of passion, and ends in cruelty, bloodshed, and desolation, which the truth of the story not warranting, as Mr. B—— tells me, makes it the more pity that the original author (for it is a French play translated, you know, madam) had not conducted it, since it was in his choice, with less terror, and greater propriety to the passions intended to be raised, and actually raised in many places.

All Richardson's criticism, then, is directed at Racine. While Addison and Steele had chosen for favorable comment certain features of Philips's tragedy that were not characteristically Racinian, a great deal

---

[22] A translation of Racine's *La Thébaïde*.
[23] *Pamela*, Vol. IV, Letter LIII. I quote from the 1902 edition (London, William Heinemann) of Richardson's novels.

of Richardson's criticism bears on tragic love as Racine portrayed it. He objects to all the characters because they are not exemplary (except, of course, Andromache). He disapproves of tragic love in general. Pamela says:

> But give me leave to say, that I think there is hardly one play I have seen or read hitherto, but has too much of love in it, as that passion is generally treated. How unnatural in some, how inflaming in others, are the descriptions of it!—In most rather rant and fury, like the loves of the fiercer brute animals, as Virgil, translated by Dryden, describes them, than the soft, sighing, fearfully hopeful murmurs, that swell the bosoms of our gentler sex; and the respectful, timorous, submissive complainings of the other, when the truth of the passion humanises, as one may say, their more rugged hearts.

In particular, he condemns, from a moral point of view, the characters of Pyrrhus and Hermione:

> Then, madam, the love of Hermione for Pyrrhus is not, I think, of that delicate sort which ought to be set before our sex for an example.—'Tis rage, not love. . . . In short, madam, I think none of the love in this piece is such love, however suited to Hermione's character and circumstances, as is fit to be recommended to our example: 'Tis a love that shocks one, and is rather rage and tumult than love, and succeeds accordingly. So that of Pyrrhus is ungoverned, wild, unjust, ungenerous caprice. Hermione's is founded in confessed ingratitude to Orestes, and she perseveres in it to Pyrrhus, when the indignities put upon her should have made her sooner wish for death than for so perjured a man. . . .

After making it plain that he disapproves of the kind of love portrayed, Richardson proceeds to commend the portrayal for naturalness. He chooses as illustrations of admirable psychological realism scenes which are characteristic of Racine and which Philips has not tampered with. Pamela continues:

> The storms, and doubts, and uncertainty of wild ungoverned love are very naturally, I humbly think, painted in several scenes of this play, in the characters of Hermione and Pyrrhus; and nowhere more affectingly than in the upbraidings of Hermione to Orestes, after she had found her bloody purpose too well complied with. . . . The staggering doubts and distress of Hermione, after she had engaged Orestes in the murder of Pyrrhus, between her love and her resentment; her questions to her woman, whether, as he approached the temple to marry her rival, in breach of his vows of betrothment to her, his countenance showed not some tokens of remorse; are very natural to one in her amorous circumstances, I fancy:

ANDROMAQUE AS THE "DISTREST MOTHER"

>"But, say, Cleone, didst thou mark him well?
>Was his brow smooth? Say, did there not appear
>Some shade of grief? Some little cloud of sorrow?
>Did he not stop? Did he not once look back?
>Didst thou approach him? Was he not confounded?
>Did he not—Oh! be quick and tell me all."

This, madam, I think is charmingly natural. And, on Cleone's answer that he went to the temple all joy and transport, unguarded, and all his cares employed to gratify Andromache in her son's safety, it is the less to be wondered at that she should be quite exasperated, and forgetting all her love for the ungrateful prince, should say:

>"Enough! He dies!—the traitor!—Where's Orestes?"

The character of Andromache has Richardson's approval with somewhat less, I suspect, of his admiration, that is, his esthetic admiration. He singles out for comment, not Philips's touches to "heighten the distress," but scenes in which he has followed Racine.[24]

Richardson's most severe criticism of an esthetic order, though apparently aimed at Racine, falls upon Philips. He is shocked at the incongruity of the superadded moralizing ending. Pamela quotes the rhyming sextet that closes Philips's play (quoted above, beginning "With open Arms I'll meet him!") and continues:

>Now, madam, good as this moral is, I should rather, in generosity, have had it recommended from any mouth than that of Andromache: For what is the consolation she receives? What are the expedients she so much rejoices in? Why, in the first place, the murder of a prince who loved her more than his own glory, and to whom she had just given her faith, as a second husband, though forced to it from a laudable motive; and next the self-murder of Hermione, the distraction of Orestes, and the prospect of succeeding with her son to the throne of the murdered prince....

Richardson criticizes severely the account of Hermione's death in *The Distrest Mother*. His criticism is of course directed at Racine but strikes only Philips. Pamela says:

>There are several circumstances of horror in this play, that made me shudder; but I think none like the description the poet puts into the mouth of Pylades, the inseparable friend of Orestes, who far from avoiding to shock the soul of his friend, by gently insinuating the fate of that Hermione, on whom he had fixed his happiness, thus terribly, with all the aggravations

---

[24] Andromache's pleas to Hermione for her son and her instructions to Cephisa for the rearing of her son after her death, and her description of her parting with Hector.

that could attend such a tragedy, points out the horrid action; taking care even to make her as impious in her reproaches of the Deity for her own rashness, as she was in the violence by which she dies; and so leaving a dreadful example (which I presume was not needful to be left) of final impenitence, especially in a suffering character, that had not merited the evils she met with.

Thus it is described; and I am affected with the transcription of a passage which the poet has laboured more than he ought, I think, to show the force of his descriptive vein:

> "Full of disorder, wildness in her looks,
> With hands expanded, and dishevelled hair,
> Breathless and pale, with shrieks, she sought the temple.
> In the midway, she met the corpse of Pyrrhus:
> She started at the sight! then, stiff with horror,
> Gazed frightful! Wakened from the dire amaze,
> She raised her eyes to heaven with such a look
> As spoke her sorrows, and reproached the gods!
> Then plunged a poniard deep within her breast,
> And fell on Pyrrhus, grasping him in death!"

The blasphemy and the gratuitous rhetoric are Philips's, not Racine's.[25]

After Richardson the only criticism of *The Distrest Mother*, in addition to that found in histories of the English stage and cited by Dorothea Canfield,[26] is to be found in various editions of Philips's plays and poetry. All this criticism falls into the English clichés of criticism of French classical tragedy. The burden of it is that, since Philips had the bad taste to imitate Racine, his play has the defects of its model; it is cold, declamatory, rhetorical. Two comments from introductions to editions of Philips's works are worthy of note. In a 1781 edition of the *Poetical Works of Ambrose Philips*, Philips is given credit for whatever

---

[25] Verses 1605-12:

> En rentrant dans ces lieux, nous l'avons rencontrée
> Qui couroit vers le temple, inquiète, égarée,
> Elle a trouvé Pyrrhus porté sur des soldats
> Que son sang excitoit à venger son trépas.
> Sans doute à cet objet sa rage s'est émue.
> Mais du haut de la porte enfin nous l'avons vue,
> Un poignard à la main, sur Pyrrhus se courber,
> Lever les yeux au ciel, se frapper et tomber.

Mesnard, in his *Notice*, makes the following comment on Richardson's criticism: "... il est à regretter qu'il n'ait pas suffisamment distingué l'un de l'autre, et qu'en quelques endroits il ait paru croire avoir affaire à Racine, tandis qu'il n'eût dû s'en prendre qu'à son copiste peu fidèle. (II, 30-31.)

[26] *Op. cit.*, pp. 144-45, 150.

ANDROMAQUE AS THE "DISTREST MOTHER"

merit the play possesses: "The first piece he brought upon the stage was his Distrest Mother, translated from the *Andromaque* of Racine, but not without such deviations as Mr. Philips thought necessary to heighten the distress; for writing to the heart is a secret which the best of the French poets have not found out."[27]

An early nineteenth-century edition[28] is noteworthy as indicating a shift of emphasis in the interpretation of the play. As Dorothea Canfield has shown,[29] the rôle of Andromache was the one most favored by the actresses of the eighteenth century[30] and apparently the rôle in which the public was most interested. By 1819 the interest seems to have shifted to the rôle of Orestes. The author of the prefatory remarks of the Oxberry edition, after the usual disparaging comment on French declamation, says: "The *Distrest Mother*, as a dramatic narrative, is intitled to applause, and the frenzy of its principal character has some temptations for expressive powers which must secure it an occasional performance." The frontispiece is an engraving of Macready as Orestes. This shift of interest does not indicate, however, a greater appreciation of Racine. To be sure, the "fureurs d'Oreste" have had great interpreters in France, beginning with Montfleury, who created the rôle. But it must be remembered that Philips prolonged the delirium of Orestes. There is little trace of Racine left in this last scene of Orestes, as the following sample will show (p. 55):

> Who talks of Reason?—Better to have none,
> Than not enough.—Run, some one, tell my Greeks,
> I will not have them touch the King.—Now!—Now!
> I blaze again!—See there!—Look where they come!
> A shoal of Furies!—How they swarm about me!
> My Terrour!—Hide me!—How they grin,
> And shake their iron Whips!—My Ears! What yelling!
> And see Hermione!—She sets them on!—
> Thrust not your Scorpions thus into my Bosom!
> Oh!—I am stung to Death!—Dispatch me soon!
> There:—Take my Heart, Hermione!—Tear it out!
> Disjoynt me!—Kill me!—Oh, my tortured Soul.—

---

[27] Edinburgh, Apollo Press, p. xvii.
[28] *The Distrest Mother. Oxberry's Drama* (London, 1819), Vol. V.
[29] *Op. cit.*, pp. 146–49.
[30] Compare the situation in France where Hermione was the favorite of the great artists. See Mesnard ed., II, 22.

Admirers of the frenzy of Orestes are admirers of Philips, not of Racine.[31]

All things considered, the great success of *The Distrest Mother* both with the critics and with the public does not indicate that the English understood or appreciated Racine during the eighteenth century. Philips failed in his attempt to imitate Racine's style and he failed not because he was an inferior poet but because he could not understand psychological drama and because he was unable to resist the momentum of traditional English poetic style. Moreover the pressure of the growing taste for *drame bourgeois* led him to pad the rôle of Andromache. The rôle of Orestes suffered from his incomprehension of psychological realism and his taste for bombastic, static poetry. Yet these two rôles most impressed the public. As for the critics, Richardson is the only one who reveals any degree of comprehension of the essence of Racine and he does not profess to know Racine. If Racine was well known and appreciated by the men of letters of the age, as Philips affirms that he was, these connoisseurs of Racine must have refrained from recording their opinions in connection with the adaptation written by Philips.

[31] *The Distrest Mother* was produced in the American colonies in the middle of the eighteenth century, and is thought to have influenced the first American play performed by a professional company in the Colonies, Thomas Godfrey's *The Prince of Parthia*. Apparently the lines of this play which echo *The Distrest Mother* are all from the delirium of Orestes and are Philips's lines, not Racine's. See L. P. Waldo, *The French Drama in America* (Baltimore, 1942), pp. 91-95. (I am indebted for this reference to one of my graduate students, Mr. Robert Hartle.)

« « CHAPTER VII » »

CHARLES JOHNSON'S
THE VICTIM

In 1714 Charles Johnson made an adaptation of *Iphigénie* under the title of *The Victim*. Doubtless Johnson was encouraged by the success of *The Distrest Mother* to try his hand at adapting Racine. But there is no evidence of the attitude of humble admiration for Racine which we find expressed in Philips's preface. In his prologue Johnson makes the following vague acknowledgment of indebtedness to Euripides and to Racine:

> *Our Author backwards looks with grateful Eyes,*
> *And on his Fathers Shoulders strives to rise;*
> *Anxious to please, he now revives the Dead,*
> *And raises* Iphigenias *mournful Shade;*
> *From* Greece, *and* France, *with equal Care and Toil,*
> *Transplants her to* Britannia's *happy Soil.*

There is scarcely anything of Euripides in Johnson's play that was not already in Racine. He introduces the character of Menelaus, who serves in the capacity of a messenger in one scene, and in another scene relents at having urged the sacrifice of Iphigenia and endeavors to help Agamemnon save his daughter. This scene was probably suggested by Euripides. There is a great deal, however, of Johnson's own invention, with perhaps some suggestions from Boyer. This "Forreign Author," who, as we have been told, had "a plaguy deal of spite in him," republished his version with Johnson's title and in an irate preface accused Johnson of stealing his translation.

Johnson undoubtedly used Boyer's translation. He changes the ending in the same way that Boyer did: the music, the chorus of priests, the eclipse of the sun, thunder, lightning—everything is there except the subterranean groans and howlings, and Diana in a machine. As in

Boyer's version, Eriphile proclaims herself the victim of love as she snatches the dagger from Calchas and stabs herself (p. 62):

> Thus, thus I bleed, the Victim of *Achilles*.
> The Son of *Thetis* strikes the pointed Steel
> Thro' that fond Heart, which only liv'd for him.[1]

Before dying she has a prophetic vision of the calamities of Agamemnon's house, ending with the following curse for Orestes (p. 63):

> Haunt him, ye Furies, seize his guilty Mind,
> Let Love, Despair and Love urge him, like me,
> To seek Relief from inexpressive Tortures
> In an untimely Grave.

This vision we owe to Johnson's imagination, as we do also the hymn to virtue, which he adds to the usual moral. The words are spoken by Agamemnon (pp. 63-64):

> Hence let us learn none can be truly happy
> But they who constantly obey the Gods,
> Who firm to Virtues Laws, strive to excel
> In all her Works and labour at Perfection.
> Oh Virtue, Daughter of Immortal Love!
> Bright Image, Representative of *Jove*:
> For thee we pant, to thee with active Fires,
> Unclog'd by Flesh, the lab'ring Soul aspires;
> There she finds Rest, whatever Lot is given.
> A brave Submission raises her to Heaven.

Johnson's changes in the dénouement do not prove conclusively that he used Boyer's version. The idea of substituting spectacle for Racine's *récit* might have occurred to anyone. The thunder, the lightning, the darkening of the sun, could all have been suggested by lines in Racine. Certainly Calchas's speech revealing Eriphile as the appointed victim came from Racine, though Johnson makes it plain that Eriphile was illegitimate and his Calchas looks upon her fate as the punishment for her illegitimacy. Eriphile's assertion that she is the victim of hopeless love points to Boyer, however. Other changes in the character of Eriphile suggest even more strongly Boyer's influence. There is the same shift of emphasis and the same alteration of the same lines of

---

[1] All references are to the first edition.

Racine. For instance, the following passages show the similar shift of emphasis in Boyer and Johnson (vss. 468-77):

> ERIPHILE
> Tu vois avec étonnement
> Que ma douleur ne souffre aucun soulagement.
> Ecoute, et tu te vas étonner que je vive.
> C'est peu d'être étrangère, inconnue et captive:
> Ce destructeur fatal des tristes Lesbiens,
> Cet Achille, l'auteur de tes maux et des miens,
> Dont la sanglante main m'enleva prisonnière,
> Qui m'arracha d'un coup ma naissance et ton père,
> De qui, jusques au nom, tout doit m'être odieux,
> Est de tous les mortels le plus cher à mes yeux.
>
> DORIS
> Ah! que me dites-vous?

Boyer translates (p. 11, italics mine):

> ERIPH. Be not surpriz'd my Griefs admit no Cure,
> But rather wonder I have liv'd so long,
> With such a load of Cares and Misery.
> I am unknown, a Stranger, and a Captive:
> *All these were little—But, oh! I'm a Lover.*
> That fierce Destroyer of the Lesbian State;
> That fatal Author of our dire Misfortunes,
> Who with Hands drench'd in Blood made me his Captive,
> And with thy Father robb'd me of my Birth,
> *Achilles* is the dearest Man I view.

Possibly Boyer did not know that the English phrase "were little" has not quite the same force when placed here as the French "c'est peu de . . ."; but the introduction of the phrase "But oh! I am a Lover" seems deliberate enough. Like Boyer, Johnson underscores the shift of emphasis and in addition misses completely the meaning of "C'est peu de. . . ." He translates (p. 15):

> ERIPH. Attend, and thou shalt hear my countless Griefs,
> And be amaz'd I bear 'em all yet live;
> Captivity . . . my Parents lost . . . my Country—
> Thy Father's Death . . . *sit lightly at my Heart.*
> Despair and Love rack my distracted Soul.
> Is there a Burden, Maid, like hopeless Love?
> DORIS. Tyrannic Love! Where will this Passion end?

Johnson mitigates or eliminates altogether the self-reproach, the aristocratic pride, the sense of persecution, and the insane malignity of Racine's Eriphile in much the same way as Boyer, placing the greatest emphasis on the suffering of unrequited love. Johnson's Eriphile gives no hint of regret at feeling no gratitude towards her benefactress nor, on the other hand, does she give any indication of an uncontrollable vindictiveness. Both the self-reproach and the blind impulse to destroy Iphigenia are in Racine's lines (vss. 503-508):

> Iphigénie en vain s'offre à me protéger
> Et me tend une main prompte à me soulager:
> Triste effet des fureurs dont je suis tourmentée!
> Je n'accepte la main qu'elle m'a présentée
> Que pour m'armer contre elle, et sans me découvrir,
> Traverser son bonheur que je ne puis souffrir.

Johnson's version of these lines conveys no more than the pangs of jealousy (p. 16):

> Yes, *Iphigenia* courts in vain my Friendship
> And loads me every Hour with Hateful Favours,
> She is my Hero's joyful promis'd Bride,
> My happy Rival ... all her Joys ... are Pangs,
> Are Daggers here, ev'n now they pierce my Heart.

The shame that will drive Johnson's Eriphile to suicide does not spring from pride of race. Instead of (vss. 523-28):

> Ou plutôt leur hymen me servira de loi.
> S'il s'achève, il suffit: tout est fini pour moi:
> Je périrai, Doris; et, par une mort prompte,
> Dans la nuit du tombeau j'enfermerai ma honte,
> Sans chercher des parents si longtemps ignorés,
> Et que ma folle amour a trop déshonorés,

Johnson has (p. 16):

> These hapless Nuptials will conclude my Fate,
> If they succeed, *Eriphile* must die;
> The silent Grave will hide my Love and Shame.

Here Johnson has appropriated Boyer's exact words:

> ... the Grave
> Will hide my Love and Shame.

CHARLES JOHNSON'S *THE VICTIM*

The malignant intent of Eriphile's insistence on accompanying Iphigenia to Aulis disappears from Johnson's version even more completely than it had done from Boyer's. Racine's Eriphile says (vss. 516-20):

> Une secrète voix m'ordonna de partir,
> Me dit qu'offrant ici ma présence importune,
> Peut-être j'y pourrois porter mon infortune;
> Que peut-être, approchant ces amants trop heureux,
> Quelqu'un de mes malheurs se répandroit sur eux.

Johnson translates (p. 16):

> A secret Impulse carried me away.
> Hurried by Fate I came . . . In hopes I here
> Shou'd heal my Love-sick Mind, and loose my Sorrows.

In Racine, Eriphile's morbid conviction that the gods have singled her out to pursue her with their hatred reaches a climax of paranoid suffering in the thought that the oracle itself which threatens Iphigénie's life is intended merely to increase her own torture. She says (vss. 1110-12):

> Tu verras que les Dieux n'ont dicté cet oracle
> Que pour croître à la fois sa gloire et mon tourment,
> Et la rendre plus belle aux yeux de son amant.

Johnson apparently does not like this morbid fancy of Racine's Eriphile. The idea expressed in Racine's third line, however, appeals to him. His translation is merely an expansion of this last line; or rather, his own explanation of the reason why Iphigenia's ordeal will make her more beautiful in the eyes of Achilles. I say Johnson's own explanation because I doubt if Racine would have given the same explanation. Here is Johnson's version (p. 38):

> Her gentle Resignation to Heav'n's Will,
> Her pious Tears, her Heart that bleeds to part
> With Life and him, and all this Pomp of Grief,
> Will more indear her to his Soul than ever.

Like Boyer, Johnson has robbed Eriphile of complexity and intensity and has made her a conventional victim of "tyrannic" love. But, though he simplifies the character, he expands the rôle. He makes some changes in the dialogue of Racine's Act II, Scene 5, and prolongs the scene. In Racine, Iphigénie reproaches Eriphile for allowing her to come to Aulis to join Achille when Eriphile might have spared her this humiliation by informing her of Achille's defection. Doubtless Eriphile's eagerness to believe that Achille loves her colors her voice as she protests that such a thing is impossible, for to Eriphile's lines (vss. 707-10):

> Avez-vous pu penser qu'au sang d'Agamemnon
> Achille préférât une fille sans nom,
> Qui de tout son destin ce qu'elle a pu comprendre,
> C'est qu'elle sort d'un sang qu'il brûle de répandre?

Iphigénie replies (vss. 711-14):

> Vous triomphez, cruelle, et bravez ma douleur.
> Je n'avais pas encor senti tout mon malheur;
> Et vous ne comparez votre exil et ma gloire
> Que pour mieux relever votre injuste victoire.

If Eriphile has a moment of hope which inflections and gestures reveal to Iphigénie and to the audience, she is soon disillusioned, for Achille enters and she learns that he still loves Iphigénie.

Doubtless Johnson wished to make more obvious this peripety in the rôle of Eriphile, which could be shown only in pantomime in Racine. He omits Iphigénie's reproaches which I have quoted above, leaving only her accusation that Eriphile loves Achilles. Eriphile replies with a brazen avowal and believes Iphigenia's assertion that Achilles loves her, Eriphile. There ensues a female "gab" contest. Eriphile fancies herself a Cleopatra and taunts Iphigenia (p. 24):

> Accuse your feeble Charms which wanted Strength
> To *Fix* a Heart, they only faintly warm'd.
> My pointed Eyes, with animated Fires,
> And Force unerring, Conquer'd all the Hero.
> When I appear'd your languid Beauties dy'd:
> My Absence only gave 'em Light and Being.
> So when from Western Hills the burning Sun
> Descends, and leaves his Empire to the Moon,
> False Meteors glare, and scatter'd Drops of Light,
> With glow-worm Spangles, dress the Gloom of Night.
> But as the Radiant God remounts his Carr,
> The borrow'd Vapours swiftly disappear,
> They fly the Force of his celestial Ray,
> Or their pale Lights are lost in Floods of Day.

To this aria on the power of profane love, Iphigenia replies with a warning that sacred love ultimately triumphs over the siren's wiles (p. 24):

CHARLES JOHNSON'S *THE VICTIM*

> Cou'd I believe a perjur'd Lover's Loss
> Worthy my Care, I might, secure to Conquer,
> Arm these neglected Eyes with killing Charms;
> And show thee how thy arrogant vain Soul
> O'er-rates thy trifling Form,—But learn from me,
> The Virgin's lasting Beauties are her Blushes;
> And she who can descend t'ensnare her Lover,
> Will lose him when the poor Deceit is known.

As in Racine, Achilles enters and Iphigenia exits to avoid him. Eriphile learns, as she does in Racine, that he still loves Iphigenia. When he asks Eriphile for an explanation of Iphigenia's conduct, she tells him that Iphigenia is in love with someone else and is being forced to marry Achilles by her parents. Eriphile does not reveal the fact that Clytemnestra and Iphigenia have come to Aulis at the request of Achilles (as reported by Agamemnon); and she does not learn that Achilles sent no such request. I can see no possible motive for Johnson's changes except the desire to introduce a bit of "cool, deliberate" villainy into Eriphile's rôle. The suspicion that she plants in Achilles' mind is never mentioned again, nor do we ever learn how or when he was informed of Agamemnon's deception.

As in Racine, Eriphile is alone on the stage (with her confidante) at the end of this act. In Racine she has learned that Agamemnon's message to Clytemnestre had been sent without Achille's knowledge or consent. She knows that all is not well with her rival. Here is her curtain speech (vss. 763-66):

> Ne désespérons point;
> Et si le sort contre elle à ma haine se joint,
> Je saurai profiter de cette intelligence
> Pour ne pas pleurer seule et mourir sans vengeance.

Johnson replaces this speech with a bouquet of rhetoric (p. 27):

> What, tho' my rigid Stars
> Shou'd still frown on, Despair will guide my Hand,
> And animate my Soul to part these Lovers.
>
> Thus when, with Jealous Rage, the Wife of *Jove*
> Saw his stoln Loves in the *Nonacrian* Grove,
> In vain the Conscious Virgin urg'd a Rape,
> The Thunderer's Power, and *Cynthia*'s borrow'd Shape:
> Rash Maid, she cry'd, 'tis Criminal to please;
> Thy Ruin only can my Wrath appease.

> Thy Beauties shall no more my Fears allarm.
> The Goddess spoke, with Indignation warm,
> And let her Vengeance loose on every Rival Charm.

The changes which Johnson makes in other rôles are slight compared with this transformation of Eriphile. Agamemnon is more the tender father than the proud king of kings. His paternal tenderness is described at length in the exposition. Clytemnestre's denunciation of his motives is omitted by Johnson. Love and glory are underscored in Achilles' rôle.

Johnson rejects throughout the Racinian rhetoric of passion, as his predecessors had done, and he uses every device invented by their unfortunate ingenuity to mar the structure of Racinian tragedy and to change the dramatic dialogue into static declamation. Like Boyer and others, he retains Racine's interrogation when it can be made oratorical. When in Racine it serves as a vehicle for the natural and spontaneous expression of emotion, he discards it. For instance, Eriphile's lines (vss. 674-78):

> Moi? vous me soupçonnez de cette perfidie?
> Moi, j'aimerois, Madame, un vainqueur furieux,
> Qui toujours tout sanglant se présente à mes yeux,
> Qui la flamme à la main, et de meurtres avide,
> Mit en cendres Lesbos . . .

become (p. 22):

> Can you believe I love that furious Man,
> Who never met my Eyes but bath'd in Blood?
> *Lesbos* in Ashes, Fire, and Flame, and Death,
> All the dread Storms of War, fore-ran his March.
> Then when I saw him first, I saw him fierce,
> Unlovely, terrible, and full of Horrour.
> Cou'd he then make impressions on my Heart?

As in Boyer, Iphigénie's ironical probing is discarded. Instead of (vss. 665-66):

> Vous ne pouviez sans moi demeurer à Mycène,
> Me verra-t-on sans vous partir avec la Reine?

Johnson has (p. 22):

> You would not leave me, when I came to *Aulis;*
> My Company was your Delight, your Life.

CHARLES JOHNSON'S *THE VICTIM*

I know you will attend me back again.

Johnson, like Boyer, is addicted to epithets. Many examples could be found of the bombastic epithet, the descriptive epithet, and the editorial epithet. He alters Racine's hemistich, "Oui, vous l'aimez, perfide," in the same way as Boyer, by substituting for the pronoun a noun with its epithet. In Racine, as Eriphile is protesting against Iphigénie's hint that she is in love with Achille, Iphigénie interrupts her, thus (vss. 674-84):

> ÉRIPHILE
> Moi? vous me soupçonnez de cette perfidie?
> Moi, j'aimerois, Madame, un vainqueur furieux,
> Qui toujours tout sanglant se présente à mes yeux,
> Qui, la flamme à la main, et de meurtres avide,
> Mit en cendres Lesbos. . . .
>
> IPHIGÉNIE
>   Oui, vous l'aimez, perfide!
> Et ces mêmes fureurs que vous me dépeignez,
> Ces bras que dans le sang vous avez vus baignés,
> Ces morts, cette Lesbos, ces cendres, cette flamme,
> Sont les traits dont l'amour l'a gravé dans votre âme;
> Et loin d'en détester le cruel souvenir,
> Vous vous plaisez encore à m'en entretenir.

Johnson understands neither the dramatic value of making Iphigénie cut short Eriphile's protestations with her accusation nor the affective value of the colloquial stress pattern and pitch pattern of Iphigénie's hemistich. Here is Johnson's rendering (p. 22):

> ERIPH. Can you believe I love that furious Man,
>   Who never met my Eyes but bath'd in Blood?
>   *Lesbos* in Ashes, Fire, and Flame, and Death,
>   All the dread Storms of War, fore-ran his March.
>   Then when I saw him first, I saw him fierce,
>   Unlovely, terrible, and full of Horrour:
>   Cou'd he then make impressions on my Heart?
> IPH.   *Eriphile*, you love this dreadful Man.

Perhaps it would be difficult to find an English equivalent of the vocative *perfide*. But "Oui, vous l'aimez" translates itself: "Yes, you *love* him," with the sentence stress concentrated on the verb. By introducing as complement the two strongly stressed words, "dreadful" and "man," Johnson makes it impossible to throw the verb into high relief without distorting the meaning of the sentence. Surely English iambic pentameter permits subtler gradations of stress than the jog-trot of "Eriphile, you love this dreadful Man."

Even in the scenes where Johnson is following Racine closely, his epithets intrude themselves and immobilize and chill the dialogue. For instance, when Agamemnon forbids Clytemnestre to accompany her daughter to the altar, Clytemnestre protests indignantly (vss. 795-801):

> Qui? moi? que remettant ma fille en d'autres bras,
> Ce que j'ai commencé, je ne l'achève pas?
> Qu'après l'avoir d'Argos amenée en Aulide,
> Je refuse à l'autel de lui servir de guide?
> Dois-je donc de Calchas être moins près que vous?
> Et qui présentera ma fille à son époux?
> Quelle autre ordonnera cette pompe sacrée?

Johnson's version is (p. 28):

> My Lord, I cannot justifie my Absence;
> I must be there; behold the pleasing Pomp
> With Transport, see the blissful Union made,
> And give the blushing Bride to her fond Lover.

Note, in addition to the superfluous adjectives, Johnson's rejection of the characteristic Racinian interrogation, which conveys the speaker's emotion.

Johnson was not content to leave intact the most moving, if not the most tense, moment in Racine's tragedy, the moment when Clytemnestre falls on her knees to beg Achille to save Iphigénie, saying (vss. 935-48):

> C'est vous que nous cherchions sur ce funeste bord;
> Et votre nom, Seigneur, l'a conduite à la mort.
> Ira-t-elle, des Dieux implorant la justice,
> Embrasser leurs autels parés pour son supplice?
> Elle n'a que vous seul: vous êtes en ces lieux
> Son père, son époux, son asile, ses Dieux.
> Je lis dans vos regards la douleur qui vous presse.
> Auprès de votre époux, ma fille, je vous laisse.
> Seigneur, daignez m'attendre, et ne la point quitter.
> A mon perfide époux je cours me présenter.
> Il ne soutiendra point la fureur qui m'anime.
> Il faudra que Calchas cherche une autre victime,
> Ou, si je ne vous puis dérober à leurs coups,
> Ma fille, ils pourront bien m'immoler avant vous.

He introduces the lines (p. 33):

> And will her Godlike Master tamely see
> The Darling of his Soul torn from his Arms?

The tumid epithet intrudes itself with deplorable results into the scene of Agamemnon's change of heart. When he decides to defy the oracle and save Iphigénie from Calchas, Iphigénie cries, "Ah! mon père" (vs. 1481). Johnson's Iphigenia exclaims, "Oh, Royal Father!" (p. 52).

Racine often conveys the *état d'âme* of a character by a brief notation of psychological fact. For instance, Iphigénie is baffled by her father's avoidance of her and perturbed by Achille's failure to come to meet her. She says (vss. 603-11):

> Pour moi, depuis deux jours qu'approchant de ces lieux,
> Leur aspect souhaité se découvre à nos yeux,
> Je l'attendois partout; et d'un regard timide
> Sans cesse parcourant les chemins de l'Aulide,
> Mon coeur pour le chercher voloit loin devant moi,
> Et je demande Achille à tout ce que je voi.
> Je viens, j'arrive enfin sans qu'il m'ait prévenue.
> Je n'ai percé qu'à peine une foule inconnue;
> Lui seul ne paraît point.

"Et je demande Achille à tout ce que je voi" is typical of Racine. Johnson drops the whole passage and substitutes (p. 19):

> ... that Godlike Hero
> Will soon relieve our Cares, and ease my Heart;
> His mighty Soul is fill'd with Love and Glory.
> In Arms he rushes dreadful to the War,
> Impetuous, rapid as contending Winds,
> Rough as the wintry Storm that plows the Deep.
> —In Peace he mildly drops the boisterous Warrior,
> Then he's all Love, soft as the balmy Air
> That gently bends the Herbage, calmly breaths
> The Morning Sweets.

Johnson probably omits the passage with the characteristic line because of his distaste for psychological realism; certainly he does not object to a character's describing his own emotions. Eriphile frequently informs the audience in asides of her state of mind. But Johnson prefers hyperbole and metaphor to precise notation of psychological fact. When

Arcas reveals Agamemnon's plan to sacrifice his daughter, Eriphile says in an aside (p. 32):

> A glimmering Dawn of Happiness strikes thro'
> The Gloom of my Despair! My Rival dies.

As Iphigenia babbles effusively of Achilles, Eriphile informs the audience of her own suffering: "Her Words are Tongues of Adders, Tails of Scorpions" (p. 19). Johnson has put into high-sounding words what Racine had left to pantomime—what could be expressed more dramatically in pantomime.

Notations of facial expression in Johnson are pretexts for description as they had been in *The Mourning Bride*. For instance, Achilles says to Iphigenia (p. 25):

> Illustrious Maid, say how have I offended.
> You shall not go—Give me to know the Cause
> Why thy bright Eyes shoot these disdainful Fires,
> Why all thy Beauties redden thus with Anger;
> What unknown Crime have I committed?

Not content with introducing descriptive poetry into the dialogue, Johnson often interrupts the action to have a character recite a lyric piece. These lyric interludes are sometimes *sententiae* with slight connection to the action of the drama. They are always adorned with metaphor and simile. Ulysses speaks Johnson's reflections on honor (p. 11):

> Honour, a Jewel plac'd in Crowns, to light
> And animate Mankind to virtuous Glory;
> Made to distinguish and adorn Desert.

Iphigenia reflects on love (p. 21):

> The Tales of faithful Love are Fictions all;
> Our Fancies Work; a fairy Land, a Bubble
> That with its borrow'd Lights pleases a Moment,
> And then expands to empty Air again.

Johnson introduces into his play one theme which is apparently topical. He reveals a marked anticlericalism, with some dramatic justification in the characters of Achilles and of Agamemnon, but hardly appropriate in Ulysses. One of Agamemnon's comments is typical both in thought and in style. Menelaus, touched by Agamemnon's grief, has

CHARLES JOHNSON'S *THE VICTIM*

offered to try to persuade Calchas to defer the sacrifice. Agamemnon says to Menelaus (pp. 46-47):

> Haste then and try to move him; tho' I doubt it.
> The Pity of that Priest is Cruelty;
> His pious Zeal mourns and destroys at once.
> In *Aegypt* thus, from the fermented Mud,
> The genial Sun raises a monstrous Brood;
> Th'amphibious Wonder quits his watry Den
> With hideous Rush, and sweeps the trembling Plain,
> Destroys all round; yet then with pious Tears
> He mourns, he murthers, weeps, but never spares.

Not only are such *sententiae* and prolonged similes alien to Racinian tragedy but they also violate French classical doctrine, which condemns them in the dramatic genre. At the end of the act, where a moralizing lyric piece was in vogue in England, they do violence to the structure of classical tragedy. Compare, for instance, the ending of Racine's first act with Johnson's. Agamemnon says to Ulysse (vss. 391-94):

> La victime bientôt marchera sur vos pas,
> Allez. Mais cependant faites taire Calchas;
> Et m'aidant à cacher ce funeste mystère,
> Laissez-moi de l'autel écarter une mère.

With this speech Racine obeys a classical rule. Agamemnon's lines explain the shift in the locale of the action which constitutes an act-ending, suggest the action which will take place in the interval, and foreshadow the conflict and the mounting tension of the next act, thus preserving the continuity of the action. In *The Victim* Agamemnon says nothing of himself preventing Clytemnestra from witnessing the sacrifice. He lingers on the stage to speak the following elegy (p. 13):

> Let *Calchas* yet preserve the fatal Secret;
>   Oh! let not *Clytemnestra* know her Child
> Must die, cut off in the gay Morn of Life;
> Hard Fate!—are these my promis'd Hopes, my Joys!
> Have I for this with Culture form'd her Mind?
> For this alone, to lose her in her Bloom?
>   The Florist thus, when Winter's Rage is o'er,
> When Frosts and Snows, and Tempests are no more,
> To the kind Soil commits the future Flower.
> Now genial Heats unbind the teeming Root,
> Swell it with Life, and make the Fibres shoot.

> He sees the rising Vegetable rear
> The tender Stalk, and trust it self in Air;
> Now Western Gales breath thro' the vernal Skie,
> Unfold the Bud, and shew its various Die.
> Secure, he views his Labour with Delight;
> When unexpected, in one piercing Night,
> His promis'd Joys are curs'd by a disastrous Blight.

Racine's exposition, as well as his act-endings, is damaged by Johnson's taste for static poetry. In Racine's tragedy, the action begins at once. Agamemnon wakes Arcas to send him to Clytemnestre with a second note that will instruct her to turn back. In order to give Arcas the necessary directions Agamemnon has to explain the situation. Johnson postpones Agamemnon's entrance and opens his play with a long conversation between two minor characters not involved in the action, Arcas and Euribates. This change gives him the opportunity to introduce such descriptions as the following (p. 2):

> All rest, but *Agamemnon*;
> Distracting Passions rend his mighty Breast,
> Alone he sits, alone in yon Pavillion,
> Sustains his Grief, his Hands support his Head,
> A winking Taper only his Companion;
> Which now and then just lifts a quivering Flame,
> And darts a melancholy Gleam around.

Ostensibly in order to substitute representation for narration, Johnson changes Racine's dénouement. But it was love of sensationalism and spectacle, not a sense of the dramatic, which prompted the change. Superfluous descriptive poetry is found even in the dénouement. Presumably scenic effects would suggest the phenomena which precede the oracle's final decree.[2] But Johnson has Calchas describe these phenomena (p. 61):

> The Planet of the Day withdraws his Beams,
> And reddens as he sinks; while thro' the Gloom
> Pale Meteors dart their subtile Fires; the Gods
> In dreadful Thunder speak; the shaking Earth
> Is torn with strong Convulsions; Nature trembles.

[2] How effectively the lighting could be controlled to suggest the eclipse no one can say. We know that thunder was often simulated. It is not clear whether this scene was played with an interior or exterior set. The stage directions call for the inside of a temple. The frontispiece of the first edition shows a smoking altar in the foreground, a pavilion and the sea in the background.

CHARLES JOHNSON'S *THE VICTIM*

Without a doubt, Calchas's heaving chest would have been clearly visible to the audience. He did not need to say: "My labouring Bosom swells."

What an English classicist calls "otiosa descriptio"[3] is Johnson's habitual sin. He is indifferent to dramatic art. Racine's tragedy is for Johnson merely the framework for a series of lyrics of his own composition. Apparently he conceived of tragedy as static poetry declaimed before an audience, and he conceived of poetry as consisting of epithet, far-fetched metaphor, and prolonged simile. Johnson's play has been called "classical."[4] If the essential characteristics of Johnson's play are aptly described as "classical," then we must abandon the term for Racine.

The Victim had a fairly successful run, but was never revived.[5] It went through four editions between 1714 and 1717. It was remembered at least as late as the thirties, for it is one of the plays satirized in the burlesque "scholarly" notes of Fielding's *Tom Thumb*.[6]

[3] Charles Gildon, *The Laws of Poetry* (London, 1721), p. 220.
[4] Allardyce Nicoll, *History of Early Eighteenth Century Drama* (Cambridge, 1929), p. 89.
[5] *Ibid.*, p. 339.
[6] Fielding, in *Tom Thumb* (ed. Felix Lindner [Berlin, 1899], p. 97), ridicules a bit of rodomontade in the rôle of Achilles:

> Though human race rise in embattled hosts
> I will oppose them all.

These verses have no counterpart in Racine.

153

« « CHAPTER VIII » »

THE SULTANESS

IN 1717 Charles Johnson presented to the English public his version of Racine's *Bajazet* under the title of *The Sultaness*. In adapting *Iphigénie*, as we have seen, Johnson did not see fit to mention his model and gave free rein to his own imagination in his adaptation. He shows a different attitude in the prologue to *The Sultaness*. He admits that his play is taken from Racine. Moreover, he presents the play as a translation, with an apology for translations:

> Our honest Author frankly bid me say,
> 'Tis to the great *Racine* he owes his Play:
> When *Rome* in Arms had gain'd immortal Fame,
> And proudly triumph'd o'er the *Grecian* Name,
> Her Poets copy'd what *Athenians* writ,
> And boasted in the Spoils of foreign Wit:
> Why then shou'd *Britons*, who so oft have broke
> The Pride of *Gaul* and bow'd her to the Yoke,
> Be blam'd if they enrich their native Tongue
> With what the *Gallic* Muse has greatly sung?
> At least, 'tis hop'd, he'll meet a kinder Fate,
> Who strives some Standard Author to translate,
> Than they who give you, without once repenting
> Long-labour'd nonsense of their own inventing.[1]

Since Johnson himself professes merely to have translated *Bajazet*, his play should be evaluated as a translation. No one has made a detailed study of the relation of the two plays, but both Dorothea Canfield and F. Y. Eccles have compared them. Canfield says:

The Sultaness, far more than most Anglicizings of French tragedy in the eighteenth century, is really a translation and not an adaptation, and it is by no means a bad one. Johnson had had much practice in writing dramatic

[1] References are to the first edition.

THE SULTANESS

blank verse in translations from the French, and this shows itself in a production agreeably free from Gallicisms and absurdities of style. The Dramatis Personae are the same as in the original and printed in the same order. . . . The disposition of the scenes is exactly the same, and the tragic ending is for once allowed to stand as it was designed by the author, without bringing to life the defunct. Johnson shows more conscience and more ability in this work than in almost any other.[2]

She continues: "It is true it is lacking somewhat in fire and spirit, both qualities rather essential in reproducing the portrait of a character like Roxane, but its lucidity and workmanlike technique make it very pleasant reading."[3] She concludes: "With all its faults this is on the whole a very fair rendition, and deserves much praise for its fidelity to the construction of the French play."[4]

These remarks leave the impression that the English reader might derive from Johnson's play a fairly accurate notion of Racine's dramatic art. Eccles rudely dispels this impression. "This piece," says he, "is not an adaptation; but it is as distant a copy of Racine as a translator, who has no notion of altering his text substantially, could execute."[5] "*The Sultaness*, considered as a translation, is inadequate; and considered as English poetry, contemptible."[6]

Perhaps any evaluation of poetry is inevitably subjective and we might expect divergence of opinion. But how could two critics hold such contradictory views of the fidelity of a translation? A difference of criteria partially accounts for the divergence. Apparently for Canfield, who had in mind the many wanton and ludicrous changes made in English adaptations from the French, an identical disposition of scenes and an unhappy ending are sufficient to warrant some praise for fidelity to the original. Eccles was doubtless more intimately acquainted with Racinian tragedy and had a more sensitive appreciation of Racine's dramatic art. He therefore demands more from a play which purports to be a translation of Racine. Johnson's translation he considers inadequate because the translator "understood neither the relations of the principal personages nor their characters."[7] He gives one illustration as

---

[2] *Corneille and Racine in England* (New York, Columbia University Press, 1904), pp. 213-14.
[3] *Ibid.*, p. 215.
[4] *Ibid.*, p. 216.
[5] *Racine in England* (Oxford, The Clarendon Press, 1922), p. 14.
[6] *Ibid.*, p. 16.
[7] *Ibid.*, p. 14.

155

evidence of Johnson's incomprehension of the characters. Furthermore he offers evidence that Johnson's knowledge of French was too superficial for his task.[8]

Neither Canfield nor Eccles attempts to determine the exact relation of Johnson's play to the original. A detailed comparison of the two plays confirms Eccles's judgment. It is true that Johnson does not drop a single scene of *Bajazet*, that he adds none of his own, and that he does not change the order of the scenes. And yet changes in the motivation of Atalide and of Roxane alter the plot considerably and destroy Racine's dramatic effects:

Racine's Roxane, at the beginning of the play, intuitively doubts Bajazet's love for her. (Her intuition has not misled her.) The time is ripe for the revolution that will place Bajazet on the throne and save Roxane and Acomat as well as Bajazet from the vengeance of Amurat, who is besieging Babylon (Bagdad) but who may, if Bagdad falls, return to Constantinople, put Bajazet to death, and punish Roxane and Acomat for not carrying out his order to execute Bajazet. Roxane will not give the signal for the *coup d'état* (and her consent to Bajazet's seizing the throne) until she has definite assurance that Bajazet returns her love.

Like all Racine's personages, she believes that involuntary gesture and facial expression are a surer index of truth than words. She plans to trap Bajazet into betraying his true feelings. She has sent for him (or plans to send for him). She will demand that he marry her or be thrown back into prison and left to Amurat's mercy even if this move should cause her own death at Amurat's hands. If she is to succeed in wrenching the truth from Bajazet, he must not know in advance what she intends to do. He must be brought before her *sans être préparé*. Surprise will cause him to reveal his true feelings.

Roxane tells Atalide of her plan. Atalide, who loves Bajazet and who is loved in return, has been bringing (false) messages of love from Bajazet to Roxane in order to induce Roxane to place Bajazet on the throne. Atalide is more skillful at deception than Bajazet, who is instinctively revolted at having to deceive the gullible Sultaness. When Roxane tells Atalide of her plan, Atalide is beside herself with fear that Bajazet will betray himself and be condemned to death. Is there no way to save him? Yes, she can intercept him on his way to the interview

[8] *Ibid.*, p. 15.

with Roxane. She can warn him to be on his guard, to mask his feelings. She can release him from his promises to her and tell him to accede to Roxane's demands (vs. 400):

> Qu'il l'epouse, en un mot, plutôt que de périr!

At this thought, she wavers. She cannot bring herself to make a move to save Bajazet from death (and to lose him to Roxane). She finds a pretext to refrain from intervening to save him, an unconscious pretext that enables her to hide her real feelings from herself. She says to herself (vss. 401–406):

> Si Roxane le veut, sans doute il faut qu'il meure.
> Il se perdra, te dis-je. Atalide, demeure;
> Laisse, sans t'alarmer, ton amant sur sa foi.
> Penses-tu mériter qu'on se perde pour toi?
> Peut-être Bajazet, secondant ton envie,
> Plus que tu ne voudras aura soin de sa vie.

She is not yet aware of the enormity of her choice. She persuades herself that Bajazet will be false to her. He will not go so far as to endanger his life for her sake. Then her confidante, Zaïre, gives her further specious reasons for refraining from warning Bajazet. She says (vss. 407–16):

> Ah! dans quels soins, Madame, allez-vous vous plonger?
> Toujours avant le temps faut-il vous affliger?
> Vous n'en pouvez douter, Bajazet vous adore.
> Suspendez ou cachez l'ennui qui vous dévore:
> N'allez point par vos pleurs déclarer vos amours.
> La main qui l'a sauvé le sauvera toujours,
> Pourvu qu'entretenue en son erreur fatale,
> Roxane jusqu'au bout ignore sa rivale.
> Venez en d'autres lieux enfermer vos regrets
> Et de leur entrevue attendre le succès.

The spectator sees the beginning of Atalide's unfounded jealousy and sees her veil from herself motives that will cause Bajazet's death and, when she recognizes them for what they are, her own suicide. The heightening of tension at the end of the act comes, not from an event, but from a psychological revelation.

Johnson begins to make changes in Scene 3 of Act I. (Roxane tells Atalide of her plan to trap Bajazet.) Johnson's Roxana, instead of insisting that Bajazet be brought before her "sans être préparé," *com-*

mands Atalida to go to Bajazet and *inform* him of the crucial nature of the interview (also to summon him to appear before Roxana, it seems). She says (p. 10):

> ROXA.   Go, Atalida,
>   Tell him his Fate depends on his Compliance.
> ATA. I'll bring you his Resolves.
> ROXA.   No, no, your Tongue
>   Expounds what he ne'er means. I'll see the Prince:
>   Tell him that Interview, that Point of Time,
>   Shall make us bless'd or wretched both for ever.

Racine's Atalide has a decision to make. Shall she (unknown to Roxane) intercept Bajazet on his way to the interview with Roxane, warn him to control his reactions to Roxane's demands and even urge him to accede to them if necessary? Or shall she allow him to go to the interview unprepared for what he will hear (as Roxane wishes), and because of his love for her, Atalide, reveal his deception to the Sultaness and endanger his life? She decides on the latter course. She persuades herself that Bajazet does not love her so deeply that he will jeopardize his life for her sake, that there is no need for her to intervene. Thus jealousy checks a generous impulse.

It would seem that Johnson's Atalida too must make a decision. Her dilemma is different from Atalide's. There is no question of frustrating Roxana's plan to surprise Bajazet. Roxana makes no such plan. She commands Atalida to summon Bajazet to the interview and to tell him that the interview will decide his fate. If she obeys Roxana's command, Atalida will see Bajazet. She can urge him to consent to marriage with Roxana, if she chooses. Or she can urge him to refuse Roxana's demand and endanger his life. Or, perhaps, she can deliberately avoid seeing him (by sending someone else to summon Bajazet to Roxana's presence?). In this situation it would be difficult for Johnson's Atalida to deceive herself about her own motives.

In the scene that follows (Atalida talks with her confidante, Zara, about Roxana's plan), Johnson merely veils Atalida's motives from the reader. At least, so it seems to me, for I can make nothing of this scene. After a few lines explaining that she and Bajazet have loved each other since childhood and that they have deceived Roxana by pretending that Bajazet returns her love, Johnson's Atalida describes her conflicting emotions in Cornelian style (p. 11):

THE SULTANESS

> If he submits to wed her (Killing Thought!)
> How can I bear his Loss? Shou'd he refuse,
> He dyes. . . . Alas! how can I bear his Death?

But Corneille's Rodrigue had to decide on a course of action. Johnson does not make it clear that his Atalida has any course of action in mind. After a few more lines of exposition of events which have occurred before the opening of the play, Atalida indulges in the following tirade (p. 12):

> Alas! my Fear to lose him will destroy him!
> My lavish Tongue has prais'd him to our Ruin.
> ZARA. Yet Bajazet, possess'd of Life and Empire
> May find a Time.
> ATA.   I must avow my Weakness
> A thousand Jealousies disturb my Rest:
> My Rival courts him with a Train of Honours;
> Opposes Empire to my feeble Charms;
> And tempts his Youth with all the Pomp of Glory.
> —My only Bribes—are Sighs, and silent Tears.
> Yes, *Zara*, 'twill be nobler to control
> These Sighs and Tears, and join to crown my Hero.
> —It shall be so; I'll counterfeit no more,
> I'll plead his Cause in earnest. But *Roxana*
> Will soon be undeceiv'd: That gallant Prince
> Knows not to feign—Her disappointed Heart
> Will ravage all, and turn to Hatred, Murther:
> —Ah! Whither will this wild Disorder drive me?
> He must not die—Cans't thou deserve, Fond Maid,
> That he shou'd perish for thee?—

Then, Zara, the confidante, says (p. 12):

>   —Oh! Conceal
> These Tears, these jealous Pangs. They'll shew
> your Love [cf. Racine].
> Roxana's interview with *Bajazet*
> Will settle all your Doubts. Look up to Heav'n:
> The Virtues of your Prince will still protect him.

The tag at the end of the act is a paraphrase of Atalide's prayer.

Some lines from Racine appear in Atalida's tirade but they are curiously transposed. In Racine, these lines are part of the exposition. Atalide tells Zaïre of an access of jealousy at the time when she and Bajazet decided, in order to preserve Bajazet's life, to allow Roxane to continue to believe that Bajazet loves her. In Racine, of course, the past tense is used. Johnson changes all past tenses in the original to the present tense and makes Atalide's description of the doubts and fears she felt in the past a sort of soul-struggle precipitated by Roxana's plan to demand that Bajazet marry her. Johnson cuts out all the lines in Racine referring to Atalide's dilemma, as he would have to do, since he has changed the dilemma. But with them he eliminates Atalide's tragic self-deception. The following passage is omitted, except for the verse in italics (vss. 395-406):

> Bajazet va se perdre. Ah! si, comme autrefois,
> Ma rivale eût voulu lui parler par ma voix!
> Au moins, si j'avais pu préparer son visage!
> Mais, Zaïre, je puis l'attendre à son passage;
> D'un mot ou d'un regard je puis le secourir.
> Qu'il l'épouse, en un mot, plutôt que de périr.
> Si Roxane le veut, sans doute il faut qu'il meure.
> Il se perdra, te dis-je. Atalide, demeure;
> Laisse, sans t'alarmer, ton amant sur sa foi.
> *Penses-tu mériter qu'on se perde pour toi?*
> Peut-être Bajazet, secondant ton envie,
> Plus que tu ne voudras aura soin de sa vie.

Johnson distorts the meaning of the one line of this passage which he includes in Atalida's tirade. Atalide says to herself: "Do you think that you deserve that a man should be willing to die rather than be false to you? Bajazet will not go to such lengths. He will save himself without your help. He may go farther than you could wish in his effort to save himself." Johnson's Atalida says: "Bajazet will die if you cannot do something to save him; and his love for you will be the cause of his death. Can you think yourself worthy of such a sacrifice? You must save him."

Johnson's Atalida, I take it, has some sort of soul struggle and apparently chooses the nobler course; but it is not clear what that nobler course is. At the end of the tirade she seems determined to save Bajazet and sacrifice herself (but we do not know just how). Then her confidante Zara admonishes her to hide her jealousy (but we do not know why Zara finds it necessary to do so). Then Zara speaks a line that is either a misinterpretation of a line of Racine's Zaïre or a deliberate alteration of it. Zaïre says: "La main qui l'a sauvé le sauvera toujours"

THE SULTANESS

(vs. 412). I take "la main qui l'a sauvé" to mean "la main de Roxane." Zara says (in a speech quoted in full above):

> ... Look up to Heav'n:
> The Virtues of your Prince will still protect him.

Certainly in English tragedy of this period Providence could usually be counted on to protect the virtuous. Johnson may have found in Racine's line what the usual English tragedy would lead him to expect. (On the other hand, Providence almost invariably rescued the virtuous in the end. And Johnson does not rescue Bajazet.) At any rate, at the end of the act, we find Atalida praying that Heaven will save Bajazet and punish only her for their deception. Are we to suppose that she has chosen the third course of action open to her: to disregard Roxana's express command and to avoid seeing Bajazet, relying on Providence to save him? If so, this shifting of responsibility to Heaven could hardly be a pretext, conscious or unconscious.

From this point on, Johnson makes similar changes, but with such baffling inconsistency that we wonder whether his changes are deliberate or inadvertent: In both plays, Bajazet refuses to marry Roxane. She calls her guards to have him thrown into prison. But when they come she does not do so. Acomat enters. She tells him that she will not permit the rebellion against Amurat. She exits leaving Acomat and Bajazet together. Bajazet explains to Acomat what has happened in his interview with Roxane. Acomat urges him to promise marriage to Roxane, and, once delivered, to break his promise. Bajazet is indignant. Acomat advances Machiavellian arguments (vss. 643-51):

> Ne rougissez point: le sang des Ottomans
> Ne doit point en esclave obéir aux serments.
> Consultez ces héros que le droit de la guerre
> Mena victorieux jusqu'au bout de la terre:
> Libres dans leur victoire, et maîtres de leur foi,
> L'intérêt de l'État fut leur unique loi;
> Et d'un trône si saint la moitié n'est fondée
> Que sur la foi promise et rarement gardée.
> Je m'emporte, Seigneur.

Bajazet stands firm. Atalide enters. Acomat (who thinks that Bajazet loves Roxane and who hopes to marry Atalide himself) urges Atalide to help him save Bajazet from himself and leaves the two together. Atalide learns that Bajazet has done exactly what she had persuaded herself he would not do: "Il falloit ou mourir ou n'être plus à vous," Bajazet tells her. Atalide now begs Bajazet to leave her and reign with Roxane. When he demurs, she confesses that at times, when she has conjured up in her imagination a picture of Roxane happy as Bajazet's consort, the image has been so painful that she has preferred Bajazet's death to losing him to Roxane. Here are her words (vss. 681–92):

> Je le veux. Je me suis consultée.
> De mille soins jaloux jusqu'alors agitée,
> Il est vrai, je n'ai pu concevoir sans effroi
> Que Bajazet pût vivre et n'être plus à moi;
> Et lorsque quelquefois de ma rivale heureuse
> Je me représentois l'image douloureuse,
> Votre mort (pardonnez aux fureurs des amants)
> Ne me paraissoit pas le plus grand des tourments.
> Mais à mes tristes yeux votre mort préparée
> Dans toute son horreur ne s'étoit pas montrée:
> Je ne vous voyois pas, ainsi que je vous vois,
> Prêt à me dire adieu pour la dernière fois.

This lucid self-analysis (rare in Racine's personages) is not psychological analysis for its own sake. Atalide's recognition of her real motives lends a desperate intensity to her plea to Bajazet to go to any lengths to save himself. In saving himself he will save her from tragic remorse. She is begging him to save her from guilt, to make it possible for her to believe herself capable of magnanimity. Later we shall see her once more draw the veil of self-deception over her own motives. Surprisingly enough, Johnson reproduces these lines of Atalide. He follows Racine rather closely to the end of the scene and the act.

Atalide thinks that Roxane will be easily persuaded to forgive Bajazet and to believe that he loves her (vss. 775–85):

> Peut-être il suffira d'un mot un peu plus doux;
> Roxane dans son coeur peut-être vous pardonne.
> Vous-même vous voyez le temps qu'elle vous donne:
> A-t-elle, en vous quittant, fait sortir le vizir?
> Des gardes à mes yeux viennent-ils vous saisir?
> Enfin, dans sa fureur implorant mon adresse,
> Ses pleurs ne m'ont-ils pas découvert sa tendresse?
> Peut-être elle n'attend qu'un espoir incertain
> Qui lui fasse tomber les armes de la main.
> Allez, Seigneur, sauvez votre vie et la mienne.

Bajazet yields to her entreaties and the act ends with Atalide's admonition to say anything to Roxane that will save him.

Act III opens with Atalide questioning Zaïre about the outcome of the interview. Zaïre has not heard what the outcome has been but all signs indicate that Roxane and Bajazet have been reconciled. This is enough to plunge Atalide once more into the *funeste aveuglement* of jealousy. She now thinks that Bajazet must have promised much in order to appease Roxane's fury, which, says Atalide, gave every evidence of being implacable (vss. 806-11):

> Et ne t'a-t-on point dit, Zaïre, par quel charme
> Ou, pour mieux dire enfin, par quel engagement
> Bajazet a pu faire un si prompt changement?
> Roxane en sa fureur paraissoit inflexible;
> A-t-elle de son coeur quelque gage infaillible?
> Parle. L'épouse-t-il?

She checks her jealous thoughts when Zaïre expresses surprise (vss. 814-28, italics mine):

> ATALIDE
> S'il l'épouse, Zaïre!
> ZAÏRE
> Quoi? vous repentez-vous des *généreux* discours
> Que vous dictoit le soin de conserver ses jours?
> ATALIDE
> Non, non: il ne fera que ce qu'il a dû faire.
> Sentiments trop jaloux, c'est à vous de vous taire:
> Si Bajazet l'épouse, il suit mes volontés;
> Respectez ma vertu qui vous a surmontés;
> A ces nobles conseils ne mêlez point le vôtre;
> Et, loin de me le peindre entre les bras d'une autre,
> Laissez-moi sans regrets me le représenter
> Au trône où mon amour l'a forcé de monter.
> Qui, je me reconnais, je suis toujours la même.
> Je voulois qu'il m'aimât, chère Zaïre, il m'aime:
> Et du moins cet espoir me console aujourd'hui
> Que je vais mourir *digne* et contente de lui.

The words *généreux* and *digne* are important. Atalide's impulse to commit suicide springs from her desire to believe in her own magnanimity as much as from her fear of believing that Bajazet is unfaithful. This is a prophetic moment. She foresees that, if she continues to live, her jealousy may destroy her and Bajazet. And that is exactly what happens.

Acomat enters and announces that Roxane and Bajazet are reconciled. He does not know for certain that they will marry but he thinks so. He has watched their interview from a distance. He reports what he has seen, with his erroneous interpretation of Bajazet's gestures and expression (vss. 882-88):

> Moi-même, résistant à mon impatience,
> Et respectant de loin leur secret entretien,
> J'ai longtemps, immobile, observé leur maintien.
> Enfin, avec des yeux qui découvroient son âme,
> L'une a tendu la main pour gage de sa flamme;
> L'autre, avec des regards éloquents, pleins d'amour,
> L'a de ses feux, Madame, assurée à son tour.

This is the terrible image which has tortured Atalide in the past, and which she fears (cf. vs. 822, above). Now Acomat has revealed that her nightmare is a reality. She does not for a moment question the accuracy of his account. (In Johnson's version, Acomat is present at the interview and hears the words spoken by Roxana and Bajazet. There is less likelihood of error.) Atalide begins to suspect that Bajazet loves Roxane:

> Ah! peut-être, après tout, que sans trop se forcer,
> Tout ce qu'il a pu dire, il a pu le penser.

At this point, Johnson obscures his Atalida's psychology by replacing these lines of Racine with:

> And yet perhaps his Words were cold and forc'd,
> To soothe *Roxana*'s Rage, as I requested.
> Perhaps tho' they were forc'd, her eager Love
> Believ'd the little that he said sincere.

Johnson's Atalida doubts Acomat's story; she finds excuses for Bajazet. Her lines give a fairly accurate account of what actually happened but are the very opposite of the thoughts which jealousy inspires in Racine's Atalide. Johnson fails to see that Atalide *wants* to believe that Bajazet is fickle in order to justify the irrational anger (or is it hate?) that she feels for him at this moment. Here and later Johnson fails to render the tortuous self-justification of jealousy.

Bajazet enters and announces the success of the interview. He is happy to be free at last to take arms against Amurat. He notices that Atalide is weeping. He questions her. Atalide's decision to commit

THE SULTANESS

suicide, prompted a moment before by generous motives, now becomes a weapon with which to wound Bajazet and perhaps a means which Atalide employs (unconsciously) to destroy the work of her generous impulses, now unbearably painful to her.

She accuses Bajazet of having given Roxane proofs of love when the mere promise of marriage was all that was necessary. If he had been content merely to promise marriage to Roxane (as she herself had urged him to), she would have killed herself because she could not live without him, but she would have gone to her death happy in the thought that she still had his love. Bajazet is amazed and alarmed at this talk of suicide, and of his love for Roxane. He realizes that someone has given her a false account of his interview with Roxane. He explains that Roxane mistook his confusion and his shame at deceiving her (she was so pitifully easy to deceive!) for signs of excessive love. Only his love for Atalide prevented him from confessing the truth to the Sultaness. And now, says Bajazet, when he tells Atalide he has preserved his life for her sake, hating himself for his deception, she greets him with threats of suicide and reproaches of inconstancy. As he speaks, Bajazet sees from the expression on Atalide's face that she has not believed a word of what he has said. Her incredulity precipitates a bitter outburst from him: He threatens to go at once to Roxane, reveal all, and take the consequences. As he threatens, Roxane appears.

Johnson makes alterations, excisions, and interpolations in this scene. Only an analysis of the dialogue itself can make his changes clear and bring out their importance. He does not change Bajazet's opening speech. But he alters Atalide's reply quite drastically. Here is Atalide's speech with the lines omitted by Johnson in italics (vss. 955–74):

> Non, Seigneur,
> Je ne murmure point contre votre bonheur.
> Le ciel, le juste ciel vous devoit ce miracle.
> Vous savez si jamais j'y formai quelque obstacle:
> Tant que j'ai respiré, vos yeux me sont témoins
> Que votre seul péril occupoit tous mes soins;
> Et puisqu'il ne pouvoit finir qu'avec ma vie,
> C'est sans regret aussi que je la sacrifie.
> Il est vrai, si le ciel eût écouté mes voeux,
> Qu'il pouvoit m'accorder un trépas plus heureux:
> *Vous n'en auriez pas moins épousé ma rivale;*
> *Vous pouviez l'assurer de la foi conjugale;*

Mais vous n'auriez pas joint à ce titre d'époux
Tous ces gages d'amour qu'elle a reçus de vous.
Roxane s'estimoit assez récompensée:
Et *j'aurois* en mourant cette douce pensée
Que, vous ayant moi-même imposé cette loi,
Je vous ai vers Roxane envoyé plein de moi;
Qu'emportant chez les morts toute votre tendresse,
Ce n'est point un amant en vous que je lui laisse.

Here is the corresponding speech in Johnson's play with his interpolations in italics (p. 28):

No, sir, I murmur not at your Success.
Heav'n, righteous Heaven, who wrought this Wonder
  for you,
Knows with what Prayers and Tears I ask'd your Life,
And while I breathe, your Eyes must witness for me,
Your Dangers only busied all my Cares.
I sacrifice my Life without Regret.
Indeed if those good Angels who preside
O'er virtuous Love, had listen'd to my Vows,
I might have hop'd for a more happy Death;
These Eyes wou'd n'er have seen you wed my Rival.
What, was there no other Way to melt
Her Stubborn Rage, no lower Price than Marriage?
Yes, you have amply recompens'd her Love:
Yet this sweet Thought *will comfort* me in Death,
That 'twas by my Command; for Love of me
You mov'd her Heart—at least so I believ'd.

Some of these lines are a distortion of corresponding lines in Racine: "Vous n'en auriez pas moins épousé ma rivale" becomes "These Eyes wou'd n'er have seen you wed my Rival." "Et j'aurois en mourant cette douce pensée" becomes "Yet this sweet Thought will comfort me." These lines in Johnson have a meaning which is the exact opposite of the meaning of the French. The change in the first is due to Johnson's failure to render the meaning of *moins*; in the second, to his substitution of the future tense for the conditional. This looks suspiciously like mistranslation. But mistranslation or not, this speech retains only one feature of Atalide's "perfide jalousie," the threat of suicide. It does not seem to be an insidious trick to undo the work of a moment of magnanimity, or a weapon of Atalida's anger or hatred used to wound Bajazet, or even a reproach to Bajazet. Atalida does not seem to blame

THE SULTANESS

Bajazet. She regrets that he had to go so far as to promise marriage to Roxana. She very definitely does not accuse Bajazet of being in love with Roxana, unless the added phrase "at least so I believ'd" is meant to imply that.

By following Racine in Bajazet's reply, Johnson makes Bajazet's words seem inconsecutive and his reaction without motive. He answers (p. 28):

> Why dost thou vainly thus disturb thy Peace?
> Why dost thou talk of Love and Marriage Joys?
> Has one injurious Accent wrong'd my Faith?
> Has my Heart feign'd one Falsehood to preserve us?

This is a reaction to the accusation of infidelity which Johnson has omitted.[9] After expressing his amazement and alarm at Atalide's accusations and reproaches, Racine's Bajazet realizes that someone must have given her an erroneous account of his interview with Roxane (Johnson omits this) and then explains what actually happened. He then tells Atalide that, when the credulous Roxane interpreted his embarrassment as excessive love, he felt unjust, criminal even, and only his great love for Atalide prevented him from telling Roxane the truth. At this point Johnson interpolates the following speech (p. 29):

> ATA.   Forgive my doubting Mind,
> If she believ'd you hers, might I not tremble?
> Millions of Fears fill each important Moment
> And crou'd my buisy Brain when thou art absent.
> Ev'n now my Love I fear.

Just what emotion do these lines imply? Two things are certain: Atalida *was* disturbed (but is no longer?) not by the suspicion that Bajazet

---

[9] Verses 975–76, 978–90:

> BAJAZET
> Que parlez-vous, Madame, et d'époux et d'amant?
> O ciel! de ce discours quel est le fondement?
> . . . .
> Moi, j'aimerois Roxane, ou je vivrois pour elle,
> Madame! Ah! croyez-vous que, loin de le penser,
> Ma bouche seulement eût pu le prononcer?

These words in Racine are Bajazet's indignant protest against Atalide's unjust accusation that Bajazet has offered Roxane "tous ces gages d'amour," that he now loves Roxane and has ceased to love her, Atalide. Johnson has omitted the accusation from the rôle of his Atalida. Thus Bajazet's protest is unmotivated if not meaningless.

loved Roxane but by the fact that Roxane thought he did; Atalida asks
Bajazet's forgiveness for doubting something or other, we do not know
what. She is still afraid of her love, why we do not know. At any rate,
this is a far cry from the accusations and reproaches of Racine's Atalide.
At this particular moment, Racine's Atalide does not speak at all. Bajazet reproaches her for doubting him and then sees from the expression
on her face that *she thinks he has been lying to her*. Johnson, after
inventing for his Atalida words that are at the very most a mild reproach to Bajazet, goes back to Racine for Bajazet's reply and makes
Bajazet's reproaches to Atalida even more bitter than those of Racine's
Bajazet (p. 29):

>   'Tis most unjust,
> Thus when my Heart, pierc'd with its own Upbraidings,
> Retires to thy lov'd Bosom for Relief,
> To beat it back again:—Unkind Atalida!
> Dost thou afflict me with a broken Heart?
> And Death, and injur'd Faith? I see thy Fears,
> Thy jealous Fears prevail o'er all my Vows,
> And paint me to thy Fancy false and perjur'd.

This is a curious scene indeed. Johnson's Atalida speaks to Bajazet and
Bajazet replies not to her but to Racine's Atalide! After this speech
Bajazet, too, departs from Racine. Instead of the bitter counter-threat
to go at once to Roxane and tell her he has been deceiving her, Johnson
has the following plea for a noble martyrdom *à deux* to faithful love
(p. 29):

> BAJA. It is not to be born! here let us fix,
>   Let us remove those Colours; they delude
>   And torture us, while we deceive *Roxana*.
>   Let us appear before the haughty Queen,
>   Such as we are; such as our Fate has made us:
>   One Heart, one Soul: let us stand up in Vertue
>   And brave our guilty Fortune;—I'll declare
>   What I have said was all pretended, feign'd,
>   To hide our mutual Passion.—But she comes,
>   *Roxana* comes: Now thou shalt see, my Love,
>   With what a steady Mind, I'll meet my Fate.[10]

[10] The words of Johnson's Bajazet are suggested by the following lines of
Racine's Bajazet. The verses in italics Johnson omits. These are the words which
indicate that Bajazet sees from Atalide's expression that she thinks Bajazet is

THE SULTANESS

It would be interesting to know what tableau met Roxana's eyes in the stage productions of Johnson's play. Perhaps she came upon Atalida and Bajazet hand in hand and starry-eyed in their pride at setting a noble example of faithful love, ready to go to the reward in Heaven which the moral at the end of the play promises to those "whom Love and Fate have join'd":

> She [*Atalida*] of her faithful *Bajazet* possess'd,
> Shall find, what greatly was on Earth confess'd,
> In endless Paradise is greatly blest.

Bajazet and Atalida do not, however, confess their deception. Johnson now takes up the thread of the action in Racine.

After Roxane comes upon the lovers quarreling, Atalide's rôle is a passive one. It would be well at this point to determine how Johnson's changes in the character of Atalide affect the tragic plot. Johnson makes his Atalida jealous only when Racine's Atalide says *in so many words* that she *is* jealous. Racine's Atalide describes in an expository *récit* the jealousy she experienced when Roxane fell in love with Bajazet and believed that her love was returned and when Atalide and Bajazet decided to take advantage of her error in order to save Bajazet. Johnson transposes this *récit* to the present, making of it Atalida's reaction to Roxana's demand that Bajazet marry her and omitting the reaction of Racine's Atalide. Johnson does not show Atalide in the process of deciding against intervening to help Bajazet in this crisis, and at the same time deluding herself about her true motives. Racine's Atalide, as the action progresses, has intermittent flashes of insight; they are prophetic of her final recognition of her motives and her suicide. Johnson,

---

lying to her. Johnson's Atalida does not accuse Bajazet, silently or otherwise, of having lied:
> Je me trouvois barbare, injuste, criminel.
> Croyez qu'il m'a fallu, dans ce moment cruel,
> Pour garder jusqu'au bout un silence perfide,
> Rappeler tout l'amour que j'ai pour Atalide.

Here Johnson interpolates Atalida's speech.
> Cependant, quand je viens, après de tels efforts,
> Chercher quelque secours contre tous mes remords,
> Vous même contre moi je vous vois, irritée,
> Reprocher votre mort à mon âme agitée.
> *Je vois enfin, je vois qu'en ce même moment*
> *Tout ce que je vous dis vous touche foiblement.*

on the other hand, places Atalida's remarks on her jealousy at a time when she sees clearly and has for the moment surmounted her jealous impulses. Whenever Racine's Atalide hides her motives from herself, Johnson either omits her words altogether or substitutes words of his own which have a meaning exactly opposite to that of the passage for which they have been substituted. Consequently his Atalida has accesses of jealousy but always surmounts them. Insight into her own motives is constant. We miss the spectacle of an instinctive destructive impulse disguising itself as reason and leading a high-minded human being inexorably to her doom. *Funeste aveuglement! Perfide jalousie!* Although he paraphrases these words of Racine's Atalide, Johnson includes in the rôle of his Atalida not one of the manifestations of the blindness and perfidy of jealousy that we find in Racine. After Roxane's last interview with Bajazet, generosity triumphs over jealousy in Atalide. She takes all the blame for the deception of Roxane, offers to take her own life, and begs Roxane to forgive Bajazet and to be happy with him. But it is too late. Though Atalide does not know it, Bajazet is already dead. The triumph of generosity in Atalide gives tragic irony to the rôle and intensifies the pathos of her recognition of her guilt when she learns of Bajazet's death. Her suicide is a vengeance on herself. But since, in Johnson's Atalida, generosity has consistently conquered jealousy, the final triumph of generosity in Atalida carries no irony. Johnson translates Atalide's recognition of her responsibility in Bajazet's death; but he has relieved his Atalida of the burden of guilt that she bore in Racine's tragedy. Whether he intended to or not, Johnson shows us in the end an Atalida so overcome with grief at Bajazet's death that she exaggerates greatly her responsibility. There is nothing tragic in her suicide.

In Racine, from the moment when Roxane begins to suspect that Atalide is her rival, Atalide's rôle is a passive one. It is mainly on Roxane that the subsequent action depends. The psychological portrait of Roxane gives a tragic turn to what is essentially a melodramatic situation. Racine's *Bajazet* is tragedy in a framework of melodrama. The Sultan, Amurat, is away from Constantinople besieging Bagdad. His Sultaness, Roxane, reigns in his stead. His younger brother, Bajazet, has been confined to prison. The absent Sultan has sent an order for the execution of Bajazet. The vizir, Acomat, now out of favor with Amurat, has had Amurat's messenger murdered and is conspiring with Roxane to incite a revolution that will place Bajazet on the throne and save all three from Amurat's vengeance. Bajazet has been released and Acomat's plans for the revolution are laid. The time is ripe for action. News from the Sultan's armies is slow and unreliable. The Sultan himself may appear at any moment. Will Acomat and Roxane carry out their plan in time to save Bajazet and themselves? Who will win the race? The plot takes on a tragic tone because Roxane refuses to run in the race for her life. She will not authorize Acomat to start the revolution. She loves Bajazet and has been assured by Atalide that Bajazet returns her love. She has doubts. She must have absolute assurance that he loves her before she will consent to his seizing Amurat's throne. Oblivious of the doom that is closing in on her, she probes for the truth. As she uncovers the truth step by step, she rejects it. She has not really wanted the truth, but reassurance. In the face of one piece of evidence after another that Bajazet does not love her, she clings to the hope that he does. She temporizes with herself. She postpones Bajazet's death from moment to moment—and Amurat's vengeance is upon her. Long before it comes we know that it is inevitable.

The changes which Johnson makes in the character of Roxane affect the tragic plot. From the point where Roxane comes upon the quarrel between Bajazet and Atalide and first suspects that they are in league against her, until Atalide falls into Roxane's trap, Johnson follows Racine. In Racine's play Bajazet replies coldly to Roxane's effusions and exits. Roxane questions Atalide. After Atalide's exit, Roxane tries to interpret what she has just seen. Can it be that Atalide is her rival? Zatime enters with a message: Orcan, a black slave of Amurat's and the most sinister of his creatures, has arrived in Constantinople and is asking for an audience with her. She is sure that he has come to demand Bajazet's death. Shall she consent? She cannot bring herself yet to allow him to die. She must have further evidence of his perfidy. She will frighten Atalide and force her to betray herself:

> Ils ont beau se cacher. L'amour le plus discret
> Laisse par quelque marque échapper son secret.
> Observons Bajazet, étonnons Atalide;
> Et couronnons l'amant ou perdons le perfide.

Johnson makes no changes in this scene except to follow the English rule of ending an act with a lyric piece. Racine's psychological generalization is the theme. He replaces "Et couronnons l'amant ou perdons le perfide" with:

> If the dumb Voice her tuneful Aid denies,
> It [love] eloquently lightens in our Eyes;
> If both are silent, the strong Passion
> Breaks its rapid Way; each Sigh and Motion speaks;
> Ev'n now Love's Power does my whole Soul employ;
> And my torn Heart will know no other Joy.

Racine's Act IV opens with Atalide and Zaïre on stage. Zaïre tells Atalide that Bajazet is being guarded and may not see Roxane unless the Sultaness summons him. Atalide has sent Bajazet a letter; Zaïre brings his reply. Atalide reads:

> "Je verrai la Sultane; et, par ma complaisance,
> "Par de nouveaux serments de ma reconnoissance,
>   "J'apaiserai, si je puis, son courroux.
> "N'exigez rien de plus: ni la mort, ni vous-même
> "Ne me ferez jamais prononcer que je l'aime,
>   "Puisque jamais je n'aimerai que vous."

Then Atalide:

> C'est Roxane, et non moi, qu'il faut persuader.
> De quelle crainte encor me laisse-t-il saisie?
> Funeste aveuglement! Perfide jalousie!

Atalide sends Zaïre to beg Bajazet to placate Roxane: "Que sa bouche, ses yeux, tout l'assure qu'il l'aime." Enter Roxane. She has received Amurat's order. She will use it to frighten Atalide. She shows Atalide the order, tells her that Amurat is coming hard on the heels of his messenger, that it is too late to oppose the Sultan. She will obey the order and have Bajazet executed. Atalide falls in a faint. Roxane orders Zatime to take the unconscious Atalide into the next room and to watch for any signs that may indicate that she and Bajazet are in love. Alone, Roxane reflects on the revelation she has just witnessed.

Johnson's excisions in this soliloquy obscure, if they do not change, Roxane's motivation from this point to the end of the play. Roxane's jealousy is the opposite of Atalide's. Atalide wanted to believe Bajazet unfaithful in order to justify her irrational anger at him. Her doubts are unfounded and she justifies them by specious reasoning. Roxane

THE SULTANESS

wants to believe that Bajazet loves her. Her doubts are well founded; but her probings are prompted by a need for reassurance rather than a desire to know the truth, as she thinks. The mechanism which she has set in motion to uncover the truth has brought her, not reassurance but more and more evidence of Bajazet's deception. In this soliloquy we find her groping for consoling illusions by means of which she can reject the truth. Here she begins to temporize with herself. What, she asks herself, has she seen in Atalide's face when Atalide heard that Bajazet's death was imminent? Surely there was proof enough of Bajazet's perfidy: "Mon malheur n'est-il pas écrit sur son visage?" For she had seen in the expression of the swooning Atalide no doubt of Bajazet, but "Un coeur dans ses douleurs content de son amant." It is clear that Atalide fears only Bajazet's death, not the loss of his love. This is the truth, but the truth is too painful. Roxane rejects it: Atalide believes Bajazet loves her, thinks Roxane; but isn't it possible that Atalide has deceived herself as she, Roxane, has done?

> Elle peut, comme moi,
> Sur des gages trompeurs s'assurer de sa foi.

It is certain that Atalide loves Bajazet but not that he loves her. She thinks of setting another trap for Bajazet; but now she fears that he may show all too plainly, not love for her, but contempt. She cannot take the step that might reveal the truth. She finds a pretext for postponing any move that might bring positive proof of Bajazet's love for Atalide and his scorn for her: Acomat is urging her to give the signal for the revolution; the Sultan has sent another order for Bajazet's execution; the Sultan himself is nearing Constantinople. Until now Roxane has been oblivious of the doom that has been drawing nearer and nearer, the wrath of the Sultan from which only Acomat's revolution can save her. She recognizes the danger only when it serves to veil her desire to hide the truth from herself. She decides to place Bajazet on the throne at once and then, if he is ungrateful enough to pursue his intrigue with Atalide, she will, at some time in the future, by some chance, surprise them in *flagrante delictu*. Then, and only then, will she take vengeance. She will kill them both and then herself. For the moment, she says, "Je veux tout ignorer." And even as she speaks Zatime enters with irrefutable proof of Bajazet's love for Atalide: his letter found on the person of the unconscious Atalide. The mechanism which Roxane has set in motion to uncover the truth brings out the truth at the very moment when she wants, above all else, to remain in ignorance of it.

Johnson's Roxana does not delude herself with the hope that Bajazet may not love Atalida. She accepts Atalida's reaction as final proof. The fear of Amurat and the need for immediate action is no longer a pretext for postponing her vengeance: Roxana does not decide to place Bajazet on the throne. She decides to have both him and Atalida killed at once. A more cruel thought occurs to her. She will arrange at once for them to meet, surprise them, and kill them both, and then herself. Of course there would be no point to having her speak the line: "Je veux tout ignorer." Johnson omits it. Zatime's entrance with the letter, instead of being an ironic reversal as in Racine, is an anticlimax.[11]

[11] The following parallel passages will show how Johnson, while paraphrasing certain lines of Racine, alters Roxane's motivation and has his Roxana make a decision that is the reverse of Roxane's (vss. 1222-50, italics added):

> Mon malheur n'est-il pas écrit sur son visage?
> Vois-je pas, au travers de son saisissement,
> Un coeur dans ses douleurs content de son amant?
> Exempte des soupçons dont je suis tourmentée,
> Ce n'est que pour ses jours qu'elle est épouvantée.
> *N'importe: poursuivons. Elle peut, comme moi,*
> *Sur des gages trompeurs s'assurer de sa foi.*
> *Pour le faire expliquer, tendons-lui quelque piège.*
> *Mais quel indigne emploi moi-même m'imposé-je!*
> *Quoi donc? à me gêner appliquant mes esprits,*
> *J'irai faire à mes yeux éclater ses mépris?*
> Lui-même il peut prévoir et tromper mon adresse.
> D'ailleurs, l'ordre, l'esclave, et le vizir me presse,
> Il faut prendre parti, l'on m'attend. Faisons mieux:
> *Sur tout ce que j'ai vu fermons plutôt les yeux;*
> *Laissons de leur amour la recherche importune;*
> *Poussons à bout l'ingrat, et tentons la fortune;*
> *Voyons si, par mes soins sur le trône élevé,*
> *Il osera trahir l'amour qui l'a sauvé,*
> *Et si, de mes bienfaits lâchement libérale,*
> *Sa main en osera couronner ma rivale.*
> *Je saurai bien toujours retrouver le moment*
> *De punir, s'il le faut, la rivale et l'amant:*
> Dans ma juste fureur, observant le perfide,
> *Je saurai* le surprendre avec son Atalide,
> Et d'un même poignard les unissant tous deux,
> Les percer l'un et l'autre, et moi-même après eux.
> Voilà, n'en doutons point, le parti qu'il faut prendre.
> Je veux tout ignorer.

Here is Roxana's soliloquy, in part, with interpolations in italics (pp. 37-38):

THE SULTANESS

Indeed, with Roxane's temporizing gone, there seems no point in continuing the play except to show Roxane stabbing the lovers and herself. But Johnson is translating, not adapting Racine's tragedy. He follows Racine *tant bien que mal* to the end: Confronted with the proof of Bajazet's love for Atalide, Roxane bursts into a vengeful fury. She will have Bajazet killed and force Atalide to view his dead body! Acomat enters and asks why she is delaying the execution of their plan. She shows him the proof of Bajazet's perfidy. He realizes that he must not at this moment oppose her rage. He offers to avenge her. Now she must choose! She demurs and finds another pretext:

> Non, Acomat:
> Laissez-moi le plaisir de confondre l'ingrat.
> Je veux voir son désordre, et jouir de sa honte.

She will see Bajazet again! She leaves and Acomat discusses the situation with Osmin. All hope is not lost. They can still save Bajazet. He decides to proceed with the revolution, against Roxane's orders.

Act V opens with Atalide seeking Bajazet. Is he dead or at this moment dying? Roxane enters. She orders her guards to arrest Atalide.

> My Misery is painted on her Visage;
> Tho' whelm'd in Grief, yet still a glimmering Hope
> Points thro', and tells her *Bajazet* is hers;
> His Life, his Life alone is all her Care,
> *But let him live or die, still I am lost.*
> *What! shall I wait 'til she explains her Perfidy*
> *With her own Mouth?* 'Tis Time to act, *Roxana*,
> The Sultan comes apace, fierce Orcan threatens;
> *Let 'em both die, I'll wait no farther Proof.*
> No, I have a better Thought; *he shall again*
> *Behold her, I'll appoint once more their Meeting*,
> Surprize 'em in their soft, unguarded Moments
> When mutually they sigh: when their fond Souls
> Brood o'er their pleasing Sorrows, then this Hand
> Shall join 'em both, with the same pointed Dagger
> Unite 'em ever; drive into my Heart,
> Into this Heart, the reeking, bloody Steel,
> And stab the perjur'd Traitor's Image here.

It would appear that Johnson did not understand the motivation of Roxane's decision to place Bajazet on the throne at once. He translates verses which, in Racine, refer to Bajazet as though they referred to Atalide:

> What! Shall I wait 'till she explains her Perfidy
> With her own Mouth?

Ignorance of the French language on Johnson's part is the most plausible explanation of the alterations that he makes in this scene.

175

We are approaching the climax, the last interview of Roxane and Bajazet.

During the preceding scenes Johnson has followed Racine fairly closely. He tries to improve on Racine's great climax. Racine prepares the audience for the highly dramatic scene of Roxane's last "piège" in a short protagonist-confidante scene. Roxane explains to Zatime her preparations for the decisive interview: Amurat's creature, the sinister Orcan, is waiting outside the room where the interview is to take place. With him are Roxane's mutes, who have orders to strangle Bajazet if he leaves the room. Roxane can save him by detaining him there with her. But if she orders him to leave her, she sends him to his death. Zatime tells Roxane that Bajazet is approaching, quite unsuspecting of the trap which has been set for him (vss. 1457-60). For a moment Roxane considers turning Bajazet over to his executioners without seeing him again. Then she yields to her impulse to see him once more. This time, however, she knows, and the audience knows, that she can no longer merely threaten him; she can no longer vacillate and temporize with herself. Bajazet appears. With deadly brevity and precision, Roxane reproaches him for feigning love for her and confronts him with the proof of his perfidy, his letter to Atalide. Bajazet confesses his deception but protests that he would have gratefully repaid Roxane in honors and power for raising him to the throne. Roxane has listened in silence to his confession. This protestation is the one thing that could impel her to bandy words with her victim. Not only is Bajazet's gratitude a poor substitute for his love; his assumption that he would be in a position to confer favors on her wounds her pride in her power. She has to punish his presumption. She says (vss. 1525-38):

> Et que pourrois-tu faire?
> Sans l'offre de ton coeur, par où peux-tu me plaire?
> Quels seroient de tes voeux les inutiles fruits?
> Ne te souvient-il plus de tout ce que je suis?
> Maîtresse du sérail, arbitre de ta vie
> Et même de l'État, qu'Amurat me confie,
> Sultane, et, ce qu'en vain j'ai cru trouver en toi,
> Souveraine d'un coeur qui n'eût aimé que moi,
> Dans ce comble de gloire où je suis arrivée,
> A quel indigne honneur m'avois-tu réservée?
> Traînerois-je en ces lieux un sort infortuné,
> Vil rebut d'un ingrat que j'aurois couronné,

> De mon rang descendue, à mille autres égale
> Ou la première esclave enfin de ma rivale?

Then she delivers her ultimatum (vss. 1539–47):

> Laissons ces vains discours; et, sans m'importuner,
> Pour la dernière fois, veux-tu vivre et régner?
> J'ai l'ordre d'Amurat et je puis t'y soustraire.
> Mais tu n'as qu'un moment: parle.
>   BAJAZET
>   Que faut-il faire?
>   ROXANE
> Ma rivale est ici: suis-moi sans différer;
> Dans les mains des muets viens la voir expirer:
> Et, libre d'un amour à ta gloire funeste,
> Viens m'engager ta foi: le temps fera le reste.
> Ta grâce est à ce prix, si tu veux l'obtenir.

In response Bajazet first denounces Roxane and then, fearing for Atalide, he tries to assume all the blame for their deception of Roxane. He begs her to spare Atalide (vss. 1560–64):

> Mais laissez-moi du moins mourir sans vous haïr.
> Amurat avec moi ne l'a point condamnée:
> Épargnez une vie assez infortunée.
> Ajoutez cette grâce à tant d'autres bontés,
> Madame; et si jamais je vous fus cher....

Roxane has listened in silence first to his denunciation of her, then to his defense of her rival and finally to his pleas for her rival's life. But his appeal to her love for him to save her rival is more than she can bear. She interrupts him with the fatal order, "Sortez." Bajazet exits in silence and Roxane does not speak again until he is gone. Then she says (vss. 1565–66):

> Pour la dernière fois, perfide, tu m'as vue,
> Et tu vas rencontrer la peine qui t'est due.

Johnson reproduces both the preparatory Roxane-Zatime scene and the final Roxane-Bajazet scene. From his translation of Roxane's words to her confidante, however, it is impossible to know whether or not his Roxana has arranged to trap Bajazet in the same way that Racine's Roxane does. Roxane says (vss. 1453–57):

> Oui, tout est prêt, Zatime;
> Orcan et les muets attendent leur victime.

>Je suis pourtant toujours maîtresse de son sort:
>Je puis le retenir. Mais s'il sort, il est mort.
>Vient-il?

Johnson translates (p. 45, italics mine):

>All Things are prepar'd,
>Fierce Orcan and the Mutes expect their Victim.
>Yet am I still the Mistress of his Fate;
>*And can defer it:*—But, *shou'd he attempt*
>*One Step beyond his Bounds, he dies.*

Can it be that Johnson failed to understand that *retenir* and *sortir* are used in their literal sense? Or does he think that he is conveying Racine's meaning but clothing it in a more elegant style? Johnson's lines fail to make clear that in the next scene the stage itself will become a trap for Bajazet and that the bounds he must not overstep are merely the limits of the stage, that death awaits him just outside this room.

Bajazet enters and Roxana makes her accusation as she does in Racine. In this speech Johnson follows Racine very closely and it is perhaps the most effective tirade in the English play. In justice to Johnson it should be quoted in full (pp. 45-46):

>I shall not tire you, Prince, with vain Reproaches;
>The Moments are too precious to be lost.
>You know what I have done.—To say no more,
>You live:—And I repine not, that my Love,
>My Benefits, cou'd merit no Regard.
>Tho', to a noble Mind, such lavish Kindness
>And such uncommon Love might have their Weight,
>And partly recompense the want of Charms.
> But, it surprizes me, you e'er could think
>Falshood and Treachery were fit Returns
>For so much Faith and Love; that you could stoop
>To feign a Passion which your Heart ne'er felt.

These lines render fairly well the simplicity, the tenseness, and the ominous restraint and irony of the original (vss. 1469-80):

>Je ne vous ferai point des reproches frivoles:
>Les moments sont trop chers pour les perdre en paroles.
>Mes soins vous sont connus: en un mot, vous vivez:
>Et je ne vous dirois que ce que vous savez.
>Malgré tout mon amour, si je n'ai pu vous plaire,
>Je n'en murmure point; quoiqu'à ne vous rien taire,

THE SULTANESS

> Ce même amour peut-être, et ces mêmes bienfaits,
> Auroient dû suppléer à mes foibles attraits.
> Mais je m'étonne enfin, que, pour reconnaissance,
> Pour prix de tant d'amour, de tant de confiance,
> Vous ayez si longtemps, par des détours si bas,
> Feint un amour pour moi que vous ne sentiez pas.

Such fidelity of translation Johnson either could not or would not maintain for long. In the rest of the scene he takes unfortunate liberties. Roxane is silent while Bajazet admits his guilt and tries with desperate eloquence to justify himself (vss. 1489–1525). It does not occur to Johnson that Roxane's silence during his long speech is more dramatic than any words could be. He interpolates the following most un-Racinian speech by Roxana (p. 46):

> Torture! Distraction! Death!
> Well, Sir, go on, go on: but still remember,
> The Time is short: This Moment is your last.

Despite this indication that Bajazet's fate has already been decided, Roxana gives him one more chance, as she does in Racine and on the same terms. But in Johnson's translation Roxana gives Bajazet information that Roxane had withheld. Roxane says (vss. 1539–42):

> Laissons ces vains discours; et, sans m'importuner,
> Pour la dernière fois, veux-tu vivre et régner?
> J'ai l'ordre d'Amurat et je puis t'y soustraire.
> Mais tu n'as qu'un moment: parle.

Roxana says (p. 47, italics mine):

> But I have done—the Moments waste. Once more
> Resolve my Doubts—Behold the Sultan's Orders,
> *The Mutes attend*—Wilt thou yet live and reign?
> Determine:—Speak:—Reply.

By inserting the words which I have italicized Johnson has Roxana reveal to Bajazet the fact that preparations have been made for his execution, that his death is imminent. His unawareness in Racine is part of the dramatic effect. This may be an inadvertence. The next change is apparently deliberate. Johnson's Bajazet refuses to ask what her terms are as Racine's had done. Instead of "Que faut-il faire?" he says "Obey the Sultan." Doubtless Johnson meant to make his Bajazet more heroic by this answer. The change makes it impossible for him to use Roxane's terse statement of the terms of her cruel bargain (vss. 1543-47):

> Ma rivale est ici: suis-moi sans différer;
> Dans les mains des muets viens la voir expirer:
> Et, libre d'un amour à ta gloire funeste,
> Viens m'engager ta foi: le temps fera le reste.
> Ta grâce est à ce prix, si tu veux l'obtenir.

Johnson substitutes the following oration (p. 47):

> No, *Bajazet*! I will defeat thy Pride!
> Thy haughty Soul aspires to perish for her!
> For curst *Atalida*.—But she shall die.
> The Mutes shall strain the fatal Cords before thee:
> Thou shalt behold each captivating Feature,
> Deform'd and swoln with suffocating Blood.
> When she is gone, I may possess thy Love.
> On these Conditions you obtain your Pardon.
> Follow me and live.

In Bajazet's reply Johnson follows Racine closely. Roxana interrupts him, as in Racine, at the point when he appeals to her love for him in order to save her rival. But instead of the famous "Sortez," Johnson's Roxana says (p. 48):

> A guard there! Take your Pris'ner—Never more,
> Perfidious Man, shalt thou behold my Face.

Johnson has destroyed all Racine's dramatic effects: Roxane's trap already set for Bajazet—and for herself; Bajazet's unawareness of the dreadful finality of the interview; the contrast between Bajazet's fecundity and Roxane's terseness; and the culmination of the scene and of Roxane's mood in the one terrible word that springs the trap, the immortal "Sortez."

An English critic describes very well the nature of the tension in such a scene as this. He refers to the first Roxane-Bajazet interview, but his remarks apply quite as well to the last. He says: "Her very restraint heightens the intensity of the scene and we can imagine the spectators, beginning to feel warm under their collars, wriggling happily in their seats and whispering to one another: 'Tu vois. Elle va éclater!' "[12] In the last interview we see the same restraint and we wait for the out-

---

[12] Martin Turnell, *The Classical Moment* (New York, New Directions, n.d.), p. 178.

THE SULTANESS

burst. The spectator knows in advance that this is Bajazet's last moment. Bajazet does not. Nor does Roxane. Sooner or later, we know, Bajazet will speak the words that will unleash Roxane's anger, that will destroy her last hope that Bajazet may return her love. It is for these words of Bajazet's that we wait. And when begging for Atalide's life, he says "Si jamais je vous fus cher," just a second before the terrible "Sortez," we whisper: "C'en est fait."

This tension is completely gone in Johnson's version. Did he mean to substitute another kind of tension, a more melodramatic kind? We get the impression that his Bajazet has a better chance to escape. The mutes are waiting to strangle him, but where? Not just outside the door. Behind the scenes Acomat's revolution is getting under way. We do not have the same feeling of the finality of this interview. What we fear is that Roxana will order Bajazet's death before the revolution has progressed far enough to save him. Twice Roxana reminds Bajazet that his last moment is at hand. Are we supposed to wonder, "Will Acomat never come?" Perhaps. But this is the technique of the last-minute, hairbreadth rescue, "probable" because "prepared," but uncertain because of the race against time. Why doesn't Johnson provide the rescue?

There is a possible explanation of this confusion of two techniques and of Johnson's changes in the motivation of Atalide and of Roxane. Johnson obviously knew very little French. Eccles has cited two examples of mistranslation. I have noted several passages that look like mistranslations. One obvious example should suffice to demonstrate Johnson's very superficial knowledge of the language: Roxane comes upon Bajazet and Atalide. Bajazet replies coldly to Roxane's effusions, turns on his heel and leaves. Roxane is amazed and begins to wonder what Atalide and Bajazet were discussing. She questions Atalide. Atalide replies: "Il vous aime toujours." To this Roxane says: "Il y va de sa vie, au moins, que je le croie." Johnson translates: "You see he throws away his Life/ Rather than counterfeit a Moment's Passion." It is patently absurd for Roxane to say such a thing at this moment. But Johnson had as little dramatic imagination as French. It is possible that many of Johnson's changes were inadvertent. When the French baffled him, he paraphrased vaguely. When his personages say the very opposite of Racine's meaning, he may be simply mistranslating.

There are, however, minor changes in the characters which are obviously deliberate. Johnson suppresses Bajazet's contempt for the former slave Roxane, and for her manner of courting him with threats and using her power to bargain for his love. He puts into Bajazet's mouth generalizations on the theme of honor which nothing in Racine justifies. For the delicacy of Racine's Bajazet, he substitutes conscious obedience to a code of love and honor. Acomat is given the ambition of a Gonsalez (*The Mourning Bride*) and of a Lycon (*Phaedra and Hippolitus*). Racine's Acomat wishes to marry a princess of the blood (Atalide) in order to strengthen his position in case Bajazet's favor should prove as fickle as Amurat's. Johnson's Acomat hopes to have a son who can claim the throne.

The changes which Johnson makes in the tragic plot of *Bajazet* are no less drastic for being inadvertent. Johnson may be said to have been faithful to the structure of Racine's *Bajazet* only if Racine's plot is considered as consisting of a series of incidents culminating in the death of the protagonists, thus: Roxane demands that Bajazet prove his love by marrying her; Bajazet refuses; Roxane orders his arrest, etc. If, on the other hand, we conceive of Racine's plot as the inexorable march of psychological events towards despair and death, Johnson does not follow Racine at all. In the exposition, we miss Atalide's self-deception which blinds her to the destructive nature of her jealous impulses, the psychological "semences" which foreshadow the catastrophe. At the central turning point, Atalide's unconscious maneuver to destroy Bajazet is obscured, well-nigh eliminated, and she should be free from the feeling of guilt which drives her to suicide—but she is not. At the climax we do not feel that Bajazet cannot escape his doom. We miss in Johnson's translation the sense of tragic inevitability.

The passages which I have quoted show plainly enough that Johnson's style bears not the slightest resemblance to Racine's. Nowhere does Racine's dialogue come closer to natural speech than in *Bajazet*. And nothing could be further from the colloquial than Johnson's mannered style. The mannered style of Roxana's speech, particularly, shows a shocking lack of dramatic imagination. The simple, direct, elemental ex-slave speaks in conceits and is addicted to epithet. Racine's Roxane, addressing Zatime, says: "Viens. J'ai reçu cet ordre. Il faut l'intimider." Johnson renders this: "These Orders, Zatima, will probe her Heart/ And find the Prince, tho' she conceals him there." Roxane's "C'est moi qui . . ./ Ai hâté les moments les plus doux de sa vie" be-

THE SULTANESS

comes: "I her most faithful Slave have watched for her,/ Guarded her softest, dearest, odious Moments." In her first interview with Bajazet, Roxane turns on him and says: "Rentre dans le néant dont je t'ai fait sortir." This is an ex-slave speaking to a prince of the blood, whose life is at her mercy. It is impossible to imagine anything more apt than the contemptuous *néant* and its implications of the ex-slave's pride in her power. But Johnson prefers: "Back to that joyless Prison/ Whence my vain Love had freed a thankless Slave." Johnson's favorite epithet is "godlike." Bajazet is, of course, referred to as "godlike." Johnson contrives to introduce the epithet into Roxana's rôle, with results disastrous to the characterization. When Roxane demands that Bajazet marry her, Bajazet reminds her of the tradition: Sultans do not marry. Roxane replies: "Mais l'amour ne suit pas ces lois imaginaires." Johnson translates: "But Love's a God-like Passion, that disdains/ Cold Policy and the dull Forms of State." It is very doubtful if Roxane—or Racine, for that matter—considered love a "godlike passion."

To merit any commendation, a translation should give some idea of the style of the original. Only in the passage which I have quoted above (Roxana's accusation of Bajazet) does Johnson's translation even approach the model. And differences in style seem trivial departures compared with Johnson's alteration of characters and tragic plot. Actually this so-called translation is much further away from its model than Ambrose Philips's adaptation of *Andromaque*. Philips leaves the tragic plot as Racine conceived it, even including death and madness for three of the leading characters. He tried to end his play on a happy note by bringing Andromache back at the end. Omit her last speech, and Racine's tragedy is almost intact. Johnson has so mutilated the tragic plot that the death of the protagonists is a non sequitur.

« « CHAPTER IX » »

THE FATAL LEGACY

The Fatal Legacy, by Mrs. J. Robe, was produced at Lincoln's-Inn-Fields Theatre in April, 1723. It had three performances and was never revived. It was printed anonymously the same year. This obscure imitation of *La Thébaïde* found at least one critic to proclaim its superiority to the original. This criticism appeared in *St. James's Journal*, April 20, 1723 (p. 310), and was signed "Dorimant." Since Dorimant's remarks are typical of a common English attitude, they should be quoted in full. He says:

"The English, in this Species of Writing, undoubtedly excel all their Neighbors; they have a Force of Thought, as well as of Style and Expression, which is no more to be described, than imitated: The Latter indeed is in good measure owing to the Strength and Manliness of our Language, but the Former is born with us; the true Poetick Spirit, that noble Enthusiasm, which distinguishes the Works of our Countrymen from the jejune and insipid, tho' possibly more correct Compositions of Foreigners.

"And therefore there are few Translations of ours, from the French especially, which do not exceed the Originals: We give them Life and Spirit; the Want of which makes them languish and tasteless in the Reading, in spite of all the Care and Correctness in their Composition. I shall produce only two instances: The first is *The Distres'd Mother* of Mr. Philips and the other, the new Tragedy, called the *Fatal Legacy*, which is to be acted, for the first time, on Tuesday next, at the Theatre Lincoln's-Inn-Fields.

"As I am a great Admirer of these Entertainments, I am not only constantly there of a Night, but I likewise very frequently attend their Rehearsals. When the new Tragedy first mention'd was rehears'd, I had the good fortune to be present, and as the Play of Racine, from whence this was taken, was fresh in my Memory, I could easily observe in how great abundance the want of this poetick Fire, (which has been spoke of before) in the French Poet, was supply'd by the English one.

"Indeed the whole Play seem'd to me (as far as I could judge from a transitory View of it) to be writ with as much Art, and Mastery of Genius, as any thing of this Kind which has lately appear'd. Racine is improv'd almost in every Scene; the English Poet borrows nothing of him which he does not repay with Interest. And whoever the Author is, (for I am inform'd he does not care to be known), he deserves all the Encouragement (not to derogate from their Merit) that any other of his Contemporaries have lately met with."

When in 1676 Racine wrote a preface for the first of his extant plays, he admitted that he had two criticisms to make: "La catastrophe de ma pièce est peut-être un peu trop sanglante. En effet, il n'y paroît presque pas un acteur qui ne meure à la fin." He further remarks that a love-intrigue among minor characters and subordinate to the main action, as it is in this play, "ne peut produire que de médiocres effets."

Mrs. J. Robe, in "improving" Racine's tragedy, did not eliminate the blemishes which Racine himself had pointed out. Indeed, in a sense, her changes all tend to exaggerate them. Racine's Hémon expresses his love for Antigone in gallant language which is incongruous in the atmosphere of horror that pervades the tragedy. Hémon would gladly die for his king but even more gladly sacrifice his life for his mistress (vss. 427-48):

>Le ciel punit sur vous et sur votre famille
>Et les crimes du père et l'amour de la fille;
>Et ce funeste amour vous nuit encore plus
>Que les crimes d'Oedipe et le sang de Laïus.
>
>####HÉMON
>Quoi? mon amour, Madame? Et qu'a-t-il de funeste?
>Est-ce un crime qu'aimer une beauté céleste?
>Et puisque sans colère il est reçu de vous,
>En quoi peut-il du ciel mériter le courroux?
>Vous seule en mes soupirs êtes intéressée:
>C'est à vous à juger s'ils vous ont offensée.
>Tels que seront pour eux vos arrêts tout-puissants,
>Ils seront criminels ou seront innocents,
>Que le ciel à son gré de ma perte dispose,
>J'en chérirai toujours et l'une et l'autre cause,
>Glorieux de mourir pour le sang de mes rois,

> Et plus heureux encor de mourir sous vos lois.
> Aussi bien que ferois-je en ce commun naufrage?
> Pourrois-je me résoudre à vivre davantage?
> En vain les Dieux voudroient différer mon trépas,
> Mon désespoir feroit ce qu'ils ne feroient pas.
> Mais peut-être, après tout, notre frayeur est vaine;
> Attendons . . . Mais voici Polynice et la Reine.

Phocias (as Mrs. Robe renamed Hémon) is quite as ready to lay down his life for love and is more hyperbolic in his expression of the sentiment (p. 33):

> Why, Madam, why this Fear? What is't a Crime
> To adore a Beauty so divinely Fair?
> Since you have deign'd to authorize my Love
> What can create the rage of those above?
> When first I nourish'd my presumptuous Flame,
> And gaz'd upon your Charms with wishing Eyes,
> Your Glances gave my Soul so fierce an Awe,
> That more I dreaded to incur your Frown,
> Than all the angry Terrors of the Skies.
> Let all the Stars conspire against me, let
> The Constellations turn to *Saturns* all,
> They strive in vain to shake my settled Love.
> Dispose of me, ye Gods, howe'er you please,
> My great Engagements bravely I'll maintain,
> Zealous for Death, in *Polynices'* Cause,
> To sacrifice my Blood; more zealous still
> To die, my dear *Antigona*, to die
> For you, before you, and to warm your Knees
> With my expiring, faithful, loving Breath,
> And take your Orders when I mount the Stars.

The catastrophe that Racine in his maturity judged too bloody Mrs. Robe makes even more bloody, not by killing off more characters, but by having two suicides take place on stage with much bloodshed referred to and presumably visible. Jocasta stabs herself off stage, then enters, "Raving and Bloody," to speak a long tirade, of which the following lines are a sample (pp. 63-64):

> *Laius*! Son! Husband! execrable Kindred!
> Unbar th'infernal Gates to give me entrance.
> Let your dark World exult at my Approach,
> And all Hell's Roof resound, *Jocasta* comes!
> . . . .

THE FATAL LEGACY

> Turn not away, my *Oedipus*! I come not
> To tempt you to the Crime of new Embraces;
> But purge away the Foulness of our past.
> Is Death so deaf he needs a second Summons?
> This purple Current flows so slowly forth,
> That it seems loth to leave my canker'd Veins.
> Hark! some officious Foes will force Life on me:
> But thus to disappoint them.

She stabs herself a second time as Antigona enters. Before she dies she bequeaths her dagger to her daughter (p. 64):

> By all my Fondness for thee, I will leave thee
> A Legacy more worth than thousand Empires,
> This Dagger—If thy Woes should e'er arise
> To vie with mine, use it as I have done.

Creon also stabs himself in sight of the audience, and his son enters to find him "weltering in his Blood."

In the dedication of her play (p. vii), Mrs. Robe admits that the first four acts of her play are "taken chiefly from *Racine*"; but she adds that the "Last is (excepting a few Lines), entirely new." This claim is hardly justified. Jocasta's death on stage and her ravings before dying we owe to Mrs. Robe. Besides this innovation, Mrs. Robe shows independence of her model only in her treatment of Creon. Even so, Racine's Creon is already made to order to appeal to English audiences. He is a plot-spinning villain motivated by political ambition. We have met the type before: Gonsalez of *The Mourning Bride*, Lycon in *Phaedra and Hippolitus*, Acomat in Johnson's *Sultaness*. Gonsalez has no counterpart in Racine. Smith had to do violence to Racine to create his Lycon. Johnson altered Acomat's motivation to make him fit the pattern. Mrs. Robe found in Creon all the elements of the run-of-the-mill villain—political ambition, exploitation of the passions of those characters who are obstacles to his ambition, and ruthlessness in the pursuit of his ambition. Nevertheless she can lay claim to some originality in her treatment of Creon. She eliminates the boldest strokes with which Racine paints Creon's ambition. She omits the lines (vss. 1433-48):

> ATTALE
> Il est vrai, vous avez toute chose prospère,
> Et vous seriez heureux si vous n'étiez point père.

> L'ambition, l'amour, n'ont rien à désirer;
> Mais, seigneur, la nature a beaucoup à pleurer:
> En perdant vos deux fils. . . .
>
> CRÉON
> Oui, leur perte m'afflige.
> Je sais ce que de moi le rang de père exige:
> Je l'étois; mais surtout j'étois né pour régner;
> Et je perds beaucoup moins que je ne crois gagner.
> Le nom de père, Attale, est un titre vulgaire:
> C'est un don que le ciel ne nous refuse guère:
> Un bonheur si commun n'a pour moi rien de doux;
> Ce n'est pas un bonheur, s'il ne fait des jaloux.
> Mais le trône est un bien dont le ciel est avare;
> Du reste des mortels ce haut rang nous sépare;
> Bien peu sont honorés d'un don si précieux:
> La terre a moins de rois que le ciel n'a de dieux.

Her technique is English, not Racinian. She adds soliloquies and asides in which her villain explains his schemes to the audience and calls attention to his giant intellect, much as Smith's Lycon had done. Her greatest claim to originality must be based on the final melodramatic peripety which she adds to the rôle.

Mrs. Robe's Creon is just as callous as Racine's but more naïvely so. When he finds Jocasta's dead body, he says (p. 66):

> My Sister breathless! Well, there's one the less
> Left to upbraid me with my Guilt's Success.

Her Creon dies as the result of the miscarriage of a stratagem. His son Phocias is not killed in an attempt to prevent the duel between Eteocles and Polynices, as Hémon is in Racine's tragedy. Racine's Créon tells Antigone how Hémon met his death and hopes that Antigone will marry him now that Hémon is dead. Mrs. Robe's Creon gives Antigona the same account of Phocias's death. But Phocias is not dead. Creon makes up the story out of whole cloth in order to trick Antigona. Into his account Mrs. Robe interpolates asides explaining his scheme and his motives. When Antigona questions him about the outcome of the duel he says in an aside (p. 67):

> Now, now's the Time
> To pay myself my promis'd Score of Vengeance
> For her Neglect of all my Vows of Love.
> I will refine upon the shocking Tale,

THE FATAL LEGACY

And make the horrid scene more horrid still:
And wound her in her very tend'rest Part.

A later aside reveals a somewhat different motive. After his false account of Phocias's death, Creon comments on his own astuteness and reveals his stratagem (p. 69):

Thanks to my good Invention, I've dispatch'd
My Rival; give her Time to relish that,
And my own Love may take a better Turn.

He then describes the death of Antigona's two brothers and, when his account is ended, presses his suit. Antigona gives him a cryptic answer, as in Racine, and exits, leaving him under the impression that she will accept him. Again he exults in his own cleverness (p. 71):

She's mine as firm
As my Extravagance of Love could wish.
She pauses, she deliberates, she yields—
Well-manag'd Story of her Lover's Death!
That Masterpiece of Thought has gain'd me all.

But his "Masterpiece of Thought" has trapped him. He learns that Antigona has killed herself. He goes into a delirium and has a vision of Oedipus, of Jocasta, and of Antigona, who, to the accompaniment of thunder and lightning, come to fetch him to Hades. He stabs himself. Phocias enters and finds his father "weltering in his Blood." Creon confesses that he has caused Antigona's death and begs his son's forgiveness as he dies. Phocias is told that he is heir to the Theban crown and the play ends with his rejection of the fatal throne.

It seems to me to be obvious that Mrs. Robe preserved Phocias's life, not in order to give the play a happy ending—how could the ending be a really happy one without the reunion of a pair of innocent lovers?—but in order to introduce a peripety of the type which we find in *The Mourning Bride*: a villain's own wiles become the instrument of his punishment and he dies confessing his guilt.

Mrs. Robe's style reveals the usual English aversion to Racine's simplicity. Her verse is cluttered with adjectives and embellished with hyperbole, simile, and strong metaphor. She follows in the footsteps of Edmund Smith but shows even less of a poetic gift than he had. Here are a few samples. Eteocles's description of the hatred between him and his brother (vss. 921-26):

> Triste et fatal effet d'un sang incestueux!
> Pendant qu'un même sein nous renfermoit tous deux
> Dans les flancs de ma mère une guerre intestine
> De nos divisions lui marqua l'origine.
> Elles ont, tu le sais, paru dans le berceau,
> Et nous suivront peut-être encor dans le tombeau:
> On diroit que le ciel, par un arrêt funeste,

becomes (p. 52):

> Our near Alliance is the Bane we curse;
> No short-liv'd Rage. Reciprocal Abhorrence
> Drawn from the Spirits of consummate Spleen,
> And riveted by long revolving Years,
> Works in our Souls, and flashes mutual Vengeance.
> Our Cradles knock'd each other, and our Nurses,
> As stung with Scorpions, quarrel'd at their tasks.
> But now the Infant Malice is Mature,
> And shall perhaps continue in the Tomb.

Mrs. Robe discards the one prolonged simile in Racine's play[1] and replaces it with a more inflated one. Créon's description of the strife between Etéocle and Polynice (vss. 215-20):

> Ce terme limité que l'on veut leur prescrire
> Accroît leur violence en bornant leur empire.
> Tous deux feront gémir les peuples tour à tour:
> Pareils à ces torrents qui ne durent qu'un jour,
> Plus leur cours est borné, plus ils font de ravage,
> Et d'horribles dégâts signalent leur passage,

is replaced by (p. 25):

> ... This fatal Legacy
> By which these rival Brothers claim the Crown,
> Confounds the Nature of all Government.
> That Nation that beholds two Partner Kings
> Mount her divided Throne, foresees with Horror
> A dreadful Age of Tyranny and Blood;
> Like Planets that shoot thwart th' affrighted Sky,
> And fiercely mingle their contending Beams,
> They shake that Empire that they war to sway.

The "poetick Fire" which "Dorimant" asserts is supplied in great

---

[1] According to Georges Le Bidois, this is the only prolonged simile in any of Racine's tragedies, *De l'action dans la tragédie de Racine* (Paris, 1900), p. 313.

abundance by the translator must consist of Senecan hyperbole and prolonged similes, a lavish use of adjectives, melodramatic asides, two suicides on stage with much bloodshed, a melodramatic peripety invented to punish a scheming villain, and a delirious vision of the dead whom he has wronged, for these are the only changes which Mrs. Robe has introduced into her adaptation.

« « CHAPTER X » »

TWO TRANSLATIONS OF *BRITANNICUS*

JOHN OZELL's translation of *Britannicus* (1714) is one of a series planned by a publisher for the purpose of acquainting the English reading public with the dramatic masterpieces of foreign literature.[1] It was to be expected, in view of the purpose of the translation, that in this case Racine's play would escape the usual mutilations—mutilations designed presumably to make the plays more stageworthy. And indeed it does. The long speeches are allowed to stand intact, without interpolations. No asides are introduced. There are no thoughtless excisions and no bumptious interpolations, no lyric effusions, no moral reflections, no prolonged similes, no great prodigality of epithet. Ozell abjures even the tags that break the continuity of the action at the end of each act in the adaptations for the stage. Nevertheless, Ozell preserves little more of the essence of Racine than the less conscientious adapters did.

Ozell's style has one characteristic which is alien to Racine's style and peculiar to Ozell among the English adapters and translators. He introduces the realistic metaphors of plebeian speech in defiance of the "style noble" of Racine and of the elevation of tone of other English adapters. To choose a few from many examples, "Britannicus le gêne" becomes "Britannicus is his Eye-Sore"; "A son épouse on donne une rivale" becomes "A Rival too is quartered on Octavia"; "Excité d'un désir curieux," "Excited by an Itch of Novelty"; "J'ignore quel projet, Burrhus, vous méditez," "I know not, Burrhus, what Designs you're

---

[1] "My purpose . . . is to present the World once a Month with a Couple of translated Tragedies sticht up together. They shall be such as are in greatest vogue in *France*, where 'tis allow'd they excel in that sort of Poem. The Reception which some of their Tragedies have met with upon our Stage, with little or no Alteration but a Language, is my Encouragement to get such of 'em put into English as are not yet done. . . ." (The English Bookseller's Advertisement.)

hatching." This trick would be enough to rob Ozell's translation of unity of tone.

In addition to this eccentricity Ozell shows the same incomprehension of Racine's rhetoric of passion that I have noted in other translators. As I have said before, when the drama is most tense Racine's dialogue often falls into short speeches with the rhythmic patterns and the pitch patterns which convey emotion in everyday speech. Displacement or omission of a single word can rob the line of all emotion or change the emotion. Ozell is particularly gauche in translating such lines. When Agrippine's suspicions of Néron's revolt are confirmed, she taxes Burrhus with encouraging Néron and trying to allay her suspicions with hypocritical reassurances. She opens her denunciation of Burrhus by quoting him ironically: "Eh! bien! je me trompois, Burrhus, dans mes soupçons?" (vs. 809). Inversion of the pronoun is enough to change the emotional tone: "Well, Burrhus, was I wrong in my Suspicions?" (p. 32)

To say, in English, "So! I was wrong in my suspicions, was I?"—and this is the meaning of the French—is to accuse an antagonist of bad faith. But, to say, instead, "Well, was I wrong in my suspicions?" is merely to say "I told you so" to an ally who has disagreed. When Néron is questioning Narcisse about Junie and Britannicus, after confessing that he loves Junie, he asks Narcisse if Britannicus loves her. Narcisse, the better to destroy Britannicus, wants Néron to have no doubt that Britannicus loves Junie. To Néron's question he replies (vss. 427-28):

Quoi! s'il l'aime,
Seigneur?

Ozell translates: "He, my Lord, love her?" (p. 22). The most natural way to speak this English question, with special emphasis on the pronouns ("*He*, my Lord, love *her*?") would make it mean: "The very idea! Of course he doesn't." Racine's lines mean just the opposite, "*Does* he *love* her, my Lord?"

I have noted how adroitly Racine throws into high relief the words that are charged with the speaker's emotion and how maladroitly his translators blur the focus of his lines. Ozell is no more skillful than his predecessors. In the venomous duel of words between Néron and Britannicus (Act III, Scene 8), when Britannicus has reminded Néron of their relative positions in the past and his (Britannicus') more legitimate claim to the throne, Néron says: "J'obéissois alors, et vous obéissez" (vs. 1042). Ozell translates the line: "I was a Subject Then as you are now" (p. 38). This line is noteworthy not because of the repetition with variation, but because all of Nero's rage is concentrated in the verb *obéissez*. Ozell's line emphasizes Nero's former position and not Britannicus' present one. An actor would have some difficulty, I suspect, in communicating Nero's threatening rage to the phrase "as you are now." In the translation of the following lines (vss. 1029-30, italics mine):

> Ce lieu le favorise, et je vous y *retiens*
> Pour lui faciliter de si *doux entretiens*.

it is Nero's irony that is weakened (p. 38):

> *I'll keep* you here, that he may *Court* the better.

Britannicus' thrusts become less deadly. His most sensational and most daring insult is in the last line of the following speech (vss. 1037-40, italics mine):

> Ils [ces lieux] ne nous ont pas vus l'un et l'autre
>   élever,
> Moi pour vous obéir, et vous pour me braver;
> Et ne s'attendoient pas, lorsqu'ils nous virent
>   naître,
> *Qu'un jour Domitius me dût parler en maître.*

The force of the line is concentrated in "Domitius" and "en maître," not only because of their position at the caesura and at the end of the line, but because no other word in the line is striking enough to arrest attention. Ozell translates: "That *Nero* e'er should check *Britannicus*" (p. 38). With the substitution of Nero for Domitius the insult disappears. The loss is to be attributed to Ozell's ignorance of Roman history, however, and not to his lack of rhetorical skill. But the verb "check" is a weak substitute for "en maître." It is further weakened by the noun complement, Britannicus, which bears stronger sentence stress but adds no force to Britannicus' defiance. When Agrippine taxes Burrhus with encouraging Nero's revolt, her last accusation is (vss. 815-16):

TWO TRANSLATIONS OF *BRITANNICUS*

>...à son épouse on donne une rivale;
>On affranchit Néron de la foi conjugale.

Her concern for Néron's "foi conjugale" is affected, for Burrhus's benefit. Alone with her confidante, she blurts out the real motive of her resentment of Néron's love for Junie (vss. 879-80):

>Quoi? tu ne vois donc pas jusqu'où l'on me ravale,
>Albine? C'est à *moi* qu'on donne une *rivale*.

The banal and colorless "donne" contributes to the effect. All the force of the line is concentrated in "moi" and "rivale." Ozell focuses attention on the verb by introducing one of his realistic metaphors: " 'Tis me they mean to saddle with a Rival." (p. 34)

Ozell is apparently baffled again and again by French words which denote moral characteristics or emotional states. When Narcisse is inciting Néron against Agrippine and against Pallas, he says: "Pallas, dont vous savez qu'elle soutient *l'audace*" (vs. 495). Ozell translates: "Pallas, whose only *Prop* she's known to be" (p. 24). The hint that Pallas is a bold and dangerous rebel against Néron is lost and the emphasis placed on the idea in "soutient." Néron, inquiring about his mother's reaction to his decree of exile for Pallas, says (vss. 761-62):

>Et de quel oeil
>Ma mère a-t-elle vu confondre son orgueil?

The word *orgueil* reveals Néron's intent in exiling Pallas and his conflict with his mother. Ozell translates: "How look'd my Mother at her *Favorite's Fall*?" (p. 31)

Note the following examples of Ozell's rejection of words with a psychological content (vss. 799, 927, 957-58, 506, 663, 695, 353; pp. 32, 35, 36, 24, 28, 29, 20):

>NÉRON. Je *souffre* trop éloigné de Junie.
>NÉRO. *'Tis Death* to be thus long from Junie.
>
>BRIT. Ne m'as tu pas *flatté* d'une *fausse* espérance?
>BRIT. Hast thou not *swell'd* me with *aerial* Hopes?
>
>JUNIE. Retirez-vous seigneur, et fuyez un *courroux*
> Que ma persévérance allume contre vous.
>JUNIA. Retire, my Lord, and shun the *lowring Storm*
> Which Junia's Steadiness has raised against ye.

NÉRON. Mon génie *étonné tremble* devant le sien.
NÉRO. My Genius trembling *bows the Head* to hers.

JUNIE. Ah! Seigneur, vos vertus m'ont toujours *ràssurée*.
JUNIA. My Lord, your Virtues ever were my *Anchor*.

BRIT. Mais, parmi ce plaisir, quel *chagrin* me *dévore*!
BRIT. But, ah! I feel a secret *Damp*, a *Worm*
That gnaws the *Core* while all looks fair without.

BRIT. Sache si du péril ses beaux yeux *sont remis*.
BRIT. Whether her beauteous Eyes *out-ride the Storm*.

In these examples Ozell apparently uses metaphor to escape from psychological precision, though he shows a taste for visual imagery and prolonged metaphor for their own sake. This taste is illustrated in a few instances where psychological precision is not a factor. For instance (vss. 861–62, p. 35; vs. 1300, p. 45):

BURR. En adoptant Néron, Claudius par son choix,
De son fils et du vôtre a confondu les droits.
BURR. Claudius, adopting Nero, broke the Pale
That fenced his Son's prerogative from yours.

NÉRON. Avec Britannicus je me réconcilie.
NERO. As for *Britannicu*s
A perfect Reconcilement shall re-tie
The knots of Friendship and ev'n strain 'em closer.

There can be no doubt, however, that Ozell fails to grasp the psychological implications of Racine's dialogue. This becomes obvious when he simply mistranslates. Sometimes mistranslation of a single word betrays incomprehension of Racinian psychology and a lack of dramatic imagination. For instance, when Junie is trying to calm Néron's rage against Britannicus, she says: "C'est votre frère. Hélas! c'est un *amant jaloux*" (vs. 1070). Ozell translates this line: "Consider he's your Brother and a *Rival*" (p. 39). The word *rival* might well aggravate Nero's fury rather than soothe it. When Narcisse is trying to inflame Néron's jealousy, he attempts to evoke in Néron's mind an image that will infuriate him and haunt him (vss. 435–42):

NÉRON. Que dis-tu? Sur son coeur il auroit quelque empire?
NAR. Je ne sais. Mais, seigneur, ce que je puis vous dire,
Je l'ai vu quelquefois s'arracher de ces lieux,

TWO TRANSLATIONS OF *BRITANNICUS*

> Le coeur plein d'un courroux qu'il cachoit à vos yeux;
> D'une cour qui le fuit pleurant l'ingratitude,
> Las de votre grandeur et de sa servitude,
> Entre l'impatience et la crainte flottant,
> Il alloit voir Junie, et revenoit *content*.

By mistranslating one word, Ozell destroys the whole effect of the picture painted by Narcissus (p. 22, italics mine):

> NERO. How? has he any Empire o'er her Heart?
> NAR. I know not. But, my Lord, this I can say,
> I've sometimes seen him flinging from the Court,
> His Breast with Anger boiling, tho' conceal'd,
> Repining at your Grandeur and his Slavery,
> Floating betwixt his Fear and his Impatience,
> Then went to wait on *Junia*, and return'd
> *Wrapt up in Thought.*

Several of the *procédés* which destroy Racine's psychological drama in Ozell's translation are illustrated in one speech of Agrippina's in Act IV, Scene 2. Ozell translates Agrippina's long narrative (vss. 1115-1222) with reasonable accuracy. During this narrative she is mindful of Burrhus's advice to refrain from upbraiding Néron and merely to justify herself. When she loses control and begins to accuse Néron, Ozell garbles the lines. Here are the two passages (vss. 1269-76, p. 44, italics mine):

> *Vous ne me trompez point, je vois tous vos détours;*
> *Vous êtes un ingrat, vous le fûtes toujours:*
> Dès vos plus jeunes ans, mes soins et mes tendresses
> N'ont arraché de vous que de *feintes caresses.*
> Rien ne vous a pu vaincre; et votre dureté
> Auroit dû dans son cours arrêter ma bonté.
> Que je suis malheureuse! Et par quelle infortune
> Faut-il que tous mes soins me rendent *importune*!

> I see your *serpentizing* wily *Turnings*;
> *Nor are my Expectations disappointed.*
> *Ingratitude was ever in your Nature.*
> Ev'n from your Infancy my Cares and Fondness
> Extorted nought from you, but *feign'd Returns.*
> Nothing could overcome that Savage Fierceness
> Which ought t' have stopt my Flow of Favours t' ye.
> Wretch that I am! by what accurst Misfortune
> Must all my Cares serve but to make me *mad*?

There is nothing to be said of "feign'd Returns" for "feintes caresses," and "mad" for "importune" except that they are unfortunate mistranslations. In the opening lines of the tirade, however, Ozell evinces a preference for certain *procédés* of his own. The tirade in Racine begins with the short sentences of an angry person. Each sentence fills a hemistich only. There are no connectives. Ozell fills in two verses without pause and ties them together with the conjunction "nor," robbing them entirely of emotional rhythm and tone. Racine's concentration on the emotion of the speaker is dissipated by the literal translation of *détours* and the introduction of the visual image in "serpentizing." The effect of this visual image is to obscure the psychological meaning of *détours*. Besides, this is no moment for Agrippina to display her descriptive vein. The line "Vous êtes un ingrat, vous le fûtes toujours" follows so closely the stress pattern and the pitch pattern into which anger would fall in everyday speech that it translates itself into English: "You're an ingrate. You always *have* been." This is prose, of course; but I cannot believe that English pentameter could not have approached the emotional pattern more closely than the stilted "Ingratitude was ever in your Nature."

Almost a century after Ozell's *Britannicus* appeared, the play was again translated into English by Sir Brooke Boothby, Bart.[2] Sir Brooke was apparently not acquainted with Ozell's version. In the long critical preface to his translation, he states his aims:

> The only pieces of Racine which remain on the English theatre, *Phèdre* and *Andromache*, are so much altered by their English dress, as scarcely to afford any idea of the *manner* of the original. I have here attempted to give him as he is, to preserve the chaste simplicity of the master. If the following is a *faithful copy, it pretends to no more*. The omission of a few love-phrases, which seemed too tender for Nero, and the restoration of a scene, which Racine, in compliance with, I think, false criticism, had been induced to leave out, are the only changes which have been made; and the former he himself appears to indicate, when he says in the preface to *Andromache*, "I confess that Pyrrhus is not sufficiently resigned to the will of his mistress, and that Celadon was a much more perfect lover; but what was to be done? Pyrrhus had never read our romances, and every hero is not made to be a Celadon." His judgment led him to censure the false taste, to which he was in some degree compelled to sacrifice.[3] [Italics mine]

[2] London, 1803.
[3] See pp. 3-4.

These words would lead us to expect, at last, a translation, not a travesty, of Racine. Let us first examine the excisions in the rôle of Nero which Boothby admits he has made. As a matter of fact I can find only one instance of the omission of a "love-phrase," if by that Boothby means the jargon of gallantry. He omits one speech in which Néron refers to "sa flamme" (vss. 567–71). But, in the same scene, he introduces the same *précieux* metaphor into a speech where Racine had not used it (vss. 636–37, p. 58):

> NÉRON. La soeur vous touche ici beaucoup moins que le frère;
> Et pour Britannicus. . . .
> NERO. Such lofty sentiments might raise suspicion
> Octavia's brother shar'd the noble flame.

Perhaps Nero is being satirical and it would be unfair to tax Boothby with preciosity. But there are two speeches of his own invention which strike me as more *précieux* than the original (vs. 799, p. 64; vs. 382, p. 52):

> NÉRON. Adieu. Je souffre trop éloigné de Junie.
> NERO. Burrhus, farewell! I go to meet my Junia,
> And when the business of my love is over,
> Affairs of state may take their turn again.

> NÉRON. Narcisse, c'en est fait, Néron est amoureux.
> NERO. Narcissus, with confusion I reveal
> The weakness that possesses all my Soul.
> 'Tis Junia reigns and Nero is subdu'd.

There are more significant changes in the rôle of Nero. Boothby drops the following line: "J'aimois jusqu'à ses pleurs [les pleurs de Junie] que je faisois couler" (vs. 402). He merely paraphrases Néron's description of how Junie's image haunted him (vss. 402–409). He cuts out also the line: "Je me fais de sa peine une image charmante"[4] (vs. 751). To some people these two lines reveal Néron as a sadist rather than a Céladon. Boothby mitigates the obsessive and the sensual quality of Néron's passion, qualities which drive him to destroy everything that frustrates his love. The translator set out to eliminate French

---

[4] He may have meant the following as a translation of the line (p. 62):
> But I will turn their love into despair.
> That pleasure still remains, nor is it little.

gallantry and succeeded only in weakening the motivation of Nero's rebellion against Agrippina and his murder of Britannicus.

Boothby has stated categorically that, except for the changes in the rôle of Nero, it is his intention to reproduce the *manner* of the original. In choosing *Britannicus* he selected a model that is not altogether typical of Racine's manner. Of the seven great secular tragedies, *Britannicus* is the only one that is strictly speaking a historical play. The color of an epoch is more important than in any of the others. It is the only one in which a protagonist is motivated solely by political ambition (Agrippine). The style, though suited to the subject, is markedly different from that of any of the other six. Rhetorical devices that Racine uses rarely if at all in his other plays appear frequently in *Britannicus*. He uses stychomythia freely in the duel of words between Néron and Britannicus in Act II, Scene 8. Throughout we find repetition with variation in perfectly symmetrical balanced Alexandrines. If force and brevity are the essential characteristics of Racine's style,[5] the force and brevity of *Britannicus* are so studied that the style is often epigrammatic and therefore undramatic since it smacks of reflection. Nevertheless there are many scenes in which the more characteristic style appears, that "négligence apparente, mais étudiée, du style, dont le contour sinueux imite en quelque sorte ce qu'il y a de plus caché dans les mouvements de la passion."[6] If the "négligence apparente" is absent in *Britannicus*, the "contour sinueux" remains.

After reading Boothby's profession of fidelity to his original and his criticism of Ambrose Philips for doing violence to Racine, I began a comparison of the English with the French *Britannicus* in excited anticipation of discovering which style the translator preferred and which one he imitated more successfully, the mannered, intellectualized style, the Cornelian element in his model, or the natural, apparently spontaneous expression of emotion, the essentially Racinian element. What was my surprise to find that Boothby had made many excisions, that much of his dialogue was not translation at all but rather loose paraphrase, and that both the Racinian and the Cornelian manners

---

[5] "Tous les mérites dramatiques du style de Racine peuvent se ramener à deux principaux, la brièveté et la force." (Georges Le Bidois, *De l'Action dans la tragédie de Racine* [Paris, 1900], p. 308.)

[6] Brunetière, *Manuel de l'Histoire de la Littérature française* (Paris, 1898), p. 193.

were replaced by a manner all Boothby's own. He does reproduce, not very successfully, some of the stychomythic dialogue of Act III, Scene 8. Some of the mannered Alexandrines he drops altogether. Among them are Racine's most audacious figures of speech, some repetition with variation, some obtrusively balanced Alexandrines. He omits (vss. 682, 747-48, 1001-1002, 690, 1042):

> J'entendrai des regards que vous croirez muets.
> Hé bien! de leur amour tu vois la violence,
> Narcisse: elle a paru jusque dans leur silence.
> De combien de soupirs interrompant le cours,
> Ai-je évité vos yeux que je cherchois toujours.
> Madame, en le voyant, songez que je vous voi.
> J'obéissois alors et vous obéissez.

Other verses of this type are altered (vs. 1528, p. 90; vs. 74, p. 41):

> Si vous craignez Néron, lui-même est-il sans crainte?
> His fears will be the pledges of his faith.

> Je le craindrois bientôt, s'il ne me craignoit plus.
> Should he once cease to fear, I, with just cause,
> Should tremble in my turn!

It would seem that Boothby tries to avoid this style. His rejection of mannered and piquant verses is apparently systematic. Nevertheless it is the typically Racinian style that suffers most. Boothby's characteristic style is one that might well have been formed by exercises in Latin prose composition which taught him to value above all else long sentences, suspensive word order, over-subordination and logical connectives. Add to this an unaccountable predilection for the passive voice and you have the mould into which he tried to force Racine's simple, natural style, which follows in its variations the flux of emotions in the mind of the speaker.

The long periods in Racine's style occur only at moments when a certain dignity and pomp are appropriate. Even Agrippine's long narrative in her interview with Néron (Act IV, Scene 2), which is impassioned enough but spoken with forced calm, contains only two long periods with suspensive word order (1123-27, 1155-58). There are 107 verses in this harangue. In the great majority, a sentence fills one Alexandrine. Some fill a hemistich only. The word order is usually direct; there is little subordination, and few connectives. Indeed, verbs serve as connectives, when there are any: "Ce n'étoit rien encore. Je fis plus," etc.[7] Here are two examples of Boothby's transformation of this style (vss. 1133-37, p. 77; vss. 1140-42, p. 77):

> Mais ce lien du sang qui nous joignoit tous deux
> Écartoit Claudius d'un lit incestueux.
> Il n'osoit épouser la fille de son frère.
> Le sénat fut séduit: une loi moins sévère
> Mit Claude dans mon lit, et Rome à mes genoux.
>
> The abject senate, with my gifts suborn'd,
> Consented to give sanction to a marriage
> Forbidden by the laws; the throne was mine.
>
> Je vous nommai son gendre, et vous donnai sa fille.
> Silanus, qui l'aimoit, s'en vit abandonné,
> Et marqua de son sang ce jour infortuné.
>
> Next I obtain'd Octavia for your wife,
> First to Silanus given; whose sudden death
> Made way for you.

Racine's style has been praised for its clarity. This clarity is achieved by many means: short sentences, direct word order, little subordination, and simple diction. But Racine's clarity is not clarity for its own sake. It is a means to an end. It enables the reader to run while he reads, and the spectator to comprehend without any effort of the intellect. This leaves him free to apprehend immediately the emotional implications of the dialogue. He is carried along in the swift flow of the lines. It is not necessary for Racine to stop the flow in order to underscore an emotion or to embroider a theme. In order to communicate the emotion immediately to the spectator Racine uses such rhetorical devices as are suitable to his end. Far and away the most important of these is interrogation. He uses it constantly but with such virtuosity that it is seldom monotonous and hardly ever oratorical. His questions are often so close to the rhythms and tones in which emotion is revealed in unreflecting natural speech that it is somewhat misleading to call it a rhetorical device. Then, too, the tones and rhythms of natural emotional speech appear elsewhere than in questions. Even the sentence structure is emotional. For instance, the short sentences themselves, as I have already pointed out, convey anger without the speaker's having to ex-

[7] See Le Bidois, *op. cit.*, p. 320.

press it. And, as I have said before, Racine's emphasis is carefully calculated to convey the emotion of the speaker. The significant words are in high relief and the attention is never diverted from them by the introduction of extraneous images and irrelevant ideas. The expressive word is, I believe, more often a verb than in the work of his English adapters, who have a predilection for epithet.

Racine has been praised or damned, according to the critic's nationality—French or English—for his psychological analysis. Analysis in this sense is an unfortunate word, for in English it implies intellectual explanation or exposition of motivation. There is no analysis of this sort in Racine. His dialogue is the fruit of subtle analysis, not of expository analysis. Much of it is rich in psychological implications but it is never cold or intellectual, to my mind at any rate. And it is apprehended emotionally with no effort of the intellect. For instance, Néron's line, "Je me fais de sa peine une image charmante" (vs. 750) is dense with psychological implications and most revealing. But it communicates an immediate *frisson*. It is evocative, not analytical. If Racine's characters do not analyze their emotions, they do define them precisely. Néron's "Je souffre trop éloigné de Junie," for instance, is more precise than the speech which Boothby substitutes for it. But it also conveys an intensity of emotion which is not found in Boothby.

All these characteristics of Racine's style are rejected by Boothby as they have been in other translations; but he seldom uses any of the rhetorical devices with which his predecessors adorn their style with the aim of elevating the tone. Indeed, you might think that Boothby did not consider it the business of the dramatist to move his audience or his readers. He almost never departs from the patterns which I have described above.

No matter how intense the speaker's emotion may be, his speech falls into the same cool, logical pattern. When, in the interview between Agrippine and Néron, Agrippine loses control and berates Néron, she says (vss. 1269–75):

> Vous ne me trompez point, je vois tous vos détours!
> Vous êtes un ingrat, vous le fûtes toujours
> Dès vos plus jeunes ans, mes soins et mes tendresses
> N'ont arraché de vous que de feintes caresses.
> Rien ne vous a pu vaincre; et votre dureté

> Auroit dû dans son cours arrêter ma bonté.
> Que je suis malheureuse!

Here is Boothby's version (p. 81):

> Your feign'd submissions never have deceiv'd me;
> Still from your infancy my fondest cares
> Have but with false caresses been return'd.
> Lives there a mother more unfortunate?

Only the most tolerant of critics would be willing to call this "translation." "Paraphrase" would, it seems to me, be a more accurate term. Indeed many of Boothby's "discours pathétiques" are mere résumés of the substance of the original. Often Boothby's conception of the substance of Racine's tirades impels him to eliminate not only the affective values of Racine's lines but the very lines which illumine in a flash the secret motivation of the characters. Agrippine's tirade in Act III, Scene 4, is a good example. Agrippine is beside herself with rage—and fear. Néron has fallen in love with Junie and has indicated that he will divorce Octavie. Agrippine has just denounced Burrhus for condoning Néron's actions. In her protestations to Burrhus she has been forced to conceal her real motives. She has pretended that her objection to Néron's love for Junie is based on indignation at his plan to repudiate Octavie, his violation of his "foi conjugale." The necessity of hiding behind such a pretext has added a feeling of frustration to her anger and fear. After Burrhus's exit, the well-meaning confidante tries to calm Agrippine's rage. But the argument she chooses for this purpose is just the one best calculated to aggravate Agrippine's frustration. The confidante interprets Agrippine's interference in Néron's love affairs as excessive concern for Britannicus and Junie. She does not see in Néron's passion for Junie a threat to Agrippine's hold on Néron. Impatience at this blindness sweeps away the last vestige of control and caution in Agrippine and provokes her sensational self-revelation. Here is Racine's dialogue (vss. 874-94):

> AGRIP. Ah! lui-même à mes yeux puisse-t-il se montrer!
> ALB. Madame, au nom des dieux, cachez votre colère.
> Quoi! pour les intérêts de la soeur ou du frère,
> Faut-il sacrifier le repos de vos jours?
> Contraindrez-vous César jusque dans ses amours?
> AGRIP. Quoi! tu ne vois donc pas jusqu'où l'on me ravale,
> Albine? C'est à moi qu'on donne une rivale.

TWO TRANSLATIONS OF *BRITANNICUS*

> Bientôt, si je ne romps ce funeste lien,
> Ma place est occupée, et je ne suis plus rien.
> Jusqu'ici d'un vain titre Octavie honorée,
> Inutile à la cour, en étoit ignorée.
> Les grâces, les honneurs par moi seule versés,
> M'attiroient des mortels les vœux intéressés.
> Une autre de César a surpris la tendresse:
> Elle aura le pouvoir d'épouse et de maîtresse.
> Le fruit de tant de soins, la pompe des Césars,
> Tout deviendra le prix d'un seul de ses regards.
> Que dis-je? l'on m'évite, et déjà délaissée . . .
> Ah! je ne puis, Albine, en souffrir la pensée.
> Quand je devrois du ciel hâter l'arrêt fatal,
> Néron, l'ingrat Néron . . . Mais voici son rival.

This dialogue is from one of those protagonist-confidant scenes which have been censured by some French and many foreign critics. The confidant or confidante, they say, is a utility character, a mechanical device to enable the protagonist to inform the audience of his or her secret thoughts. Even the most hostile of critics would have to admit that here Racine masks a mechanical device very skillfully. The scene is highly dramatic. This is no calm confession made to a bosom friend; it is an involuntary self-betrayal occurring at a moment when violent emotion has swept away all control. Such sudden unveiling of secret motives is a psychological *coup de théâtre*. Here is Boothby's version (pp. 67–68):

> CURIA. Why, for *Britannicus* or *Junia*,
>   Are you to sacrifice your own repose
>   Or interfere with *Nero* in his love?
> AGRIP. See'st thou not then this blow is aim'd at me?
>   To break this fatal marriage should I fail,
>   My place, my name, my power are lost for ever.
>   *Octavia*, honored with an empty title,
>   Takes no concern in the affairs of state.
>   . . . .
>   Should *Junia* reign, won by her youthful charms,
>   *Nero* will lay the empire at her feet;
>   And *Agrippina* from that hour is nothing.
>   The thought alone is not to be endur'd.

Boothby's stylistic changes rob Agrippine's tirade of emotion; his excisions eliminate the psychological revelation. First he fails to see that the word "donc" has an emotional value in Agrippine's impatient protest against her confidante's blindness. This word could only be rendered by intonation in English ("Can't you *see* . . . ?"). Boothby translates it with the cool argumentative "then." The verb *ravale* is a tragic "mot de caractère." It is replaced by the banal metaphor, "this blow is aim'd at me." The impassioned "C'est à moi qu'on donne une rivale," with its psychological revelation, disappears altogether. The words

> Should *Junia* reign, won by her youthful charms,
> *Nero* will lay the empire at her feet;
> And *Agrippina* from that hour is nothing

are a tame substitute for

> Une autre de Néron a surpris la tendresse
> Elle aura le pouvoir d'épouse et de maîtresse.

Finally Boothby greatly weakens the last lines by omitting "l'on m'évite, et déjà délaissée . . ." and by changing "je ne puis, Albine, en souffrir la pensée" to the passive voice, "the thought alone is not to be endur'd."

Agrippina's was the rôle which most appealed to Boothby.[8] If he mutilates her tirades in this fashion we can hardly expect him to do justice to the scenes between Britannicus and Junie, for he had the usual English contempt for French gallantry. As might be expected, he makes more drastic excisions there. He omits Britannicus' agonizing doubts of Junie, expressed in characteristic questions (vss. 736-41). His Nero, then, did not witness Britannicus' anguish and cannot say, "Je l'ai *vu* douter du coeur de son amante" or "Je me fais de sa peine une image charmante." Boothby reduces to a five-line summary Junie's plea to Britannicus to believe her, her description of her suffering during the interview which Néron had watched (vss. 998-1019). In the last scene between the young lovers, he cuts out entirely the bit of dialogue which Ozell had garbled ("Vous m'aimez? Hélas! Si je vous aime!). He omits all of Junie's fearsome suppositions (vss. 1541-47), retaining only her presentiment of disaster.

Considering the English love for villains, it is surprising that Narcisse did not inspire Boothby to more effective translation than we find in the scenes where he appears. Boothby is no more dramatic in Narcisse's two big scenes than elsewhere. In the first of these scenes he employs

---

[8] See his Preface, p. 23, note.

his usual method of résumé. The series of poisonous insinuations with which Racine's villain goads Néron into an ominous fury of jealousy —his astonishment that Néron should doubt for a moment that Britannicus is in love with Junie, his insistence in the face of Néron's reluctance to believe it, his tantalizing hint that Junie perhaps returns Britannicus' love, and finally the image that he plants in Néron's mind to haunt him, the picture of a wretched Britannicus fleeing from Néron's palace to seek comfort with Junie and returning content—all this Boothby's Narcissus delivers in one dose, thus (p. 53):

NERO.   But say, Narcissus
    Think'st thou the boy Britannicus her lover?
NAR. Oh yes, with all the fervour of his years,
    Tender, submissive to her least desires,
    He shares her griefs, and softens all her pains.
    Stung with some mark of insolent neglect,
    When anger unconceal'd has fired his breast,
    Soon, by her side, his passion sooth'd to peace,
    He has return'd with pleasure in his eyes.
    Her inexperienc'd heart, I fear, is his.

Narcisse's last big scene, on the other hand, is one of the few that are translated, not merely paraphrased. A detailed analysis should show how close Boothby was able to come to his model. Burrhus has persuaded Néron to give up Junie and to seek a reconciliation with Britannicus. In a few words, carefully chosen and deftly arranged, Racine's villain undoes all that Burrhus had accomplished by his impassioned plea. When Néron reveals his change of heart, Narcisse begins goading him. In every line he speaks, his own comment is in the overtones. Having failed to persuade Néron to pursue his plan for poisoning Britannicus, he tries to inflame his jealousy (vss. 1410-11):

    Et l'hymen de Junie en est-il le lien?
    Seigneur, lui faites-vous encor ce sacrifice?

Narcisse's amazement at the abjectness of Néron's surrender is implicit in the questioning "Seigneur" placed at the beginning of the line, and in the word "encor." Both disappear in Boothby's translation (p. 86):

    And Junia is the cement of your friendship;
    You are no doubt to make that sacrifice.

If Boothby intended to inject Narcissus' comment into these lines, I cannot divine what it is. It is certainly not feigned amazement at Nero's abject surrender. Racine's Néron is stung by Narcisse's implied criticism. He tries to cut off the discussion (vss. 1412-13):

> C'est prendre trop de soin. Quoi qu'il en soit, Narcisse,
> Je ne le compte plus parmi mes ennemis.

Narcisse tries another tack. He is resigned, but he is chagrined that Néron has played into his mother's hands (vss. 1414-15):

> Agrippine, Seigneur, se l'étoit bien promis.
> Elle a repris sur vous son souverain empire.

The emotional tone is set by the word "bien." The sting for Néron is made more venomous by "souverain." Boothby translates (p. 86):

> It seems then Agrippina knew her strength,
> And has again resum'd her boasted empire.

Bien, like *donc*, is a word that can be rendered in English only by intonation. "Agrippina knew her strength" is not a bad translation and could be spoken with the proper tone. The proper intonation is no longer possible when it is introduced by "It seems *then*." By replacing the telling *souverain* with "boasted," Boothby thoughtlessly anticipates Narcisse's next thrust and removes the emphasis from the idea in "souverain empire," i.e., Néron's complete subjection. Racine's Narcisse had hinted vaguely in his first remark ("Agrippine, Seigneur, se l'étoit bien promis") that Agrippine had been counting on just that; but he reserves the revelation of her boasts for his next thrust. Néron is angry and curious: "Quoi donc? Qu'a-t-elle dit? et que voulez-vous dire?" (vs. 1416). This is what Narcisse had been building up to. He can now be explicit in response to a command from Néron. He delivers two thrusts in succession in his next speech: Agrippine has *boasted*; Agrippine has boasted *publicly*: "Elle s'en est vantée assez publiquement" (vs. 1417). Boothby telescopes the two ideas and ends his verse lamely with a superfluous verb in the passive voice: "Her public vauntings have not been restrain'd" (p. 86). When Néron insists that Narcisse be still more explicit, Narcisse delivers his masterly *coup de grâce* (vss. 1418-22):

> Qu'elle n'avoit qu'à vous voir un moment;
> Qu'à tout ce grand éclat, à ce courroux funeste,
> On verroit succéder un silence modeste;

TWO TRANSLATIONS OF *BRITANNICUS*

> Que vous-même à la paix souscririez le premier,
> Heureux que sa bonté daignât tout oublier.

His work is done and Britannicus' doom is sealed. In his report of the facts Narcisse contrives to sketch a picture of Agrippine as she utters her boasts. She not only boasts of her power over her son; she expresses her contempt for him, depicting the emperor as an ineffectual and childish creature who storms and rages when safely out of ear-shot but who, at a word from her, is reduced to shamefaced submission. Her contemptuous and satirical tone (as Narcisse imagines it and doubtless imitates it) are conveyed in *tout ce* modifying *grand éclat*, and the repetition of *ce* with "courroux funeste." The pompous and tragic words *courroux funeste* are themselves used mockingly, and, placed at the end of the verse, they prepare for the anticlimax of *silence modeste* which balances them in the next line. Not one of these effects is preserved in Boothby's translation (p. 86):

> That she should but see you for a moment
> Reduc'd to modest silence in her presence,
> Your angry menaces would all subside.
> Yourself would be the first to sue for peace,
> Too happy if she deign'd to pardon you.

The two pictures which Narcisse sketches—Agrippine's boasting in a mocking, satirical tone, and her own caricature of Néron—these two pictures disappear altogether. Boothby's lines could be spoken, perhaps, with Narcissus' comment in the overtones. Racine's lines may be said to dictate the innuendo to the actor. Boothby's hardly suggest it; but an actor could impose it on the lines. Not even that is possible in some of the other speeches. With Narcissus' innuendo gone the spectacle of Nero's reaction must go too. Boothby has come very near to spoiling completely what was in Racine an exciting psychological peripety.

Throughout the play what Boothby eliminates is nothing less than the action itself. His version is for the most part a summary in rather prosaic verse of Racine's tragedy. Except for the numerous excisions, the substance of what the personages actually say is preserved, but what they feel is eliminated almost entirely, for the manner in which they say it is seldom reproduced. I think it may be said that in general Boothby imposes a narrative style on Racine's dramatic dialogue. It is not, however, the narrative style of an art-form like the epic. It is that of an *argumentum*.

It is obvious that Boothby's version of *Britannicus* is much farther from the original than *The Distrest Mother* from *Andromaque*. Yet, in making his translation, he was impelled by a desire to give the English public a more faithful copy of Racine than Ambrose Philips had done. How can we account for his distortion of his model in the face of his professed intention of reproducing the "manner" of the original, and of preserving the "chaste simplicity of the master"? The two paragraphs following the statement of his aims throw considerable light on what he meant by the "manner" of the original and the "chaste simplicity" of the master. He says:

> That so chaste and simple a tragedy as the Britannicus of Racine should be received on the English stage, is less than ever to be expected; to succeed at present, a piece must comprise, in one incoherent jumble, every manner at once, except that which is simple and natural—tragedy, farce, opera, pantomime, without sense, or feeling, or conduct, or interest. (p. 4)

In the next paragraph he continues:

> To have given this tragedy some better chance for a temporary success, might not perhaps have been difficult; but the alteration, like those of Philips and Smith, would neither have been of a piece with the rest, nor have been Racine. The banquet of Nero, the death of Britannicus, Junia embracing the statue of Augustus, and borne by the people to the temple of Vesta, the stabbing of Narcissus on the way and her reception into the vestal choir, would, for example, have furnished a fifth act with plenty of bustle and show. The giant arm of Shakespeare might have played with such machinery, but the severe Greek manner would have been no more. (p. 5)

To reproduce Racine's manner, then, he had only to avoid a mélange of genres and to refrain from sensationalism in the last act. What of Racine's psychological drama which his excisions and his undramatic style have eliminated everywhere? He had no reason not to attempt to reproduce it. He was not writing with one eye on Racine and the other on an English audience. His purpose was to acquaint the English with Racine as he is. Why then did he eliminate Racine's psychological drama? There can be only one answer. He simply did not see it. Therefore, he did not realize that to alter the style as he did was to destroy the drama. Nearly a century before, another translator of the same play, with substantially the same aim but by different methods, had destroyed the same essential characteristics of Racine's dialogue. In discussing the adaptations for the stage I have hesitated to attribute loss of psychological drama entirely to incomprehension of Racine. I could not ignore the possibility of canny alteration to suit English taste. Would not the failure of two disinterested translators, separated by nearly a century, tip the balance in favor of incomprehension as the explanation of the loss of Racinian psychology in one adaptation after another?

« « II » »

RACINE AND ENGLISH CLASSICISM

CHAPTER XI

NEO-CLASSICAL THEORY OF TRAGEDY IN ENGLAND
1674–1699

EXCEPT FOR the unimportant translation of *Andromaque* and Otway's *Titus and Berenice*, at the very beginning of Aristotelian formalism in England, there were no translations or adaptations of Racine made during the ascendancy of Thomas Rymer in English criticism. The trends of criticism in this period are important, however, because of the light they throw on the methods of English adapters of Racine during the early years of the eighteenth century. It has been pointed out that the English theory of tragedy which developed during the last quarter of the seventeenth century is based largely on Aristotle as interpreted by French critics.[1] This fact naturally suggests the question: Why is it that the impact of French classical doctrine on English criticism did not lead to an understanding and appreciation of Racine which might have prevented adapters from presenting as classical tragedies their travesties of Racine? I propose to examine English classical theory with a view to answering this question.

Aristotelian formalism was introduced into England by Thomas Rymer, whose translation of Rapin's *Réflexions sur la Poétique d'Aristote* appeared in 1674. Certain remarks of Rapin were destined to become commonplaces of English criticism, notably his comments on the French genius as compared with the English and the French language as compared with the English. The high points of Rapin's comparison are:

[1] *Critical Essays of the Seventeenth Century*, ed. J. E. Spingarn (Oxford, 1908), Introduction; George Burwell Dutton, "The French Aristotelian Formalists and Thomas Rymer," *Publications of the Modern Language Association*, XXIX (1914), 152–88; Baxter Hathaway, "John Dryden and the Function of Tragedy," *Publications of the Modern Language Association*, LVIII (1943), 665–73; John C. Sherwood, "Dryden and the Rules: The Preface to *Troilus and Cressida*," *Comparative Literature*, II (1950), 73–83.

RACINE AND ENGLISH CLASSICISM

The *English* have more of *Genius* for *Tragedy* than other People, as well by the Spirit of their Nation which delights in Cruelty, as also by the Character of their Language which is proper for great Expressions.[2]

We may flatter ourselves with our Wit, and the *Genius* of our (the *French*) Nation; but our *Soul* is not enough exalted to frame great *Ideas*, we are busied with petty *Subjects*, and by that means it is that we prove so Cold in the Great; and that in our Works scarce appears any shadow of that sublime *Poesie*, of which the Ancient Poets have left such *excellent Models*, and above all *Homer* and *Virgil*; for *great Poetry* must be animated and sustained by *great Thoughts* and *great Sentiments*; but these we ordinarily want, either because our Wit is too much limited, or because we take not care to exercise on *important Matters*.[3]

Of love as a subject for tragedy, Rapin says:

The genius of our (the *French*) Nation is not strong enough to sustain an *Action* on the *Theatre* by moving only *Terror* and *Pity*. These are *Machines* that will not play as they ought, but by great *Thoughts* and noble *Expressions*, of which we are not indeed altogether as capable as the *Greeks*. Perhaps our Nation which is naturally *Gallant*, has been oblig'd by the necessity of our *Character* to form for our selves a *New System* of *Tragedy* to suit with our *Humour*.[4]

He admits, somewhat reluctantly, that the French are justified in admitting love as a subject because "... the Passions represented become deform'd and insipid unless they are founded on *Sentiments* conformable to those of the *Spectator*."[5] Nevertheless he thinks that "... 'tis to degrade *Tragedy* from that *Majesty* which is proper to it, to mingle in it *Love*, which is of a Character always *Light*. ... For *Love* is of a Character that always degenerates from that *Heroic Air*, of which *Tragedy* must never divest it self. And nothing to me shews so mean and sensless, as for one to amuse himself with *Whining* about frivolous *Kindnesses*, when he may be *Admirable* by *Great* and *Noble Thoughts*, and *Sublime Expressions*."[6] He believes that "... these *Tragedies mixed* with *Gallantries*, never make such admirable Impressions on the Spirit, as did those of *Sophocles* and *Euripides*."[7]

While recommending highly figurative language, Rapin distinguishes

---

[2] *The Whole Critical Works of Monsieur Rapin* (London, 1706), II, 217-18.
[3] *Ibid.*, p. 162.
[4] *Ibid.*, pp. 209-10.
[5] *Ibid.*, p. 210.
[6] *Ibid.*, p. 211.
[7] *Ibid.*

between the true and the false sublime. Of the false sublime, he says: "For this haughty and pompous kind of Speech becomes Vain and Cold, if not supported with great Thoughts, and the great Words that are indiscreetly affected to heighten the Discourse, for the most part only make a Noise."[8] But he thinks contemporary French writers go too far in the other direction:

Of late some have fallen into another Extremity, by a too scrupulous Care of *Purity of Language*: they have begun to take from *Poesie* all its *Nerves* [this word is Rymer's translation of the French word "force"], and all its *Majesty*, by a too *timorous* Reservedness, and *false Modesty*, which some thought to make the *Character* of the *French* Tongue by Robbing it of all those *wise and judicious Boldnesses* that *Poesie* demands; they would Retrench, without Reason, the use of *Metaphors*, and of all those *Figures* that give Life and Lustre to the *Expressions*; and study to confine all the Excellency of this admirable Art within the Bounds of a *pure* and *corrected* Discourse, without exposing it to the Danger of any high and bold Flight.[9]

All these ideas, simplified and sometimes distorted, appear in Rymer's preface and in his two essays on English tragedy. Of French tragedy, Rymer says: "*Rapin* tells us, for his own *Countrey-men*, that none of them had writ a good *Tragedy*, nor was ever like to write one."[10] "But I have elsewhere declar'd my opinion, that the *English* want neither *genius* nor *language* for so great a work."[11] Rapin's remarks on the style of contemporary French poets probably inspired the following comment on the French language: ". . . their language it self wants strength and sinews, is too feeble for the Weight and Majesty of Tragedy. We see their Consonants spread on Paper, but they stick in the Hedge; they pass not the Teeth in their Pronunciation."[12] Rapin had protested against a stylistic trend which was banishing imagery from French poetry and which "some thought to make the Character of the French Tongue." According to Rymer, the weakness of the French language is an irremediable one: a dearth of consonant sounds.

Rymer again echoes Rapin in his comments on love as a subject of

[8] *Ibid.*, pp. 166–67.
[9] *Ibid.*, pp. 168–69.
[10] Thomas Rymer, *The Tragedies of the Last Age Consider'd* (London, 1678), p. 10.
[11] *Ibid.*, p. 11.
[12] Thomas Rymer, *A Short View of Tragedy* (London, 1693), p. 64.

tragedy: "Nor did their Love come whining on the Stage to effeminate the Majesty of their [the Greek] Tragedy."[13]

In the preface to his translation, Rymer had said of Rapin: "The author of the *Reflections* is as well known to the *Criticks*, as *Aristotle* to the *Philosophers*."[14] Rapin's reputation endured in England for at least half a century.[15] His comparison of the English genius with the

[13] *Ibid.*, p 62.
[14] *Op. cit.*, II, 111.
[15] "The *Poet* and *Critick* were seldom as Conspicuous and Illustrious in one man as in him [Dryden] except Rapin." ("A Short History of Criticism," in *Essays of John Dryden*, ed. W. P. Ker [Oxford, 1926], II, 314.)

Dryden thought that were all other critics lost Rapin alone would suffice to teach anew the rules of writing. ("The Author's Apology for Heroique Poetry and Poetique Licence," prefixed to *The State of Innocence and the Fall of Man*, in *Works*, ed. Scott-Saintsbury, V, 115.)

Langbaine thought that if Shakespeare's plots were more irregular than Dryden's it was because Shakespeare had not read Aristotle or Rapin. ("Essay on Dryden," in Spingarn, *op. cit.*, III, 119.)

"Rapin, Dacier, and Bossu, those great masters among the French." (Sir Richard Blackmore, "Preface to Prince Arthur" [1695], in Spingarn, *op. cit.*, III, 240.)

Congreve quotes Rapin to support his argument for nobles as characters in comedy. (*Amendments of Mr. Collier's False and Imperfect Citations* [London, 1698], p. 82.)

Collier cites Rapin to support his theory of the moral end of poetry. (*A Short View of the Immorality and Profaneness of the English Stage* [London, 1698], p. 157.)

Oldmixon mentions favorably Aristotle, Horace, Boileau, Dacier, and Rapin. (*Essay on Criticism* [4th ed., London, 1728], p. 2.)

"Rapin, Saint-Evremont, and Rymer are candid, judicious, and learned critics." (*The English Theophrastus* [1702], quoted by Spingarn, *op. cit.*, I, lxxix.)

John Dennis quotes Rapin at length to combat Addison on the subject of simplicity of style. In Rapin he finds support for his contention that poetry demands figurative language. (*The Critical Works of John Dennis*, ed. E. N. Hooker, II, 35.)

Rebels against the rules bear witness to Rapin's influence by naming him among the French critics who have enslaved English neo-classicists. Robert Wolsey accuses Mulgrave of picking up "scraps of Bossu, Rapin and Boileau." ("Preface to *Valentinian*," in Spingarn, *op. cit.*, III, 11.)

Farquhar describes the methods of the classicists: "Heinsius, Hedelin, Rapin, with some half a Dozen more, are thumb'd and toss'd about, to teach the Gentlemen forsooth, to write a Comedy." ("Discourse upon Comedy," in *Critical Essays of the Eighteenth Century*, ed. W. H. Durham [New Haven, 1915], p. 260.)

Addison describes the neo-classical critic: "He has formed his Judgment upon *Homer*, *Horace*, and *Virgil*, not from their own Works, but from those of Rapin

NEO-CLASSICAL THEORY OF TRAGEDY

French was repeated with some variations by one English critic after another. His criticism of love as a subject of tragedy became a tenet of English neo-classicism, though playwrights for the most part ignored it. Critics of various shades of opinion accepted with the greatest self-complacency and with complete linguistic naïveté the notion of the superior endowments of the English for tragedy and the great superiority of the English language over the French as a medium for tragedy. Some thought the English had already surpassed the ancients; others believed they had only to submit to the rules in order to do so. It never occurred to anyone that a French dramatist ever had produced or ever could produce a tragedy to equal the English. The following pronouncement is typical:

Rapin, in his *Reflexions on Poetry,* owns, that Tragedy seems to be our Talent, but gives those reasons for't, that discover plainly, he knew little of our Language or Genius, which one may venture to affirm are much more adapted to the sublime than the *French,* and the Pathetick of our Tragedies, where the passions have been well mov'd, is much above what they can boast of. Yet 'tis not Terrour only in which we excel 'em, and we are not too hard for them there, because, as he insinuates, we *are Insularies, and a people fond of Slaughter and Cruelty* but from the greatness of our Minds and the excellence of our Reason.[16]

---

and Bossu." His comic neo-classical critic, Sir Timothy Tittle, tells the frivolous young lady who laughed at an irregular comedy that there are such people in the world as Rapin and Dacier who should have checked her unseemly mirth. (*Tatler,* No. 165.)

James Ralph refers scornfully to critics who are "displeased with every thing that will not stand the test of Aristotle and Rapin." (*The Taste of the Town* [London, 1731], p. 13.)

[16] John Oldmixon, *Reflections on the Stage* (London, 1699), p. 176. This attitude persisted to the end of the eighteenth century. Dryden thinks the English have a "stronger genius" for writing than the French. ("Heads of an Answer to Rymer," in *Dramatic Essays of the Neoclassic Age,* ed. Adams and Hathaway [New York, 1950], p. 157.) The Earl of Roscommon believes the French language incapable of succinctness, the English being immeasurably superior in that respect. ("An Essay on Translated Verse" [1684], in Spingarn, *op. cit.,* II, 298.) Sir William Temple says he has conversed with men of other nations, but has nowhere observed so much true genius as among the English. ("Of Poetry," in Spingarn, *op. cit.,* III, 105.)

Dryden says: "Our authors as far surpass them in genius, as our soldiers excel theirs in courage." ("Dedication of the *Examen Poeticum*" [1693], in Ker, *op. cit.,* II, 7.) Because of the taste of English audiences, Dryden thinks, English writers take too much license with the "mechanic rules" of the ancients. "But

RACINE AND ENGLISH CLASSICISM

In exalting Rapin above other French critics, Rymer launched the reputation of a critic who was in some respects not representative of French classical doctrine of his own generation. Rapin's praise of the English language and the English genius for tragedy is unique in French criticism of his generation. In his ideas of poetic diction he is opposed to contemporary trends in French criticism. Ferdinand Brunot devotes a chapter of his *Histoire de la langue française* to an analysis of the war on imagery conducted by French critics and rhetoricians in the second half of the seventeenth century. The typical attitude he summarizes thus:

> C'est qu'à cette époque les théoriciens, grammariens ou critiques, sont hostiles non à l'abus des images, mais aux images mêmes. . . . Elles sont non pas une forme supérieure de l'expression, mais un pis aller, par lequel on

---

if our audience had their [the French] taste, our poets could more easily comply with them than the French writers could come up to the sublimity of our thoughts or to the difficult variety of our designs." (*Loc. cit.*) The French language, he thinks, is "not strung with sinews, like our English; it has the nimbleness of a greyhound, but not the bulk and body of a mastiff." ("Dedication of the *Aeneis*" [1697], in *ibid.*, II, 218.) In 1697, Dryden praised French criticism and damned French poetry: ". . . impartially speaking, the French are as much better critics than the English, as they are worse poets." (*Ibid.*, p. 179.)

William Wotton thinks the "French Language wants strength to temper and support its Smoothness for the nobler Parts of Poesie." He draws a highly interesting conclusion from this supposed weakness of the French language. Because of the weakness of their language the French critics "are always setting Rules, and telling Men what must be done and what omitted if they would be Poets. . . . They are too fond of their language to admit where the Fault lies; and therefore the chief thing they tell us is that Sence, Connexion, and Method are the principal Things to be minded." ("Antient and Modern Learning" [1694], in Spingarn, *op. cit.*, III, 222.)

John Dennis's attitude toward rules is the opposite of Wotton's, but he agrees on the subject of the French and English languages. According to him, English writers have "naturally more Elevation" and "both our Writers and Language more Force; we want only Art, to make ourselves as superior to them in Poetry, as we formerly were in Empire." ("Advancement and Reformation of Poetry" [1701], *op. cit.*, I, 206.) Like Rymer, he apparently attributes the "force" of the English language to the abundance of consonants. (*Ibid.*, I, 389.)

For the persistence in the eighteenth century of the English belief in the superiority of their genius and their language to the French, see Henry Felton, *A Dissertation upon Reading the Classics* (2d ed., London, 1715), pp. 264-65, 267-68; Joseph Trapp, *Lectures on Poetry* (London, 1742), pp. 326-27, 298; William Guthrie, *An Essay upon English Tragedy* (London, n.d.), pp. 4-5; the Earl of Orrery, *The Greek Theatre of Father Brumoy* (London, 1759), I, ii.

remplace des phrases simples qui manquent. Ecoutons Bouhours: "Elle [la langue française] ne s'en sert que quand elle ne peut s'en passer."[17]

The passage from Rapin which inspired or lent authority to the many English strictures on the French language is cited by Brunot as among the earliest protests against this attitude.[18] Rapin differs from theorists of the drama too on one important point: he makes no distinction between epic and dramatic styles.

A theory of a style peculiarly suited to the dramatic genre had been propounded at length by La Mesnardière.[19] He had in mind two conditions of dramatic poetry which necessitate a style different from that of epic poetry: (1) Dramatic poetry is heard, not read, and consequently the significance of the dialogue must be immediately apprehended by the spectator, who cannot ponder, reflect, or reread in order to understand; (2) the characters of the play are speaking, not the poet himself. These two conditions demand two qualities of style: (1) It must be clear; (2) it must be appropriate to the personage speaking and the circumstances under which he speaks. "Il faut écrire," says La Mesnardière, "de sorte que personne n'ait le pouuoir de ne les [nos écrits] entendre pas."[20] The poet should remember that "l'on n'entreprend pas d'écrire pour *trauailler* les Auditeurs; mais que l'on tasche à les instruire et que l'on veut les diuertir."[21] The personages of tragedy are moved by violent passions, and violent passion does not express itself in eloquent or recherché diction. "I'aimerai bien mieux que Niobe exprime son désespoir par vne effusion de larmes, & par vne stupidité qui marquent son abattement, que si elle rompt le silence pour déployer vn tas de Fleurs, de Pointes & d'Antithèses."[22] The tragic poet "doit éuiter ainsi qu'un chant de Sirénes, la sublimité des pensées, le pompeux éclat des parolles, & l'agencement du Discours."[23] La Mesnardière thinks that the worst faults of diction in tragedy spring from a confusion of the dramatic with the epic genre. Tragic poets make their characters speak like epic poets. They introduce into the dialogue the flowery descriptions of

---

[17] *Histoire de la langue française* (Paris, 1913), Bk. IV, Part I, pp. 553-54.
[18] *Ibid.*, p. 565.
[19] Jules de la Mesnardière, *La Poëtique* (Paris, 1640).
[20] *Ibid.*, p. 395.
[21] *Loc. cit.*
[22] *Ibid.*, p. 386.
[23] *Ibid.*, p. 364.

heroic poetry.²⁴ He censures Euripides for having the bad taste to "mesler parmi les sanglots des pensées qui les démentent: Comme lors qu'il lui arriue d'étaller des *Moralitez* parmi les soupirs & les plaintes lors qu'à peine la douleur lui doit permettre de parler."²⁵ Euripides is guilty of "cet étrange vice de vouloir estre élevé en tous les endroits."²⁶ Seneca is condemned for "sentences mal placées" and for "descriptions vicieuses."²⁷ Gratuitous descriptions are objectionable in all genres but particularly so in "la poésie théâtrale," where superfluities are even more offensive than in other genres.²⁸ Similes are particularly unsuited to the tragic genre, characterized as it is by "les mouuemens rapides," for it requires tranquillity of mind and clarity of judgment to make a beautiful comparison.²⁹ Tropes and figures are unsuitable to oratory if they occur too frequently but more unsuitable to the tragic genre than any other, since the greatest beauties of tragedy "consistent dans les Actions & dans les Passions violentes."³⁰

La Mesnardière recommends the elimination from tragic dialogue of simile, sententiae, and descriptive passages. For him the chief beauty of dramatic dialogue is the *oratio morata* to which he gives the name of *oraison agissante*. In the *oraison agissante*, "il faut que les desseins de la Personne paroissent dans ce qu'elle dit mais comme au trauers d'vn voile, & non pas à découuert."³¹ He implies here, and his examples make it clear, that he considers dialogue most dramatic when the speaker betrays to his interlocutor or to the spectator or to both feelings which he intends to conceal or of which he may not himself be aware. When he does not express or describe his feelings but unintentionally reveals them, his speech becomes a "Discours expressif des Moeurs secrettes."³² La Mesnardière commends this "discours agissant" as one of the greatest, possibly the greatest, beauty of "la Poésie de Theatre."³³ The poet should use the *discours agissant* frequently for

---

[24] *Ibid.*, p. 392.
[25] *Ibid.*, p. 378.
[26] *Ibid.*, p. 386.
[27] *Ibid.*, p. 338.
[28] *Ibid.*, pp. 338–41.
[29] *Ibid.*, p. 390.
[30] *Ibid.*, p. 360.
[31] *Ibid.*, p. 131.
[32] *Loc. cit.*
[33] *Ibid.*, p. 135.

". . . non seulement il fait voir que le Poëte est fort sçauant en l'Art d'imiter la Nature & les diuers mouuemens de toutes sortes de personnes, mais il oblige l'Acteur de faire voir sa science dans leur representation, qui touche les Auditeurs, & les pique sensiblement quand elle est faite avec addresse."[34]

It seems to me that La Mesnardière is here suggesting a style suitable to psychological tragedy, in which the action is the flux of emotion in the minds of the speakers, emotion which the speaker himself may not recognize for what it is or may wish to hide but which he involuntarily reveals. To introduce into such dialogue the moralizing generalizations, the studied descriptions, or the elaborate comparisons of the epic could only be the poet's own comment on the emotions of his characters, and would change drama into declamation. The task of the dramatist, then, is to write dialogue colored by the emotion of the speakers and this dialogue stands in need of the collaboration of the actor for its psychological significance to become apparent to the spectator.

D'Aubignac[85] is in accord with La Mesnardière. He commends La Mesnardière's comments on the passions.[86] He condemns sententious speeches, which are ordinarily "defectueux sur le Theatre, parce qu'ils sont de leur nature froids et languissans";[87] many moderns have failed because "se jettant . . . dans le Didactique et les enseignemens, ils s'écartent de l'Intrigue du Theatre, et en laissent ralentir l'activité."[38] The moralizing generalizations appropriate to astrologers or High Priests make such personages inappropriate for the theatre. Didactic speeches are often very effective in the epic, a fact which has led some dramatists to introduce them into dramatic poems, where they are quite out of place, for "quelque conformité qu'en apparence et par esprit on remarque entre ces deux sortes de Poësie, je puis assurer que, hors les endroits pathétiques, il n'y en a presque point."[39] Narrations, like moralizing generalizations, "refroidissent et relâchent"[40] when they are

---

[84] *Loc. cit.*
[85] Aubignac (François Hédelin, Abbé d'), *La Pratique du Théâtre*, ed. Pierre Martino (Paris, 1927; 1st ed., 1657).
[86] *Ibid.*, p. 332.
[87] *Ibid.*, p. 314.
[88] *Ibid.*, p. 315.
[89] *Ibid.*, pp. 316–17.
[40] *Ibid.*, p. 293.

long. The "discours pathétique," D'Aubignac thinks, should make use of figures but of "les grandes figures qui sont aux choses et aux sentimens, et non pas celles qui ne sont que dans les paroles; comme sont les Antitheses et les autres jeux de mots."[41] Certain figures are appropriate to dramatic style, others are not. The poet should attend the theater and observe which figures are effective and which cause the action to languish.[42] D'Aubignac does not mention metaphor or simile among the figures which he considers theatrical. Even in "narrations," he objects to a lavish use of epithets, adverbs, "et autres termes peu necessaires."[43] Irony, he thinks, is by its very nature, "theatrale."[44] Exclamation too is proper in dramatic style because it reveals a mind agitated by violent emotion.[45] The same may be said for hyperbole.[46] Interrogation he recommends because it is the mark of "un esprit agité."[47] Imprecation is theatrical because it springs from a violent transport.[48] Apostrophe is effective only if used sparingly and if it doesn't exceed two verses in length.[49] These ideas are reflected in other French critics.[50]

[41] *Ibid.*, p. 344.
[42] *Ibid.*, p. 347.
[43] *Ibid.*, p. 291.
[44] *Ibid.*, p. 353.
[45] *Loc. cit.*
[46] *Loc. cit.*
[47] *Loc. cit.*
[48] *Loc. cit.*
[49] *Ibid.*, p. 350.
[50] Corneille believes that the diction of tragedy should be more elevated than that of prose but should not go so far as "l'enflure du poëme épique." (*Oeuvres*, ed. Charles Marty-Laveaux [Paris, 1862], I, 40.) Saint-Évremond believes that comparisons are more appropriate to the epic than to the tragic genre: ". . . Dans la tragédie, l'âme pleine de sentiments & possédée de passions, se tourne malaisément au simple éclat d'une ressemblance." ("Sur les Auteurs tragiques," in *Oeuvres*, ed. René Planhol [Paris, 1927], I, 193.) Boileau condemns bombast and superfluous description in Hecuba's expression of grief in Seneca's *Troades*. (*Art Poétique*, Bk. III, in *Oeuvres* [Paris, 1871], I, 204.) He thinks the sublime does not consist in "ambitiosa ornamenta." Old Horace's "qu'il mourût" and Médée's "moi," "mots de caractère," and "mots de situation" in the simplest language, he cites as examples of sublimity in Corneille. (*Ibid.*, II, 106–107.) In the preface to his translation of Longinus he insists on a distinction between "le style sublime" and "le sublime." (*Ibid.*, II, 123.) Le Bossu prefers epic style to tragic *because* the epic permits highly figurative language but he does not doubt the inappropriateness of highly figurative style for tragedy: ". . . l'Epopée l'emportera par la grande liberté qu'elle a d'user de métaphores & d'allusions perpetuelles aux

Despite the fact that La Mesnardière's is probably the most important single influence on Rymer's theory of tragedy, the English critic, as we shall see later, seems to have passed over completely La Mesnardière's theory of dramatic or theatrical style. Rymer uses the term "discours agissant" but in an entirely different sense from La Mesnardière.[51] He also rails against fustian, but his remarks are apparently inspired by Rapin's criticism of the false sublime.[52]

The French theories of a style peculiarly suited to the dramatic genre made a little headway in England. Simile was condemned in the language of passion, in any genre. There was some protest against the abuse of metaphor and simile in the dialogue of drama. But no one except Charles Gildon expounded a theory of a style exclusively and peculiarly suited to the dramatic genre.[53] Gildon's theory was belated,

---

Fables. Les expressions allégoriques feroient plus d'obscurité sur le Théatre, & auroient quelque chose de moins vrai-semblable en la bouche des personnes que l'on entend parler, que dans le récit d'un Poëte qui écrit pour être lû." (*Traité du Poëme épique* [Paris, 1675], p. 28.) Dacier's remarks on style are in line with these. He objects even more strongly to ornate diction than his predecessors: "Les endroits qui éclatent par la beauté des sentimens n'ont pas besoin des ornemens de la diction, parce que ces ornemens ne feroient que les offusquer; jamais un beau sentiment ne paroît mieux, que dans un stile simple." (*La Poëtique d'Aristote Traduite en François avec des Remarques* [Paris, 1692], p. 414.) Of contemporary tragedy he says: "Nous avons peu de Tragedies où les personnages parlent *politiquement* pour me servir du terme d'Aristote, c'est à dire communement & simplement; ils ne cherchent qu'à étaler tous les ornemens de la Rhétorique, & sont bien plus Déclamateurs qu'Acteurs, & de là vient qu'on y trouve tant de faux brillans, & que les moeurs y sont si rarement marquées, car il n'y a rien de plus contraire aux moeurs & aux sentimens qu'une diction enflée & un stile trop recherché." (*Ibid.*, p. 415.)

[51] *A Short View of Tragedy*, p. 5.

[52] *Ibid.*, pp. 141, 158.

[53] I cannot find in English criticism of the seventeenth and early eighteenth centuries any theory of a style peculiarly appropriate to "la poésie théâtrale" such as we find in La Mesnardière and D'Aubignac. There are echoes in English criticism of the French idea that a man under stress of violent emotion is incapable of impersonal moralizing generalizations or prolonged similes. Dryden apparently accepts this view (Preface to "Troilus and Cressida," *op. cit.*, VI, 278) and regrets his own inappropriate use of simile in his *Indian Emperor*. He thinks abuse of figurative language makes Shakespeare's style obscure (*ibid.*, p. 255); but he reveals his taste for descriptive poetry in the dramatic genre when he praises Shakespeare's "passionate descriptions," quoting one which begins with a four-verse simile (*ibid.*, p. 281). The Earl of Mulgrave satirizes the inappropriate use of figures in the drama ("Essay upon Poetry," in Spingarn, *op. cit.*, II, 291-92). John Dennis objects to simile in the language of grief in any genre (*op. cit.*,

coming after the movement of imitation of Racine was over, and after

---

I, 2) and criticizes the abuse of simile in the dialogue of an epic (*ibid.*, I, 91). He also criticizes the lavish use of epithet (*ibid.*, I, 43). But, for Dennis, imagery is the essence of poetry. For him, "Poetry is Poetry because 'tis more passionate and sensual than Prose. . . . A Discourse that is writ in smooth and tolerable Numbers, if 'tis not figurative can be but measur'd Prose; but a Discourse that is everywhere bold and figurative, and consequently everywhere extremely pathetick, is certainly Poetry without Numbers" (*ibid.*, II, 34). Actually, Dennis is here quoting Le Bossu: "Mais, il y faut, sur-tout, un tour & des manières de parler relevées, hardies, & métaphoriques; & ces manières sont tellement propres à ce genre d'écrire, que sans cela l'arrangement le plus exact des longues, & des brèves, fait beaucoup moins des Vers que de la Prose mesurée: et au contraire, ces expressions hardies & propres aux Vers, étant dans un discours qui n'auroit point les pieds & les mesures Poëtiques, lui donneroient tellement l'air de Vers, que ce seroit moins de la Prose qu'une espèce de Poésie sans mesure" (*op. cit.*, Bk. I, pp. 24–25). But, as I have pointed out above (n. 50), Le Bossu, despite his taste for metaphor, does not question the French dictum that highly figurative language is inappropriate in the *theater*. Dennis, like Bysshe, has a taste for the pictorial: "But these passions that attend upon our Thoughts, are seldom so strong, as they are in those kind of Thought, which we call Images. For they being the lively Pictures of the Thoughts which they represent, set them, as it were, before our very Eyes" (*op. cit.*, I, 218). Commenting on a passage from Milton, he says: "What a number of admirable Images are here crouding upon one another . . . at the same Time the Eye is ravishingly entertain'd, Admiration is rais'd to a Height" (*ibid.*, I, 277).

Later critics, while often objecting to the abuse of simile and epithet, nevertheless reveal an ineluctable taste for imagery in poetry. Henry Felton satirizes the style of the "so so Writers" (*op. cit.*, pp. 100–101); but he believes that metaphors and similes enliven and adorn a discourse (*ibid.*, pp. 97–98). Addison and Ambrose Philips object to figurative language because it obscures noble sentiments (see above, Chap. VI), but both yield to the English taste for simile in their own tragedies. Joseph Trapp commends homely, simple language for the expression of grief but, for him, imagery distinguishes poetry from prose (*op. cit.*, pp. 305–306, 51, 48, 138). Epithets, he thinks, are essential to poetic style (*ibid.*, pp. 78–79). Fielding satirizes the vogue of simile in English tragedy (*Tom Thumb*, ed. Felix Lindner [Berlin, 1899], p. 92). Aaron Hill berates the French for banishing imagery from dramatic poetry. ("Advertisement to the Reader," in *Meropé* [London, 1749]).

The idea that *sententiae* are inappropriate to the dramatic genres made even less headway in England. Rymer objected to Seneca's "dry Morals, and a tedious train of Sentences" as inappropriate in the *drama* (*A Short View of Tragedy*, p. 6). Collier took the opposite view (*op. cit.*, p. 30). John Dennis objects to *sententiae* in the *epic* (*op. cit.*, I, 58, 74). Rapin had taken a stand opposite to that of La Mesnardière, D'Aubignac, and other theorists of the drama: he believed *sententiae* more appropriate to the drama than to the epic (see comparison of Homer and Virgil in *Works*, I, 195–96). Le Bossu objects to the *excessive* use of *sententiae* in the *epic* (*op. cit.*, p. 214).

the tide of criticism had turned and the French were showing signs of the influence of English style.[54]

In general, English critics of the late seventeenth and early eighteenth centuries were less interested in making a distinction between dramatic and nondramatic style than in defining the difference between poetry and prose. This preoccupation is illustrated in the controversy over the style of Congreve's *The Mourning Bride*. In vigorous and picturesque language, Collier attacks the abuse of epithet in Congreve's dialogue. He refers to one of Osmyn's speeches as a "Rant of Smut and Profaneness." He then comments on the following verses:

> O my Almeria;
> What do the Damn'd endure but to despair,
> But knowing Heav'n, to know it lost for ever.
> What are the Wracks, and Whips, and Wheels to this?
> Are they not soothing Softness, sinking Ease,
> And wasting [*sic*] Air to this?

"This Litter of *Epithetes*," says Collier, "makes the *Poem* look like a Bitch over-stock'd with Puppies, and sucks the Sense almost to Skin and Bone."[55]

This thrust rankled in Congreve's breast. He is bitterly sarcastic about it.[56] In defending his style, he takes a position opposite to that of French critics of Racine's generation:

> ... every body knows that *Discourses of men in Passion, naturally abound in Epithets and Figures,* in Agravations and Hyperboles. To this I add, That the Diction of Poetry consists of Figures; by the frequent use of bold and daring Figures, it is distinguished from Prose and Oratory. Epithets are beautiful in Poetry, but make Prose languishing and cold. ... If Figures and Epithets are natural to Passion, and if they compose the Diction of Poetry, certainly Tragedy, which is of the sublime and first-rate Poetry, and which ought every where to abound in *Passion*, may very well be allow'd to use Epithets and Figures, more especially in a Scene consisting entirely of Passion, and still more particularly in the most violent part of that Scene.[57]

---

[54] Particularly in the Abbé du Bos's *Réflexions critiques sur la poésie et la peinture.*

[55] Jeremy Collier, *op. cit.*, p. 34.

[56] William Congreve, *Amendments of Mr. Collier's False and Imperfect Citations* (London, 1698), p. 29.

[57] *Ibid.*, pp. 30–31. Italics mine.

Collier replies:

The Figures and Flights of Poetry are Bold; but then the Fancy should be Natural, the Figures Just, and the Effect hold some proportion with the Cause. Zara . . . rails bitterly on the King, in *Astronomy*. And, as far as I can discover, she goes somewhat upon the System of *Copernicus*:

> Rain, rain, ye Stars spout from your burning Orbs,
> Precipitated Fires, and pour in Sheets,
> The blazing Torrent on the Tyrant's Head.

Well. Tho' this Lady has not much Wit in her Anger, she has a great deal of Learning: I must own this is a very Scholar-like piece of Distraction.[58]

Again he quotes:

> The swarming Populace spread every Wall
> And cling as if with Claws they did enforce
> Their Hold through clifted Stones, etc.

On this he comments: "*Cling* and *Claws* are extremely magnificent in solemn Description, and strangely proper for Tragedy. . . . To give him his due, I think these two Lines are the best Image of a parcel of Cats running up a Wall, that I have met with."[59] He later makes merry over the inept use of that favored epithet "Godlike" in one of Zara's speeches and over a "most terrible fit of Fustian" (Zara's tirade on discovering the headless body which she supposes to be Osmyn's). He says: "One would think by this Rant, that Zara had Bloud enough in her Veins to fill the Bay of Biscay or the Gulph of Lions."[60] Despite his attacks, Collier, like Congreve, is concerned with poetry, not with drama, and with the appropriateness or inappropriateness of Congreve's images to tragic poetry. There is nothing to suggest that he objected to imagery as inappropriate to the dramatic genre.

Oldmixon defends Congreve's style. Of two expressions criticized by Collier, he says: "*Respiring Lips* and *noon of Night*, I am sure as Mr. *Congreve* has us'd them, are expressions proper enough in Poetry, though they had been outrageous in Prose."[61]

The point of view of Congreve and of other English critics interested in the distinction between poetry and prose rather than in the distinction between dramatic and nondramatic poetry is reflected in Edward

---

[58] *An Answer to Mr. Congreve's Amendments* [London, 1699], p. 95.
[59] *Ibid.*, p. 92.
[60] *Ibid.*, pp. 92-94.
[61] *Reflections on the Stage*, p. 94.

Bysshe's *The Art of English Poetry*.[62] Bysshe says in his Introduction that the poet's art consists chiefly in "beauty of coloring." The title page of the fourth edition tells us that the book contains a "Collection of the Most Natural, Agreeable, and sublime Thoughts, viz. Allusions, Similes, Descriptions and Characters of Persons and Things; that are to be found in the best English Poets." A few samples of his favorite passages from dramatic poetry will indicate what kind of poetry Bysshe considered "sublime" and "natural." From Congreve he quotes the description of the scaling of the wall which Collier had criticized. Of many quotations from Shakespeare, the following are characteristic:

> Behold a Charnel-House,
> O'er cover'd quite with dead Men's ratling Bones,
> With reeky Shanks, and yellow, chapless Skulls.

> Hung be the Heav'ns with Black, yield Day to Night,
> Comets, importing Change to Times and States,
> Brandish your golden Tresses in the Skies,
> And with them scourge the bad revolted Stars
> That have consented unto Henry's Death.

> I do remember an apothecary,
> And hereabouts he dwells, which late I noted
> In tatter'd weeds, with overwhelming brows,
> Culling of simples; meagre were his looks,
> Sharp misery had worn him to the bones:
> And in his needy shop a tortoise hung, etc.

> Ambition's like a Circle on the Water,
> Which never ceases to enlarge it self,
> Till by broad spreading it disperse to nought.

Among those from Otway is the following:

> For my Castalio's false!
> False as the *W*ind, the *W*ater, or the *W*eather!
> Cruel as Tyger's o'er their trembling Prey!
> I feel him in my Heart, he tears my Breast.
> And at each Sigh he drinks the gushing Blood.

As a sample from Dryden there is a description of anger from *All for Love*:

> With fiery Eyes, and with contracted Brows,

[62] 4th ed., London, 1710, Preface.

> He coin'd his Face in the severest Stamp,
> And Fury shook his Fabrick like an Earth-quake.
> He heav'd for Vent, and burst, like bellowing Aetna,
> In Sounds scarce human.

Bysshe's taste obviously runs to the pictorial and the grandiose. Since his book went through eight editions between 1702 and 1725, we may conclude that many of his countrymen shared his tastes. It is significant that features of style looked upon by French critics as undramatic and untheatrical constituted for the English the peculiar essence of great poetry. Though French theories of style made some headway in England, Bysshe's theory represents a view most widely accepted and constant in England during the classical period.

If Rymer was scarcely influenced at all by La Mesnardière's theory of dramatic style, he was greatly influenced by his concept of tragedy. Like La Mesnardière he made poetic justice the foundation of his whole system. Rymer might have picked a French theorist at random and found the rule of distributive justice formulated. But nowhere could he have found all other rules so completely subordinated to it as in La Mesnardière. La Mesnardière insists that the catastrophe must show the perfect equity of Divine Justice, lest the people grumble at seeing virtue unfortunate and vice triumphant. He believes that ". . . non seulement *le Peuple n'absout pas Dieu de tout peché* . . . mais que les plus grans esprits . . . ne voyent pas sans murmure la prosperité des impies, & le malheur des gens de bien."[63] The virtuous in the audience should see their opposites punished and the vicious should witness the exemplary punishment of people like themselves;[64] lest the virtuous, seeing "la Vertu dans l'infamie & le Vice sur le thrône,"[65] waver in their holy resolutions and the wicked persist in vice, considering that the only reward of virtue is misfortune.[66] He concludes that *"les plus iustes Tragedies sont celles où les forfaits ont leurs punitions légitimes & les vertus leurs recompenses."*[67]

This insistence on the equitable distribution of rewards and punishments inevitably favors above other patterns of tragedy the "double fable," with the happy outcome for the good and the unhappy for the

---

[63] *Op. cit.*, pp. 171–72.
[64] *Ibid.*, p. 170.
[65] *Ibid.*, p. 171.
[66] *Ibid.*, p. 170.
[67] *Ibid.*, p. 222.

wicked. Indeed it must lead to portraying characters as either wholly virtuous or wholly wicked. La Mesnardière was a worshipper of Aristotle and looked upon himself as his disciple and defender; but he obviously had a taste for melodrama in the modern sense which conflicted with Aristotle's conception of the tragic. The result of this conflict is inconsistency. At times La Mesnardière is quite Aristotelian; but his own taste leads him to favor especially a type of tragedy that is pure melodrama. He accepts tragicomedy, or *la tragédie heureuse*,[68] as he calls it. Pity and fear are the essential passions of tragedy; but pity is aroused by *les actions pitoyables* and fear by *les odieuses*, if a single adventure does not arouse both, as the *Oedipus*[69] does. He thinks he is quoting Aristotle when he says: "Nous mourons de compassion quand nous voyons souffrir quelqu'un *sans qu'il ait fait aucune faute*; et nous mourons de frayeur lors que nous voyons chastier les criminels qui nous ressemblent."[70] Not only are pity and fear aroused by different personages of a tragedy but they are experienced by different spectators. Pity he values above fear as a tragic emotion: "La commiseration est infiniment plus douce, plus humaine, & plus agreable que la terreur & l'effroy."[71] Fear, however, is a "useful" passion. The poet should not introduce too often detestable criminals since the virtuous in the audience have a natural hatred of vice and do not stand in need of the poet's lesson. But the theatre should occasionally represent the exemplary punishment of the detestable actions of the wicked in order to frighten the wicked in the audience, who "tremblent iusqu'au fonds du coeur en voyant punir à leurs yeux les crimes qu'ils ont commis, ou dont ils se sentent capables; & se resoluent de l'instant d'éuiter de si grans malheurs par l'amandement de leur vie."[72] For this reason it is necessary that the poet introduce occasionally "des meschans, & qu'ils paroissent revestus au moins de quelque partie de leurs mauvaises habitudes."[73] For him the manners must be *exemplaires* rather than morally good. They are exemplary, to be sure, if the poet portrays personages with "de nobles habitudes et des sentimens exemplaires."[74] But they are also

---

[68] *Ibid.*, p. 42.
[69] *Ibid.*, p. 105.
[70] *Ibid.*, p. 26. Italics mine.
[71] *Ibid.*, p. 19.
[72] *Ibid.*, p. 26.
[73] *Ibid.*, p. 222.
[74] *Ibid.*, pp. 141–42.

exemplary if the wicked are signally punished at the end. "Discovery" is more common in tragicomedy than in tragedy. In tragicomedy discovery "vient fort à propos pour garantir les Innocens de quelque insigne malheur qui alloit tomber sur eux."[75] Peripeteia occurs more frequently in tragedy where "elle vient convertir les extremes felicitez de la personne coupable en d'extremes infortunes."[76] The simple fable, in which "le Héros devient mal-heureux peu à peu" is inferior to the complex, where "on voit tout d'un coup le Héros estre accablé de misères & tomber du faiste dans les abysmes, . . . le mouuement de l'âme excité par cette surprise, est l'vn des plus beaux effets que produise le Theatre."[77] Peripeteia La Mesnardière defines as "Vn euenement impréueu, qui dement les apparences, & par une Réuolution qui n'étoit point attendue, vient changer la face des choses."[78] This kind of peripety La Mesnardière considers very beautiful:

> Ce soudain Renuersement est la plus grande beauté du Sujet de la Tragedie. C'est lui qui touche l'esprit avec le plus de véhémence, & qui le met en vn état où étonné par les disgraces qui arrivent à l'improuiste, il admire & craint tout ensemble cette souueraine Iustice, qui punit rigoureusement les Personnes vicieuses, & ruinant des entreprises qui leur sembloient infaillibles, leur arrache l'Ame du corps, ou la Couronne de la teste, lors qu'elles se préparoient à opprimer les innocens.[79]

He ranks the peripeties of Greek tragedies. At the top of his hierarchy he places those which, according to his interpretation, show the punishment of the completely wicked. A perfect peripety is that of Sophocles's *Electra*, which he describes thus:

> Ainsi nous voyons dans Sophocle, qu'Egysthe & Clytemnestre, insolens par le succés d'vn meurtre & d'vn adultére, sont accablez soudainement par la Iustice de Dieu qui fait arriuer Oreste, dont ils célébroient la mort, pour venger celle de son Pere, & pour noyer la tyrannie dans le sang de ses meurtriers.
>
> Iamais vn rigoureux supplice ne parut mieux appliqué que celui que le Poëte ordonne à ces esprits sanguinaires, qui se treuuent enueloppez de mal-heurs inéuitables, lors qu'ils pensoient que la Fortune se déclarast ouuertement pour leurs intentions criminelles, qui tendoient à exterminer

---

[75] *Ibid.*, p. 106.
[76] *Loc. cit.*
[77] *Ibid.*, p. 54.
[78] *Ibid.*, p. 55.
[79] *Loc. cit.*

tous les enfans d'Agamemnon aprés l'auoir tué lui-mesme, pour s'assurer de son throsne.[80]

The pattern of the double fable is implicit in these remarks, but La Mesnardière never recommends it explicitly. It remained for Corneille, *who opposed poetic justice*,[81] to become the apologist of the plot with the double thread ending with the triumph of the virtuous and the downfall of the wicked. Corneille was chiefly concerned with finding rules to justify his own practice. Since his favorite among his tragedies, *Rodogune*, follows this pattern, he naturally argues for it as one acceptable form of tragedy. He maintains that there are several patterns for tragedy which have succeeded in modern times, but which Aristotle does not discuss because there were no examples in the Greek theater. The first of these is "quand un homme très-vertueux est persecuté par un très-méchant, et qu'il échappe du peril où le méchant demeure enveloppé, comme dans *Rodogune* et dans *Héraclius*."[82] He returns to the defense of these two plays in discussing Aristotle's four tragic situations. *Rodogune*, he realizes, has the sort of dénouement which Aristotle condemns: a protagonist intends to kill a kinsman whom he knows to be his kinsman but does not carry out his intention. Commenting on this type of situation and dénouement, Corneille says:

> Disons donc qu'elle [la condamnation d'Aristote] ne doit s'entendre que de ceux qui connoissant la personne qu'ils veulent perdre, s'en dédisent par un simple changement de volonté, sans aucun événement notable qui les y oblige, et sans aucun manque de pouvoir de leur part. J'ai déjà marqué cette sorte de dénouement pour vicieux; mais quand ils y font de leur côté tout ce qu'ils peuvent, et qu'ils sont empêchés d'en venir à l'effet par quelque puissance supérieure, ou par quelque changement de fortune qui les fait périr eux-mêmes, ou les réduit sous le pouvoir de ceux qu'ils vouloient perdre, il est hors de doute que cela fait une tragédie d'un genre peut-être plus sublime que les trois qu'Aristote avoue; et que s'il n'en a point parlé, c'est qu'il n'en voyoit point d'exemples sur les théâtres de son temps où ce n'étoit pas la mode de sauver les bons par la perte des méchans, à moins que de les souiller eux-mêmes de quelque crime, comme Electre.[83]

Corneille is proud of his "invention" in the dénouement of *Rodogune*.

---
[80] *Ibid.*, pp. 55–56.
[81] See Corneille as quoted below in this chapter.
[82] Pierre Corneille, "De la tragédie," in *Oeuvres*, ed. Charles Marty-Laveaux (Paris, 1862), I, 63.
[83] *Ibid.*, pp. 68–69.

History tells us, he says, that Antiochus, discovering his mother's plot, forces her to drink the poison she has prepared for him. In his version, Cléopatre, seeing that Antiochus and Rodogune suspect her of having poisoned the wine she offers them, decides to drink first: she will die but she hopes that her gesture will allay their suspicions and that they will drink after her and die with her. But her plot fails because they notice the effects of the poison on her just in time to prevent them from drinking. Commenting on his happy alteration of the story, Corneille says:

> Si j'eusse fait voir cette action sans y rien changer, c'eût été punir un parricide par un autre parricide; on eût pris aversion pour Antiochus, et il a été bien plus doux de faire qu'elle-même [i.e., Cléopatre], voyant que sa haine et sa noire perfidie alloient être découvertes, s'empoisonne dans son désespoir, à dessein d'envelopper ces deux amants [Antiochus et Rodogune] dans sa perte, en leur ôtant tout sujet de défiance. Cela fait deux effets. La punition de cette impitoyable mère laisse un plus fort exemple, puisque elle devient un effet de la justice du ciel, et non pas de la vengeance des hommes; d'autre côté, Antiochus ne perd rien de la compassion et de l'amitié qu'on avoit pour lui. . . .[84]

It is the character of Cléopatre that leads Corneille to argue against the interpretation of the adjective "good" as meaning "morally good" in the rule of character which demands that the "moeurs" of the characters be "bonnes,"[85] and to make an apology for the villain in tragedy. The "moeurs" are "bonnes," he thinks, if we see

> . . . le caractère brillant et élevé d'une habitude vertueuse ou criminelle. . . . Cléopatre dans *Rodogune*, est très-méchante; il n'y a point de parricide qui lui fasse horreur, pourvu qu'il la puisse conserver sur un trône qu'elle préfère à toutes choses, tant son attachement à la domination est violent; mais tous ces crimes sont accompagnés d'une grandeur d'âme qui a quelque chose de si haut, qu'en même temps qu'on déteste ses actions on admire la source dont elles partent.[86]

Doubtless such passages as Corneille's comment on the dénouement of *Rodogune* led Spingarn to believe that Corneille's was the most important French influence on Rymer's doctrine.[87] I believe, however, that Dutton is right in saying that La Mesnardière's was the dominant

[84] *Ibid.*, p. 79.
[85] "Du Poëme dramatique," *Oeuvres*, I, 31.
[86] *Ibid.*, p. 32.
[87] *Op. cit.*, Introduction.

influence.[88] The doctrine of poetic justice is the core of Rymer's theory of tragedy. Corneille never accepted it wholeheartedly. In 1643 he had said: "Cette règle imaginaire est entièrement contre la pratique des anciens."[89] In 1660 he still refuses to accept it as an inviolable rule.[90]

Rymer's attitude is best illustrated by his distinction between poetry and history and his comments on *Othello*. He says that Sophocles and Euripides

... were for teaching by *examples*. ... And, finding in History, the same *end* happen to the *righteous* and to the *unjust*, *vertue* often *opprest*, and *wickedness* on the Throne: they saw these particular *yesterday-truths* were imperfect and unproper to illustrate the *universal* and *eternal* truths by them intended. Finding also that this *unequal* distribution of rewards and punishments did perplex the *Wisest*, and by the Atheist was made a scandle to the *Divine Providence*. They concluded that a *Poet* must of necessity see *justice* exactly administred, if he intended to please.[91]

Of *Othello* Rymer says that the play has some semblance of a "fable" and that the fable is very instructive: it is a

... caution to all Maidens of Quality how, without their Parents consent, they run away with Blackamoors ... a warning to all good Wives, that they look well to their Linnen; ... a lesson to Husbands, that before their Jealousie be Tragical, the proofs may be Mathematical.[92]

On the dénouement Rymer has this to say:

Then after a little spurt of villany and Murder, we are brought to the most lamentable [*sic*], that ever appear'd on any Stage. A noble Venetian Lady is to be murdered by our Poet; in sober sadness, purely for being a Fool. No Pagan Poet but wou'd have found some *Machine* for her deliverance. ... What instruction can we make out of this Catastrophe? Or whither must our reflection lead us? Is not this to envenome and sour our Spirits, to make us repine and grumble at Providence and the government of the World? If this be our end, what boots it to be Vertuous?[93]

Here are his suggestions for a more satisfactory dénouement:

Desdemona dropt the Handkerchief, and missed it that very day after her

---
[88] *Op. cit.*, p. 185.
[89] "Epitre de la Suite du Menteur," *Oeuvres*, IV, 282.
[90] *Oeuvres*, I, 21-23.
[91] Thomas Rymer, *The Tragedies of the Last Age Considered*, pp. 13-14.
[92] *A Short View of Tragedy*, p. 89.
[93] *Ibid.*, pp. 137-38.

Marriage; it might have been rumpl'd up with her Wedding sheets: And this Night that she lay in her wedding sheets, the *Fairey* Napkin (whilst *Othello* was stifling her) might have started up to disarm his fury, and stop his ungracious mouth. Then might she (in a Trance for fear) have lain as dead. Then might he, believeing her dead, touch'd with remorse, have honestly cut his own Throat, by the good leave, and with the applause of all the Spectators, who might thereupon have gone home with a quiet mind, admiring the beauty of Providence: fairly and truly represented on the Theatre.[94]

Rymer would make of *Othello* a school for husbands and wives. Is he ironical in these remarks? To the Frenchman, Louis Charlanne, the comments on the moral of the fable of *Othello* seem ironical. It apparently never occurs to Charlanne that they could be anything else.[95] The remarks on the dénouement, however, Charlanne takes seriously. It seems to me that if Rymer's remarks on the fable are interpreted as ironical, those on the dénouement must be so interpreted. And there is the possibility, nay, the probability, that both are serious. The distinction between poetry and history is certainly so. If we are to take seriously Rymer's remarks on *Othello*, his conception of the moral function of tragedy differs in one respect from La Mesnardière's and from that of all other French critics: Rymer conceives of the teachings of tragedy as copybook maxims of bourgeois morality. As we shall see, other English critics share this conception. Rymer's theory resembles La Mesnardière's in the great emphasis placed on the equitable distribution of rewards and punishments and particularly in the insistence that a play must leave the audience convinced of the equity of Divine Justice or Divine Providence. There must be no occasion to grumble at the injustice of Heaven.

Second in importance only to his doctrine of poetic justice is Rymer's preoccupation with decorum. He is particularly concerned with that part of the rule of manners which demands that characters be portrayed according to their rank. Here again we see the influence of La Mesnardière, for La Mesnardière all but substituted protocol for characterization. Of the many remarks showing La Mesnardière's preoccupation with court etiquette, the following will suffice to illustrate his attitude:

[94] *Ibid.*, p. 138.
[95] Louis Charlanne, *L'Influence française en Angleterre au XVIIe Siècle* (Paris, 1906), p. 576.

NEO-CLASSICAL THEORY OF TRAGEDY

Surtout, qu'il [le poète] n'ignore pas de quel air usent entre elles les Personnes de condition dans leurs amours, dans leurs querelles & dans leurs civilitez. Comment les Rois se font servir, comment ils traitent les Princes & comment les Ambassadeurs. De quelle manière ils parlent aux Souverains leurs égaux, aux Reines, aux Seigneurs, aux Dames, aux Officiers aux Soldats. En quels termes on parle aux Rois, aux Reines, & et aux Princesses, etc.[96]

Again and again Rymer criticizes breaches of decorum in this narrow and superficial sense on the part of Fletcher and Shakespeare. For instance, Arbaces (*A King and No King*) "should have been endu'd with all the greatness of mind and *generosity* of a King and also the *modesty* of a Subject." Instead of that, he is not respectful to his father and not humble in the presence of Blood Royal.[97] "A King should not be found drolling and quibbling with Buffoons."[98] When Arbaces suggests marriage to Panthea, after she is discovered to be queen and he not her brother, Rymer thinks she "should have call'd him impudent Slave and discharg'd a frown that should have struck him dead."[99] "There is nothing in the noble *Desdemona*, that is not below any Countrey Chamber-maid with us."[100]

Thus, at the inception of neo-classical theory of tragedy in England, the complex French rule of decorum appears simplified and in its narrowest and most extreme form. The French rule demanded that the characters of tragedy be portrayed in a manner appropriate to the epoch and country in which they lived, their age, sex, and social situation (*condition*). Rymer chose to emphasize the last aspect; and disregarding the French notion that nobility of birth is accompanied by nobility of soul, he identified the part of the rule demanding characterization appropriate to rank with observance of the rules of court etiquette. La Mesnardière was probably the source of Rymer's doctrine of decorum.[101]

---

[96] *Op. cit.*, p. 239.
[97] *Tragedies of the Last Age Consider'd*, pp. 63–64.
[98] *Loc. cit.*
[99] *Ibid.*, p. 67.
[100] *A Short View of Tragedy*, p. 91.
[101] Dutton, quite rightly, I believe, attributes Rymer's rules of decorum to the influence of La Mesnardière (*op. cit.*, p. 185). La Mesnardière is the only major theorist of the drama who carries the rule of the "bienséances" so far as to demand strict observance of French court etiquette in the characters of tragedy. D'Aubignac thought that tragedy was more pleasing than comedy to the French

Other rules that Rymer laid down he could have found in La Mesnardière and numbers of other critics. He applies to tragedy Le Bossu's theory of the moral, allegorical "fable" of the epic. Like Aristotle he

nobility because it reflected their own life: "Dans ce Royaume les personnes, ou de naissance, ou nourries parmy les Grands, ne s'entretiennent que de sentimens genereux, et ne se portent qu'à de hauts desseins, ou par les mouvemens de la vertu, ou par les emportemens de l'ambition; de sorte que leur vie a beaucoup de rapport aux representations du Theatre Tragique" (op. cit., pp. 74-75). Tragedy does not admit meanness or pettiness. Certain passions, such as avarice and cowardice, are the field of comedy (ibid., p. 335). Valère's vengeance on Horace for the murder of Camille is a middle-class vengeance: ". . . selon l'humeur des François il faut que Valere cherche une plus noble voye pour venger sa Maistresse; et nous souffririons plus volontiers qu'il étranglast Horace que de luy faire un procez; un coup de fureur seroit plus conforme à la generosité de nostre Noblesse, qu'une action de Chicane, qui tient un peu de la lâcheté et que nous haïssons" (ibid., p. 340). A King should speak with the dignity befitting his rank (ibid., p. 78). Princesses should not bustle about the stage like slaves (ibid., p. 232). These things he demands in the name of verisimilitude. An audience would not be convinced or moved if it saw heroes, kings, and princesses acting like bourgeois or the slaves of comedy.

Minor French critics did carry the rule of decorum to ridiculous lengths. Pradon presents his Hippolyte to the Duchesse de Bouillon thus: ". . . ce jeune Héros auroit eu mauvaise grace de venir tout herissé des épines du Grec, dans une cour si galante que la nostre." ("Dedicatory epistle of Pradon's *Phèdre et Hippolyte*" [1677], in *Oeuvres* [Paris, 1682], p. 11.) Barbier d'Aucour criticizes Racine for making of Orestes, King of Argos, a simple ambassador and for having him address Pylades, himself a king, as a master would address a valet. (*Appollon, vendeur de Mithridate* [1675], as quoted in the Larousse edition of *Andromaque*, p. 80.) Subligny criticizes Act I, Scene 2 of Racine's *Phèdre* for breaches of court etiquette. Oenone tells Hippolyte that the queen is approaching and wishes to see no one. Hippolyte retires coldly without mentioning his intention of leaving the court in order to search for his father. Subligny comments: "C'est manquer de civilité: c'est choquer les régles de la bienséance: c'est ignorer l'usage de la cour, qui ne veut pas, que les ordres généraux, comme celui-là, soient donnés pour le fils du Roi: c'est pécher contre le bon sens, qui veut qu'en pareille rencontre, une personne chargée d'un ordre si général, ne l'annonce point à un Prince du sang sans une exception civile, & sans lui demander, s'il veut qu'on aille avertir la Reine de son dessein. Car enfin un homme comme Hippolyte, devoit du moins prier Oenone, de dire à la Reine, qu'il étoit venu pour lui dire adieu: De bonne foi, je ne crois pas que Monsieur Racine eût commis cette faute, si son esprit appliqué tout entier à embellir la Scène qui suit, eût pû faire un petit retour sur cette action incivile" ("Dissertation sur les tragédies de *Phèdre et Hippolyte*" [1677], in François Granet, *Recueil de Dissertations sur plusieurs Tragédies de Racine & de Corneille* [Paris, 1740], II, 369-70).

By a process of reasoning which remains a mystery to me, Clarence C. Green manages to bring Boileau into the camp of the apostles of court etiquette. He says: "In the same year Boileau drew up the rule [of decorum] in a couplet:

NEO-CLASSICAL THEORY OF TRAGEDY

considers plot the soul of tragedy. His criticism of rambling plots resembles Saint-Évremond's criticism of Elizabethan tragedies. "When," says Rymer, "some mangl'd, abus'd, undigested, interlarded History on our Stage impiously assumed the sacred name of Tragedy, it is no wonder if the Theatre grow corrupt and scandalous."[102] Saint-Évre-

---

> Ne faites point parler vos acteurs au hasard,
> Un vieillard en jeune homme, un jeune homme en vieillard."

And the next couplet indicates the almost complete identity between decorum and courtly etiquette:

> Etudiez la cour et connoissez la ville;
> L'une et l'autre est toujours en modèles fertile.

(*The Neo-classic Theory of Tragedy in England during the Eighteenth Century* [Cambridge, 1934], p. 35). If the couplets quoted by Green are placed in their context, his misinterpretation is at once apparent. Boileau had ended his discussion of tragedy 175 verses before the first couplet quoted by Green occurs. The discussion of tragedy is followed by that of the epic. Then follows the discussion of comedy, in which both couplets quoted occur. Boileau begins to lay down his precepts for the comic poet with the following admonition:

> Que la nature donc soit votre étude unique,
> Auteurs qui prétendez aux honneurs du comique.

This is the topic sentence of his discussion, in which he recommends observation of contemporary life as the method of the comic writer. Later, he says:

> La nature, féconde en bizarres portraits,
> Dans chaque âme est marquée à de différents traits,
> Un geste la découvre, un rien la fait paraître:
> Mais tout esprit n'a pas des yeux pour la connaître.

He then launches into his description of the characteristics of youth, middle age, and old age, a part of the rule of decorum more often applied to comedy than to tragedy. This description ends with the first couplet quoted by Green. It is followed, at the beginning of another paragraph, by the one in which Green sees evidence of "the almost complete identity of decorum and courtly etiquette." As a matter of fact, this couplet merely recommends to comic poets the method of observation and indicates that writers of comedies can find comic types at court and in Paris. This is evident when the verses which follow this couplet are added:

> Etudiez la cour et connoissez la ville;
> L'une et l'autre est toujours en modèles fertile.
> C'est par là que Molière, illustrant ses écrits,
> Peut-être de son art eût remporté le prix,
> Si moins ami du peuple, en ses doctes peintures
> Il n'eût point fait souvent grimacer ses figures.

If Boileau is talking about court etiquette in tragedy, what in the devil is Molière doing in that galley?

[102] *A Short View of Tragedy*, p. 164.

mond had said that Elizabethan tragedies with few exceptions were "une matière informe & mal digérée, un amas d'événemens confus."[103]

To Rymer, unity of action is important but he does not stress the unities of time and place. In his *Tragedies of the Last Age*, he says: "I would not examin the *proportions*, the *unities*, and *outward* regularities, the *mechanical* part of Tragedies: there is no talking of Beauties when there wants Essentials."[104] Later, he states that unity of action entails a certain limitation of time and place.[105] In his introductory chapter to *A Short View of Tragedy*, he espouses Dacier's idea that the chorus should be restored because it forces the poet to conform strictly to the unities. But he does not discuss violations of the unities in his critique of Shakespeare.

Dryden's critical theories were of great importance during the neoclassical age. In his very influential *Essay of Dramatic Poesy*, which antedates Rymer's translation of Rapin by six years, Neander, the speaker presenting Dryden's own views, accuses the French of being cold and declamatory, and of wearying the spectator with long and tiresome speeches. He is thinking of such plays as *Cinna* and *Pompey*, which he says are "not so properly to be called plays, as long discourses of reason of state."[106] He criticizes the mythological fable of *Andromède* as incredible.[107] In the same essay the function of tragedy is defined by the apologist of the French system thus: "The end of tragedies or serious plays, says Aristotle, is to beget admiration, compassion, or concernment."[108] "Admiration" is Cornelian, not Aristotelian. By "concernment," a word that occurs again and again in this essay, Dryden apparently means apprehension felt for the sympathetic characters. He all but identifies tragic fear with suspense. He criticizes the Greeks for using threadbare stories, the outcome of which is already known to the audience. His Neander comments: "The novelty being gone, the pleasure vanished."[109] Even Corneille, that apostle of "l'agréable sus-

---

[103] *Sur les Auteurs tragiques*, in *Oeuvres*, ed. René Planhol (Paris, 1927), Vol. I, p. 195.

[104] *Tragedies of the Last Age*, pp. 3-4.

[105] *Ibid.*, p. 24.

[106] *Essay of Dramatic Poesy*, in *Dramatic Essays of the Neoclassic Age*, ed. Adams and Hathaway (New York, 1950), p. 75.

[107] *Ibid.*, p. 77.

[108] *Ibid.*, p. 65.

[109] *Ibid.*, p. 57.

pension," he accuses of being content with some "flat design, which, like an ill riddle, is found out ere it be half proposed."[110] He finds it "infinitely pleasing to be led in a labyrinth of design, where you see some of your way before you, yet discern not the end till you arrive at it."[111] Although Dryden is here criticizing French plays as lacking in interest of this kind, when he stresses suspense and the surprise ending, he is in perfect accord with French classical doctrine.[112]

After the publication of Rymer's *Tragedies of the Last Age*, Dryden was enthusiastic about the book, with some reservations.[113] His Preface to *Troilus and Cressida* shows that he has drawn somewhat closer to Aristotle as interpreted by French Aristotelians. He professes to be following Aristotle, Horace, and Longinus. In reality he shows the influence of Rymer, of Rapin, and of Le Bossu.[114] Like Rymer, he applies to tragedy Le Bossu's theory of the moral fable of the epic. He condemns double plots. He is now concerned with the tragic emotions of pity and fear, rather than with admiration. He believes that both should be aroused by the protagonist, who must be virtuous in order to excite pity but must have "alloys of frailty" leaving room for "punishment on the one side and pity on the other." The punishment of a wicked character cannot arouse pity. "We are glad," says he, "when we behold his crimes punished, and that poetical justice is done upon him." He does not think, however, that villains should be banished altogether from tragedy. Only the hero need have "virtuous inclinations." But villains must have other motives than a "natural inclination to villainy."

The most significant passage is the one dealing with catharsis. Dry-

[110] *Ibid.*, p. 79.
[111] *Ibid.*, p. 76.
[112] "Suspendre l'attention pour laisser entier au dénouement le plaisir de la surprise, préparer le dénouement pour que le plaisir ne soit pas détruit par l'invraisemblance. Suspendre et préparer, voilà tout le secret. Tous les critiques le répètent." (René Bray, *La Formation de la doctrine classique en France* [Lausanne, 1931], p. 322.) It should be noted, however, that D'Aubignac, though he certainly favors suspense and surprise in tragedy, admits the appeal of tragedies without plot complication, believes that those depending for their appeal solely on surprising incidents do not wear well, and favors above all those which are "meslez d'incidents et de passions" (*La Pratique du Théâtre*, pp. 70–71). He also defines and apparently approves of the appeal of tragedies whose outcome is known in advance to the spectator (*ibid.*, p. 138).
[113] See below, p. 388.
[114] See John C. Sherwood, "Dryden and the Rules: The Preface to *Troilus and Cressida*," *Comparative Literature*, II, No. 1 (Winter, 1950), 73–83.

den professes to be following Rapin here. His theory differs from Aristotle's, from any of the French theories, and even from Rapin's. Fear, says Dryden, is aroused by the spectacle of the downfall of the great. This vicarious fear does not, however, moderate the passion of fear in real life: it purges the spectator of another passion, namely, pride. Here he is following Rapin. By arousing pity, on the other hand, the tragic dramatist is supposed to increase the spectator's capacity for pity in real life, for the sight of the misfortunes of the "most virtuous as well as the greatest . . . insensibly works us to be helpful to, and tender over, the distressed; which is the noblest and most godlike of moral virtues."[115] Dryden differs from Rapin when he particularizes the sources of pity. Rapin does not say that the suffering of the innocent arouses pity. More important still is the fact that Dryden disregards a paragraph of Rapin, in which the French theorist recommends the purging of any excess of those two weaknesses, pity and fear.[116] Dryden agrees with La Mesnardière, who considers pity "une

---

[115] *Works*, VI, 263.

[116] "Ce philosophe [Aristote] avoit reconnu deux defauts importans à regler dans l'homme, l'orgueil & la dureté, & il trouva le remede à ces deux defauts dans la Tragedie; car elle rend l'homme modeste, en luy representant des Grands humiliés & elle le rend sensible & pitoyable, en luy faisant voir sur le theatre les étranges accidens de la vie & les disgraces impreveues, auxquelles sont sujettes les personnes les plus importantes. Mais parce que l'homme est naturellement timide, & compatissant, il peut tomber dans une autre extremité, d'estre ou trop craintif, ou trop pitoyable: la trop grande crainte peut diminuer la fermeté de l'ame, & la trop grande compassion en peut diminuer l'equité. La Tragedie s'occupe à regler ces deux foiblesses: elle fait qu'on s'apprivoise aux disgraces, en les voyant si frequentes dans les personnes les plus considerables: & qu'on cesse de craindre les accidens ordinaires quand on en voit arriver de si extraordinaires aux Grands. Mais comme la fin de la Tragedie est d'apprendre aux hommes à ne pas craindre trop foiblement des disgraces communes, & à menager leur crainte: elle fait état aussi de leur apprendre à menager leur compassion, pour des sujets qui la meritent. Car il y a de l'injustice d'estre touché des malheurs de ceux, qui meritent d'estre miserables." (*Réflexions sur la Poëtique d'Aristote*, Sec. XVII, pp. 169-71.)

Rapin's attitude towards the passion of pity lies halfway between the extreme of sentimentality expressed by Dryden and the opposite, as expressed by La Rochefoucauld, who said: "C'est une passion qui n'est bonne à rien au dedans d'une âme bien faite, qui ne sert qu'à affoiblir le coeur, et qu'on doit laisser au peuple, qui, n'exécutant jamais rien par raison, a besoin de passions pour le porter à faire les choses." (*Maximes & Réflexions Diverses*, ed. Henry A. Grubbs, Jr. [Princeton, 1929], p. 181.)

passion plus douce et plus humaine que la terreur,"[117] but departs from him and, I believe, from all other French critics when he recommends the vicarious experience of pity in order to increase capacity for pity in real life because this emotion (in real life) is the "noblest and most godlike of moral virtues."[118]

Some two years later we find that Dryden has reverted to a position nearer to that of the *Essay of Dramatic Poesy*. In the preface to *Troilus and Cressida*, he is concerned with poetic justice to the extent of recommending the punishment of the wicked. He says nothing of the rescue of the innocent. In the preface to *The Spanish Friar* (1681), we find an apology for the happy outcome for tragedy not because of the principle of poetic justice but because it is a more difficult artistic feat to end a tragedy happily than to kill the characters off. He indicates that it requires great art to lead the spectator to believe that the sympathetic characters are doomed to unhappiness and then surprise him with a happy outcome, unforeseen but convincing.

Rymer's doctrines were accepted by many minor critics. I find only one protest against the doctrine of the moral function of tragedy. Oldmixon maintains that the chief aim of the dramatist should be to please, and he quotes Racine to support his position. He quotes the preface to *Bérénice*: "La principale règle est de plaire."[119] Collier ac-

[117] See above, p. 231.
[118] *Loc. cit.*
[119] *Reflections on the Stage*, p. 22. In 1711 Addison protested against the tyranny of the rule of poetic justice and expressed his preference for the original ending of *Lear*. But the very terms in which this protest is couched indicate that the rule was universally accepted. He speaks only of the rescue of the innocent, saying nothing of the punishment of the wicked: "The English writers of tragedy are possessed with a notion that when they represent a virtuous person in distress, they ought not to leave him till they have delivered him out of his troubles, or made him triumph over his enemies. This error they have been led into by a ridiculous doctrine in modern criticism, that they are obliged to an equal distribution of rewards and punishments, and an impartial execution of poetical justice. . . . *I do not . . . dispute against this way of writing tragedies, but against the criticism that would establish this as the only method*" (*Spectator*, No. 40; italics mine).

Despite Addison's objection to Tate's alteration of the ending of *Lear*, Tate's version held the boards in the eighteenth century. Everybody knows that Dr. Johnson approved of the rescue of Cordelia. The version which Garrick used is printed in the Bell edition with notes by the author of the *Dramatic Censor*. These notes throw some light on the interpretation of poetic justice and the tragic emotions in the second half of the eighteenth century. On the happy

cepted the doctrine of poetic justice. His opponents did not dispute it. Congreve's defense of *The Mourning Bride* rests largely on the moral teaching of the play. His comment on the dénouement of his play is notable because he specifies the virtues that are rewarded and the vices that are punished. We see here, as we did in Rymer's curious comments on the fable of *Othello*, the copybook maxims of bourgeois morality. Congreve calls attention to "The Reward of Matrimonial Constancy in *Almeria*, of the same Virtue, together with filial Piety and Love to his Country in *Osmin*; the Punishment of Tyranny in *Manuel*, of Ambition in *Gonzales*, of violent Passions, and unlawful Love in *Zara*."[120] James Drake's *Antient and Modern Stages Survey'd* (1699) proclaims the superiority of modern plays to the ancient. Their superiority lies in their morality. Modern poets, he tells us, "show more respect to Providence and the Divine administration." Of *The Mourning Bride* he says: "The Fable of this Play is one of the most just, and regular that the Stage, either Antient or Modern, can boast of. I mean, for the distribution of Rewards, and Punishments. For no virtuous person misses his Recompence and no vitious one escapes Vengeance."[121]

Drake is particularly impressed with the form of peripeteia which we find in *The Mourning Bride*, that is, the type in which the villain is the engineer hoist with his own petard. "Manuel in the prosecution and exercise of his Cruelty and Tyranny, is taken in a Trap of his own laying, and falls himself a Sacrifice in the room of him, whom he in his

---

ending, the Censor says: "Though the king's restauration is a pleasing circumstance, and Tate piqued himself upon it, the true tragic feelings, and poetical justice would, according to the opinion of some critics, have been better maintained by making him fall a sacrifice to his obstinate pride and frantic rashness as in the original. But we venture to differ with them as the faults of Lear arose from weakness, and not vice; besides that, there would be no sort of sacrifice to poetical justice, to have involved the spotless Cordelia in his misfortunes." In these comments we see the persistence of the notion that the dénouement of tragedy should represent the punishment of wholly vicious characters rather than that of a hero with a tragic flaw. Lear, as described by the Censor, is the ideal Aristotelian protagonist; but the tragic flaw, in the Censor's opinion, is not enough to warrant punishment. (Bell's edition of Shakespeare [London, 1774], II, 76.)

For further evidence of the general acceptance of the rule of poetic justice in the eighteenth century, see Clarence C. Green, *The Neo-classic Theory of Tragedy in England during the Eighteenth Century* (Cambridge, 1934), pp. 139-49.

[120] *Amendments*, p. 36.
[121] See p. 215.

rage had devoted. Gonsalez villainous cunning returns upon his own head." The virtuous are unharmed in the downfall of the wicked: "Thus every one's own Wickedness or Miscarriage determines his Fate, without shedding any Malignity upon the Persons of others."[122] In *Hamlet* he finds the same type of peripeteia. The moral of Shakespeare's tragedy is "that the Greatness of the Offender does not qualifie the Offense, and that no Humane Power, or Policy are a sufficient Guard against the Impartial Hand, and the Eye of Providence, which defeats their wicked purposes, and turns their dangerous Machinations upon their own heads."[123]

According to Drake, modern dramatists have improved on the structure of Greek tragedy by combining two types, the moral and the pathetic:

> The *Moderns*, who were sensible of the use of one and the power of t'other sort of Tragedy, have taken a happy Liberty of compounding 'em and throwing the *simple* tragedy quite aside, stick altogether to an Implex kind, which is at once both *Moral* and *Pathetick*. . . . Wherein they must to their honour be acknowledg'd, to have made a considerable improvement of Tragedy, and to have had singular regard to Probity and Virtue.[124]

A Defence of Dramatick Poetry (by Edward Filmer?) is noteworthy for its interpretation of tragic pity and for the information it affords concerning audience reaction. "*Tragedy* indeed," says the author, "does raise the Passions; and its chief work is to raise *Compassion*: For the great entertainment of Tragedy is the moving that tenderest and noblest Humane Passion, *Pity*."[125] So far he is in accord with some French classical doctrine, notably La Mesnardière. But he adds:

> And what is it we pity there, but the Distresses, Calamities and Ruins of *Honour, Loyalty,* or *Love?* . . . thus *Virtue*, like *Religion*, by its *Martyrdom*, is rendered more shining by its *Sufferings*, and the Impression we receive from *Tragedy* is only making us in Love with *Virtue* and out of Love with Vice, for at the same time we pity the suffering Virtue, it raises our Aversions and Hate to the Treachery or Tyranny in the *Tragedy*, from whence and by whom that Virtue suffers.[126]

---

[122] *Loc. cit.*
[123] *Ibid.*, p. 205.
[124] *Ibid.*, pp. 225–26.
[125] See p. 71.
[126] *Ibid.*, pp. 71–72.

Obviously his ideal of tragedy is the pattern which shows completely virtuous characters persecuted by completely wicked ones. He does not, however, specifically recommend poetic justice. He tells us that audiences insist on seeing "Virtue made Lovely, and Vice made Odious." "That Expectation," says he, "brings us to the Play; and if we find not that very Expectation answer'd, instead of any satisfactory Delight we receive, or any Applause we return, we explode and Hiss our Entertainment; the Play sinks, and the Performance is lost."[127] As an illustration of the audience's hostility to villains, he notes that often a good actor playing a villain's rôle, such as Iago, arouses the audience's ire, "such a natural Affection and commiseration of *Innocence* does Tragedy raise, and such an Abhorrence of Villainy."[128]

A treatise which appeared anonymously in 1698 represents the extreme point of view of the "irregulars." It is noteworthy because the author considers Corneille the great master of the unities and the dictator of the rules! The unknown author, possibly Elkanah Settle, remarks that the "Corneillean Rules" are "as Dissonant to the *English* Constitution of the State, as the *French* Slavery to our English Liberty."[129] The French, who are the "dullest of Mankind at their Playhouses"[130] are content to hear a Play made up of a short-winded Plot, and a few long-winded Speeches."[131] He refers satirically to "modern would-be Criticks, that are wonderfully tickl'd with their own nicer Stage Performances, under this strict *Cornelian* Model of the Unities."[132] "The Subjects of our English Tragedies," says he, "are generally the whole Revolutions of Governments, States, or Families. . . . Our *Genius* of Stage-Poetry can no more reach the Heights that can please our Audience under his [Corneille's] Unity Shakles than an Eagle can soar in a Hen-coop. Corneille may reign Master of

---

[127] *Ibid.*, p. 72.
[128] *Loc. cit.* Compare Rymer (*A Short View of Tragedy*, p. 118), who describes the delight with which audiences watch the scene in *Othello* in which Iago, "by shrugs, half words, and ambiguous reflections, works *Othello* up to be jealous." This is the scene, Rymer thinks, which in the opinion of spectators, "raises *Othello* above all other Tragedies on our Theatres." Rymer is here criticizing the spectators' taste for pantomime, "the Mops and the Mows, the Grimaces, the Grins and Gesticulations."
[129] *A Farther Defence of Dramatick Poetry* (1698), p. 28.
[130] *Loc. cit.*
[131] *Loc. cit.*
[132] See p. 29.

his own Revels; but he is neither a Rule-maker nor a Play-maker for our Stage."[133]

John Dennis, who had read more French criticism and read it more reflectively than either Dryden or Rymer, and who, in addition, was thoroughly familiar with Racine's prefaces and with the plays themselves, nevertheless shows that he accepts some of the doctrine of Rymer even in its aspects that are apparently peculiar to the English. Dennis thinks that tragedy makes men virtuous because it "moderates the Passions, whose Excesses cause their Vices; Secondly, because it instructs them in their Duties, both by its Fable, and by its Sentences."[134] Love, in tragedy, he thinks, is "lawful and regular, or it is not. If it is not, why then in a Play, which is writ as it should be . . . it is shewn unfortunate in the Catastrophe, which is sufficient to make an Audience averse from engaging in the Excesses of that Passion. But if Love that is shewn is lawful and regular, nothing makes a Man happier than that Passion."[135] Tragedy is useful to the advancement of religion, especially of the "reformed Religion."[136] He is in accord with La Mesnardière in the following statement of the function of tragedy: "I conceive that every Tragedy, ought to be a very Solemn Lecture, inculcating a particular Providence, and showing it plainly protecting the Good, and chastizing the Bad."[137] He follows English critics in his remarks on lawful and unlawful love and in the following comment on Otway's *The Orphan*:

> . . . the Calamities of all three [i.e., Castalio, Monimia, and Polidor] are occasion'd by Faults which *Aristotle* terms involuntary, that is, by Faults occasion'd by the Force of an outrageous Passion. The Fault of *Castalio* is dissembling with his Brother, and marrying *Monimia*, without the Knowledge or Consent of his Father; that of *Monimia* is the marrying *Castalio*, without the Knowledge and Consent of his Father, who was her Benefactor; that of *Polidor*, is dissembling with his Brother, and the debauching *Monimia* without her Consent, contrary to the Rights of Hospitality, and that Veneration that was due to his Father's Protection and Guardianship; which Faults in all of them proceed from the Violence of a Passion, which is

---

[133] See pp. 32–33.
[134] "The Usefulness of the Stage," in *op. cit.*, I, 153.
[135] *Loc. cit.*
[136] *Ibid.*, p. 184.
[137] "The Advancement and Reformation of Poetry," *op. cit.*, I, 200. La Mesnardière says that a tragedy ending with the punishment of vices is "vne Prédication active & vn Sermon délicieux" (*Poëtique*, pp. 216–17).

admirably painted by the most ingenious Author. And the Moral, tho' not express'd at the End of the Play, yet most intelligibly implied, is *a wholesome, but terrible Instruction to an Audience to beware of clandestine Marriages*, which involv'd a Family so happy before in such fatal Disasters.[138]

Plays conforming to the rule of poetic justice with the double fable showing suffering virtue rescued in the end and punishment finally overtaking the villain, had been written before Rymer suggested an ideal ending for *Othello*. A notorious example and one that is particularly pertinent here is Nahum Tate's version of *King Lear* (1681).[139] Tate introduces a romance between Edgar and Cordelia. They then become the pair of innocent lovers whose lives are imperiled by the machinations of a trio of villains, Edmund, Goneril, and Regan. In Act V we find Albany and Goneril triumphant. Lear and Cordelia are prisoners. Albany orders their guards to treat them well. But Goneril countermands the order and instructs them, in an aside, to put his prisoners to death. Edgar enters in disguise and accuses Edmund of treason to Albany and "of Foulest Practice 'gainst your Life and Honour." (Both Goneril and Regan are in love with Edmund and he is secretly carrying on an intrigue with both.) Edgar promises to produce a champion who will meet the traitor in single combat to prove his charges. Albany makes the appointment for "anon—before our Tent." The scene shifts to Albany's camp before his tent. A herald calls for a champion to fight Edmund. Enter Edgar. He has thrown off his disguise and confronts his villainous half-brother. They have a duel of words—original with Tate—before coming to blows. Edgar taunts Edmund with his illegitimacy, saying that he draws his villainy from his licentious mother. Edmund has a Cornelian greatness of soul in wickedness. He replies that his mother's licentiousness gives him reason to suspect that he may not be Gloster's son but

> Who 'twas that had the hit to Father me
> I know not; 'tis enough that I am I.

Edgar wounds him mortally. When he falls Goneril and Regan rush to him. Each discovers that the other is her rival. Each reveals that she has poisoned the other at a banquet which they attended. The sisters accompany the dying Edmund off stage and all three die in the wings.

---

[138] "Remarks upon *Cato*," *op. cit.*, II, 66–67. Italics mine.
[139] Passages quoted are from the first edition.

NEO-CLASSICAL THEORY OF TRAGEDY

In the meantime, what of Lear and Cordelia? The last scene shows them in prison. Lear is asleep, his head in Cordelia's lap. Enter the assassins. The captain reveals his orders to Lear and Cordelia. Cordelia asks to be killed first. Lear seizes a partisan and lays about him, killing two of the assassins. He is about to succumb to the others when Edgar and Albany enter. Upon the timely entrance of her rescuers, Cordelia says, "Then there are Gods, and Vertue is their Care." Albany restores Lear to the throne. Lear bestows the kingdom on Cordelia. Edgar speaks the moral:

> Our drooping Country now erects her Head
> Peace spreads her balmy Wings, and Plenty blooms.
> Divine Cordelia, all the Gods can witness
> How much thy Love to Empire I prefer!
> Thy bright example shall convince the World
> (Whatever Storms of Fortune are decreed)
> That Truth and Vertue shall at last succeed.

In a dedicatory epistle Tate explains his reasons for the changes he has made:

'Twas my good fortune to light on one Expedient to rectifie what was wanting in the Regularity and probability of the Tale, which was to run through the whole a Love betwixt Edgar and Cordelia. . . . This renders Cordelia's indifference and her Father's Passion in the first scene, probable. It likewise gives Countenance to Edgar's Disguise, making that a generous Design that was before a poor Shift to save his Life. The Distress of the Story is evidently heightened by it; and it particularly gave Occasion of a New Scene or Two, of more Success (perhaps) than Merit. This Method necessarily threw me on making the Tale conclude in a Success to the innocent distrest Persons. Otherwise I must have incumbred the Stage with Dead Bodies, which Conduct makes many Tragedies conclude with unseasonable Jests. Yet was I wrackt with no small Fears for so bold a Change, till I found it well receiv'd by my Audience; and if this will not satisfiy the Reader, I can produce an Authority that questionless will. Neither is it of so Trivial an Undertaking to make a Tragedy end happily, for 'tis more difficult to save than 'tis to kill. The Dagger and Cup of Poison are always in Readiness; but to bring the Action to the last extremity, and then by probable Means to recover All, will require the Art and Judgment of a Writer, and cost him many a Pang in the Performance.

A note printed in the margin indicates that the source of this apology for tragicomedy is Dryden's preface to *The Spanish Friar*. We may conclude from these remarks of Tate that in altering Shakespeare's tragedy he had in mind, first, verisimilitude, which seemed to him to be violated by Cordelia's lack of motivation in the first act; second, to make the hero's motivation more noble than in Shakespeare; and third, to increase the pathos by showing the peril of a pair of noble and innocent lovers. Furthermore he reveals that to him the acme of dramatic art lies in the suspense created by their peril and the surprising last-minute rescue of the sympathetic pair.

Poetic justice is not mentioned in the dedicatory epistle; but the idea of a particular Providence watching over the innocent and rescuing them in the end is sufficiently plain in Cordelia's words on seeing Edgar enter and in the moral spoken by Edgar at the end. This version of *Lear* held the boards for a century and met with little unfavorable criticism. It was approved not only because of conformity to the law of poetic justice but because of the suspense and surprise it afforded.[140] This mutilation of Shakespeare is not exactly the pitiable sacrifice to poetic justice that it has been called.[141] It is indeed a pitiable sacrifice. But to what? Poetic justice or a taste for melodrama? A quarter of a century later, Racine's *Phèdre* was to be transformed in exactly the same way, so that Shakespeare and Racine, far from appearing as the great representatives of two contrasting systems, are rather fellow victims of a taste for melodrama dignified by the name of dramatic art and reinforced by an excessive regard for the supposedly classical doctrine of poetic justice.

The doctrine of poetic justice undoubtedly came from France, and specifically from La Mesnardière. French theory might well have been responsible for the acceptance by the English of the double fable with the double catastrophe as the ideal form of tragedy. Despite La Mesnardière's worshipful attitude towards Aristotle, he not only recognizes tragicomedy as a classical genre, but he places tremendous emphasis on distributive justice; he divorces the tragic emotions the one from the other, both as to source and effect. Though he values pity more than fear, he recommends the latter emotion for its moral effect on the vicious individuals in an audience and he admits villains in tragedy because their punishment is the source of the terror experienced by the wicked spectator. Moreover, in his comments on peripeteia, he praises the surprise ending consisting in the sudden and unexpected punishment

---

[140] See below, n. 142.
[141] Hazleton Spencer, *Shakespeare Improved* (Cambridge, 1927), p. 252.

of the villain plotting the destruction of the innocent. In his evaluation of peripeties in Greek tragedy, he places at the top of his hierarchy the type which shows the punishment of the completely wicked. Without favoring poetic justice and without favoring exclusively the double fable, Corneille did write an apology for the pattern, which he had illustrated in his favorite among his tragedies, *Rodogune*, and in *Héraclius*. Rymer, in introducing Aristotelian formalism into England, was greatly indebted to La Mesnardière. Dryden had already indicated that he considered plot complication and suspense the acme of dramatic art. Rymer introduced, or gave new emphasis to, the rule of poetic justice and rejected the panoramic drama of Shakespeare and the heroic school in favor of classical concentration. After the appearance of Rymer's first book, Dryden accepted certain aspects of the doctrine of poetic justice and Le Bossu's theory of the moral fable. In practice he began to approach French concentration in his plots. I have found little or no evidence anywhere in English theory that anyone conceived of the possibility of a tragedy without surprising incidents and dependent only on the passions for its appeal. Nor did the English ever cease to consider as the ultimate in dramatic art the skillful unraveling of a plot that has kept the spectator in ignorance of the outcome until the very end.[142]

[142] In 1713, John Dennis indicates that he believes surprise (for the spectator) to be the source of the wonderful, the terrible, and the deplorable in tragedy ("Remarks upon Cato," in *op. cit.*, II, 47).

In 1729 James Thomson says of Congreve:

> . . . Closely wrought
> His meaning Fable, with deep art perplex'd,
> With striking ease unravel'd; no thin plot,
> Seen thro' at once and scorn'd; or ill conceal'd
> By borrow'd aids of mimickry or farce.

("A Poem to the Memory of Wm. Congreve," in *Early English Poetry and Ballads* [London, 1844], IX, 22.)

In 1731, James Ralph thinks the conduct of a play artful because the catastrophe is "to the last degree *surprenant* and *merveilleux*, and gives the Audience all that can be imagin'd of an agreeable Astonishment, which is the chief End of Poetry" (*The Taste of the Town*, p. 54).

Joseph Trapp thinks the happy ending requires more art and quotes the same passage from the dedicatory epistle of the *Spanish Friar* which Tate had quoted to justify his alteration of *Lear* (*Lectures on Poetry*, 1742, pp. 314–15). Trapp thinks the catastrophe "ought to turn, as we say, upon a Point, to start up, on a sudden; as soon as that is discover'd, the Play should conclude; and this End once obtain'd, all Action cease: Otherwise, the Curiosity of the Audience will be pall'd, and what promis'd Pleasure will then appear insipid and tedious" (*ibid.*,

This view of dramatic art had abundant support in French theory. Tate cites Dryden as his authority for the type of ending which he

p. 267). The poet should take care, he thinks to conceal the outcome from the audience till the conclusion of the play. He thinks that the title of *Venice Preserv'd* shows a lack of art since it reveals the catastrophe (*ibid.*, pp. 268-69). Trapp approves of poetic justice. He thinks, however, that the innocent *may* be shown laboring under distress even at the end; but that the wicked "should never come off in real Triumph, and Satisfaction." If the innocent meet death in the end, the dramatist should remind the spectators that "there certainly will be eternal Punishments and Rewards hereafter" (*ibid.*, p. 315).

New support for these theories came from France with the publication in 1742 of Fontenelle's *Reflexions sur la poétique*. For Fontenelle, the apologist of the Cornelian system, the ultimate in dramatic art is to appeal to the curiosity of the spectator. He recommends concealing the outcome until the very end, indeed, contriving, if possible, to make the spectator fear that the ending will be unhappy. If the subject is well known so that the outcome is known in advance to the spectator, the best the dramatist can do is to arrange the material so that events will surprise the personages of the play. Fontenelle considers the type of play which affords surprises for the characters only and not for the spectators inferior to the type which keeps the spectators in doubt as to the outcome until the last moment. Perhaps he would not have commended the former type at all if the younger Corneille had not written plays of this type. He cites *Ariane* as an example of this technique (*Reflexions sur la poétique*, in *Oeuvres* [Paris, 1752], III, 144).

David Hume read Fontenelle's treatise and was influenced by it. In his essay on tragedy, Hume is concerned not with dramatic art but with explaining the psychological paradox of the pleasure derived from the spectacle of suffering presented by tragedy. But Hume implies that he accepts the common English concept of tragedy. He does not intimate that he thinks an unhappy ending more truly tragic, although he does say that "one scene of full joy and contentment and security is the utmost, that any composition of this kind can bear; and it is sure always to be the concluding one" (*Of Tragedy*, in *Philosophical Essays* [Georgetown, 1817], I, 233). Later he implies that the dénouement with some measure of poetic justice is necessary to make the spectacle agreeable to the audience: "The mere suffering of plaintive virtue, under the triumphant tyranny and oppression of vice, forms a disagreeable spectacle, and is carefully avoided by all masters of the drama. In order to dismiss the audience with entire satisfaction and contentment, the virtue must either convert itself into a noble courageous despair, or the vice receive its proper punishment" (*ibid.*, p. 241). Suspense and novelty, he thinks, add to the force of the prevailing passion (*ibid.*, p. 238).

The author of the *Dramatic Censor* commends the suspense created in Tate's version of *Lear* by the peril of Lear and Cordelia and the nick-of-time rescue: "The tender feelings of apprehension are here finely tremulated; the timely rescue is most agreably thrown in" (Bell's edition of Shakespeare [London, 1774], II, 76).

imposed on Shakespeare's tragedy. But Dryden himself might have been inspired by French critics, notably Corneille. Corneille might easily have suggested to him the idea that a high degree of dramatic art is necessary "to bring the Action to the last extremity and then by probable Means to recover All." Corneille says, speaking of the last act of a play:

> ... il faut, s'il se peut, lui réserver toute la catastrophe, et même la reculer vers la fin autant qu'il est possible. Plus on la diffère, plus les esprits demeurent suspendus, et, l'impatience qu'ils ont de savoir de quel côté elle tournera est cause qu'ils la reçoivent avec plus de plaisir: ce qui n'arrive pas quand elle commence avec cet acte. L'auditeur qui la sait trop tôt n'a plus de curiosité; et son attention languit durant tout le reste, qui ne lui apprend rien de nouveau.[143]

We have seen that he was proud of the surprise happy ending of *Rodogune*. Rapin, too, finds the appeal of tragedy in the surprises it affords the spectator. The pleasure of the spectator, according to him, is to expect constantly something surprising. Nothing is more important in the theater than suspense because the greatest pleasure which drama offers the spectator is surprise. "For the pleasure of the spectators is to expect always something that may *surprize*, and that is contrary to their *Prejudgments*. And nothing ought to be predominant on the Theatre so much as the *Suspension*, because the chief delight to be receiv'd there, is the *Surprize*."[144]

If there is anything peculiarly English in English neo-classical theory of tragedy, it is the idea that the moral function of tragedy is to teach conformity to the conventions of bourgeois morality—that is, to inculcate domestic virtues—and the sentimental and humanitarian interpretation of tragic pity which we find in Dryden.

Despite the French origin of English neo-classical doctrine, however, it is, in almost every respect, inimical to Racinian tragedy. Racine is amoral (except in the Biblical plays), antiheroic, and antimelodramatic. In his tragedies the innocent perish with the guilty (Britannicus, Bajazet, Hippolyte). "Lawful love" is indistinguishable from hate when embittered by jealousy (Hermione). "Lawful love," even when requited, is capable of destroying the beloved object (Atalide). Racine asks us to pity "unlawful love" even when it plots the destruction of

[143] "Du Poëme dramatique," in *Oeuvres*, I, 48.
[144] *Op. cit.*, p. 130.

the innocent (Eriphile).[145] To the apostles of great thoughts and noble sentiments Racine must certainly have appeared wanting. Duty and "gloire" become pretexts for temporizing and dissimulation, and the handmaidens of submission to instinct (Hermione). Racine's characters conceive of magnanimity and cannot achieve it (Atalide, Eriphile, Phèdre). Magnanimity is an unattainable ideal; the concept of magnanimity merely serves to underscore the fatality of instinct and increase the pathos of heroines who recognize the fact that their generous impulses are checked, beguiled, and overruled at the crucial moment by powerful destructive forces within themselves (Atalide, Phèdre). Of Racine's tragedies only *Iphigénie, Mithridate,* and *Athalie* have a double fable ending with the rescue of the innocent. Only in these three is there any possible doubt of the outcome until the last minute. In the others, suspense and foreshadowing are for the most part of a psychological order, arising from the audience's knowledge that the characters deceive themselves as well as others and that they are subject to rash and violent impulses. The psychological action reaches its climax in Act IV (*Andromaque, Britannicus, Phèdre*) or early in Act V (*Bajazet*) and here it turns definitely towards catastrophe and the dénouement begins. Indeed with such well-known subjects as those of *Andromaque, Britannicus, Bérénice, Phèdre,* and *Athalie* the outcome must have been known to the audiences from the beginning.

Only in the trend towards concentration in plot does English neo-classicism favor the Racinian genre rather than native panoramic drama. This is more than counterbalanced by the cult of the sublime, the grandiose, and the pictorial in poetic style, which must have made Racine's simple, natural style seem anything but poetry worthy of the noble genre of tragedy.

It might be said that English neo-classicism completely passed over the Racinian moment in French classical tragedy. The reason is not far to seek. In their search for that regularity which would bring to fruition their native genius for tragedy, the English read French theory in preference to French dramatists, whom they looked upon as handicapped in the first place by a want of natural genius and in the second place by a language better suited to courting and to billets-doux than to sublime poetry.[146] Now Racinian tragedy found no apologists among

---

[145] Preface to *Iphigénie,* in *Oeuvres,* III, 160.
[146] Louis Charlanne, *op. cit.,* pp. 202–11.

the French theorists themselves. D'Aubignac had foreshadowed the Racinian genre by recognizing a genre with a minimum of incident, depending for its interest on the passions, and by admitting the appeal of a tragedy whose outcome is known in advance. But he merely gave this genre a place alongside the one with plot complication, suspense, and surprise for the spectator.[147] Racine's contemporary, Rapin, the most revered of the French critics in England, definitely favored the latter genre.[148]

Racine obviously appealed to the Parisian public. They liked to weep at his tragedies and many were probably weary of Cornelian heroics. Bussy-Rabutin, though no partisan of Racine, speaking for his circle, and writing in 1688, said: "Nous avons été ravis de nous délasser avec Molière des grands sentimens de Corneille. On est si fâché en le lisant de n'être pas Romain et d'être forcé d'admirer ce qu'on n'est plus capable ni de faire ni de penser, qu'on sort tout abattu de cette lecture."[149] Among the professional critics, the partisans of Racine were aware of his originality and the nature of the appeal of his tragedies. Boileau saw that the fatality of instinct was the source of the tragic in Phèdre: "... Phèdre, malgré soi, perfide, incestueuse...." But, if the first part of Canto III of the *Art Poétique* is a codification of Racine's system, there are verses which could not but lend support to the pattern of plot complication and surprise ending:

> Que le trouble toujours croissant de scène en scène,
> A son comble arrivé se débrouille sans peine.
> L'esprit ne se sent point plus vivement frappé,
> Que lorsqu'en un sujet d'intrigue enveloppé,
> D'un secret tout à coup la vérité connue
> Change tout, donne à tout une face imprévue.[150]

La Bruyère perceived the psychological realism of Racine's portrayal of passion: "ce qu'il y a de plus flatteur et de plus délicat dans la passion."[151] He saw that the appeal of Racine's tragedies was a purely emotional one: "l'on est plus occupé aux pièces de Corneille, l'on est plus ébranlé et plus attendri à celles de Racine; Corneille est plus moral,

---

[147] See above, n. 112.
[148] See above, n. 142.
[149] *Correspondance*, ed. Ludovic Lalanne (Paris, 1859), VI, 142.
[150] Boileau, *Oeuvres* (Paris, 1871), I, 202.
[151] La Bruyère, *Oeuvres* (Paris, 1865), I, 142.

Racine plus naturel. . . ."[152] But certain remarks of his might also be interpreted as favoring suspense and surprise. He refers to "l'incertitude," "l'espérance," and "les surprises" in tragedy.[153]

The partisans of Corneille were more prejudiced and more vociferous than the critics who favored Racine. They continued to extol Corneille at the expense of Racine after Racine had eclipsed his great rival in the public favor. Cornelian heroics found a champion in Saint-Évremond who was the apologist of admiration as a tragic emotion.[154] The "Moderns" were partisans of Corneille. They lauded the heroic quality of his characters and spoke disdainfully of Racine's realism.[155] But it was not only the heroic in Corneille that was held up for admiration to the detriment of Racine. The structure of Cornelian tragedy was proclaimed more "regular" than the Racinian genre. Saint-Évremond, in some respects a "Modern," is definitely on the side of the "Ancients" when he needs an argument to prove Corneille's superiority. At the moment when Racine's triumph over his great rival was complete, Saint-Évremond plainly implied that Corneille had followed the precepts of the Aristotelians while Racine had no guide but the current bad taste of his public.[156] Earlier he had hoped that the public would soon recover

[152] *Loc. cit.*
[153] *Ibid.*, p. 138.
[154] Saint-Évremond recommends as the subject of tragedy "des actions principales qui soient reçues dans notre créance comme humaines, & qui nous donnent de l'admiration comme rares & élevées au-dessus des autres" ("De la Tragédie ancienne et moderne," in *Oeuvres*, ed. René Planhol [Paris, 1927], I, 176). He notes that fear has become in modern tragedy—he does not mention any particular tragedies—little more than "une agréable inquiétude qui subsiste dans la suspension des esprits; c'est un cher intérêt que prend notre âme aux sujets qui attirent son affection" (*ibid.*, p. 179). Of pity in modern tragedy, he says: "Nous la dépouillons de toute sa faiblesse, & nous lui laissons tout ce qu'elle peut avoir de charitable et d'humain." He approves of pity for "un grand homme malheureux" but thinks pity should be mingled with "une admiration animée" (*loc. cit.*).
[155] In 1687 Perrault praises in Corneille "L'héroïque beauté des nobles sentiments" (*Le Siècle de Louis le Grand*, quoted by Pierre Mélèse, *Le Théâtre et le Public à Paris sous Louis XIV* [Paris, 1934], p. 141). In 1693 Fontenelle writes: "Les caractères de Corneille sont vrais, quoiqu'ils ne soient pas communs. Les caractères de Racine ne sont vrais, que parce qu'ils sont communs. . . . Quand on a le coeur noble, on voudroit ressembler aux héros de Corneille; et quand on a le coeur petit, on est bien aise que les héros de Racine nous ressemblent." (*Ibid.*, p. 145.)
[156] Around 1677 we find Saint-Évremond desperately defending Corneille

NEO-CLASSICAL THEORY OF TRAGEDY

from its aberration.[157] There were others who considered Corneille's tragedies "regular," Racine's "irregular."[158]

After Corneille was dead and Racine had written his last tragedy, a different appraisal of the two great French dramatists is brought to the attention of the English with the appearance of André Dacier's commentary on Aristotle.[159] Dacier is not a partisan of either. With one exception, he takes issue with Corneille on points of theory.[160] He

---

against the criticism of certain members of the London salon of the Duchesse de Mazarin. He says, with biting irony: "Vous avez raison, messieurs, vous avez raison de vous moquer des songes d'Aristote et d'Horace; des reveries de Heinsius et de Grotius; des caprices de Corneille et de Ben Jonson, des fantaisies de Rapin & de Boileau. La seule règle des honnêtes gens, c'est la mode. Que sert une raison qui n'est point reçue, & qui peut trouver à redire à une extravagance qui plaît?" (from the third letter in the series which has been entitled "Defense de quelques Pièces de Théâtre de M. Corneille," in *Oeuvres*, I, 215). He does not name Racine at once but it is plain that Racine's is the "extravagance qui plaît." He continues: "J'avoue qu'il y a eu des temps où il fallait choisir de beaux sujets & les bien traiter; il ne faut plus aujourd'hui que des caractères" (*loc. cit.*). Later he shows his hand: "Racine est préféré à Corneille & les caractères l'emportent sur les sujets" (*ibid.*, p. 217).

[157] The letter which has been entitled "A un Auteur qui me demandait mon sentiment d'une pièce où l'Héroïne ne faisait que se lamenter" (1672) is perhaps an oblique attack on Racine, specifically on *Bérénice* which had been a "succès de larmes," while Corneille's treatment of the same subject (*Tite et Bérénice*), presented at the same time to the Parisian public, had been far less successful. This was Racine's first triumph over Corneille. In 1672 Saint-Évremond was hoping that the taste of the Parisian public would soon improve: He says to the author of the "tragédie larmoyante," ". . . il [Corneille] ouvre le coeur avec tout son secret. . . . Quelques autres [Racine and Quinault?] ont suivi plus heureusement la disposition des esprits, qui n'aiment aujourd'hui que la douleur & les larmes; mais je crains pour vous quelque retour du bon goût justement sur votre pièce, & qu'on ne vienne 'a désapprouver le trop grand usage d'une passion dont on enchante présentement tout le monde'" (*Oeuvres*, I, 218-19).

[158] After the triumph of *Bérénice*, l'Abbé de Villars says that Corneille has written plays "dans toutes les règles," and is admired for the form of his tragedies, while Racine's *Bérénice* touches only those who are ignorant of the rules (*La Critique de Bérénice*, in G. Michaut, *La Bérénice de Racine* [Paris, 1907], pp. 241-42).

[159] *La Poëtique d'Aristote Traduite en François avec des Remarques*, Paris, 1692.

[160] He thinks that Corneille effectively refutes the opinion that, in saying that the manners of tragedy should be "good," Aristotle meant *morally* good. Dacier thinks, like Corneille, that Aristotle meant that the character of the personages should be "well-marked" (*op. cit.*, p. 233). On the other hand, he thinks that Corneille misinterpreted the meaning of Aristotle's phrase, "tragédie sans moeurs"

criticizes irregularities in several of Corneille's tragedies.[161] He rejects admiration as a tragic passion.[162] He finds the double catastrophe inferior to the simple.[163] He considers Racine's *Phèdre* the only French tragedy which follows exactly one of the two patterns which Aristotle ranked first.[164] He points out that Racine has violated a rule by making his Hippolyte a lover; but recognizes the necessity for a change.[165] He thinks that Racine has improved on Euripides in the character of Iphigénie.[166] On the other hand, although he does not rank high the double fable with the happy ending for the good and the unhappy for

---

(p. 90). Corneille's notion of unity of place is quite erronneous (p. 278). He argues against Corneille for continuity of action (p. 279). He takes issue with Corneille on the question of choruses (p. 313). He thinks Corneille erred in substituting admiration for pity and fear in *Nicomède* (p. 141).

[161] He criticizes *Oedipe* (p. 140), *Nicomède* (p. 141), *Héraclius* (pp. 154–55), *Polyeucte* (p. 177), *Rodogune* (p. 219), *Médée* (p. 246), and *Cinna* (p. 276).

[162] Admiration is the emotion proper to the epic; the proper tragic emotions are pity and fear (p. 77). Corneille was wrong in thinking that catharsis could be effected in tragedy by admiration alone: ". . . ce n'est nullement le but de la Tragédie de purger les passions par l'admiration, qui est une passion trop douce pour produire un si grand effet; elle n'emploie que la crainte & la pitié et laisse regner l'admiration dans le Poëme épique" (p. 141).

[163] Dacier defines the "fable simple" as "celle qui n'expose que les malheurs d'un seul personnage" and the "fable double" as "celle qui a une double catastrophe, c'est à dire, qui finit par une catastrophe qui est heureuse pour les bons & funeste pour les méchans" (p. 187). The latter type he disapproves of because "la prospérité des bons n'a rien de tragique; & il n'y a rien de terrible ni de pitoyable dans la punition des méchans" (p. 188). The double catastrophe, "bien loin d'être d'un genre plus sublime que les autres, comme l'a prétendu M. Corneille, ne tient que le second ou même le troisième rang, comme Aristote l'a déjà prouvé" (p. 218).

[164] "Mais si je m'en souviens bien, hors la seule Phedre de M. Racine, qui est une pièce Greque, nous n'en avons pas une seule, qui soit précisément dans l'une ou l'autre de ces deux regles; c'est à dire qu'il n'y en a point dont le Héros, n'étant ny bon ny méchant, tombe dans un grand malheur par sa faute; ou qui étant plûtôt bon que méchant, s'attire par une faute involontaire une catastrophe funeste. Notre Theatre ne peut donc proprement se vanter d'avoir les deux especes de Tragédie ausquelles Aristote donne le premier rang" (pp. 188–89).

[165] "M. Racine a peché contre la ressemblance dans le caractere de son Hippolite, car en le faisant amoureux, il a bien sçu qu'il s'éloignoit de la vérité, mais pour cacher ce defaut & pour ratrapper en quelque maniere la ressemblance, il luy a donné un amour farouche & sauvage, persuadé que nôtre Theatre ne pourroit souffrir un homme entierement ennemy de l'amour" (p. 244).

[166] "M. Racine a beaucoup mieux réussi; en empruntant les beautez d'Euripide, il a évité ses défauts, & a fait un caractere d'Iphigénie toujours noble, sans aucune inégalité" (p. 243).

the wicked characters, he praises French tragedies which follow this pattern.[167] Moreover, he favors a last-minute surprise ending, whether happy or unhappy.[168] He mentions Racine less frequently than Corneille and, though he takes issue with Corneille, he refers often to his great genius.[169]

After the appearance of his treatise, Dacier took his place in England, along with Rapin and Le Bossu, as the third of the great triumvirate of dictators of the rules.[170] He may have called *Phèdre* and *Iphigénie* to the attention of English classicists as examples of regular Aristotelian tragedies.[171] He furnished the classicists with one argument for the rules when he asserted that Corneille's later plays were more regular—and greater—than his earlier ones.[172] On the other hand, since he presents Corneille as a "great irregular genius," he might conceivably have enhanced Corneille's reputation with the English "Moderns." He might

---

[167] "Nous en avons pourtant de cette espèce parmi nos plus belles, mais il est certain qu'Aristote en condamnant le dessein de ces pièces, n'auroit pû s'empêcher d'admirer les beautés infinies sous lesquelles ce défaut est presque caché" (p. 200).

[168] "C'est une vérité constante, où il n'y a point de surprise, il n'y a pour l'ordinaire, ni crainte ni compassion" (p. 142). "Le noeud comprend la plus grande partie de la Tragédie, car il embrasse ordinairement les quatre premiers Actes & quelquefois même la plus grande partie du cinquieme, en un mot il dure autant que l'esprit du spectateur est suspendu sur l'issuë des desseins du Héros, & des obstacles qui le traversent. Dans l'Iphigénie & dans la Phedre de M. Racine, comme dans l'Hippolyte & dans l'Iphigénie d'Euripide, le noeud dure jusqu'à la derniere Scene, où se fait le denouëment. Et cela est beaucoup plus beau que, quand le noeud ne va que jusques au milieu du quatrieme Acte. Car alors il est difficile, ou plutot impossible que le reste ne soit bien languissant" (pp. 294–95). ". . . le meilleur denouement c'est toujours le plus reculé, & celui qui ne vient qu'à la fin, c'est à dire, à la derniere Scene" (p. 305).

It is difficult to understand how he can believe that the dénouement of *Phèdre* does not begin until the last scene. Surely there can be no doubt of the outcome after Phèdre learns of Hippolyte's love for Aricie and does not carry out her intention of confessing in order to save Hippolyte (Act IV, Scene 4).

[169] Corneille he cites as an example of a great genius whose plays improved as he became acquainted with the rules (p. 120). Cf. Rymer, *A Short View of Tragedy*, p. 62. "M. Corneille a été," says Dacier, "sans contredit pour le Theatre un des plus grands génies que l'on ait jamais veu." He points out the fallacies in Corneille's notion of unity of place in order to show "dans quelles erreurs les plus grands Hommes ne peuvent s'empêcher de tomber, quand ils violent les regles, & qu'ils s'éloignent de la Nature & de la Vérité" (p. 278).

[170] See above, n. 15.
[171] See above, n. 164 and n. 166.
[172] See above, n. 169.

even have suggested to them some kinship between Corneille and their own "great irregular genius," Shakespeare.

Racine altered the content and somewhat modified the form of tragedy.[178] But French theory of tragedy was scarcely influenced by this change. The English, reading French theorists in preference to French dramatists, and even more addicted than the French to the sublime and to great and noble thoughts, developed a conception of tragedy as heroic melodrama. Psychological naturalism and Racinian pathos had no effect on their concept of tragedy. It was the spirit of sentimental melodrama, the spirit of the *drame bourgeois* which encroached on the heroic in England. Despite its French origin, English neo-classicism was a formidable barrier to the appreciation of the Racinian genre in England. Racine's style was suited to his psychological realism and his conception of the dramatic as psychological conflict. The English, failing to perceive either the psychological realism or the psychological drama, could hardly have appreciated the simple, natural style. It may have appeared undramatic; it certainly must have seemed unpoetic to critics for whom the essence of poetry as distinguished from prose was ornament, in the form of prolonged metaphor and simile, and epithet.

There was little in the English neo-classical theory of tragedy to encourage a sympathetic exploration of Racine's tragedies and much to encourage the exploitation and distortion or his plays which we find in the adaptations of the early eighteenth century.

[178] Two recent studies point out the antithesis of Racinian and Cornelian tragedy. Paul Bénichou notes the radical change in content: *Morales du Grand Siècle*, Paris, 1948. Georges May analyzes the contrast in structure and appeal: *Tragédie Cornélienne, Tragédie Racinienne*, Urbana, 1948.

« « CHAPTER XII » »

ENGLISH JUDGMENTS OF RACINE
1675 – 1699

IN ENGLISH CRITICISM of the period of Dryden and Rymer there appeared only two criticisms of Racine sufficiently particularized to be of any importance: John Crowne's remarks on *Andromaque*[1] and Dryden's criticism of *Phèdre* in the preface to *All for Love*. These two bits of Racine criticism have something in common. Both are strictures on the French poet. Both are so intemperate in tone and so ill-considered as to suggest that they sprang from motives other than purely esthetic. John Crowne, as I have shown,[2] was too ignorant of the French language to be capable of criticism of Racine that could be taken seriously. Nor is there evidence that his criticism exerted any influence in England. On the other hand, Dryden's remarks on *Phèdre* set a pattern in English criticism. These remarks have been quoted again and again; but, as far as I know, no one has interpreted them in the light of the context in which they appear, the moment at which Dryden wrote them, and their relation to his dramatic theory. Here are Dryden's remarks on French poets and his strictures on *Phèdre*:

"The faults my enemies have found are . . . cavils concerning little and not essential decencies; which a master of the ceremonies may decide betwixt us. The French poets, I confess, are strict observers of these punctilios: They would not, for example, have suffered Cleopatra and Octavia to have met; or, if they had met, there must have only passed betwixt them some cold civilities, but no eagerness of repartee, for fear of offending against the greatness of their characters and the modesty of their sex. This objection I foresaw, and at the same time contemned; for I judged it both natural and probable, that Octavia, proud of her new-gained conquest, would search out Cleopatra to triumph over her; and that Cleopatra, thus attacked, was not of a

[1] See above, Chap. I.
[2] See above, Chap. I.

spirit to shun the encounter: And it is not unlikely, that two exasperated rivals should use such satire as I have put into their mouths; for, after all, though the one were a Roman, and the other a queen, they were both women.... in this nicety of manners does the excellency of French poetry consist. Their heroes are the most civil people breathing; but their good breeding seldom extends to a word of sense; all their wit is in their ceremony; they want the genius which animates our stage; and therefore it is but necessary, when they cannot please, that they should take care not to offend. But, as the civilest man in the company is commonly the dullest, so these authors, while they are afraid to make you laugh or cry, out of pure good manners make you sleep. They are so careful not to exasperate a critic, that they never leave him any work; so busy with the broom, and make so clean a riddance, that there is little left either for censure or for praise: For no part of a poem is worth our discommending, where the whole is insipid; as when we have once tasted of palled wine, we stay not to examine it glass by glass. But while they affect to shine in trifles, they are often careless in essentials. Thus, their Hippolytus is so scrupulous in point of decency, that he will rather expose himself to death, than accuse his step-mother to his father; and my critics I am sure will commend him for it. But we of grosser apprehensions are apt to think that this excess of generosity is not practicable, but with fools and madmen. This was good manners with a vengeance; and the audience is like to be much concerned at the misfortunes of this admirable hero. But take Hippolytus out of his poetic fit, and I suppose he would think it a wiser part to set the saddle on the right horse, and choose rather to live with the reputation of a plain-spoken, honest man, than to die with the infamy of an incestuous villain. In the meantime we may take notice, that where the poet ought to have preserved the character as it was delivered to us by antiquity, when he should have given us the picture of a rough young man, of the Amazonian strain, a jolly huntsman, and both by his profession and his early rising a mortal enemy to love, he has chosen to give him the turn of gallantry, sent him to travel from Athens to Paris, taught him to make love, and transformed the Hippolytus of Euripides into Monsieur Hippolyte. I should not have troubled myself thus far with French poets, but that I find our *Chedreux* critics wholly form their judgments by them."[3]

[3] *Works*, ed. Scott-Saintsbury (Edinburgh, 1883), V, 327-31.

ENGLISH JUDGMENTS OF RACINE

Dryden brings three charges against Racine: he has changed the traditional character of Hippolytus; he has Gallicized the Greek hero; his Hippolytus shows an absurd concern for decency and good manners characteristic of the French. The first two charges are not uniquely English. Some French critics had censured Racine for making his Hippolytus a lover.[4] As early as 1666, Saint-Évremond had criticized Racine for making Frenchmen of the characters of antiquity.[5] This criticism was frequently made by partisans of Corneille and reportedly by Corneille himself.[6] Racine, like D'Aubignac, thought that the characters of a tragedy should be portrayed in such a way as to conform to the tastes and beliefs of the contemporary audience.[7] Corneille and his partisans espoused the old literary doctrine of historical realism. Dryden himself refers later to the French criticism of *Bajazet* on this score.[8]

It is noteworthy that Dryden advocates historical realism only when

---

[4] In the "Dissertation sur les tragedies de Phèdre et Hippolyte," attributed to Subligny and published in 1677, we find the following criticism of the character of Hippolyte: "Je ne pense pas que vous approuviez M. Racine d'avoir souillé l'innocence d'Hippolyte, que tant de siecles et d'auteurs ont respectée, et de l'avoir, par cette tendresse criminelle, rendu capable d'une révolte si ingrate à l'égard de son père et si dangereuse pour lui. . . . C'est vouloir faire passer . . . un Joseph pour un Absalon" (p. 392). Subligny is less shocked by a Hippolytus in love than by the fact that Hippolyte's passion causes him to plan a rebellion against his father. Dryden's objection is of the same order as Saint-Évremond's objection to Racine's Alexander. "Mais gardons-nous," says Saint-Évremond, "de faire un Antoine d'un Alexandre, & ne ruinons pas le héros établi par tant de siècles, en faveur de l'amant que nous formons à notre fantaisie." ("Dissertation sur la tragédie de Racine intitulée *Alexandre*," *Oeuvres*, ed. René de Planhol [Paris, 1927], I, 204.)

[5] "Je m'imaginais en Porus une grandeur d'âme qui nous fût plus étrangère, le héros des Indes devait avoir un caractère différent de celui des nôtres. Un autre ciel, pour ainsi parler, un autre soleil, une autre terre y produisent d'autres animaux & d'autres fruits: les hommes y paraissent tout autres par la différence des visages, & plus encore, si je l'ose dire, par une diversité de raison: une morale, une sagesse singulière à la région y semble régler & conduire d'autres esprits dans un autre monde. Porus cependant, que Quinte-Curse dépeint tout étranger aux Grecs & aux Perses, est ici purement Français: au lieu de nous transporter aux Indes, on l'amène en France, où il s'accoutume si bien à notre humeur qu'il semble être né parmi nous, ou du moins y avoir vécu toute sa vie." (*Ibid.*, p. 199.)

[6] See Pierre Mélèse, *Le Théâtre et le public à Paris sous Louis XIV* (Paris, 1934), pp. 267–68, p. 268, n. 1.

[7] See particularly Racine's second preface to *Andromaque* and D'Aubignac, *La Pratique du théâtre*, ed. Martino (Paris, 1927), pp. 72–74.

[8] *Works*, VI, 271.

he is criticizing Racine. As early as 1670 he had commended, as a sure road to success, conformity to the taste of an audience (*Conquest of Granada*, Part II, Epilogue):

> They, who have best succeeded on the stage,
> Have still conform'd their genius to their age.

In *Heads of an Answer to Rymer*[9] he attributes Shakespeare's success in part to his conformity to the taste of his age and his countrymen:

> And one reason of that success is, in my opinion, this: that Shakespeare and Fletcher have written to the genius of the age and nation in which they lived; for though nature, as he objects, is the same in all places, and reason too the same, yet the climate, the age, the disposition of the people to whom a poet writes may be so different that what pleased the Greeks would not satisfy an English audience.[10]

[9] There have been contradictory conjectures concerning the date of composition of Dryden's *Heads of an Answer to Rymer*. The original manuscript is not extant. The piece was first published in the 1711 edition of the works of Beaumont and Fletcher (Preface, pp. xii–xxvi), with the following note: "Mr. *Rymer* sent one of his Books as a Present to Mr. *Dryden*, who on the Blank Leaves, before the beginning, and after the End of the Book, made several Remarks, as if he design'd an Answer to Mr. *Rymer*'s Reflections; they are of Mr. Dryden's own Hand Writing, and may be seen at the Publisher's of this Book; 'tis to be wish'd he had put his last Hand to 'em, and made the Connection closer, but just as he left them, be pleas'd to take them here *verbatim* inserted" (p. xii). Dr. Johnson reprinted it in his life of Dryden, with the remark that Dryden had written his observations on the blank leaves of the copy of *Tragedies of the Last Age* which Rymer had sent him (*Lives of the English Poets*, ed. George Birkbeck Hill [Oxford, 1905], I, 471). Birkbeck Hill believed it likely that Dryden, when he wrote *Heads of an Answer*, had before him not only *Tragedies of the Last Age* but also *A Short View of Tragedy*, 1693 (*ibid.*, p. 471, n. 1). The one passage in *A Short View of Tragedy* to which Hill sees a possible allusion in Dryden's piece does not strike me as convincing evidence (*ibid.*, p. 476, n. 2). The Scott-Saintsbury edition of Dryden merely notes that Dryden's observations were written on the blank leaves of "Rymer's book," i.e., *Tragedies of the Last Age* (1677). Fred G. Wolcott advances the theory that the Preface to *Troilus and Cressida* is the completed essay, of which *Heads of an Answer* was the outline ("John Dryden's Answer to Thomas Rymer," *Philological Quarterly*, XV [1936], 194–214). If Wolcott's theory is correct, Dryden composed *Heads of an Answer to Rymer* as early as 1678. On the other hand, Henry Hitch Adams and Baxter Hathaway give 1693 as the date of composition of Dryden's piece and state without evidence that it comes from notes which Dryden scribbled in his copy of *A Short View of Tragedy*. (*Dramatic Essays of the Neoclassic Age*, ed. Adams and Hathaway [New York, 1950], p. 157.)

[10] *Dramatic Essays of the Neoclassic Age*, p. 163.

ENGLISH JUDGMENTS OF RACINE

Peculiar to Dryden in this criticism of *Phèdre* is the interpretation of Hippolyte's motive in remaining silent in the face of his father's accusation. Dryden would have it that Hippolyte chooses to die or at least to "expose" himself to death rather than to be unmannerly. The lines of Racine's play make it clear that Hippolyte's choice is not between *death* and denouncing his stepmother, but between *exile* and causing his *father* pain and shame.[11] Racine speaks in his preface of Hippolyte's "grandeur d'âme" in sparing Phèdre's honor.[12] But could anyone seriously think that Hippolyte was merely obeying a rule of etiquette?

Dryden's criticism of the French for an undue regard for court etiquette is justified by some French critics and dramatists, notably Jacques Pradon, author of the rival *Phèdre*.[13] La Mesnardière and his English follower Rymer are the examples of the identification of decorum in the portrayal of character with the mere rules of court etiquette. But Dryden did not make this criticism of Rymer's book when it appeared.[14] On the contrary, he was most enthusiastic:

> Mr. Rymer sent me his booke, which has been my best entertainment hetherto: 'tis certainly very learned, & the best piece of Criticism in the English tongue; perhaps in any other of the Moderns; if I am not altogether of his opinion I am so, in most of what he sayes; and thinke my selfe happy that he has not fallen upon me, as severely and as wittily as he has upon Shakespeare, and Fletcher, for he is the only man I know capable of finding out a poet's blind sides; and if he can hold here without exposing his Edgar to be censured by his Enemyes; I thinke there is no man will dare to answer him, or can.[15]

---

[11] Thésée's prayer to Neptune in Hippolytus' presence is ambiguous (vs. 1075). Hippolyte mentions exile (vs. 114). Aricie fears for his life (vs. 1334) but he trusts in the justice of the gods (vs. 1351) and urges her to flee with him and join her in a rebellion against Thésée and Phèdre (vss. 1357-70). He explains his motive in remaining silent (vss. 1340-43).

[12] Mesnard ed., II, 301.

[13] In his dedicatory epistle to the Duchesse de Bouillon, Pradon says of his Hippolytus: "Ce jeune Héros auroit eu mauvaise grace de venir tout hérissé des épines du Grec, dans une cour si galante que la nostre." (Pradon, *Oeuvres* [Paris, 1682], I, 11.)

[14] The title page of Rymer's *The Tragedies of the Last Age Consider'd* bears the date 1678; but there is evidence that the book had appeared in the late summer of 1677. See *Letters of John Dryden*, ed. Charles E. Ward (Durham, 1942), p. 148.

[15] *Ibid.*, pp. 13-14.

Perhaps undue stress of etiquette was one point on which Dryden differed from Rymer. If so, it scarcely dampened his enthusiasm. But Racine's fancied regard for good manners is enough to damn his play in Dryden's eyes. Dryden's choice of Racine as an example of the French obsession with etiquette is singularly wanting in aptness. In France Racine was the butt rather than the exemplar of the sticklers for etiquette.[16] Dryden had to distort fact somewhat and offer an unconvincing interpretation of Hippolyte's motives in order to prove Racine guilty of a fault with which he might quite rightly have charged other French writers. And, as I have pointed out, he had to shift his critical position in order to condemn Racine for Gallicizing a hero of Greek legend. Why did he go out of his way to attack Racine? The context of his criticism suggests circumstances similar to those which brought forth John Crowne's strictures on *Andromaque*. As Dryden himself tells us, he set about writing *All for Love* in accordance with Rymer's precepts: ". . . I have endeavoured in this play to follow the practise of the ancients, who, as Mr. Rymer has judiciously observ'd, are and ought to be our masters."[17] Dryden says he is imitating the ancients. Could it be that actually he was imitating the French while pretending to imitate the ancients? Such tactics were often resorted to in England during this period.[18]

In *All for Love* Dryden approached for the first time the concentration of French classical tragedy. Did he have a particular French model? There is evidence that he had read Racine's *Bérénice* before writing his tragedy on a similar theme. There are verbal echoes that cannot be attributed to chance. For instance (vss. 545-46, 655-62):

---

[16] See above, Chap. XI, n. 101.

[17] *Op. cit.*, p. 16.

[18] Rymer claims to be following the ancients and never mentions the name of La Mesnardière, his most important source. Dryden is more indebted to French critics than to the ancients in his preface to *Troilus and Cressida* but states that Aristotle, Horace, and Longinus were his guides (see John C. Sherwood, "Dryden and the Rules: The Preface to Troilus and Cressida," *Comparative Literature*, II [1950], 73-83). In the dialogue entitled *A Comparison between the two Stages* (1702), a speaker who admires Dryden replies thus to a charge of wholesale plagiarism brought by his interlocutor against Dryden: "I believe he has not borrow'd a Thought from any other Author, but he has mended it. I'le grant you he was a notorious Plagiary, and what's worse, he always contemns those from whom he takes." (*A Comparison between the two Stages*, ed. Staring B. Wells [Princeton, 1942], p. 34.)

ENGLISH JUDGMENTS OF RACINE

Titus
Depuis cinq ans entiers, chaque jour je la vois,
Et crois toujours la voir pour la première fois.

Antony
I saw you every day, and all the day;
And every day was still but as the first,
So eager was I still to see you more.

Bérénice
Je ne te vante point cette foible victoire,
Titus. Ah! plût au ciel que, sans blesser ta gloire,
Un rival plus puissant voulût tenter ma foi
Et pût mettre à mes pieds plus d'empires que toi;
Que de sceptres sans nombre il pût payer ma flamme;
Que ton amour n'eût rien à donner que ton âme!
C'est alors, cher Titus, qu'aimé, victorieux,
Tu verrois de quel prix ton coeur est à mes yeux.

Cleopatra
How often have I wished some other Caesar,
Great as the first, and as the second young,
Would court my love, to be refused for you.[19]

If Dryden turned to Racine for guidance when he set out to classicize Shakespeare's tragedy, only to be censured by Gallophile critics[20] whom he might have expected to please, resentment might well have clouded his judgment sufficiently to account for his choice of Racine as his victim and for the injustice of his attack. It is ironical that his estimate of Racine should have had such a lasting influence in England.

---

[19] These and other passages are quoted by Dorothy Burrows in her unpublished doctoral dissertation. Miss Burrows points out that the plot of *Aureng-Zebe* is that of *Mithridate*, with further complications (Dorothy Burrows, "The Relation of Dryden's Serious Plays and Dramatic Criticism to Contemporary French Literature," thesis [University of Illinois, 1933], p. 245). She thinks that Nourmahal suggests (but does not parallel) Roxane and also Hermione; but she is of the opinion that Dryden came closest to the Racinian manner in *All for Love* (*ibid.*, p. 247) and that the relative absence of incident and the concentration of interest on the psychological study in this play "strongly suggest imitation of Racine" (*ibid.*, p. 248).

[20] None of Dryden's editors has any suggestion to make concerning the identity of the critics of Dryden's *All for Love*. The Earl of Rochester had attacked Dryden's plays in general in his *Horace's 10th Satyr of the First Book Imitated* (*Works* [London, 1709], Part II, pp. 1-3). Dryden attacks Rochester violently in the preface to *All for Love* (*op. cit.*, pp. 12-16).

If Dryden's young admirer John Dennis had chosen to devote a critical essay to Racine, he would doubtless have contributed to English criticism a more judicious and enlightened estimate of the French tragic poet. Unfortunately his only judgment of Racine was written at a time when his admiration for Dryden was great. In January, 1693/4, he writes an adulatory letter to Dryden in which we find the following indirect compliment to Racine: ". . . tho I can but hope that the Confederate Forces will give chase to De Lorges and Luxemburgh, I am very confident that Boileau and Racine will be forced to submit to you."[21] Such praise of Racine is hardly satisfying to his admirers. Nevertheless it implies great admiration for Racine, if only because, in casting about for a comparison that would be most flattering to Dryden, Dennis chose Racine rather than Corneille. Incidental remarks of Dennis's indicate that he had an unusually thorough knowledge of Racine's tragedies and prefaces, in addition to a wider and more profound knowledge of the French critics than either Dryden or Rymer.[22] In

---

[21] *The Letters of John Dryden*, ed. Ward, p. 66. This letter is dated January, 1693/4.

[22] A glance at the index of E. N. Hooker's edition of the *Critical Works* of Dennis will reveal the frequency with which Dennis cites Boileau, Dacier, Rapin, and Saint-Évremond. It is obvious that he had read and digested Dacier's remarks on Aristotle before he took issue with Rymer in *The Impartial Critick*, though he does once misquote Dacier. (Dennis says: "How did Corneille do it before him, who was certainly a great Man, too? And if you'll believe *Dacier, C'etoit le plus grand genie pour le Theatre qu'on avoit Jamais veu*" [I, 21]. Dacier had said: "M. Corneille a été sans contredit pour le Theatre *un des plus grands génies* que l'on ait jamais veu" [André Dacier, *La Poëtique d'Aristote Traduite en François, avec Des Remarques* (Paris, 1692), p. 120; italics mine].) So well does he know Dacier that he sometimes couches his critical remarks in Dacier's very phrases (see below, n. 26 and n. 28). Dennis admired Boileau as much as a Gallophobe could admire a Frenchman. He translated Boileau's speech of reception to the French Academy as an example of the distortion of historical facts by French writers, who, he maintains, were constrained to praise Louis XIV. In the letter accompanying his translation, he deplores Boileau's flattery of Louis, but expresses the greatest admiration for his genius, his art, and his critical integrity. The panegyric of Louis "is scarce to be supported" despite the "most admirable Genius of the Author, which shines throughout it and an Art to which nothing can be added." He thinks Boileau "in the main a Man of Sincerity and a lover of Truth." (*Familiar Letters written by the Right Honourable John, late Earl of Rochester, and other letters, by persons of Honour and Quality* [London, 1705], I, 104.) Dennis knows Rapin and Le Bossu at least as well as Dryden did. Le Bossu seems to have had some influence on his theory of tragedy. But he is apparently less familiar with Corneille's critical writings

view of the dearth of published criticism of Racine, and the absence of evidence in print of a knowledge or appreciation of Racine in England, Dennis's incidental remarks take on some importance.

Dennis's first mention of Racine occurs in *The Impartial Critick* (1693), in connection with the discussion of the restoration of the chorus, recommended by Rymer. Dennis attacks the assertion that the French "have lately seen the necessity" for restoring the chorus in tragedy. To refute this argument, Dennis maintains that, in the preface to *Esther*, "the first tragedy that has been lately writ with a Chorus," Racine says that both the subject and the form of his play were suggested by Madame de Maintenon. The purpose of the chorus, as stated by Freeman (who represents Dennis in the dialogue), is, for all its flippancy of tone, an accurate digest of a passage in Racine's preface:

FREEM. So that what Mr. R—— calls a necessity, was but at best a conveniency.
BEAUM. A conveniency!
FREEM. Aye; for upon the Writing this Religious Play with a Chorus, the cloister'd Beauties of that blooming Society, had a favorable occasion of shewing their Parts in a Religious way, to the French Court.[23]

Racine had no intention of modifying the structure of tragedy. He does say:

... je m'aperçus qu'en travaillant sur le plan qu'on m'avoit donné, j'exécutois en quelque sorte un dessein qui m'avoit souvent passé dans l'esprit, qui étoit de lier, comme dans les anciennes tragédies grecques, le

---

than Dryden and certainly he was less influenced by La Mesnardière than Rymer. A great admiration for Boileau and a thorough knowledge of Dacier might well have inclined him towards a greater appreciation of Racine than critics who derived their doctrine from La Mesnardière, Corneille, Le Bossu, and Rapin.

[23] *Op. cit.*, I, 31. Cf. Racine's preface: "On a soin aussi de faire apprendre à chanter à celles [des demoiselles de Saint-Cyr] qui ont de la voix, et on ne leur laisse pas perdre un talent qui les peut amuser innocemment, et qu'elles peuvent employer un jour à chanter les louanges de Dieu. Mais la plupart des plus excellents vers de notre langue ayant été composés sur des paroles extrêmement molles et efféminées, capables de faire des impressions dangereuses sur de jeunes esprits, les personnes illustres qui ont bien voulu prendre la principale direction de cette maison ont souhaité qu'il y eût quelque ouvrage qui sans avoir tous ces défauts, pût produire une partie de ces bons effets. Elles me firent l'honneur de me communiquer leur dessein, et même de me demander si je ne pourrois pas faire, sur quelque sujet de piété et de morale, une espèce de poëme où le chant fût mêlé avec le récit, le tout lié par une action qui rendît la chose plus vive et moins capable d'ennuyer." (Mesnard ed., III, 454-55.)

choeur et le chant avec l'action, et d'employer à chanter les louanges du vrai Dieu cette partie du choeur que les païens employoient à chanter les louanges de leurs fausses divinités.[24]

But he does not indicate that he had any notion of changing the accepted form of tragedy. He does not even use the word "tragédie" in referring to *Esther*; "pièce" is used throughout his preface. A second time in this dialogue Dennis cites the preface to *Esther* to refute a statement of Rymer's. Rymer affirms, says Dennis, that the chorus is necessary to "confine a poet to unity of place." Dennis points out that Racine's first tragedy with a chorus is also the first one in which he violates the rule of unity of place, and that he admits as much in his preface.[25] These comments by Dennis reveal familiarity with the preface of *Esther* and comprehension of Racine's point of view.

Dennis's next reference to Racine occurs in a comment on the *Hippolytus* of Euripides in his *Remarks on Prince Arthur* (1696). He criticizes Euripides for violating the rule of the "convenience" of the manners in having his Phaedra speak too philosophically for her sex on her present condition. "For," says Dennis, "a Speculative or Sententious Discourse; besides that it puts a stop to the Action of the poem, is by no means the Language of a very violent Passion." He reproves Rymer for commending rather than condemning Euripides here. He then goes on to say that he had once imitated this scene when he had intended to translate Euripides' tragedy for the English stage. In his imitation of the scene he says that he "took care to avoid his Defects, as *Racine* had judiciously shewn me the way; who has copied all the Beauties of the *Grecian*, and has prudently declined his Faults."[26] Dennis shows con-

---

[24] Mesnard ed., III, 455.
[25] *Op. cit.*, I, 32. As Dennis says, Racine does admit this violation. He indicates that while adhering to the older rule of unity of place, *i.e.*, confining the action to one locality but not limiting it to the same scene throughout, he has violated the later and stricter conception of unity of place, to which he had conformed in his profane tragedies. This passage from Racine's preface is worth quoting because it shows quite clearly that he did not take *Esther* seriously as a development of the tragic genre: "On peut dire que l'unité de lieu est observée dans cette pièce, en ce que toute l'action se passe dans le palais d'Assuérus. Cependant, comme *on* vouloit rendre ce *divertissement* plus agréable *à des enfants*, en jetant quelque variété dans les décorations, cela a été cause que je n'ai pas gardé cette unité avec la même rigueur que j'ai fait autrefois dans mes tragédies." (Mesnard ed., III, 457. Italics mine.)
[26] *Op. cit.*, I, 74. Dennis praises *Phèdre* in the same words which Dacier had

siderable independence of judgment in affirming Racine's superiority to Euripides and admitting that he intended to be guided by the former in avoiding the latter's defects. As a matter of fact, his supposed adaptation of the scene from Euripides is a translation of a scene from Racine's *Phèdre*, the scene of Phèdre's confession of her secret to her nurse, which Racine had imitated from Euripides. Dennis omits the Greek's sententious speeches, and also includes much of Racine's original.[27]

In Chapter III of his *Remarks on Prince Arthur*, Dennis gives his reasons for abandoning his plan to write a play in imitation of Euripides' *Hippolytus*. One reason he gives is the dilemma in which the character of Hippolytus places him. He must violate the rule of "likeness" of the characters or present to his contemporaries a hero distasteful to them. If he portrays Hippolytus as Euripides has portrayed him, the character will be "improper for the English Stage, which will never endure that the principal Person of the Drama should be averse from Love."[28] Legend has it that Racine made his Hippolyte a lover because a hero patterned after Euripides' Hippolytus would have called forth quips from the French fops.[29]

In the preface to his *Iphigenia* (1700) Dennis quotes Racine verbatim without, however, mentioning his name. He says:

That the present Tragedy is more Regular than most of our Tragedies are, I have some grounds to believe. Whether there is in it what is requir'd

---

used to praise *Iphigénie*: "M. Racine a beaucoup mieux réussi; en empruntant les beautés d'Euripide, il a évité ses défauts." (*Op. cit.*, p. 243.)

[27] Notably Phèdre's apostrophe to the sun and her description of her vain attempts to forget Hippolytus, including the characteristically Racinian lines (vss. 289-90):

> Je l'évitois partout. O comble de misère!
> Mes yeux le retrouvoient dans les traits de son père.

For Dennis's translation, see *Remarks on a Book entituled, Prince Arthur, an Heroick Poem* (London, 1696), pp. 58-68.

[28] *Op. cit.*, I, 79. Dennis's words are those of Dacier: "M. Racine a peché ... contre la ressemblance dans le caractére de son Hyppolite, car en le faisant amoureux, il a bien sçû qu'il s'éloignoit de la vérité; mais pour cacher ce défaut, & pour ratraper en quelque maniére la ressemblance, il luy a donné un amour farouche & sauvage, persuadé que *nôtre Theatre ne pourroit souffrir un homme entierement ennemy de l'amour.*" (*Op. cit.*, p. 244. Italics mine.)

[29] Sister Marie Philip Haley argues convincingly that Racine changed the character of his hero at least partly from consideration of the opinion and taste of his public. (*Racine and the "Art Poétique" of Boileau* [Baltimore, 1938], pp. 193-96.)

on the account of Genius, must be determined by the knowing Impartial Reader; that is, whether the *Passions are touch'd*, whether the Expressions are worthy of the Passions, and whether there *reigns throughout it that majestick Sadness which makes the pleasure of Tragedy*.[30]

Undoubtedly he had Racine's preface in mind when he wrote this one of his own.

These verbal echoes of Racine's preface suggest that Dennis read and reflected upon Racine's theories before writing his classical tragedy. There are points of similarity between the critical ideas expressed by Dennis and those found in Racine's prefaces. Like Racine, Dennis set great store by audience-reaction; the rules he considered a means to an end, that end being to move an audience; like Racine, Dennis satirizes pedantic critics who are afraid to enjoy a play which may have violated a rule; like Racine he thinks that a play which pleases a discerning public cannot possibly be accused of violating a rule.[31]

---

[30] *Op. cit.*, II, 390. Italics mine. Cf. Racine: "Ce n'est point une nécessité qu'il y ait du sang et des morts dans une tragédie; il suffit que l'action en soit grande, que les *passions y soient excitées*, et que *tout s'y ressente de cette tristesse majestueuse qui fait tout le plaisir de la tragédie*." (Preface to *Bérénice*, Mesnard ed., II, 376. Italics mine.)

[31] Compare: "Mais je n'aurois jamais fait si je m'arrêtois aux subtilités de quelques critiques, qui prétendent assujettir le goût du public aux dégoûts d'un esprit malade, qui vont au théâtre avec un ferme dessein de n'y point prendre de plaisir, et qui croient prouver à tous les spectateurs, par un branlement de tête et par des grimaces affectées, qu'ils ont étudié à fond la *Poétique* d'Aristote." (First Preface to *Alexandre*, Mesnard ed., I, 527.)

"Mais de quoi se plaignent-ils [carping critics who pretend to know the rules] si . . . j'ai été assez heureux pour faire une pièce qui les a peut-être attachés malgré eux, depuis le commencement jusqu'à la fin?" (*ibid.*, p. 529).

"Je m'informai s'ils se plaignoient qu'elle [sa tragédie] les eût ennuyés. On me dit qu'ils avouoient tous qu'elle n'ennuyoit point, qu'elle les touchoit même en plusieurs endroits, et qu'ils la verroient encore avec plaisir. Que veulent-ils d'avantage? Je les conjure d'avoir assez bonne opinion d'eux-mêmes pour ne pas croire qu'une pièce qui les touche et qui leur donne du plaisir puisse être absolument contre les règles. La principale règle est de plaire et de toucher. Toutes les autres ne sont faites que pour parvenir à cette première" (Preface to *Bérénice*, Mesnard ed., II, 378).

"Il [a critic] se plaint que la trop grande connoissance des règles l'empêche de se divertir à la comédie" (*ibid.*, p. 380).

"Ceux mêmes qui s'y étoient le plus divertis eurent peur de n'avoir pas ri dans les règles, et trouvèrent mauvais que je n'eusse pas songé plus sérieusement à les faire rire" (Preface to *Les Plaideurs*, Mesnard ed., II, 147).

"I never in my life at any Play took notice of a more strict attention or a more profound silence. And there was something like what happen'd at the

ENGLISH JUDGMENTS OF RACINE

When his tragedy *Iphigenia* proved a failure, Dennis turned to more profitable subjects, namely patriotic themes. Except for a reference to the preface to Racine's *Iphigénie*, Dennis makes no further mention of Racine until 1720, when he came to Racine's defense after Steele had attacked French classical tragedy.[32]

The only other Racine criticism of this period is a sort of parallel of English and French dramatists which appeared in *Reflections on the Stage* (1699), attributed to John Oldmixon. The author awards the palm to the English. He says:

All that are conversant with Mr. Dryden's *All for Love* and *Oedipus*, Shakespeare's *Hamlet* and *Macbeth*, and part of Lee's *Lucius Junius Brutus*, know that I am not guilty of the least flattery, and that they can't give an instance of one play in French, even of Corneille's where the passion of Terrour is better touch'd, than in these Authors. The French fancy they are particularly happy in moving Pity in their Tragedies, yet this passion has appear'd on our Stage as lively, as ever Racine brought it on theirs. Otway's *Venice Preserv'd*, and *Orphan*, part of Lee's *Brutus*, some scenes of Mr. Southerne's *Fatal Marriage*, and part of *The Mourning Bride* are examples of as penetrating tenderness as any we can find in the *Bérénice* or *Bajazet*, or, in short, in the best of Racine's pieces, who is most excellent when he is touching that passion.[33]

This, then, is Racine's balance sheet in England during the period when English criticism was dominated by French classical doctrine: on the credit side, a few incidental remarks scattered here and there in the critical essays of John Dennis, remarks which imply some admiration for Racine and which show an acquaintance with his plays and prefaces; on the debit side, two outbursts of abuse from disgruntled playwrights, and a comparison placing on an equal footing with Racine's masterpieces a melodrama so naïve as to be ludicrous.

Representation of *Pacuvius* his Tragedy. For upon *Orestes* discovering his passion to *Iphigenia* in the fourth Act, there ran a general murmur through the Pit, which is what I have never seen before. But after three or four representations, several people, who during that time had wholly abandon'd themselves to the Impression which Nature had made on them, began to study how to be discontented by Art; and repented heartily at having been pleas'd with what *Athens* and *Rome* and *Paris* had been pleas'd before" (Dennis, *op. cit.*, II, 390).

". . . when any Man of Judgment, who has for a long Time frequented Plays, happens to be very much touch'd by a Scene, we may conclude, That that Scene is very well writ, both for Nature and Art" (*ibid.*, I, 152).

[32] See below, Chap. XIII.
[33] *Op. cit.*, p. 177.

« « CHAPTER XIII » »

RACINE AND THE CRITICS
1700–1721

DURING THE PERIOD of the vogue of translation and adaptation of Racine, English classical criticism was dominated by three men: Joseph Addison, John Dennis, and Charles Gildon, while Addison's colleague and friend, Richard Steele, was a champion of sentimental drama and an enemy of classical tragedy.

As the author of the most successful of all English classical tragedies, and as perhaps the most influential critic of this period, Addison might be expected to give us particularly revealing comments on Racine. Nowhere in his writings, however, do we find as much as a single sentence devoted to Racine. From incidental references and from comments on English adaptations of Racine, we must divine Addison's opinion.

Addison first mentions Racine's name in a letter to Bishop Hough, written towards the end of Addison's sojourn in France at the turn of the century. In this letter he describes a visit which he made to Boileau. Apparently he had some admiration for Boileau; but the context in which he mentions Racine shows quite plainly that at the time he had no interest in Racine. He writes:

... I had the good fortune to be introduc'd to Monsr. Boileau. ... He is Old and Deaf but talks incomparably well in his own Calling. He heartily hates an Ill poet, and puts himself in a passion when he talks of any one that has not a high respect for the Ancients. I dont know where is more of old Age Or Truth in his censure of the French Authors; but he wonderfully cries down their present writers and extolls his former Contemporaries very much, especially his two intimate Friends Arnaud and Racine. I ask'd him whether he thought Telemach was not a good Modern piece: he spoke of it with a great deal of Esteem. ...
He talk'd I thought extremely well on several other French Authors, but

I only mention this Romance because it is the great Book that is at present most in vogue.[1]

It is obvious that Addison is not in the least interested in Boileau's opinion of Racine. Boileau's talk about Racine is merely the boring rambling of an old man living in the past. The young Englishman is impatient to divert the critic's attention from his old friends and elicit his opinion of the current best seller.

There is only one other mention of Racine in Addison's printed works. A decade later, when Addison is commending simplicity of style, he names Racine along with Corneille to illustrate the effectiveness of a simple style for the expression of noble sentiments. What he thought of Racinian tragedy must be a matter of conjecture. In 1707 he is reported to have been very active in promoting Edmund Smith's *Phaedra and Hippolitus*. Not until four years later, however, does he offer an opinion of the play in print. He says: "Would one think it was possible (at a time when an author lived that was able to write the *Phaedra and Hippolitus*) for a people to be so stupidly fond of the Italian opera, as scarce to give a third day's hearing to that admirable tragedy?" (*Spectator*, No. 18).

This judgment is now notorious. The sincerity of the praise has been questioned.[2] One critic asks whether if Addison sincerely admired Smith's *Phaedra and Hippolitus* he could at the same time have ap-

---

[1] *Letters*, ed. Walter Graham (Oxford, 1941), pp. 25-26. In the Bohn edition of Addison's *Works* (ed. Richard Hurd [London, 1856], V, 333), we find in this letter the following comments of Boileau on Corneille: "He talked very much of Corneille, allowing him to be an excellent poet, but at the same time none of the best tragic writers, for that he declaimed too frequently and made very fine descriptions, often where there was no occasion for them. Aristotle, says he, proposes two passions that are proper to be raised by tragedy, terror and pity, but Corneille endeavors at a new one, which is admiration. He instanced in his Pompey, (which he told us the late Duke of Condé thought the best tragedy that was ever written), where in the first scene the king of Egypt runs into a very pompous and long description of the battle of Pharsalia, though he was in a great hurry of affairs and had not himself been present at it."

This passage does not appear in Professor Graham's edition. He doubtless considered it spurious. Without this passage, the letter shows no interest at all on Addison's part in French tragedy.

[2] Dorothea Canfield, *Corneille and Racine in England* (New York, Columbia University Press, 1904), p. 21; F. Y. Eccles, *Racine in England* (Oxford, The Clarendon Press, 1922), p. 10.

preciated Racine's *Phèdre*.[8] I think there can be no doubt that an admirer of Smith's play could not possibly appreciate Racine's. And I believe too that Addison's praise of Smith's play is quite sincere. His dislike of opera may conceivably have led him to express a somewhat greater admiration of *Phaedra and Hippolitus* than he actually felt. But he praises the play in another connection and here if anywhere one might expect him to mention Racine's tragedy. When he attacked the narrow interpretation of poetic justice which demanded the rescue of innocent characters at the end, he cited Tate's *Lear* as opposed to Shakespeare's in support of his opinion. He considered Tate's dénouement, which conformed to the narrow rule of poetic justice, greatly inferior to Shakespeare's, which violated the rule. Tate, as we have seen, ends his tragedy with a last-minute rescue of the innocent Cordelia. Similarly Smith ends his *Phaedra* with a surprise rescue of Ismena by the resuscitated Hippolitus. If he had known and admired Racine's *Phèdre*, in which the innocent Hippolyte is allowed to die, he might have cited Racine's tragedy in further support of his argument for the unhappy ending. But far from citing Racine's tragedy as superior to Smith's, he mentions Smith's *Phaedra and Hippolitus* in a concession to the doctrine which he was attacking. He prefers the unhappy ending for tragedy but does not condemn altogether the happy ending. He says: "At the same time, I must allow, that there are very noble Tragedies which have been framed upon the other Plan, and have ended happily." Among his examples of "noble Tragedies" with happy endings, we find *The Mourning Bride* and *Phaedra and Hippolitus* (*Spectator*, No. 40). If Addison knew Racine's *Phèdre*, he probably had no great admiration for it.

A second occasion on which Addison might have been expected to make some comment on a tragedy of Racine's was that of the presentation of *The Distrest Mother*. He devoted a paper in *The Spectator* (No. 335) to a description of a performance of his friend's tragedy. Philips himself paid a handsome tribute to Racine in his preface and there is no reason to believe that he would have objected to anything Addison might have said of Racine in connection with his adaptation. As a matter of fact, Addison was interested in *The Distrest Mother* chiefly because it illustrated certain principles of dramaturgy which he

---

[8] Eccles, *op. cit.*, p. 21.

had been advocating. In a series of essays in *The Spectator*, he had criticized the English stage and the taste of the audience for rant and for the use of accessories such as lighting effects, elaborate costumes, and sets. He sometimes mentions a French convention as preferable to an English one. He prefers the French method of having kings appear unattended and wishes the English would imitate the French in "banishing from our stage the noise of drums, trumpets, and huzzas" (No. 42). He thinks a good poet can give the spectator a more lively idea of an army or a battle in a description than by actually showing them "drawn up in battalions, or engaged in the spectacle of a fight" (No. 42). Of the tricks used in the English theater to arouse terror in the spectators, he mentions thunder and lightning, and, above all, the rising of ghosts. Of the English love of ghosts he says: "But there is nothing which delights and terrifies our English theatre so much as a ghost, especially when he appears in a bloody shirt. A spectre has very often saved a play, though he has done nothing but stalked across the stage, or rose through a cleft of it, and sunk again without speaking one word" (No. 44). Among the "machines" for the moving of pity, he mentions handkerchiefs and widow's weeds. "A disconsolate mother," says he,

with a child in her hand, has frequently drawn compassion from the audience, and has therefore gained a place in several tragedies. A modern writer, that observed how this had took in other plays, being resolved to double the distress, and melt his audience twice as much as those before him had done, brought a princess upon the stage with a little boy in one hand and a girl in the other. This too had a very good effect. A third poet being resolved to out-write all his predecessors, a few years ago introduced three children, with great success; and as I am informed, a young gentleman who is fully determined to break the most obdurate hearts, has a tragedy by him, where the first person that appears upon the stage is an afflicted widow, with half a dozen fatherless children attending her, like those that usually attend about the figure of Charity [No. 44].

Most of all Addison objects to

... that dreadful butchery of one another, which is so very frequent upon the English stage. To delight in seeing men stabbed, poisoned, racked, or impaled is certainly the sign of a cruel temper. . . . It is indeed very odd to see our stage strewn with carcasses in the last scene of a tragedy; and to observe in the ward-robe of the play-house several daggers, poinards, wheels, bowls for poison, and many other instruments of death. Murders and executions are always transacted behind the scenes in the French theatre; which in general is very agreeable to the manners of a polite and civilized people [No. 44].

Addison's purpose in reviewing *The Distrest Mother* (*Spectator*, No. 335) was to point out that such tricks are unnecessary to hold the interest of even the most naïve of spectators. He casts Sir Roger in the rôle of the untutored spectator. The old knight, who has not been to the theatre in some years, attends a performance of *The Distrest Mother*. Addison is interested in his remarks "because I looked upon them as a piece of natural criticism, and was well pleased to hear him at the conclusion of almost every scene, telling me that he could not imagine how the play would end." Sir Roger, then, found that the play had suspense. He was somewhat puzzled at certain departures from English tradition. The simplicity of the style gave him pause. "But pray," says he to Addison, "you that are a critic, is this play according to your dramatic rules as you call them? Should your people in tragedy always talk to be understood? Why, there is not a single sentence in the play that I do not know the meaning of." Sir Roger resumes his seat at the beginning of Act IV confidently expecting to see Hector's ghost; but is not greatly disappointed when no ghost appears. He mistakes one of Andromache's pages for Astyanax but again is not too disappointed at not seeing Astyanax, though "he owned he should have been very glad to have seen the little boy." He finds the confidants interesting personages. Between acts, to people who are praising Orestes, he says that he thinks "his friend Pylades ... a very sensible man." To applauders of Pyrrhus he remarks: "And let me tell you ... though he speaks but little, I like the old fellow in whiskers as well as any of them [i.e., Phoenix]." He is wonderfully attentive" to the *récit* of Pyrrhus's death and remarks that "it was such a bloody piece of work, that he was glad it was not done upon the stage."

If Addison admired anything in *The Distrest Mother* or the original other than the simplicity and clarity of the style and certain "mechanic rules" which he might have found illustrated in almost any French tragedy, he gives us no hint in his printed work. When he himself composed a tragedy on the classical pattern, Racine was certainly not his model.

There is reason to suppose that if Addison knew Racine's tragedies at all, he had no particular taste for them. In addition to his undoubted admiration for Edmund Smith's *Phaedra and Hippolitus*, certain remarks of his concerning the French moralistes would indicate a distaste for psychological naturalism. In 1709 he commented:

> ... it is impossible to read a page in Plato, Tully, and a thousand other ancient moralists, without being a better man for it. On the contrary, I could never read any of our modish French authors or those of our own country, who are imitators and admirers of that trifling nation, without being for some time out of humour with myself, and at everything about me. Their business is to depreciate human nature, and consider it under its worst appearances. They give mean interpretations and base motives to the worthiest actions: they resolve virtue and vice into constitution. In short, they endeavor to make no distinction between man and man, or between the species of men and that of brutes. As an instance of this kind of authors, among many others, let any one examine the celebrated Rochefoucauld, who is the great philosopher for administering of consolation to the idle, the envious, and worthless part of mankind" [*Tatler*, No. 108].

If he was so offended by La Rochefoucauld's psychological naturalism, could he have admired Racinian tragedy? Racine had introduced the fatality of instinct into the tragic genre, where, as Addison himself tells us, "our minds should be open to great conceptions and inflamed with glorious sentiments" (*Spectator*, No. 42).

Addison's friend, Richard Steele, had no liking for the tragedy of his day. Of contemporary English tragedy he said: "It is a common fault of you gentlemen who write in the buskin style, that you give us rather the sentiments of such who behold the tragical events, than of such who bear a part in them themselves. ... The way of common writers in this kind is, rather the description than the expression of sorrow" (*Tatler*, No. 47). Steele's critical doctrine is implicit in the condescending prologue which he wrote for Philips's *The Distrest Mother*. Propriety is the refuge of authors who lack genius. By obeying the French rules, Philips "does his feeble Force confess." The French original (he does not name Racine) has contributed "correctness" to Philips's play. What "fire" it has is of British origin. Steele was impressed by the play, as his comments in the *Spectator* show (No. 290). His sense of the tragic may be judged by the fact that Andromache appeals to him because her distress springs not from weakness but misfortune. She is heroic in the practice of "domestic virtues."

In 1720, after Addison's death, Steele attacked the French theater. In the second number of *The Theatre*, he makes the following pronouncement:

> Nations are known, as well as private persons, by their pleasures, and the general inclination cannot be understood so well as by their diversions. In France they are delighted either with low and fantastical farces, or tedious declamatory tragedies. Their best plays are chiefly recommended by a rigid affectation of regularity within which the genius is cramped and fettered, so as to waste all its force in struggling to perform a work not to be gratefully executed under that restraint. They fall into the absurdity of thinking it more masterly to do little or nothing in a short time, than to invade the rules of time and place to adorn their plays with greatness and variety: thus they are finical and mechanic when they would highly please; and when they labour for admiration, they have it for performing what they might have better deserved, if they had neglected.

Steele's attack on the French theater was the occasion of the two most favorable judgments of Racine in English criticism of the period. John Dennis replied to Steele with a mixture of virulent personal abuse and sound literary criticism.[4] Here is Dennis's comment on the paragraph which I have quoted above:

> The Paragraph that begins at the bottom of the Third Column, in this Second Paper, is an unparallel'd one, and shews what vast Improvement of the Stage we are to expect from you, and how perfectly you understand it. You say that in *France*, they are delighted with Low and Fantastical Farces, or Tedious and Declamatory Tragedies. How rarely this sounds from one now, who has himself brought their Plays upon the *English* Stage, and set his own Name to them; from one of whose Poetical Works they make up the better Half; and lastly, from one, who in his Speculations has so often, and so fulsomely commended the bare Translations of those Originals which he here decries. 'Tis true, one of their own celebrated Authors has accus'd *Corneille* of being sometimes a little Declamatory, but neither he, nor any one before your self, has ever accus'd *Racine* of it. How angry you were once with the Town, for not liking that wretched *Rhapsody*, the *Phedra* of Captain *Rag*, which is nothing but a Medley of Two Tragedies of Racine, *The Phedra*, and *The Bajazet*, both murdered in the mingling them. And now *Racine* himself, it seems, is grown contemptible to one, who formerly so much admir'd an absurd Imitation of him.[5]

To Dennis goes the honor of being the only critic of the period who

---

[4] "The Characters and Conduct of Sir John Edgar," in *Critical Works*, ed. E. N. Hooker, II, 181–99.
[5] *Ibid.*, pp. 194–95.

recognized (or at least admitted) the superiority of Racine's *Phèdre* to Smith's ridiculous melodrama, indeed the only English critic of any period who has realized that Smith used material from *Bajazet* as well as from *Phèdre*. And he has given us the most judicious criticism, the only judicious criticism, of Smith's play, of the English neo-classical period. The phrase "wretched Rhapsody"[6] would indicate that he recognized the fact that Smith had slung together bits of Racine's dialogue with complete disregard for the structure of the tragedy. His remark that *Bajazet* and *Phèdre* are "murder'd in the mingling them" suggests that he considers Smith's Phaedra a monstrous creation, combining as she does Phèdre and Roxane. Unfortunately this criticism was belated, and, just though it was, Dennis was impelled to make it by personal animosity toward Steele.

Charles Gildon came to the defense of both Molière and Racine. He is indignant at the ignorance displayed by Steele. He writes: "As what he [Steele] has said on the *French Comedy* is false in fact, so what he says on their *Tragedy* is nothing but a mixture of folly and ignorance. If we may judge by the *Tragedies* of *Racine*, his charge of the *French Tragedies* being tedious and declamatory is absolutely false."[7]

Later in the same work Gildon gives us the most favorable judgment of Racine on record for the period which concerns us. He quotes Roscommon:

> Vain are our Neighbors hopes and vain their cares,
> The fault is more their languages than theirs.
> 'Tis courtly, florid, and abounds in words
> Of softer sound than ours perhaps affords;
> But who did ever in *French Authors* see
> The comprehensive *English Energy*?
> The weighty bullion of One Sterling Line,

---

[6] Dennis uses the word "rhapsody" on several other occasions when he is criticizing a work severely ("Rhapsody," *ibid.*, II, 23; "wretched rhapsody," *ibid.*, II, 123). "Wretched rhapsody" is Molière's term. In the *Critique de l'Ecole des femmes*, Climène says: "Je viens de voir, pour mes péchés, cette méchante rapsodie de l'*Ecole des femmes*" (*La Critique*, Scene III). Molière is here using the word in the etymological sense of a patchwork of bits drawn from various other works. Lack of unity and plagiarism are implied. Dennis quite probably took the term from Molière. He knew Molière's little play very well. He cites a passage verbatim from it on one occasion (*op. cit.*, II, 313) and he echoes the same passage on three other occasions (*ibid.*, II, 259, 233, 187).

[7] *The Laws of Poetry* (London, 1721), p. 179.

> Drawn to *French Wire,* would thro' whole pages shine.
> I speak my *private* but *impartial* sense
> With Freedom, and (I hope) without offense,
> For I'le Recant, when France can shew me Wit,
> As strong as *Ours,* and as *succinctly Writ.*

Having agreed with Roscommon on the superiority of the English language to the French, Gildon makes the following exceptions:

> ... tho' I am as willing as any man to think well of my own country, yet I must needs say, that the advantage we receive from this judgment will not reach all our poets; as it will not be over all the *French*: for *Boileau*, I fancy, will very well bear an exception and, I am very sure, that *Racine* has excell'd most of our tragic writers; perhaps by being better acquainted with the ancients, than much the greater part of those, who have ventur'd to give us plays of that kind, have been.[8]

When Gildon says he is very sure that Racine "has excell'd most of our tragic writers," he is apparently not referring merely to Racine's style, but to Racinian tragedy. His ideal both of tragedy and of dramatic dialogue would incline him to admire the Racinian genre. What strikes one about his theory of tragedy is his emancipation from the English neo-classical ideal of the end of the seventeenth century, the ideal illustrated by such plays as *The Mourning Bride* and Smith's *Phaedra and Hippolitus*. He reflects Dacier's theory rather than Rymer's. He rejects admiration as a tragic emotion: unless a poem arouses "*Terror and Compassion,* it cannot be called a tragedy."[9] He objects to completely innocent or completely wicked characters.[10] He remarks that the English stage is "full of those villainous characters which are properly punish'd only by the *hangman,* and not by the poet."[11] He considers the unhappy ending "more delightful and more instructive" than the happy ending.[12] The plot with the double catastrophe, happy for the good and unhappy for the wicked, is all very well for comedy but not for tragedy.[13]

---

[8] *Ibid.,* pp. 291–93.

[9] *The Complete Art of Poetry* (London, 1719), I, 198–99, 243; "The Art, Rise, and Progress of the Stage in Greece, Rome, and England," in *The Works of* Mr. *William Shakespeare* (London, E. Curll, 1710), VII, xlii.

[10] *The Laws of Poetry,* pp. 238–39; *Complete Art,* I, 243.

[11] *The Laws of Poetry,* pp. 239–40.

[12] *Complete Art,* I, 189.

[13] *Ibid.,* I, 244.

Gildon's theory of dramatic dialogue is particularly noteworthy. He takes issue with Bysshe's statement that the poet's art consists chiefly in the "Beauty of Colouring": "But I have in the Body of the Book prov'd that the *Poet's Art* does not chiefly consist in the *Colouring*, any more than that of the Painter, but in the Design."[14] He is not content merely to protest against the abuse of metaphor and simile in dialogue. Like D'Aubignac, he believes that certain figures are appropriate to the theatre, others are not. Among the figures most appropriate to dramatic dialogue, he mentions exclamation and interrogation, as being "naturally and immediately concern'd in the expression of the *passions*." These are among the figures recommended by D'Aubignac. He recognizes the dramatic effectiveness of the "mot de situation" in the simplest language.[15]

Gildon shares Steele's contempt for contemporary English tragedy, without, of course, extending his condemnation to French tragedy. His remarks on the taste of English audiences suggest an explanation of the wanton mutilation of Racine which we find in the so-called classical tragedies based on Racine. English tragic poets, says Gildon, place the chief excellence of poetry in the diction, which is the least important part of tragedy. They are mere dabblers in rhetoric who cram figures of speech into dramatic dialogue, where they are inappropriate.[16] He attributes this "false way of dialogue" to the influence of Seneca, "one of the worst *dramatic* poets that ever writ in any language: for he knew nothing of the *fable*, the *manners*, or the *sentiments*. He had indeed a solemn and pompous *diction*, and that made him admir'd by our unnatural writers."[17] Dryden, whom he had once admired, he now places among these "unnatural writers."[18] Dryden, he thinks, did little good by his "nearer approach to regularity." "But, on the other hand, the injury they [Dryden and his imitators] did to *Tragedy*, by their affectation of what they call fine language, and idle descriptions, remains to this day, and has debauch'd the taste of the people, to relish a company of worthless scribblers, and give them the name of great poets, merely for a *diction* that is unnatural, and destructive of all the

[14] *Ibid.*, I, Preface.
[15] *The Laws of Poetry*, pp. 210–11.
[16] *Ibid.*, p. 209.
[17] *Ibid.*, p. 234.
[18] *Loc. cit.*

true beauties of the *tragic* poem."[19] Now, thinks Gildon, the dramatists merely give the audiences what they like:

A *simile*, a *metaphor*, an *epithet*, some common-place reflections, and at most an idle description, are their principal aim, the highest ambition of their muse; and if the getting a full third day, and the pleasing the great vulgar and the small, be the true aim of *tragic* writing, they have certainly obtain'd it, for they cannot write more stupidly and more ignorantly than their audience judge. I have many times heard some of the principal frequenters of the *theatre* who take it very much amiss to have their sense and understanding call'd in question, cry up plays to an extravagant degree. But if you ask them, Pray, gentlemen, what are the beauties of this piece? Is the *fable* masterly? Are the *characters* justly distinguish'd? Are the *manners* truly mark'd? Are the *sentiments* natural? Are the *incidents* well prepar'd? And do they justly produce *terror* and *compassion* as well as the *catastrophe*? They will stare at you full of amazement, and reply, we know not what you mean by these hard questions. But this we know, that the language is wonderfully fine, the similes surprizing and pleasing to the last degree, the descriptions nice, and the reflections divine.[20]

Gildon's protest came too late. The vogue of translation and adaptation of Racine was over. The adapters and translators had already "improved" Racine by forcing his tragedies into the pattern of melodrama favored by Rymer and illustrated by *The Mourning Bride* and Tate's *Lear*, replacing Racine's dramatic dialogue with the traditional fine language. Moreover, Gildon gives no evidence of having read reflectively Racine's tragedies themselves. Like the great majority of the English critics of the period, he apparently read French criticism with more attention than French drama. If his theories favor the Racinian genre, it is most probably because he was influenced more strongly by D'Aubignac, Boileau, and Dacier than by La Mesnardière, Corneille, Le Bossu, and Rapin.

[19] *Ibid.*, pp. 213–14.
[20] *Ibid.*, pp. 221–22.

« « CHAPTER XIV » »

SUMMARY AND CONCLUSION

ENGLISH ADAPTATIONS and translations of Racine made during the English neo-classical period are very much farther from the originals than has hitherto been supposed. Little of the spirit of Racine has passed into any of these versions, not even the ones purporting to be faithful translations. There is an almost total loss of the essentially Racinian: Racinian psychology, as shown in the motivation of the personages and in the psychological drama, the typical structure of Racinian tragedy, the Racinian sense of the tragic, and the Racinian style which is primarily a vehicle for the drama. This fact invalidates any conclusions based on the assumption that failure of these adaptations on the English stage indicates a rejection of Racine by the English public. The adapters and translators, so-called, had eliminated Racine from his tragedies before they presented them to the public. What must be accounted for is the fact that no English dramatist could or would present Racine as he is to the English public of the neo-classical period.

With one exception, critics who have commented on English adaptations of Racine have looked upon these adaptations as Racinian tragedies still, despite certain changes—they note only the most obvious and superficial of these—and have interpreted their failure on the English stage as proof that Racine had no appeal for the English public. F. Y. Eccles alone seems to recognize changes made by English adapters as serious distortions of Racinian tragedy. Consequently only Eccles is concerned with the question of why English adapters were impelled to alter Racinian tragedy. Eccles thinks that these "romantic cobblers" were aiming in the right direction but did not go far enough. This explanation implies that adapters attempted to accommodate Racine's classical tragedies to the ineluctably romantic taste of the public but failed to make them romantic enough to succeed on the English stage.

He thus makes the romantic taste of the English public responsible for both the serious distortion of Racine in English adaptations and the failure of the adaptations, which he assumes were not sufficiently distorted to please this taste. He does not attempt to determine the relation of the adaptations to English neo-classical theory of tragedy and therefore fails to recognize the possibility that what we would call "romantic" today might have seemed "regular" to English classicists.

English adapters and translators eliminated almost completely the peculiar essence of Racine. The changes they made are of two kinds: deliberate and drastic alterations in plot and characters and more subtle changes, often apparently inadvertent, which can be attributed only to incomprehension of Racinian psychology.

If the adaptations of the eighteenth century are considered in relation to the English neo-classical theory of tragedy, it is obvious that deliberate alterations made by the English, far from violating classical tenets, bring Racine's tragedies closer to the English neo-classical ideal than they were to begin with; and this despite the fact that some tenets of English doctrine came from the French and that others, if not derived from French critics, paralleled tenets widely accepted in France. In the last analysis French classical doctrine itself was a barrier to the understanding of Racinian tragedy in England, and an incentive to the mutilations practiced upon it by adapters—mutilations which made certain adaptations ludicrous travesties of the originals.

This fact seems paradoxical only if you consider Racine the epitome of French classicism and his dramatic system the culmination and embodiment of French classical dramatic theory. Historically, this view is a fallacy. The two great representatives of French classical tragedy, Corneille and Racine, are opposed in many respects. Racine did not continue the Cornelian tradition; he broke with it. To the triumphant egotism of souls above the ordinary run of mortals, which we see in Corneille, Racine opposed human beings who conceived of magnanimity and could not achieve it, in whom primitive amoral instinct triumphed over their will to magnanimity. This contrast was obvious to contemporaries of the two and was doubtless one cause for the sharp alignment of partisans of the one or the other. In criticism, the contrast was pointed out in the "parallel," a form of criticism that seems inevitable whenever a critic deals with one or the other of the two great representatives of French classical tragedy. Moreover, French

SUMMARY AND CONCLUSION

classical theory of tragedy is complex and we find critics disagreeing on many points. Racine's system is opposed to certain tenets which were widely accepted by critics. The vast majority of critics favored a form of tragedy which afforded suspense and surprise for the spectator. Conceal the outcome from the spectator until the last possible moment, then surprise him by a sudden reversal of fortune which, though unexpected, is plausible because "prepared." This was the ideal of most French Aristotelians. They favored a plot composed of a series of incidents which would delight the spectator with unexpected turns of event and keep him in doubt until the very end, when the plot would be unraveled in an unforeseen but convincing manner. Racine fell short in this ideal. Suspense in Racine is of a psychological order. His personages are violent and impulsive, capriciously reversing their own intentions. They are the victims of the self-deception induced by passion. The spectator, aware that they are beguiled by their emotions, watches the inexorable march of psychological events towards despair and death. As early as Act IV or the beginning of Act V, the psychological action veers definitely towards catastrophe. The outcome is no longer in doubt.[1] The absence of incidents in Racine's tragedies

---

[1] Given the characters and the event which has precipitated the crisis between them, the outcome is determined. Lanson considered Cornelian tragedy psychological tragedy of this type, though he had to make exceptions of *Rodogune* and *Héraclius*. These two he considers "tout à fait en dehors du caractère de la tragédie classique." (For him, "classique" is equivalent to "psychologique.") M. Georges May has recently taken issue with Lanson, pointing out Corneille's devices for hiding the dénouement and the incidents introduced which make the outcome dependent on chance even in those pieces of Corneille in which the action is psychological. His study is closely reasoned and carefully documented. It should make clear how radically Racine departed from Corneille in dramatic technique and in the structure of his tragedies. (*Tragédie Cornélienne, Tragédie Racinienne* [Urbana, 1948], especially pp. 94-99.) It seems to me that there is suspense in Racine but suspense of a different order from that in Corneille. The peril that threatens a Racinian protagonist comes from within himself. The psychological action often turns in the direction of a happy outcome: Pyrrhus's decision to give up Andromaque and marry Hermione; Atalide's decision to plead with Bajazet to seek a reconciliation with Roxane, Néron's consent to a reconciliation with Britannicus; Phèdre's decision to save Hippolyte at any cost, etc. But we know that the resolution that will save a Racinian protagonist is precarious and may be suddenly reversed. We know that one moment of weakness will be sufficient to turn the action definitively towards catastrophe. We know that this moment will come. We do not know how or when. When it does come, there is some surprise as well as recognition of its inevitability.

made him appear to more than one critic less "regular" than Corneille. Racine triumphed in France with the public rather than with pseudo-Aristotelian theorists. Even after Racine's triumph over his rival, there were critics who praised Cornelian heroics to the detriment of Racine's psychological realism and who considered the system based on plot complication as a means of furnishing suspense and surprise for the spectator as well as the protagonists superior to Racinian dramatic irony. The critical climate in France was not too favorable to the Racinian genre. It is not surprising, then, that French classical doctrine, when it invaded England, should be a barrier to the understanding of Racine in England.

There was no reason why English classicists should set up as their ideal of regular tragedy a dramatic system based on the practice of Racine rather than on French theory. Without exception their critics expressed contempt for French dramatists. One after another they affirmed the superiority of the English genius for tragedy to the French and the intrinsic superiority of the English language to the French as a vehicle for the sublime genre of tragedy. They even found support for this view in certain remarks of a French Aristotelian, René Rapin. The success of French dramatists they attributed to the skill with which they applied the rules of dramatic art which their critics had propounded for them. Since, to the minds of English Aristotelians, English tragedy of the past lacked only art in the construction of a plot to surpass even the Ancients, they naturally turned to French critics to find the secret of the art that had won fame for French dramatists despite the handicaps under which they labored—a language better suited to billets-doux than to the majesty of tragedy and a national genius incapable of the sublimity of tragic terror. There was no reason why English Aristotelians should even read Racine and there is little evidence that any of them did. But they did read French criticism. They derived much of their doctrine from French critics, they expressed a certain admiration for French critics, and they sometimes acknowledged a debt to them, though they preferred to be considered followers of Aristotle, Horace, and the Greek dramatists.

Rymer criticized the rambling plots of English panoramic drama of the past and recommended a unified plot as the "soul of tragedy." Without mentioning La Mesnardière's name, he expounded La Mesnardière's doctrine of poetic justice. Indeed, Rymer gave it the name of "poetical justice." The essence of the doctrine of poetic justice as propounded by La Mesnardière and Rymer was the conception of Divine Justice or Providence watching over the virtuous, rescuing them from the machinations of the vicious, and visiting exemplary punishment on the wicked persecutors of innocence. La Mesnardière and Rymer insist, sometimes in the same words, that the dénouement of a tragedy must convince the spectators of the perfect equity of divine justice. The tragic poet must never give his audience occasion to grumble at the injustice of Heaven. Such a doctrine, if followed to the letter, could not but eliminate the tragic from the genre called "tragedy." A tragic view of life implies inscrutable and ironic forces at work in human suffering. The mystery of human suffering resides in the injustice, from a human point of view, of the forces which crush and destroy man.

"La souveraine justice," as La Mesnardière conceived it, and Providence, as the English thought of it, stays its hand until the last possible moment, rescues the innocent just when all hope seems lost, and strikes down the wicked at the moment of their apparent triumph, thus providing the spectator with prolonged apprehension for the fate of the wholly virtuous sympathetic characters and surprising him with a nick-of-time rescue or delighting him by the ultimate ironical frustration of the nefarious schemes of the wicked. According to La Mesnardière, Aristotelian "discovery" was a device most often used in tragicomedy to rescue the innocent; Aristotelian peripeteia, occurring most often in tragedy, brought about the unexpected and awful punishment of the guilty. La Mesnardière admired Aristotle but misinterpreted him. It is obvious that he himself had a taste for the melodramatic in the modern sense of the word. Like Aristotle, he praised the *Oedipus*, but when he ranked the *peripéties* of Greek tragedies, he did not rank first the dénouement of the *Oedipus*. He considered the most perfect *peripétie* that of Sophocles's *Electra*, where Aegisthus and Clytemnestra, murderers and adulterers scheming to hold the throne of Agamemnon, are struck down at the very moment when they are exulting in the success of their crimes and when the spectator, too, as La Mesnardière thought, believes wickedness about to triumph.

If La Mesnardière's concept of tragicomedy (innocence rescued at the end by means of a discovery) be combined in one play with his concept of tragedy (sudden and unexpected reversal of the fortunes of the wicked), we have the double fable, with the happy ending for the virtuous and the unhappy ending for the vicious. This was the form of tragedy favored in England at the end of the seventeenth century. It is the form best suited to demonstrate the perfect equity of Heaven and to keep the spectators in suspense, finally surprising them with the reversals in the catastrophe.

Pierre Corneille was the most important apologist of this pattern in France, and that despite the fact that he did not accept the doctrine of poetic justice. Corneille's theory of tragedy is for the most part special pleading after the fact for his own pieces. He was particularly fond of *Rodogune* and he maintained that in this play he had found a pattern of tragedy unknown to the Greeks but perhaps more "sublime" than any pattern known to Aristotle. His objection to the *Electra* is that, in order to punish the wicked, Sophocles made his sympathetic characters guilty of a horrible crime. In his own *Rodogune* the criminal but awe-inspiring Cléopatre is punished, not by her son, as in history, but by what appears to be an effect of the justice of Heaven. The virtuous characters are rescued from peril without becoming criminals. Here is his description of the pattern which he commends as more sublime than any of which Aristotle conceived: ". . . quand un homme très-vertueux est persécuté par un très-méchant, et qu'il échappe du péril où le méchant demeure enveloppé, comme dans *Rodogune* et dans *Héraclius*." Corneille consistently advocated "l'agréable suspension" but only in his remarks on *Rodogune* do we find him concerned with poetic justice. In the play itself the dénouement is shown on the stage, not related. Divine Justice has due regard for suspense and surprise, rescuing unexpectedly and very near the end of the play the sympathetic pair of lovers. The unexpected rescue comes at the very moment when they seem doomed to fall into the trap laid for them by Cléopatre, who, in order to destroy them, has finally taken the desperate measure of drinking first of the poison cup.

In 1681 Dryden presented a play (*The Spanish Friar*), in which a pair of lovers, the sympathetic characters, are "rescued" by a last-minute "discovery." A character believed by the sympathetic pair to have been executed at the command of one of them, is discovered to be alive. The burden of guilt is lifted and the play ends with their definitive happiness. In his preface Dryden says: "Neither is it of so Trivial an Undertaking to make a Tragedy end happily, for 'tis more difficult to save than 'tis to kill. The Dagger and Cup of Poison are always in Readiness; but to bring the Action to the last extremity, and then by probable Means to recover All, will require the Art and Judgment of a Writer, and cost him many a Pang in the Performance."

Justifying himself by this ideal of dramatic art, Nahum Tate altered Shakespeare's *Lear*. Edgar and Cordelia become the sympathetic pair of lovers. They are persecuted by the bastard Edmund, whom Tate endows with Cornelian pride in his superiority to the common run of mortals, and by his two paramours, the wicked sisters of Cordelia. Edgar kills the villain, Edmund, and the wicked sisters poison each other. But Goneril has sent assassins to murder Lear and Cordelia. The assassins enter the tent where Lear and Cordelia are held prisoner. They set upon Lear, who defends himself, killing two of the assassins. He is about to succumb to the others when Albany and Edgar rush in and save him. Tate does not fail to pay his respects, in Cordelia's lines and in the moral, to Heaven's concern with protecting virtue, but undoubtedly the suspense and the nick-of-time rescue were partly responsible for the success of this version of Shakespeare's tragedy.

In the last decade of the century Rymer criticized *Othello* as violating the rule of poetic justice. He maintained that no Greek poet would have allowed Desdemona to die but would have found a "machine" to rescue her. He suggests a fantastic device by means of which Othello would kill himself out of remorse for Desdemona's supposed death at his hands but Desdemona would be discovered merely to have fainted.

Finally in 1697 this ideal of tragedy flowered in Congreve's *The Mourning Bride*. It was a brilliant success with the public and won praise from critics as a "regular" play. It fulfilled all the requirements of the classicists. It had a skilfully constructed plot with suspense maintained to the end, the heroine being unexpectedly preserved from suicide and reunited with the hero, who had escaped from peril. It had a "discovery" which English and French critics alike might well have considered Greek. The hero and heroine are noble lovers, secretly married, separated by a shipwreck, and each thinking the other dead. The hero, really a Spanish prince, appears first in the guise of a Moorish warrior, captive of the heroine's father. His real identity is discovered by his mourning bride and the discovery is a surprise to the spectators as well as to the heroine. It had Aristotelian peripeteia, *à la* Mesnardière: The villain's wicked plan to destroy the hero miscarries and destroys the villain himself just when he is exulting in his triumph.

Congreve points out this peripeteia in the lines of the play itself. Every vice is punished and every virtue rewarded.

Especially noteworthy in *The Mourning Bride* is the "machine" used by Congreve to rescue the heroine and bring death to her rival. The villain, an ambitious minister, has killed his master and benefactor, the king, whom he had mistaken for the hero, because the king had donned the robes of the hero for his own nefarious purposes. The hero, having escaped from prison, is leading a rebellion against the king. (The spectator knows this.) The rebels are driving the king's forces back on the palace. In order to conceal the king's death from his already demoralized soldiers, the king's henchmen sever the head from the body of the king and leave the body lying upstage, disguised in the hero's garb. The Moorish queen who loves the hero and is loved by the king, having learned that the king is aware of her treachery, enters on her way to her beloved's cell. She is resolved to die with the hero by poison. Her black mutes follow her with two poison bowls. She sees the headless body, mistakes it for that of the hero, drinks one of the bowls of poison, and dies. Enter the heroine. She sees first the body of the Moorish queen and the two poison bowls; then she catches sight of the disguised body lying upstage. Her beloved husband is dead! She takes one of the poison bowls and lifts it to her lips. It is empty. (Will this delay be long enough for the hero to reach her?) She finds the second bowl. She lifts it to her lips. (The hero will come too late!) Just as she is about to drink the poison, a thought strikes her. She will kiss the lips of her beloved before she dies. She moves upstage towards the body. She discovers that it is headless. The shock causes her to drop the bowl just as the hero enters victorious.

The macabre variant of the motif of disguised identity may have been suggested by an episode in Shakespeare's *Cymbeline*, though there it is not a "machine" used to unravel the plot. The manner in which the business with the poison bowls is used to prolong suspense is reminiscent of the dénouement of Corneille's *Rodogune*. Racine himself made a contribution to this so-called tragedy, which is, in all important respects, antipodal to the Racinian genre. Congreve took from Racine's *Bajazet* the Amurat-Roxane-Bajazet triangle. His captive Moorish queen whom he names Zara loves the hero and is loved by the king. She woos and threatens the hero after the manner of Roxane. She uses the power bestowed on her by the king's love alternately to

SUMMARY AND CONCLUSION

punish the hero for rejecting her love and to rescue him from the peril in which she has placed him. Frustrated love turns to hate and hate to love as in Hermione and Roxane. But, while Racine was content to show the effects of ambivalence, Congreve explains it in a *sententia* which has given the play a sort of anonymous immortality, since it is quoted by many although few know its source:

> Heav'n has no Rage, like Love to Hatred turn'd,
> Nor Hell a Fury, like a Woman scorn'd.

Congreve's Zara differs from Roxane in that she is of royal birth and rank, not a slave and concubine elevated to imperial power. Whereas Racine's Bajazet expresses contempt for Roxane's low birth and her ex-slave's manner of wooing him with threats, the hero of Congreve's play admires Zara's soul of "godlike" mould. But this character type—Roxane, raised to royal birth—apparently appealed greatly to the English. She has a prototype in Dryden's *Aureng-Zebe* (perhaps inspired also by Roxane). And we shall see her progeny in several eighteenth-century adaptations of Racine. The character type may be described as an "anti-heroine," an imperious and heroic villainess who burns with a violent, illicit, unrequited passion for the hero. She is the heroic representative of what the English critics were wont to call "unlawful love." The rôle of Congreve's Zara was played by Mrs. Barry, the greatest actress of the age. It was among her most successful rôles.

There is in Congreve's play a second character type which appealed greatly to the English at the end of the seventeenth century, the villain. Congreve's villain is not a king or a prince. He is a minister, Gonsalez by name, an ambitious politician, heroic by virtue of his towering ambition. He covets a throne—for his son. He is a "cool, deliberate villain" (the words are Edmund Smith's description of his own villain). His great advantage over the suffering sympathetic characters and over the passionate anti-heroine lies in his coolness and his shrewd insight. He lays plans to murder the hero. He is caught in the trap which he has set for the hero and he *recognizes* in the awful miscarriage of his plans Heaven's punishment of his ambition. The popularity of villains at the end of the seventeenth century is reflected in the remarks of two English critics. One, Edward Filmer, describes the hatred of villains displayed by English audiences. This means, I take it, that spectators enjoyed feeling hatred for villains and were delighted to witness their punishment. Rymer describes the delight which spectators took in the spectacle of Iago's machinations to "work up" Othello's jealousy.

Thus, by the last decade of the seventeenth century, the surprise happy ending for virtuous characters had received the accolade of critical approval both for morality and for dramatic art. And the most successful tragedy of the decade followed the pattern of the double fable with the happy ending for the innocent characters and the unhappy for the guilty. If English critics did not derive their ideal of tragedy from French critics, they certainly found ample support in French doctrine for such a conception of "regular" tragedy. Yet this pattern is antithetical to the typical Racinian pattern.

English neo-classical doctrine diverged most sharply from the French on the question of style suitable to the tragic genre. Rymer, while taking over La Mesnardière's doctrine of poetic justice, overlooked entirely his theory of dramatic dialogue. English critics never had the attitude towards style which was characteristic of Racine's generation in France.

In the France of Racine's generation style was not an end in itself. A style was not considered to have any value independent of its function. It was good or bad according to the effectiveness with which it performed its function. And, of course, its function varied with the genre. Tragedy and the epic were both noble genres. They had in common the importance and the seriousness of the action and the rank of the personages. But they differed in what Aristotle called the manner of imitation. This difference demanded different styles for the epic and tragedy.

The epic poet is telling a story. He is at liberty to indulge in description, moralizing generalization, and comment. He may display his own poetic vein. The reader may read and reread and ponder over the meaning of what he has read. He may admire the poet's descriptive skill as manifested in metaphors, similes, and epithets.

The ideal style of tragedy differs in almost every respect from that of the epic. Tragedy represents men acting and speaking to one another on a platform where they can be seen and heard by a group of spectators who must be persuaded by every possible means that they are hearing the very words of the persons represented by the actors. The poet may not intrude. He may not make poets of his personages at will. They must speak in a manner appropriate to them and to the moment at which they speak. They are often in the grip of violent emotion.

SUMMARY AND CONCLUSION

This is no time for a display of verbal dexterity: antithesis, simile, abundance of epithet. All this smacks of studied stylistic effect or detached and deliberate comment, of which a man in agony of soul would be incapable. What the rhetoricians call "figures of words" are inappropriate to the tragic genre.

Drama is movement. The spectator comes to watch this movement, not to listen to the author's comment on it. Moralizing generalizations, in addition to being inappropriate to the situations in which tragic protagonists find themselves, retard the movement of the drama, and are "languissants" for the spectator. Preachers and pedagogues are the most boring of characters in the theatre. It would be both boring and undramatic to introduce into the rôle of a tragic protagonist in the throes of violent emotion the calm reflections characteristic of a detached observer.

Moralizing generalizations and "figures of words," then, are most inappropriate to tragic poetry. The only figures appropriate to "la poésie théâtrale" are certain "figures of thought." Among those recommended by D'Aubignac are irony and interrogation. Irony indicates tension between the speakers. Interrogation is the sign of agitation of mind. According to La Mesnardière, the chief beauty of "la poésie théâtrale" is the "oraison agissante," which he defines as a discourse in which a personage reveals involuntarily motives which he is trying to conceal. Such an ideal of style would preclude all poetry that might be termed static, lyric effusions, moralizing generalizations, prolonged similes. It would preclude any obtrusive display of verbal dexterity. And it would preclude the explicit.

English critics paid little attention to these theories of dialogue. There was some protest against the abuse of metaphor, simile, and epithet in emotional dialogue; but no one apparently (except perhaps Charles Gildon) conceived of a style peculiarly appropriate to what French critics called "la poésie théâtrale." On the contrary, the English show a very marked tendency to value dramatic poetry as poetry rather than as drama. And, for them, poetry, as distinguished from prose, consists primarily of metaphor, simile, and epithet. The taste of the age is attested by the popularity of Bysshe's *Art of Poetry* with its collection of commonplaces. Many of these commonplaces are taken from English drama and they reveal a predilection for the pictorial and the grandiose in static poetry.

Racine alone perhaps succeeded in attaining the ideal of dramatic style conceived by La Mesnardière and D'Aubignac. Moreover, he imposed on his dialogue a function more difficult than any that these critics had assigned to "la poésie théâtrale." He all but eliminates incidents from his plots. The action is a series of psychological events. All the drama is in the flux of emotion in the minds of the speakers. To use the phrase contemptuously applied by an English critic to classical tragedy, Racine's tragedies are a "series of confrontations." These confrontations are dramatic by virtue of the fact that in each of the confrontations we see the protagonists moving nearer and nearer to the final paroxysm of emotion that will translate itself in the dénouement into the act of violence that will destroy them. The protagonists who confront each other are helpless against the tide of emotion which sweeps them towards catastrophe. The tension between them is so great that they cannot be said to be talking to one another; they react to a word, an involuntary gesture, a tone. Needless to say they could not, in this swift interplay of emotion, be explicit, even if they would. In most cases, far from wishing to be explicit, they wish to hide their real feelings; but they involuntarily betray them. Moreover, they are aware that words are designed to hide motives and they watch for the revealing shades of emotion that flit across a face; they respond not to the words but to a tone that chills words intended to appear warm, the color of a voice that belies the words it speaks. Often they are hiding their real motives from themselves. In describing the quality of Racinian dialogue which distinguishes it from Cornelian dialogue, a French critic says: "Le langage d'Hermione n'est pas, comme celui de Chimène ou d'Emilie, à l'image de ses actes et de leurs mobiles vrais; il ne renseigne sur l'Hermione véritable qu'à travers une déformation qu'il appartient à nous de corriger si nous voulons saisir les vrais ressorts qui la font agir, et que ses propos sont destinés à dissimuler à nos yeux comme aux siens."[2] It is a striking coincidence that these words should be almost a paraphrase of La Mesnardière's definition of the "oraison agissante," where "il faut que les desseins de la Personne paroissent dans ce qu'elle dit, mais comme au travers d'un voile, et non pas à découvert." In scenes between two protagonists Racine's personages do not explain their emotions or describe them. The emotion is implicit not in what they say but in the way they say it. The style then is the drama itself.

[2] Paul Bénichou, *Morales du Grand Siècle* (Paris, 1948), p. 139.

SUMMARY AND CONCLUSION

As Brunetière puts it, Racine's style is marked by a "négligence apparente mais étudiée." In its contour it imitates "ce qu'il y a de plus caché dans les mouvements de la passion."

What is the studied negligence of Racine's style and how does it convey emotion? For one thing, Racine casts his Alexandrines in the patterns of emotional speech. He avoids, as La Mesnardière says the dramatic poet should, "l'agencement du discours." No long periods, no logical connectives, little suspensive word order. The Alexandrine has the sentence structure, the rhythms, and the pitch patterns of emotional speech, spontaneous and unstudied. Racine's favorite rhetorical device is one of D'Aubignac's "figures of thought," namely, interrogation. Le Bidois remarks that by means of this device Racine effects "la désagrégation de la phrase par la passion." He does more than this with this one simple device. He uses interrogation to charge with emotion the simple words of everyday speech. Often his questions are of the type that has rising pitch. His personages scream their impatience, their frustration, their despair, in Alexandrines ending on high pitch, just as people under stress of violent emotion are wont to do. When irony is most bitter and meant to be most stinging, irony too takes the form of a question with rising pitch. Interrogation is also the figure best suited to convey emotional tension between two speakers. Racine employs the technique very skillfully to heighten this effect.

But where is the poetry of this dialogue which is primarily dramatic, not poetic, and which is emotional because it is colloquial? The poetry is in what might be called lyric overtones. There is subjective lyricism in the protagonist-confidant scenes, when the protagonists are impelled to speak of the passion that obsesses them. There is also a subjective lyricism in the more dramatic scenes. Here emotion is so intense that a single line reveals in a flash the agony from which it springs. Racine's poetry is always dense and evocative. It is never interpolated into the drama to retard the movement. I believe with Thierry Maulnier that Racine was primarily concerned with drama. The poetry with which he clothed his dialogue is dictated by the intensity of emotion which drives his protagonists but is incidental and subordinate to the drama: "Jamais peut-être le plus grand de nos poètes n'a chéri et cherché la poésie pour elle-même," says Thierry Maulnier. "La poésie pour Racine doit émaner des êtres sans ralentir le drame, et le drame ne garde toute sa précipitation que si les héros ne se détournent pas de lui, et ne disent que lui."[3] Because they serve the ends of drama, "Les mots de Racine ne vont donc pas à la recherche de la poésie, ils ne tendent pas à elle, elle naît en eux par surcroît, et si dans l'expression aussi rigoureuse et nécessaire qu'il se peut des passions à leur paroxysme, il y a quelque chose qui rappelle la simplicité du commun langage, le héros de Racine a cette simplicité."[4]

English critics at the end of the seventeenth century, as I have pointed out, were greatly concerned with poetry. They attached perhaps a higher value to poetry than to drama. The essence of poetry, as distinguished from prose, lay in those very "figures of words" which the French of Racine's generation considered undramatic and "languissants." To the English, who sought poetry rather than drama in the dramatic genre, it mattered very little if that poetry happened to be static rather than dramatic. Indeed, they probably found little or no poetry in Racine's unadorned style. And it is quite likely that they attributed this lack of poetry to an irremediable weakness of the French language itself. When English dramatists began to exploit Racine, we could hardly expect them to do otherwise than to attempt to introduce poetry, as they conceived of poetry, into dialogue that to them was so signally lacking in poetry. In so doing they doubtless thought that they were merely bestowing on Racinian tragedy those qualities which the French language itself prevented it from having and which the English language made possible. When one of them attempted to imitate Racine's simple style—and it is nothing short of miraculous that even one should have attempted to imitate Racinian simplicity—he did so not for the sake of drama but for the sake of clarity and he failed to reproduce the drama of Racine's dialogue.

When the vogue of adaptation of Racine began in England at the end of the seventeenth century, English neo-classical doctrine, sometimes inspired by French criticism, always supported by it, had set up as the ideal of regular tragedy what strikes us today as heroic melodrama. This ideal had been realized in Congreve's *The Mourning Bride*. In opposition to the French ideal of dramatic dialogue, expounded by La Mesnardiére and D'Aubignac and illustrated by Racine, the English displayed an ineluctable taste for static poetry in the dramatic genre.

[3] *Racine* (Paris, 1936), p. 131.
[4] *Ibid.*, p. 135.

SUMMARY AND CONCLUSION

The critical biases of the last decade of the seventeenth century in England appear to be largely responsible for the choice of Racinian tragedies to be imitated and the deliberate mutilation of the tragedies chosen. Imitators chose most often *Iphigénie* and *Bajazet*. *Bajazet* appealed because of the character of Roxane. Roxane had inspired Congreve's Zara. When Edmund Smith adapted *Phèdre*, he all but eliminated Phèdre herself from his piece, substituting Roxane. Finally Roxane appears under her own name in Charles Johnson's *The Sultaness*, a piece purporting to be a translation of Racine's *Bajazet*. In *Iphigénie* Racine had come close to the pattern of *The Mourning Bride*, the double fable with the happy ending for the virtuous and the unhappy ending for the wicked. The outcome is in doubt until the end, and the dénouement is brought about by a discovery of identity which turns the villainess's wicked purpose back upon her own head. *Iphigénie* was twice adapted for the English stage. Thus *Bajazet* and *Iphigénie* served as models for four of the five adaptations of Racine made when his vogue was at its height.

The pattern of the plot of *The Mourning Bride*, representing the ideal of regular tragedy and the character types of this melodrama—largely dictated by the pattern—together with the current English ideal of tragic style, apparently accounts for deliberate alterations made in all six of the adaptations. The two adapters of *Iphigénie* deliberately changed the original in the way we should expect, considering English theory of tragedy and ideal of style at the time. Both showed the dénouement in action, exploiting the possibilities for spectacle and making the most of the final peripety, the type most favored by English critics, namely, the villain caught in the trap laid for the innocent. Both attempted to embellish the style. Abel Boyer, the first of the adapters, was content to introduce as many epithets as possible and an occasional simile. The fact that Boyer, a Frenchman, was willing to do violence to Racine's style is perhaps the most puzzling thing about this adaptation. Boyer admits, however, that Thomas Cheek helped him with the verse and one contemporary document indicates that the collaboration of Boyer and Cheek is responsible for the piece. The abuse of epithet is perhaps the work of Cheek.

The general trend—evident in all the English versions—away from the dramatic towards the static reaches its extreme limit in Johnson's *The Victim*. It would appear that Johnson's prime purpose in adapting

RACINE AND ENGLISH CLASSICISM

Racine's piece was to win for himself recognition in the books of commonplaces of the future. Wherever possible he introduces objective, detachable lyrics on commonplace themes. His themes are sometimes traditional and sometimes they reflect current ideas. They range from a variant of the Renaissance motif of the pathos of the rose—introduced into Agamemnon's rôle as a reflection on the pathos of Iphigenia's early death—and of the "belle matineuse" conceit of *précieux* poetry—introduced into the rôle of Eriphile—to the anticlericalism of the age of enlightenment. This static poetry which Johnson introduces is always adorned with elaborate similes. Comparisons are chosen with due regard for sublimity. The dialogue abounds in images drawn from grandiose nature, mythology, and legendary natural history. These objective lyrics are introduced everywhere.

The difference between Racine's lyricism and Johnson's may be illustrated by one comparison: Iphigénie recounts her anxiety at Achille's failure to meet her:

> Pour moi, depuis deux jours qu'approchant de ces lieux,
> Leur aspect souhaité se découvre à nos yeux,
> Je l'attendois partout; et d'un regard timide
> Sans cesse parcourant les chemins de l'Aulide,
> Mon coeur pour le chercher voloit loin devant moi,
> Et je demande Achille à tout ce que je voi.

Racine evokes an "état d'âme" by exact notation of psychological fact in the simplest language.

Johnson omits these lines, replacing them with:

> Achilles—that Godlike Hero
> Will soon relieve our Cares, and ease my Heart;
> His mighty Soul is fill'd with Love and Glory
> In Arms he rushes dreadful to the War,
> Impetuous, rapid as contending Winds
> Rough as the wintry Storm that plows the Deep:
> —In Peace he mildly drops the boisterous Warrior,
> Then he's all Love, soft as the balmy Air
> That gently bends the Herbage, calmly breaths
> The Morning Sweets.

This change is not merely a rejection of Racine's style. Johnson is quite oblivious of Iphigénie's anxiety and foreboding at the moment. His interpolated lyric, if it has any psychological significance at all, is

SUMMARY AND CONCLUSION

an expression of confidence in Achilles. With characteristic inconsequence, Johnson now returns to Iphigenia's state of mind with the following prosaic verses:

> IPH: . . . Is he not more than Divine, *Eriphile*
> —And yet I wonder he so long is absent.
> He must have heard of our Arrival here.

Edmund Smith's *Phaedra and Hippolitus* is the extreme example of the general trend away from the tragic towards the melodramatic. Smith used material from Racine's *Phèdre* and Racine's *Bajazet* to construct a melodrama on the pattern of Congreve's *Mourning Bride*. From the point of view of English classicists, the most obvious fault of Racine's *Phèdre* was, of course, the death of the innocent Hippolyte. Smith invents an ending similar to that of *The Mourning Bride*. Theseus has commanded the captain of his guards to force Hippolitus to stab himself. Ismena, beloved of Hippolitus, thinking Hippolitus dead, is about to stab herself, when Hippolitus rushes in and stays her hand. He has outwitted his executioner—a turn of events for which the spectators are not prepared. This surprise happy ending provides the rescue of the innocent characters demanded by English doctrine. However, it is of less importance than other alterations in the transformation of Racine's *Phèdre* into a melodrama conforming to the English ideal. This rescue of the innocent pair is trivial compared with Smith's other changes. Much more important is the displacement of Phaedra's discovery that Hippolitus loves someone else. Smith's Phaedra makes this discovery before the return of Theseus, when she hears that Hippolitus and Ismena have eloped. She then speaks some of Racine's lines: "O douleur non encore, . . ." Ironically enough, by this displacement, the climax of Racine's tragedy becomes merely a bit of that static poetry which Racine and contemporary critics considered inappropriate to the dramatic genre.

The "discovery" in Racine, coming at the climax of *Phèdre*, embodies, I believe, a typically Racinian use of Aristotelian discovery and peripeteia. The discovery results in an ironical reversal of Phèdre's magnanimous intention. When Phèdre resolves to save the innocent Hippolyte—at what awful cost to herself—she is obeying an inclination to magnanimity which she considers her birthright and an obligation placed upon her by her illustrious ancestry. Theseus, himself unaware of the import of his words, reveals to Phèdre the fact that she has a rival. The sudden irruption of jealousy is so violent a shock that it produces in Phèdre a savage desire to destroy Aricie, an impulse that verges on insanity, since she proposes to destroy her rival by denouncing her to Theseus, the very person most wronged by her own love for Hippolyte. Racine has been very careful to make the shock of the discovery violent enough to justify the delirium which it precipitates. Phèdre has believed all along that Hippolyte has rejected her love because he hates all women. In his supposed misogyny Phèdre finds her greatest consolation. She is sure that in all her atrocious suffering she will at least be spared that of jealousy. When reason returns, Phèdre realizes that there are within her monstrous amoral forces against which her ideal of generosity is helpless. She has betrayed most shamefully her illustrious birth. Her self-loathing, present from the beginning, is now so intense that it can be placated only by self-destruction:

> Je respire à la fois l'inceste et l'imposture.
> Mes homicides mains, promptes à me venger,
> Dans le sang innocent brûlent de se plonger.
> Misérable! et je vis? Et je soutiens la vue
> De ce sacré soleil dont je suis descendue?

Her suicide is a vengeance on herself.

All this, of course, Smith deliberately eliminates from his so-called "tragedy." He is not imitating Racine. He is improving on him. He could not, indeed, have used Phèdre's discovery as Racine had used it without giving his Phaedra the qualities which make her a tragic figure —her conviction that magnanimity is her birthright and her obligation, her sense of guilt and her longing for purity, her intense self-loathing. Racine's Phèdre quite obviously did not appeal to Smith. He is at pains to eliminate all these qualities. He remakes the character on the model of Roxane. His Phaedra differs from Roxane only in her occasional and rather unconvincing expression of scruples against violating her marriage vows. Her passion for Hippolitus is less sinful than Phèdre's, since she has been a wife to Theseus in name only. But for this extenuating circumstance, she woos Hippolitus as shamelessly as Roxane woos Bajazet.

With this very different heroine Smith could not retain Racine's discovery and peripeteia nor could he motivate her suicide as Racine had done. Instead of a Phaedra destroying herself because of a guilt

SUMMARY AND CONCLUSION

so horrible in her own eyes that her very existence stains the pure light of day, he shows us at the end a Senecan Phaedra delirious and impenitent pursuing the beautiful Hippolitus, beyond the gates of Hell itself.

In remaking his Phaedra, Smith was doubtless attempting to bring her closer to a favorite type with the English at the moment, the type which I have called the "anti-heroine," inspired in the first place by Roxane and popularized by Mrs. Barry in the role of Zara in Congreve's *The Mourning Bride*. He may have known or hoped that Mrs. Barry would play Phaedra, as indeed she did.

In order to introduce planned and passionless villainy, Smith transforms Racine's Oenone. Oenone, motivated in Racine by the blind devotion of a woman of the people to the child she has suckled, becomes Lycon, a "mighty politician," minister of state and kinsman and confidant to Phaedra. Lycon sets out to destroy both Phaedra and Hippolitus in order to mount the throne himself. He has the motive of Congreve's villain and the method of Iago. He feigns devotion to Phaedra. (This enables him to speak many of Oenone's lines.) He plans to arouse Phaedra's wrath against Hippolitus by having her offer her love and meet with scornful rejection. In soliloquies and asides—a device condemned by French critics but an indispensable appurtenance of the cool, deliberate, self-confident villain—he confides his plan and explains his motives to the audience:

> With humble, fawning, wise, obsequious Arts
> I'll rule the Whirl and Transport of her Soul.

He urges Phaedra to woo Hippolitus with "soft allurements" and she falls in with his plan. He stirs up her anger at Hippolitus in order to gain her consent to the false accusation. The machinations of a villain replace the self-deception of Racine's Phèdre. Smith's Phaedra needs no pretext to send for Hippolitus and declare her love. Lycon's wiles rather than Phaedra's imagination lead her to consent to the calumny. In Racine, Phèdre is haunted by the image of Hippolyte's face, where, at the moment when she had snatched his sword to stab herself, she had seen no pity, only horror and revulsion. Now Phèdre sees Hippolyte as a "monstre effroyable." When Hippolyte appears with Thésée, Phèdre misinterprets Hippolyte's expression:

RACINE AND ENGLISH CLASSICISM

> Ah! je vois Hippolyte;
> Dans ses yeux insolents je vois ma perte écrite.

This misinterpretation precipitates the fear which leads Phèdre to consent to the calumny:

> Fais ce que tu voudras, je m'abandonne à toi,
> Dans le trouble où je suis, je ne puis rien pour moi.

For the paralyzing fear engendered by Phèdre's imagination, Smith substitutes a jealous rage induced by a villain's deliberate misrepresentation of Hippolitus' character. Lycon says:

> Then the fierce Scythian—Now methinks I see
> His fiery Eyes with sullen Pleasures glow,
> Survey your Tortures, and insult your Pangs;
> I see him, smiling on the pleas'd Ismena,
> Point out with Scorn the once proud Tyrant Phaedra.

Phaedra reacts in the manner of Roxane:

> Curst be his Name! May Infamy attend him;
> May swift Destruction fall upon his Head,
> Hurl'd by the Hand of those he most adores.

(After this, Smith has his Phaedra speak lines of Racine's Phèdre: "Oh Heavens! accuse the guiltless?" and "Do you resolve, for *Phaedra* can do nothing." Such inconsequence makes one wonder if Smith knew what he was about and justifies John Dennis's remark that Smith has combined *Phèdre* and *Bajazet* and murdered both in mingling them.)

In his hodgepodge of ill-assorted scenes from *Phèdre* and *Bajazet*, with several *de son cru*, Smith uses many of the lines of *Phèdre*. By virtue of the many verbal reminiscences Racine's *Phèdre* is the chief source of Smith's piece. But Smith shows remarkable ingenuity in reproducing the lines spoken by Racine's personages while altering the motivation of their acts and in utilizing the incidents of Racine's plot while destroying the structure of Racine's tragedy and eliminating the Racinian sense of the tragic.

Today Smith strikes us as the most outrageous of the "romantic cobblers" who patched up Racine for English consumption. But his play fell far short of the success of *The Mourning Bride* and found no champions among the enemies of classicism. English classicists, on the other hand, praised the piece extravagantly. No voice was raised in

SUMMARY AND CONCLUSION

protest at the mutilation of Racine. The classicists who praise Smith's play do not mention *Phèdre* as a source. One proclaims the *superiority* of Smith's piece to Euripides, Seneca, and Racine. Only one English classicist, John Dennis, appears to have been cognizant either of Smith's debt to Racine or of the enormity of his mutilation of his Racinian sources. And Dennis pointed this out only when he needed a weapon to attack Steele, not through any love of Racine.

As a matter of fact, Smith's piece had all the perquisites of "regular" tragedy as the English classicists conceived of regular tragedy at the end of the seventeenth century. Smith's alterations of material from Racine merely brought it closer to regularity. An age which accepted Tate's "improvements" on Shakespeare's *Lear* could hardly be expected to object to Smith's improvements on Racine. Smith altered Racine's *Phèdre* in the same way that Tate had altered *Lear*. Today Smith seems to us to have transformed classical tragedy into *bas-romantisme*. But, from the point of view of English neo-classical doctrine, he merely made Racine's tragedy more regular. If Tate has classicized *Lear*, Smith has classicized *Phèdre*.

The initial failure of Smith's melodrama to capture the public is harder to explain than its success with classical critics. Certainly, Racine cannot be blamed for the play's failure. I should guess that it fell short of the success of Congreve's melodrama chiefly because Smith was far less skillful than Congreve in constructing a plot with *coups de théâtre* and suspense. Congreve's *Mourning Bride* is good *bas-romantisme*. Smith's is bad *bas-romantisme*. But both plays maintained their reputation as "noble tragedies" until the end of the eighteenth century. The only objection to Smith's *Phaedra and Hippolitus* voiced at the end of the century was that it *was* classical. It was mentioned, along with *Cato* and *Irene* as a noble achievement in a discredited art form.

No other adapters altered a Racinian model as drastically as Johnson had altered *Iphigénie* stylistically and as Smith had altered *Phèdre* in structure and in characterization. The taste for melodrama and the taste for the pictorial and the grandiose in style are evident, however, in other adaptations of the early eighteenth century. When Ambrose Philips chose *Andromaque* for imitation (*The Distrest Mother*, 1712) he was attracted by the blameless heroine, a shining example of domestic virtues. In paraphrasing Racine's preface, he makes this clear. In the play itself he pads the rôle of Andromaque and he provides a semblance of a happy ending by showing her at the end rejoicing in the imminent reunion with her child. He was, of course, doing his best to conform to the pattern of melodrama by showing the virtuous heroine, rescued by Providence, in a state of definitive happiness. But Philips did not introduce a "cool, deliberate villain." Most incongruously he shows us an Andromache first grieving for the death of Pyrrhus and then, referring to Pyrrhus's death as the "unforeseen expedient" by which the Gods have brought her relief. When Charles Johnson adapted *Iphigénie*, it was the rôle of Eriphile which most appealed to him. He expanded the rôle, while simplifying the character. To him obviously Eriphile was the anti-heroine so popular in the drama of the period. Iphigénie and Achille needed no alteration. He stresses Agamemnon's paternal love rather than his ambition, thus making him somewhat more admirable than Racine's personage, and more of a bourgeois figure. When later he chose *Bajazet* for translation, doubtless it was because of the character of Roxane, the prototype of the anti-heroine. To bring her closer to the English type he eliminates Bajazet's contemptuous references to her lowly origin. Bajazet he tries to make more heroic by giving him a touch of the *vertu parleuse* of a Cornelian hero. Johnson's Bajazet affirms rather ostentatiously his devotion to Love and Honor.

When Mrs. J. Robe adapted *La Thébaïde*, she was obviously most interested in Creon, the villain. She brings Creon closer to the Gonsalez type by having him attempt to trick Antigona and, with the miscarriage of his plans, bring misfortune on his own head. In all these changes the influence of melodrama can be detected. Adapters chose for imitation those tragedies of Racine which offered protagonists who, with a bit of pruning and a bit of touching up, could be made into the stock characters popular at the moment.

Only a small part of the loss of Racinian psychology in eighteenth-century adaptations can be attributed to deliberate alterations dictated by the taste of the moment. All the adapters and translators, apparently without realizing what they are doing, distort or obscure Racinian motivation, destroy dramatic tension, and eliminate the tragic. The loss is the result of thoughtless excisions, incongruous interpolations, or stylistic changes. These slight but damaging changes are wholly unnecessary, and for that reason, are doubtless inadvertent.

The most striking example of the apparently inadvertent elimination

SUMMARY AND CONCLUSION

of all that is characteristic of Racine from an English version is Charles Johnson's *The Sultaness*. In his prologue Johnson introduces his play to the English public as a "translation" from "the great Racine." It is evident that he had no intention of eliminating the tragic in favor of the melodramatic, for his Bajazet, his Roxana, and his Atalida all die in the end and in the same way as Racine's protagonists. Indeed he doesn't omit a single scene, and all the scenes are in the same order as in the original. Most of the dialogue is translated or paraphrased. And yet all that is tragic disappears from Johnson's piece quite as completely as it had from Edmund Smith's melodrama with its surprise happy ending for the innocent young lovers and its planned and passionless villainy.

Distortion of the motivation of Atalide at two crucial moments is largely responsible for the loss of the tragic as I believe Racine conceived of the tragic. At the end of Act I, Atalide learns that Roxane, doubting the sincerity of Bajazet's assurances of his love for her—he speaks warm words in too cool a tone to be convincing—has planned to trap him into revealing his true feelings. She will send for him without giving him any inkling of her intentions. She will then surprise him with the demand that he marry her. His involuntary reaction to this demand will reveal his true feelings. Roxane forbids Atalide to see him before the interview. Atalide fears that the interview will be fatal to Bajazet. He will be unable to feign love for Roxane or accede to her demand. Then she thinks of a way to save him. She can intercept him on his way to the interview, warn him of Roxane's intentions, urge him even to consent to the marriage. This she cannot bring herself to do. The thought of losing Bajazet to Roxane is too painful. Perhaps she would rather see him dead, as she confesses later she has sometimes felt. She persuades herself that her fears are groundless. Why should she believe that Bajazet loves her, Atalide, so well that he would endanger his life for her sake? Is she worthy of such love? Bajazet, she tells herself, can be trusted to do and say all that is necessary to save himself—more perhaps than she would like.

Thus Racine shows us love choosing to risk destroying the beloved object which it cannot possess. Jealousy disguised as reason has checked a generous impulse. Johnson changes all this. His Roxana commands Atalida to summon Bajazet and to tell him he will have to marry her or die. This change alone eliminates something characteristic of Racine. The belief that truth can be discovered not in words spoken but in involuntary gesture and facial expression characterizes all Racinian personages. Johnson has retained an incident of Racine's plot while robbing it of Racinian psychology. The Racinian sense of the tragic is completely lost in Atalida's reaction to Roxana's announcement. Atalida has a soul struggle somewhat reminiscent, stylistically, of Rodrigue's *stances* but for the most part expressed in violent words, the whole so vague and so incoherent that we hardly know what is going on in Atalida's mind. At the end she is apparently resolved to take the "nobler course." We get the impression that magnanimity has conquered jealousy.

Apparently Johnson conceives of Atalida as a noble princess, subject to accesses of jealousy but always recognizing her jealous impulses for what they are and strong enough in her will to magnanimity to overcome them, while Racine conceived of his Atalide as a noble and generous princess whose reason is beguiled at crucial moments by a ruthless, selfish instinct. Racine's Atalide commits the acts which destroy Bajazet and herself at moments when she is unaware of her real motives. Johnson's Atalida is never beguiled by jealousy. What Johnson eliminates from the rôle of Atalida is self-deception. When Atalide learns that Bajazet has effected a reconciliation with Roxane, as Atalide herself had so desperately begged him to do, at any cost, her reaction is not one of relief at Bajazet's escape from death but bitter resentment of Bajazet's happiness attained at the cost of her own pain, perhaps even hatred of Bajazet. She justifies this shocking reaction by persuading herself that Bajazet now loves Roxane and has abandoned her, Atalide. She convinces herself by the specious reasoning characteristic of Racine's personages. When begging Bajazet to placate Roxane, she has said:

> Peut-être il suffira d'un mot un peu plus doux;
> Roxane dans son coeur peut-être vous pardonne.

This we know to be the truth. Roxane has shown herself to be only too eager to believe that Bajazet loves her and consequently very gullible. After the reconciliation Atalide says:

> Roxane en sa fureur paroissoit inflexible.
> A-t-elle de son coeur quelque gage infaillible?

She has now persuaded herself that only the most ardent and sincere

SUMMARY AND CONCLUSION

protestations of love could have touched the implacable Roxane. When Bajazet appears, she accuses him of being unfaithful to her and of sending her to her death without the consoling knowledge that he still loves her. He could have promised marriage to Roxane. He need not have offered proof of his love (vss. 970-74):

> Et j'aurois en mourant cette douce pensée
> Que vous ayant moi-même imposé cette loi,
> Je vous ai vers Roxane envoyé plein de moi;
> Qu'emportant chez les morts toute votre tendresse,
> Ce n'est point un amant en vous que je lui laisse.

Johnson's Atalida refuses to believe that Bajazet has given Roxana proof of his ardent love for her. She guesses correctly how the reconciliation came about. She does not accuse Bajazet of being false to her or of sending her to her death without the consolation of his love. By changing the conditional to the future, Johnson has his Atalida speak Racine's lines but say just the opposite of what Atalide has said (italics mine):

> Yet this sweet Thought *will comfort* me in Death,
> That 'twas by my Command; for Love of me
> You mov'd her Heart—at least so I believ'd.

(I admit I am baffled by "at least so I believ'd.")

When Bajazet explains that the gullible Sultaness, only too eager to believe that he loves her, has interpreted his confusion as evidence of love, Racine's Atalide says nothing but reveals all too plainly by her expression that she does not believe him. It is her silent accusation that he is lying which precipitates Bajazet's angry threat to tell Roxane the truth. At this moment Roxane suddenly appears, and, in the faces of Atalide and Bajazet, surprises the signs of emotional strain which betray their secret and seal their doom.

Johnson's Atalida does not accuse Bajazet of lying. She begs his forgiveness for any fleeting doubts she may have had of his constancy. Apparently Johnson does not understand the psychological principle that is repeatedly noted by French moralists of the age and described in all its effects—the principle that La Rochefoucauld has stated most succinctly: "L'esprit est toujours la dupe du coeur." Nor does he seem to be aware of Racine's use of it in constructing his tragic plot. In Racine passion assumes the guise of reason and beguiles and betrays even the noblest of human beings. Atalide's jealousy is an active force in the tragic plot only when Atalide herself does not recognize it as jealousy. Apparently Johnson is as unaware of it as Atalide herself. His Atalida is jealous only when Racine's Atalide says in so many words that she is jealous, that is, in moments of lucidity when she is able to conquer jealousy and act magnanimously. He even translates her line "Funeste aveuglement. Perfide jalousie." But in his Atalida jealousy is neither blind, nor fatal, nor perfidious. In short it is not tragic. It is merely a trivial fault for which Atalida chides herself, rather than a powerful, amoral, insidious force within her which drives her against her will to destroy Bajazet and herself.

Having lifted from his Atalida the burden of guilt that Racine's Atalide bore, Johnson has robbed of tragic irony the magnificent triumph of generosity in Atalide when she offers her life for Bajazet's sake, unaware that he is already dead; in Johnson this magnanimous act is merely the culmination of a generosity that is constant and never seriously impaired by jealousy. Atalida's death itself becomes pathetic rather than tragic. Johnson translates Atalide's last speech. But in Johnson it is no longer the moral recognition scene characteristic of Racinian tragedy. Atalide sees with awful lucidity the evil in herself which has driven her to destroy Bajazet. She, not Roxane, has knotted the bowstring that strangled her beloved. By her own death she avenges the death of Bajazet. Johnson's Atalida, speaking Atalide's words, seems to be exaggerating beyond all reason her responsibility in the death of Bajazet.

It would seem that Johnson was unaware that he was changing the character of Atalide. I can see no other explanation of his procedure in the crucial scene in which Atalide's insanely unjust accusations of Bajazet provoke Bajazet's anger and his threat to reveal the truth to Roxane and take the consequences. Johnson omits Atalide's accusations of infidelity but retains Bajazet's reaction to them. So we have Atalida speaking to Bajazet and Bajazet replying, not to her, but to Racine's Atalide. Both personages are talking in a vacuum, so to speak. As a result, all Racine's psychological drama disappears from this crucial scene.

If Johnson could not see that by changing the motivation of Atalida's crucial decisions and acts he was eliminating the tragic from Racine's tragedy, he might at least be expected to see that he was destroying the drama. But obviously he did not. He is apparently baffled by Racinian

SUMMARY AND CONCLUSION

psychology. It is possible, however, that it was not so much Racinian psychology that baffled him, as it was the French language. When French syntax eluded him, he guessed at Racine's meaning and it is quite natural that he should be guided by a preconceived notion of what a young heroine of tragedy should be.

To my mind, Atalide is Racine's tragic heroine, but many people consider Roxane the tragic protagonist. Of all Racine's personages, Roxane was the one who had the greatest appeal for the English. Yet, even in this character, Johnson failed to see the essentially Racinian and the tragic element: the fatal blindness of heart. Roxane is motivated by the psychological principle stated in La Rochefoucauld's paradox: "Quand on aime on doute souvent de ce qu'on croit le plus." She cannot decide to make Bajazet sultan while she still has doubts of his love. She cannot have him executed while she still believes that he loves her, and in her heart she is stubbornly clinging to this belief. Roxane can save herself by carrying out the absent Sultan's order to execute Bajazet or by giving Acomat the signal to set in motion the revolution that will place Bajazet on the throne and save them all from Amurat. She cannot make up her mind to do either. She doubts Bajazet's love for her and probes for the truth but what she really wants is reassurance. As each piece of evidence of Bajazet's deception is uncovered, she finds a pretext for delaying his execution because she clings to the belief that he loves her. As she temporizes, her doom is closing in on her. She ignores Acomat's pleas to allow him to start the revolution and Amurat's repeated order to execute Bajazet until these pleas and these threats themselves serve as a pretext for further temporizing, an excuse for making Bajazet sultan without being certain that he loves her. Roxane is now afraid to continue probing for the truth. Since the absent Sultan and Acomat are both pressing her—she argues—she will at once give the order to start the revolution and place Bajazet on the throne. There will always be time enough to take vengeance on Bajazet and Atalide, if, after he is sultan, Bajazet is ungrateful enough to be unfaithful to her. She will then be able to surprise him and Atalide and kill them both. For the moment, "Je veux tout ignorer," says she and even as she speaks, her confidante enters with irrefutable proof that Bajazet loves Atalide and has only contempt for Roxane, namely, the letter that Bajazet has written to Atalide. It is at this moment, if anywhere, that Roxane is pitiable. Johnson seems quite unaware of her motives in temporizing with herself—her fear of uncovering a truth too painful to bear. His Roxana makes the opposite decision. She decides not to consent to the coup d'état, but to kill Bajazet and Atalida. Johnson omits all mention of consent to Acomat's revolution and translates the words in which Roxane describes her plan to kill the lovers in the vague and distant future as though it were a plan for the immediate future. Roxane's "Je veux tout ignorer" is of course omitted.

Since Johnson's Roxana has already definitely decided to kill Bajazet and Atalida, there is no point to having the confidante enter here and give Roxana the letter which proves Bajazet's deception. But Johnson retains this incident. What was in Racine an ironic reversal of Roxane's intention—and, incidentally, exciting theater—becomes in Johnson's version an anticlimax. Throughout the play Johnson's *procédé* is to retain the incidents of Racine's plot and, by distortion of the motivation of the protagonists' decisions, to rob them of tragic irony; to retain the protagonist-protagonist scenes and garble the dialogue so as to eliminate the dramatic tension.

Johnson, failing to understand the motivation of Racine's personages, inadvertently omitted the psychological events which constitute the tragic plot: Atalide's decision against intervening to save Bajazet; Atalide's sudden reversal of her resolution to save Bajazet from death by renouncing him, and the wholly unjustified conviction that Bajazet has abandoned her, by means of which she hides her real motives from herself and justifies her accusation of Bajazet, an accusation which results in Roxane's discovery of their love; and finally Roxane's temporizing with herself until it is too late to make the decision which would have saved her no matter which course she chose. Johnson's incomprehension of Racinian psychology has resulted in quite as complete a loss of the Racinian sense of the tragic as Smith's deliberate mutilation of the tragic plot of *Phèdre* and his transformation of Racine's personages into the stock characters of heroic melodrama. But Johnson fails to supply the happy ending that would be appropriate. The death of his protagonists is a non sequitur.

Nowhere else do we find elimination of the tragic so obviously deliberate as in Smith's *Phaedra and Hippolitus* or so obviously unconscious as in Johnson's *The Sultaness*. But in Johnson's *The Victim* and in Philips's *The Distrest Mother*, there is alteration of the motivation of Racine's tragic protagonists which is comparable to alterations made

SUMMARY AND CONCLUSION

by Smith in his *Phaedra* and Johnson in his *Sultaness*, because here the same traits are eliminated, that is, the very qualities which make Racine's personages tragic.

Racine's style is so rigorously designed to serve the ends of psychological tragedy that it is not possible to discuss style and the psychological tragedy separately. By a change in style a translator may unwittingly eliminate something essential to Racine's psychological tragedy. In making stylistic changes, he may be merely in quest of poetry as the English conceived of poetry at the time and, wholly preoccupied with making Racine's style poetic, he may overlook the psychological implications of the passage he sets out to embellish. And so we cannot always say whether the elements of Racine's psychological tragedy disappear because of the translator's incomprehension of Racinian psychology itself or distaste for it or merely distaste for the *procédés* which Racine employs to convey it.

The qualities of Racine's tragic style which elude translators (or repel them, as the case may be) are psychological precision, economy, and density, qualities which make his poetry evocative and reveal in a flash the intensity and complexity of the emotions which drive his protagonists. Racine's protagonists never affirm the violence of their emotions in Senecan hyperbole or prolonged and grandiose simile, which is the English way. The English never convey the intensity of an emotion by defining it exactly, which is the Racinian way.

The contrast between the characteristic *procédés* of Racine and the characteristic *procédés* of English tragic poets of the age can be illustrated by one example from Edmund Smith, two lines from a scene where he is following closely Racine's *Phèdre*, the expository scene of Phèdre's confession to Oenone of her guilty passion for Hippolyte. Phèdre is describing the obsessive quality of her love for Hippolyte. She says:

> Je l'évitois partout. O comble de misère!
> Mes yeux le retrouvoient dans les traits de son père.

For this Smith substitutes:

> I sent him, drove him from my longing sight:
> In vain I drove him, for his Tyrant Form
> Reign'd in my Heart, and dwelt before my Eyes.

By an exact notation of psychological fact in simple words, Racine describes the *manner* in which thoughts of Hippolyte intrude themselves into Phèdre's consciousness against her will. Phèdre has been struggling to escape from her shameful passion for Hippolyte. She is in that morbid state of mind where all sensory impressions convey some reminder of him. She is trapped and helpless. Racine's words evoke her agony and foreshadow her doom. Her passion at the outset has the stamp of tragic inevitability. Smith's lines, on the other hand, do not have this quality because they do not describe the *manner* in which the memory of Hippolitus obsesses Phaedra. They merely state in metaphor that Phaedra thinks constantly of Hippolitus. They convey nothing of the trance-like despair of Racine's Phèdre, and they fail to do so because they do not have the psychological precision of Racine's lines. Smith's metaphor is an escape from psychological precision.

This *procédé* is characteristic of translators of the eighteenth century. Considering the ideal of tragic poetry of the age, it might well be that in their determined quest for poetry they failed to see the importance of Racinian precision in conveying the intensity and complexity of the emotions that drive Racine's tragic protagonists.

Racine himself uses metaphor, but in Racine metaphor itself is an instrument of psychological precision. Racine's metaphors are usually in one word, often a verb. The metaphor, rich in psychological implications, seems to spring unbidden from the inner intensity of the speaker. It never gives the effect of a conscious effort on his part to assert in sublime words the violence of his emotions, which is the English way.

Ambrose Philips sets out with the express purpose of imitating Racine's simple style. But, in the rôle of Orestes, he quite deliberately departs from the master. With the rejection of Racine's style, he rejects also all the Racinian sense of the tragic that is in the rôle. What we miss in his Orestes is the morbid intensity engendered by his helpless struggle against himself and his despairing surrender to an impulsion which will lead him he knows not where. Even in the opening scene, Oreste himself feels and the spectator feels that he has already been brushed by the wing of death. A few samples of Philips's translation will serve to show how, perhaps unwittingly, he robs the rôle of Oreste of what is ominous and tragic. "Je me livre en aveugle au destin qui m'entraîne," says Racine's *homme fatal*. This is the reading of the 1697 edition. In earlier editions the reading is: "Je me livre en aveugle au *transport* qui m'entraîne." Whether or not Philips used the 1697 edition

SUMMARY AND CONCLUSION

I have not been able to determine, but there is evidence elsewhere that he consulted earlier editions. Here it would seem that, ignoring "en aveugle," he is inspired by "transport" to have his Orestes burst into the following most un-Racinian effusion:

> OREST. Oh, would he render up *Hermione*
> And keep *Astynax*; I should be blest!
> He must; he shall: *Hermione* is my Life,
> My Soul, my Rapture!—I'll no longer curb
> The strong Desire, that hurries me to Madness:
> I'll give a Loose to Love; I'll bear her hence;
> I'll tear her from his Arms; I'll—O, ye Gods!
> Give me *Hermione*; or let me die!—

Such epileptic outbursts in series of short exclamations are characteristic of Philips's Orestes. There is nothing of the melancholy, paranoid Oreste in this outburst. The tirade in Philips gives the impression of heroic resolution to win rapturous happiness at the risk of his life. Orestes shouts, "Let me die!" but we do not get the impression that he is reluctantly yielding to an impulsion that will lead him not to rapture but to spiritual destruction.

Similar alteration of the emotional tone of the rôle of Oreste is illustrated in Philips's translation of the first interview of Oreste and Hermione. Compare:

> ORESTE
> Tel est de mon amour l'aveuglement funeste.
> Vous le savez, Madame; et le destin d'Oreste
> Est de venir sans cesse adorer vos attraits,
> Et de jurer toujours qu'il n'y viendra jamais.
> Je sais que vos regards vont rouvrir mes blessures,
> Que tous mes pas vers vous sont autant de parjures;
> Je le sais, j'en rougis. Mais j'atteste les Dieux
> Témoins de la fureur de mes derniers adieux,
> Que j'ai couru partout où ma perte certaine
> Dégageoit mes serments et finissoit ma peine.
> J'ai mendié la mort chez des peuples cruels . . .
>
> ORESTES
> Madam, you know my Weakness. 'Tis my Fate
> To Love, unpity'd: To desire to see you;
> And still to swear each time shall be the last.
> My Passion breaks through my repeated Oaths;
> And every time I visit you I am perjur'd.

> Even now, I find my Wounds all bleed afresh:
> I blush to own it; but I know no Cure
> I call the Gods to Witness, I have try'd
> Whatever Man could do (but try'd in vain)
> To wear you from my Mind. Through stormy Seas,
> And savage Climes, in a whole Year of Absence,
> I courted Dangers, and I longed for Death.

The tragic poetry of this speech is in the two lines: "Que tous mes pas vers vous sont autant de parjures" and "J'ai mendié la mort chez des peuples cruels." These two lines leaven the whole speech. After ". . . tous mes pas vers vous sont autant de parjures," the simple prosaic "j'en rougis" takes on a certain tragic dignity. The jargon of gallantry —"regards," "blessures"—recedes into the background and becomes unobtrusive. Philips's unaccountable substitution of "Weakness" for "funeste aveuglement," his interpolated "To Love, unpity'd," and the prosaic explicitness of his rendering of the two Racinian metaphors throw the gallantry into high relief. "I blush to own it" becomes ludicrous understatement.

In Oreste's love there is always a hint of the kinship with hate. This element of hatred becomes overt when Pyrrhus reverses his decision to protect Astyanax against the Greeks, when he decides to surrender Astyanax to them and to marry Hermione. Oreste conceives the mad plan of abducting Hermione. He is driven to do this by so strong a desire to torture Hermione that to Pylade's wise protestations, he replies:

> Non, non, à mes tourments je veux l'associer
> C'est trop gémir tout seul. Je suis las qu'on me plaigne,
> Je prétends qu'à mon tour l'inhumaine me craigne,
> Et que ses yeux cruels, à pleurer condamnés,
> Me rendent tous les noms que je leur ai donnés.

These lines Philips replaces with:

> Talk no more!
> I cannot bear the Thought! She must be mine!
> Did *Pyrrhus* carry Thunder in his Hand;
> I'd stand the Bolt, and challenge all his Fury
> Ere I resigned *Hermione*—By Force
> I'll snatch her hence, and bear her to my Ships!
> Have we forgot her Mother *Helen's* Rape?

SUMMARY AND CONCLUSION

It is impossible to guess what impelled Philips to make such a change. Did he find the unadorned simplicity, precision, and directness of Oreste's words inadequate to express the violence of his emotion? Did he feel the need of the traditional hyperbolic rodomontade? Was he aware of the drastic change he effected in Oreste's motivation? Did he consider the sadistic impulse to which Oreste yields unworthy of a "parfait amant"? Whatever impelled him, he has made his Orestes a "héros de roman" defying his rival. Moreover he has introduced a patriotic motive in the line "Have we forgot her Mother Helen's Rape?" This more than anything does violence to Racine's sense of the tragic. It is clear that Racine meant to show Oreste's impulse to torture Hermione overriding all considerations not only of his own happiness but of the obligations to society placed on him by his rank. ("Oreste, ravisseur!" Pylade exclaims with horror.)

Later, Philips omits the famous tirade beginning: "Mon innocence enfin commence à me peser." He thus eliminates the most obvious manifestation of Oreste's paranoia, the moment when Oreste, in defiance of the unjust deities that are persecuting him, resolves to justify their persecution by committing crimes worthy of the misfortunes visited upon him. Orestes appealed to Philips as one of those tragic personages who "run mad" at the end in a burst of Senecan rant. He lovingly prolongs the delirium. But he has omitted the stages through which Racine's Oreste passed on his way to spiritual destruction.

In Charles Johnson's *The Victim* Eriphile is transformed in somewhat the same way. Racine's Eriphile suffers because she has something of the self-loathing of Phèdre and the paranoia of Oreste. Her love for Achille would be a source of suffering even if it were requited, for she considers it mad and shameful to love the conqueror of her country and the murderer of her friends. Her love itself is a passion unworthy of her illustrious birth; though she does not know who her parents were, she knows that they were of royal rank and she feels that her love for Achille has dishonored them. She has a pride of race which intensifies her sense of guilt. It is not without self-reproach that she yields to the jealousy which causes her to hate her kind benefactress, Iphigénie, but she is driven by an unconquerable impulse to destroy her rival. Her love she looks upon as the crowning irony in a long series of misfortunes visited upon her by malignant and unjust gods of whom she is the chosen victim.

All the Racinian motivation disappears in Johnson's version: pride of race, the paranoia, the self-loathing. We miss particularly in Johnson's Eriphile the feeling that she is being driven against her will to crime and self-destruction by the ominous intensity of her emotions. In Johnson's Eriphile the fact that her love is unrequited is the only source of her feeling of shame or of her suffering. When she accompanies Iphigenia to Aulis, she is not motivated by the hope that in some way she may bring misfortune upon her beloved and her rival simply because she finds their happiness unbearably painful to her. Johnson's Eriphile has no malignant intent in coming to Aulis. She comes merely in the hope of healing her "love-sick mind." She does not feel, as Racine's Eriphile does, that she hates where she should love (Iphigénie) and loves where she should hate (Achille) and is betraying her illustrious birth by this immoral passion. Her betrayal of Iphigenia is not foreshadowed at the beginning of the play nor does it seem to Johnson to need any other justification than elemental jealousy. The spectacle of her rival's happiness causes intense pain, but apparently does not engender the will to destroy. The intensity is conveyed in a characteristically English and most un-Racinian metaphor. The pangs of jealousy are "tongues of adders" and "tails of scorpions." Her suffering is not compounded of insane malignity and paranoia. In short, Johnson's Eriphile is no more than the stock character of English melodrama, the antiheroine. She often asserts that she is the victim of Tyrannic Love, but the *manner* in which love tyrannizes over her is never shown.

Did Johnson deliberately cut down Racine's Eriphile to fit the pattern of the anti-heroine? It would seem that he did wilfully delete the motif of pride of race. All references to her pride in her illustrious birth are systematically dropped. And, in the end, Calchas proclaims that her death is the punishment of her illegitimacy. If Racine meant his Eriphile to be illegitimate, he is carefully vague about it. Be it said in passing that the motif of aristocratic pride entailing obligation is systematically eliminated in all translations and sometimes replaced, as in Smith's Phaedra, by scruples against violating the conventions of bourgeois morality.

The elimination of Eriphile's aristocratic pride is deliberate in Johnson's version. It would seem that other alterations of Eriphile's motivation are due to Johnson's failure to see the implications of Racine's dialogue because he was baffled by the psychological precision and

SUMMARY AND CONCLUSION

compression of the style. In the following passage, for instance, failure to render the words "triste" and "souffrir" is largely responsible for the loss in Johnson's Eriphile of self-reproach and reluctant surrender to a blind impulse to destroy her rival. Racine's Eriphile says:

> Iphigénie en vain s'offre à me protéger,
> Et me tend une main prompte à me soulager:
> *Triste* effet des fureurs dont je suis tourmentée!
> Je n'accepte la main qu'elle m'a présentée
> Que pour m'armer contre elle, et sans me découvrir
> Traverser son bonheur que je ne puis *souffrir*.

Johnson translates:

> Yes, *Iphigenia* courts in vain my Friendship
> And loads me every Hour with Hateful Favours,
> She is my Hero's joyful promis'd Bride,
> My happy Rival . . . all her Joys . . . are Pangs,
> Are Daggers here, ev'n now they pierce my Heart.

Racinian tragedy is the poetry of the fatality of instinct. To say that Racine portrayed personages of exalted rank as impulsive human beings who yield to their savage instincts just as the least civilized of human creatures do is the truth but not all the truth. To say that the morality of Racine's personages is the morality of the jungle is not true at all. Racine ennobles his tragic protagonists and makes them pitiable by endowing them with noble inclinations inspired by pride of race. We see in them a peculiarly Racinian variant of the caste spirit of the age of chivalry. In Corneille and in the theory of tragedy of the seventeenth century we see a survival of this caste spirit in the notion that nobility of birth gives nobility of soul. A Cornelian hero boasts of his superiority to the common run of mortals, his "âme peu commune," welcomes the assaults of fortune that put his superiority to the test, and never succumbs to them. The Racinian protagonist conceives of magnanimity as an obligation laid upon him by illustrious birth and cannot achieve it. The reader or spectator perceives this, and sometimes the protagonist himself is aware from the beginning that he is driven by a force within him that his will to magnanimity cannot combat. This awareness is the source of the self-loathing that engenders the wish for death and culminates in suicide. For in the end Racine's lost souls recognize the awful disparity between their ideals and their acts. They have been betrayed, not by a scheming villain but by what is false within. Whether or not there is an ideal of generosity, the will to destroy or torture is engendered by an intensity of suffering that makes them pitiable.

The loss of the Racinian sense of the tragic, in eighteenth-century English adaptations, where it is not to be attributed to the critical tenets of an age greatly preoccupied with the theory of tragedy but signally lacking in a sense of the tragic, seems to result from incomprehension of the psychological principles which are the stuff of tragedy in Racine. The English chose to imitate the very plays in which love and jealousy are the springs of tragedy but failed to see in Racine's portrayal of love and jealousy the elements which make these passions tragic. The union of love and hate and of love and cruelty and the process of self-deception they understood only in their least subtle form, as they appear in Hermione and in Roxane. Hermione's love of Pyrrhus is not a source of shame to her and her hatred has some moral and rational justification. Pyrrhus has abandoned her despite his betrothal to her (cf. Samuel Richardson's comments on Hermione in Philips's adaptation). Roxane's vengeful fury is in some measure justified by the deception practiced upon her by Bajazet and Atalide. In both Hermione and Roxane self-delusion appears in a natural and obvious form: the tendency to cling to the belief that they are loved by those whom they love and who have professed love for them. English adapters did not understand love as a completely amoral passion so possessive that it turns to hate when denied possession and without other justification. They fail to render the intensity of suffering that engenders the will to torture and destroy and at the same time makes Racine's personages pitiable. They eliminate the ideal of magnanimity inspired by pride of race which ennobles Racine's protagonists, and at the same time eliminate the spectacle, both pitiable and terrifying, of the triumph of instinct over the will to magnanimity. They do not understand the kind of self-deception which causes Racine's most noble protagonists to succumb to irrational destructive impulses: the specious reasoning by which they justify the acts inspired by their irrational impulses and hide their real motives from themselves. The characteristic moral recognition scene, where they see clearly the evil in themselves or realize when it is too late what they have forfeited, disappears or loses its significance.

Racinian drama eluded English adapters as completely as the Racinian sense of the tragic. Rejection or incomprehension of the Racinian rhetoric of passion is an even more vital factor in the loss of the dramatic

SUMMARY AND CONCLUSION

than in the loss of the tragic. Much of the loss of the tragic is due to failure on the part of the English adapters to render with any precision the passions that drive Racine's tragic protagonists to catastrophe. These springs of tragedy are revealed for the most part in protagonist-confidant scenes. Here some explicit self-revelation is possible because there is no tension between the speakers. These scenes are themselves dramatic because the confidant is a foil to the protagonist, not a passive listener. A confidant may needle a protagonist by pointing out motives that the protagonist would fain hide even from himself, he may provoke self-revelation by admonitions based on a misinterpretation of the protagonist's motives, or he may enrage a protagonist by rational arguments against a course which the protagonist is impelled to take by the blind intensity of his emotions. But the confidant himself has not the power to provoke in the protagonist emotions that will cause him to reverse his decisions or that will drive him to the emotional paroxysm which causes him to destroy himself and others. In the protagonist-protagonist scenes each of the speakers has the power to sway the other. The tension between the two is so great that they scarcely ever consider the express meaning of the words spoken by the interlocutor. They react not to what is said but the manner in which it is said. They talk at cross purposes; they speak to wound, or they wound unintentionally. They provoke unexpected reactions. They react spontaneously to a word that stings, to an involuntary gesture, to a revealing shade of emotion that flits unbidden across a face, to a tone that belies the sentiment that words are intended to express. In short, the emotional implications of the dialogue create the interplay of emotion that is the drama. The devices by means of which Racine projects the flux of emotion in the minds of the speakers are of paramount importance.

Mere stylistic changes can result in a loss of Racinian psychological drama. Stylistic changes made by English adapters often cause all dramatic movement to disappear. The style in vogue in England at the time when Racine's tragedies were adapted is as far removed from the dramatic as any style could conceivably be. The English valued above all else in the tragic genre ornate descriptive poetry. It was inevitable that in many scenes English adapters should reject Racine's dramatic dialogue in favor of static declamation: hyperbolic descriptions of the passions that drive the protagonists, lyric effusions, grandiloquent *sententiae*.

RACINE AND ENGLISH CLASSICISM

One stylistic feature which the English considered of the essence of poetry, epithet, intrudes itself into every scene everywhere, even in the style of the most conscientious of all the English adapters, and the only one whose professed purpose it was to imitate Racine's style, Ambrose Philips. The epithets which English adapters introduce into the dialogue are usually inept or superfluous. Often they give the effect of deliberate and detached comment. Sometimes this comment is so remote from anything the speaker might conceivably say under the circumstances that the lines become a reader's gloss on Racine's dialogue. Sometimes an epithet introduces visual imagery which obscures psychological significance. Often an adapter rejects the *procédés* which give Racine's style its dramatic quality in favor of a lavish and indiscriminate use of epithet. Racine's swift-flowing style in which verbs are so vital is converted into stagnant pools of nouns and adjectives. Racine's favorite rhetorical device, interrogation, is rejected by all adapters and is often replaced by a plethora of epithets. One example from Charles Johnson's *The Victim* and from a scene where Johnson is following Racine closely, will illustrate the manner of English adapters. Agamemnon has advised Clytemnestre not to attend the wedding of Achille and Iphigénie. Clytemnestre protests:

> Qui? moi? que remettant ma fille en d'autres bras,
> Ce que j'ai commencé je ne l'achève pas?
> Qu'après l'avoir d'Argos amenée en Aulide,
> Je refuse à l'autel de lui servir de guide?
> Dois-je donc de Calchas être moins près que vous?
> Et qui présentera ma fille à son époux?
> Quelle autre ordonnera cette pompe sacrée?

Johnson translates:

> My Lord, I cannot justifie my Absence;
> I must be there; behold the pleasing Pomp
> With Transport, see the blissful Union made,
> And give the blushing Bride to her fond Lover:

Racine's rhetorical questions, here as almost always, are rhetorical only in the sense that they do not demand an answer. They convey the agitation of the speaker. The language is colloquial. Such questions are more dramatic than others of D'Aubignac's "grandes figures." Exclamation, for instance, implies no tension between the speaker and his interlocutor. Questions such as these necessarily imply great tension between the speakers. Here Racine's questions convey shock and indignation, perhaps some suspicion of Agamemnon. In an effort to use poetic rather than colloquial diction Johnson has eliminated all emotion. His epithets, banal or inept, have robbed the lines of the tragic dignity they had in Racine despite the colloquial language. Johnson's Clytemnestra gives the impression that she is daydreaming about a beautiful wedding that her husband has forbidden her to attend.

Even Ambrose Philips's *The Distrest Mother* furnishes examples of apparently unconscious loss of Racinian psychological drama through stylistic changes. Philips tells us in his preface that he intends to imitate Racine's simple style because he believes that imagery obscures noble sentiments. His reason for imitating Racinian simplicity betrays the fact that he valued only the negative qualities of Racine's style. His translation shows that he is insensitive to Racine's rhetoric of passion. Irony he misses or makes heavy or awkward. Interrogation he discards or translates as a simple request for information rather than as a vehicle for emotion. Two passages will illustrate his manner. Hermione is ecstatically happy at Pyrrhus's return to her, and impelled by her delirious happiness to dwell in thought on Pyrrhus and only Pyrrhus. She sees the disconsolate Andromaque approaching—Andromaque threatened with the death of her son. Hermione is irritated and impatient at the intrusion of her rival's grief upon her own happy musings. Racine conveys her emotion with the characteristic interrogation:

> Dieux! ne puis-je à ma joie abandonner mon âme?
> Sortons: que lui dirois-je?

Philips translates:

> I would indulge the Gladness of my Heart!
> Let us retire: Her Grief is out of Season.

Philips has substituted an explanation of the emotion for the emotion itself. His lines are not a translation of Racine's. They are a reader's gloss on them.

Andromaque has stung Pyrrhus by insinuating that he is being gratuitously cruel in separating her from her son. Pyrrhus has replied to the barb by hinting cryptically that his supposed persecution of her is trivial compared with the danger that threatens her from the Greeks. Andromaque retorts:

> Et quelle est cette peur dont leur cœur est frappé,
> Seigneur? Quelque Troyen vous est-il échappé?

Philips translates:

> Alas! What Threats? What can alarm the Greeks?
> There are no Trojans left!

Andromaque's first question is cast in the form which, in emotional speech, inevitably conveys contemptuous disbelief, in English as well as in French: "And what, pray, may this fear be, my Lord?" Add "Can it be that some Trojan has escaped you?" and Andromaque has noted the fact that no Trojan is alive to threaten the Greeks but she has also implied contempt for what she believes to be a wretched pretext on Pyrrhus's part to alarm her and punish her for her reproaches to him. By innuendo she has reminded him of his merciless slaughter of the Trojans. By substituting "Alas!" for "Et," and following the interjection with two questions conveying merely anxiety on the part of Andromache and the desire to know what has stirred the Greeks to threats against her and her son, Philips has eliminated the tension between Andromaque and Pyrrhus that was in Racine's lines. By changing the second question to a statement of fact, with the telling "vous" omitted, Philips has eliminated the irony and the barb for Pyrrhus. This statement (following the anxious plea for more details about the danger to her and her son) indicates merely alarm and bewilderment. In this bit Philips has made of Pyrrhus merely a messenger bearing ill tidings, and Andromache's lines convey her reaction to the tidings, not to Pyrrhus.

Ambrose Philips was the most humble, the most admiring, the most conscientious, and, next to Otway, the most gifted of the adapters. He was probably the most competent linguist among them. Yet it would seem that even he could not always see the emotional implications and the innuendo of Racine's dialogue. The *procédés* of the other adapters and translators show quite plainly that they were baffled by Racine's psychological dráma. Their incomprehension is revealed by their thoughtless excisions and their incongruous interpolations.

English adapters systematically cut out all lines which indicate a reaction to facial expression, to tone of voice, to involuntary gesture.

SUMMARY AND CONCLUSION

Sometimes such a reaction is crucial in the plot. I have noted how English adapters reject psychological turning points. (Hermione is convinced of Pyrrhus's complete indifference to her and enraged by it when she perceives from the expression in his eyes that he is completely absorbed in thoughts of Andromaque, that he wants nothing so much as to put an end to this interview with her, Hermione; Bajazet perceives from Atalide's expression that she does not believe his account of the reconciliation with Roxane; Phèdre misinterprets the expression in Hippolyte's eyes and consents to the calumny.) The omission of these particular psychological events would perhaps indicate only that English adapters could not conceive of a tragic plot turning on a mere reaction to facial expression. The systematic elimination everywhere of the Racinian *procédé* suggests that no English adapter could conceive of a conversation between two people where the speakers do not respond to words but to what might be called the psychological obligato to the words, which may either supplement the meaning of the words or contradict it.

On the other hand, English translators appear to see nothing strange in *répliques* which are not responses to anything in the preceding *réplique* and which themselves provoke no response. A striking example of this type of dialogue is the Atalida-Bajazet interview in Act III of Johnson's *The Sultaness*. Johnson changes Atalide's *répliques* and introduces additional ones (for example, Atalide's silent accusation that Bajazet is lying is replaced by an apology for ever having doubted him). But he retains Bajazet's speeches. Throughout the scene Atalida speaks to Bajazet and he replies not to her but to Racine's Atalide. The scene in Johnson's adaptation is not unique. It is extreme but typical. All English adapters and translators, regardless of their attitude towards Racine, regardless of their intent, regardless of the English taste of the moment, obscure or destroy Racinian psychological drama in the same way as Johnson. The tension between the personages is mitigated. There is nothing of the current of violent emotion that plays between them and sweeps them in a dramatic crescendo towards the state of agitation which finally destroys them.

Thomas Otway could not have had the same reasons as eighteenth-century adapters for altering the structure of his Racinian model or transforming Racine's characters. When Otway adapted *Bérénice* (1678), English Aristotelians had not yet formulated their rules for regular tragedy, that is, heroic melodrama. Nor was Otway influenced by the Senecan rhetoric of English tragic style. He aimed at simplicity of style. Otway is nevertheless a "romantic cobbler" and a romantic cobbler à la française.

In transforming Racine's Antiochus, Otway reverts with a vengeance to the French romanesque tradition of which there is only the merest vestige in Racine's Antiochus. He introduces into the rôle of Antiochus a struggle between love and friendship. In the Titus-Antiochus interview, where Titus asks Antiochus to deliver his message of banishment to Berenice, Otway has Antiochus confess to his friend Titus that he is his rival. The scene becomes a contest of generosity between the two friends. The scene is expanded, but most of Racine's dialogue is cut out. Otway introduces a scene entirely of his own invention, in which Antiochus declares his love to Berenice for the second time. In this scene Otway's Antiochus is a veritable caricature of the conventional "mourant" of French *précieux* poetry. Here is one sample, from this scene, of Otway's "poésie mourante":

> Pity the pains and anguish I endure,
> In Wounds which you and none but you can cure.
> Look back, whilst at your feet my self I cast,
> And think the sigh that's coming is the last.

The sentiments of Otway's "mourant" are repeatedly expressed in *précieux* metaphors. Otway apparently considers such metaphors the proper language of strong emotion. There are traces of the jargon of gallantry in Racine's *Bérénice*, not nearly so much, however, as we find in *Andromaque*. We do find Antiochus referring to "le premier trait qui partit de vos yeux" and Bérénice refers to Antiochus's "fers," while Titus says: "Mon coeur saignera." These metaphors, if not dead metaphors in Racine, are certainly inconspicuous. Otway revives the image in a dead metaphor by elaborating it. For instance, his Titus says, "My heart bleeds now/ I feel the drops run down." His Antiochus says, "My poor heart lies bleeding at your feet," a mixed metaphor almost as ludicrous as Mascarille's heart "écorché de la tête aux pieds." "Fers" occurs in such contexts as this: "No Slave that wears her Chains,/ Upon such easie terms his Freedom gains."

Otway has conventionalized his Antiochus in language and in sentiments, for he has deprived him, unnecessarily it seems to me, of the

SUMMARY AND CONCLUSION

tenderness, the delicacy, and the perceptiveness of Racine's Antiochus which make him much more than a "mourant." He did so, I believe, because he did not understand the relation of Racine's Antiochus to Bérénice. Bérénice's cruelty to Antiochus is the unconscious cruelty of a woman completely absorbed in her love for someone else. For Bérénice, Antiochus hardly exists except as a friend of Titus to whom she can talk of Titus. Antiochus realizes this and it is the cause of his suffering. The following bit of the dialogue from the first Antiochus-Bérénice interview strongly suggests incomprehension both of Bérénice's unconscious cruelty and Antiochus' suffering because of it:

> BÉRÉNICE
> Je n'attendois que vous pour témoin de ma joie.
> Avec tout l'univers j'honorois vos vertus.
> Titus vous chérissoit, vous admiriez Titus.
> Cent fois je me suis fait une douceur extrême
> D'entretenir Titus dans un autre lui-même.
> ANTIOCHUS
> Et c'est ce que je fuis. J'évite, mais trop tard,
> Ces cruels entretiens où je n'ai point de part.
> Je fuis Titus: je fuis ce nom qui m'inquiète,
> Ce nom qu'à tous moments votre bouche répète.
> Que vous dirois-je enfin? Je fuis des yeux distraits
> Qui, me voyant toujours, ne me voyoient jamais.
> . . . .
> BER.   ... your parting I with trouble hear,
>   For you, next him [Cesar] are to my Soul most dear.
> ANT. In justice to my Memory and Fame,
>   I fly from *Titus* that unlucky Name.
>   A name, which every Moment you repeat,
>   Whilst my poor heart lies bleeding at your feet.

Otway omits the lines which convey Bérénice's unconscious cruelty (her repetition of the name Titus and the reminder that Antiochus has been to her no more than a proxy for Titus), translates Antiochus' response to the lines that are no longer there, and replaces the exact notation of Antiochus' suffering with a banal metaphor ludicrously elaborated. Racine's Antiochus is aware that Bérénice's cruelty is unconscious. He applies the word "cruelle" to her only once and then only in speaking to his confidant after Bérénice has accused him of lying out of jealousy. Otway having cut out of the rôle of his Berenice the manifestation of unconscious cruelty, which defines the relation of Antiochus to Bérénice, proceeds to introduce into the rôle of his Antiochus repeated accusations of calculated cruelty not provoked by anything Berenice has said or done. For instance, in the first Bérénice-Antiochus scene, when Racine's Bérénice, in reply to Antiochus' inquiry, tells him that she believes Titus will make her empress that very day, Antiochus says only: "Et je viens donc vous dire un éternel adieu." Here is the *réplique* in Otway:

> How she insults and triumphs in my ill!
> Sh'as with long practice learnt to smile and kill.
> Oh, *Berenice*, Eternally Farewell.

Having changed, consciously or unconsciously, the relation of Antiochus to Bérénice, Otway could not be expected to render with any accuracy the psychological drama of the second Bérénice-Antiochus interview, the scene in which Antiochus is forced against his will to deliver to Bérénice Titus's message of banishment. The scene in the original is a fine example of Racinian psychological drama, one of those scenes which I have called a chain explosion of emotions which the speakers are powerless to check. Antiochus is forced in the end to deliver the painful message to Bérénice. (He had had no intention of doing so.) Bérénice, in her pain and humiliation, accuses Antiochus of having lied out of jealousy, only to recognize the unjust and perfidious accusation as a feeble pretext to hide from herself a truth too painful to accept. ("Hélas! pour me tromper, je fais ce que je puis.") In Otway's version a few thoughtless excisions and many incongruous interpolations transform the scene completely. The swift interplay of emotions that is the drama disappears. Where I can make anything of the dialogue, it seems to me to be first an exchange of gallantries, then a *dépit amoureux* in the manner of the courtly romance, consisting of a debate between Antiochus and Berenice on the question of whether Antiochus has shown a submission to his mistress's will sufficiently abject to prove himself a *fin amant*.

The opening lines of this scene will show how Otway obscures Racine's psychological drama. Racine's Bérénice, after her first interview with Titus, is beside herself with anxiety over Titus's mysterious coldness and his avoidance of her, which she now knows to be intentional. She has consoled herself with a farfetched explanation. (Titus must be

SUMMARY AND CONCLUSION

jealous of Antiochus and, if he is jealous, he must still love her. Otway omits this.) But she must find Titus and end her misgivings and her agonizing doubts. She enters seeking Titus and finds, not Titus, but Antiochus, who, she had supposed, had already left Rome as he had announced that he intended to do. His presence now can only frustrate her and delay the explanation she so desperately needs. On seeing him she expresses surprise to find him still in Rome: "Et quoi, Seigneur! vous n'êtes point parti?" In the earlier editions the line read: "Enfin, Seigneur, vous n'êtes point parti" and this is of course the line which Otway is translating. The earlier reading does not convey unflattering surprise so unmistakably as the emended reading, but Antiochus' reply reveals that Bérénice's words have been accompanied by a *jeu de visage* betraying her disappointment at finding him when she was seeking Titus. Antiochus is stung by the look of disappointment on her face. Always sensitive to Bérénice's involuntary betrayals of her absorption in Titus and her indifference to him, he is now impelled to defend himself against the implication that he is lingering unnecessarily at Rome. He has been detained by Titus's command, he says. Thus, intending merely to defend himself, he has aggravated Bérénice's anxiety. He has revealed to her the fact that Titus, who is obviously avoiding her, seeks Antiochus' company. The chain explosion has begun.

These, I believe are the psychological implications of Racine's lines:

> BÉRÉNICE
> Et quoi, Seigneur! vous n'êtes point parti?
> ANTIOCHUS
> Madame, je vois bien que vous êtes déçue
> Et que c'étoit César que cherchoit votre vue.
> Mais n'accusez que lui, si malgré mes adieux
> De ma présence encor j'importune vos yeux.
> Peut-être en ce moment je serois dans Ostie,
> S'il ne m'eût de sa cour défendu la sortie.

Here is Otway's version of these lines:

> BER. My Lord, I see you are not gone;
> Perhaps 'tis me alone that you would shun.
> ANT. You came not here *Antiochus* to find,
> The Visit to another was design'd;
> Cesar: and 'tis on him the Blame must light,
> If now my Presence here offend your Sight.

They're his commands are guilty of the Sin.
It may be else I had at *Ostia* been.

Otway has interpolated "Perhaps 'tis me alone that you would shun," which can be interpreted only as coquetry on Berenice's part, a coquetry that is out of character and shocking considering the state of anxiety Berenice is in at the moment. From Antiochus' reply Otway has omitted the reference to Bérénice's facial expression revealing disappointment. Antiochus' lines become a reproof to Berenice for *pretending* to be looking for him. But how has she indicated that she means to leave that impression? And if she has pretended to be looking for him, how does Antiochus get the idea that his presence offends her sight? For Otway has retained Antiochus' reaction to the disappointment in Bérénice's face after cutting out the reference to her facial expression. I cannot discover in Otway's lines the psychological continuity that would prove that they are deliberate alteration rather than unwitting distortion of Racinian psychology. Otway had no clear idea of what was going on in the minds of Bérénice and Antiochus and his translation reflects his own confusion. This confusion is evident throughout the scene.

Otway comes much closer to Racine in the first two scenes between Titus and Berenice. They are indeed the only scenes which might possibly be called translation of Racine. (The term has been used by several critics in speaking of the relation of Otway's play to Racine's. Edmund Gosse, for one, says that the play owes so little to its English dress that it does not merit any comment as a work of Otway.) In the second scene, however, there are excisions and there is some loss of psychological precision. Otway does not render adequately certain lines which convey Titus's love for Bérénice and his despair at having to send her away, nor does he render the quality of tenderness of Bérénice's love for Titus. Titus's

> N'accablez point, Madame, un prince malheureux,
> Il ne faut point ici nous attendrir tous deux

is translated:

> O! stop the deluge, which so fiercely flows:
> This is no Time t'allay each others woes.

Titus's

SUMMARY AND CONCLUSION

> Mais il ne s'agit plus de vivre, il faut régner

becomes

> And now I would not a dispute maintain,
> Whether I lov'd [sic], but whether I must Reign.

One mistranslation of a characteristic Racinian metaphor robs the line of all the qualities with which both poets are often accredited—tenderness, poignancy, pathos. Bérénice, who asks nothing but to be near Titus, sees in his decision to banish her only gratuitous cruelty. She says:

> Pourquoi m'enviez-vous l'air que vous respirez?

Otway translates:

> Or why d'ye envy me the air I breath?

Did Otway prefer to have his Berenice accuse Titus of wanting to kill her (literally or figuratively?) or was he merely misled by cognates (envier-envy) into a sophomoric mistranslation?

The career of Racinian tragedy in England during the neo-classical period began and ended with an ironical contretemps. John Crowne's *Andromache* deserves mention only because of the circumstances attending Racine's début in England. The English play is composed of a verse translation of Act V, a mixture of prose and verse in Act IV, and a prose translation of the first three acts. After the play's failure on the stage and criticism from admirers of Racine, Crowne tells us (in his preface) that he has turned into prose a poor verse translation offered him by a "young gentleman" who admired Racine. He says nothing of the parts which he has left in heroic couplets. Internal evidence shows that Crowne merely completed a fragmentary verse translation by translating the remainder of the play directly from the French into prose. There are bits of the verse translation which deserve to be commended both for accuracy and for rather successful imitation of Racine's style. In fact, I should be willing to call one or two of the speeches in heroic couplets the best translation of Racine in English. The prose, on the other hand, is the kind of version of a French original which you might expect from a second-semester French student who has not yet reached the point when it dawns on him that the original has a meaning and that a translation needs to have any meaning at all, let alone the same meaning as the original. In his preface Crowne admits that the play is a poor thing but remarks contemptuously that the fault is Racine's since his own version has everything that was in the original verbatim. Here are two samples of this conscientious translation:

> HERMIONE
> Ah! je l'ai trop aimé pour ne le point haïr.
> And yet I fear I have loved him too well, ever to
>   hate him cordially.

Here we have the sophomoric method of substituting one's own mental bias for syntax. The following lines show the translator's ignorance of the value of tenses:

> CEPHISE
> Je croirois ses conseils, et je verrois Pyrrhus.
> Un regard confondroit Hermione et la Grèce . . .
> . . . I saw *Pyrrhus* and methought one regard mixt
>   *Hermione* and *Greece.*

As they say in the classroom, Crowne had not "had" the conditional. He would have been incapable of translating *Colomba,* let alone Racine.

The last translator, too, claims fidelity to the original. Indeed Sir Brooke Boothby tells us in the preface to his translation of *Britannicus* (1802) that a scrupulous fidelity to Racine's *Britannicus* is his only aim and the only merit which he claims for his piece. He knows that a chaste classical piece would have no chance of succeeding on the stage. He could have made the play acceptable to English audiences of the day if he had chosen to show the dénouement in action: the banquet, the poisoning of Britannicus, the death of Narcisse at the hands of an angry mob, and Junie fleeing to sanctuary with the Vestals. But his intention is to give to the reading public as exact a notion of classical tragedy as possible. The only two translations of Racine which are still being played, he says, do not give the English public any notion of what the originals are like. He is referring to Edmund Smith's *Phaedra and Hippolitus* and Ambrose Philips's *The Distrest Mother.* He is careful to point out the only excisions which he has made. He has cut out the jargon of gallantry in the rôle of Nero, he tells us.

Boothby, unlike Crowne, admired Racine. His admiration was qualified, however. His criterion was that of the *difficulté vaincue.* Racine does exceedingly well, he thinks, considering the handicaps

SUMMARY AND CONCLUSION

under which he labored: the unities of time and place and a language without accent and without compound epithets. Unlike Crowne, too, he is a competent linguist in that he apparently could at least extract the meaning of the original. Colloquial French eludes him as it had eluded his predecessors. But there are no evidences in his translation of ignorance of the printed language such as we find in Charles Johnson's translation of *Bajazet* or the earlier translation of *Britannicus*.

It is a surprise to find on examining this translation that Boothby has made a great many excisions and that he has failed everywhere to render adequately the psychological drama of the original. He eliminates all the lines in Racine which convey Néron's sadism and some lines which reveal Agrippine's motives. He abridges many scenes.

The style of this translation is different from that of any other translation of Racine but just as remote from the characteristic style of Racine as that of any of the other translations or adaptations. Boothby paraphrases Racine's dialogue in long, complex sentences characterized by over-subordination, suspensive word order, and logical connectives. Here is an example of Boothby's rendering of Racine's narrative style:

> AGRIPPINE
> Je vous nommai son gendre, et vous donnai sa fille.
> Silanus, qui l'amoit, s'en vit abandonné,
> Et marqua de son sang ce jour infortuné.
> Next I obtain'd Octavia for your wife,
> First to Silanus given; whose sudden death
> Made way for you.

In most of the dramatic scenes Boothby uses just such narrative style. For the most part his translation is a reader's summary of the substance of what Racine's personages say. He never reproduces the way they say it, and of course in Racine's dialogue a speaker often reveals his emotion without intending to, and he reveals it by following the pitch patterns and stress patterns of emotional speech. All emotion is lost in Boothby's labored narrative style.

Racine uses his characteristic *procédés* in the rôle of his Narcisse, but in a somewhat different way. Narcisse is Racine's only cool, deliberate villain. He plays upon Néron's vicious inclinations by insinuation and innuendo. He contrives to include in a mere statement of fact or a mere request for information what he wishes Néron to believe is his own reaction to the matter under discussion. These are the methods he uses, for instance, to goad Néron into a jealous fury against Britannicus. Néron has fallen in love with Junie. He must know if Britannicus is a threat to his love as he is to his power. He asks Narcisse:

> Dis-moi: Britannicus l'aime-t-il?
> NARCISSE
> Quoi? s'il l'aime
> Seigneur?
> [What? *Does* he *love* her? You amaze me. How could anyone have the slightest doubt that he loves her?]
> NÉRON
> Si jeune encor, se connoît-il lui même?
> D'un regard enchanteur connoît-il le poison?
> [Why shouldn't I doubt it? Britannicus is too *young*.]
> NARCISSE
> Seigneur, l'amour n'attend pas la raison.
> N'en doutez point, il l'aime. . . .
> Et peut-être déjà sait-il persuader.
> [Who knows? He may even have inspired love.]
> NÉRON
> Que dis-tu? Sur son coeur il auroit quelque empire?
> [Do you mean to tell me *she* loves *him*?]
> NARCISSE
> Je ne sais; mais, Seigneur, ce que je puis vous dire,
> Je l'ai vu quelquefois s'arracher de ces lieux,
> Le coeur plein d'un courroux qu'il cachoit à vos yeux,
> D'une cour qui le fuit pleurant l'ingratitude,
> Entre l'impatience et la crainte flottant:
> Il alloit voir Junie, et revenoit content.
> [Of course I don't *know*. I don't want to upset you by saying she *does* love him when I can't be absolutely certain. But I can say this: I have seen him many a time, etc.]

Here is Boothby's version of this dialogue:

> *Nero.* But say, Narcissus
> Think'st thou the boy Britannicus her lover?
> *Nar.* Oh yes, with all the fervour of his years,
> Tender, submissive to her least desires,
> He shares her griefs, and softens all her pains.
> Stung with some mark of insolent neglect,
> When anger unconceal'd [*sic*] has fired his breast,

SUMMARY AND CONCLUSION

> Soon, by her side, his passion sooth'd to peace,
> He has return'd with pleasure in his eyes.
> Her inexperienc'd heart, I fear, is his.

In the Néron-Narcisse scene which is the climax of the tragedy, the psychological *peripétie*, Boothby abandons his method of résumé and follows the dialogue line by line. But he manages to eliminate the innuendo from Narcisse's speeches and it is this innuendo that causes Nero's rebellion against his mother. The "monstre" is unleashed.

Of all translators and adapters, Sir Brooke Boothby is the only one who set out to translate Racine with the intention of revealing to the English the beauties—such as they were to him—of Racine's classical manner. For him, it would seem, judging from his translation, that the peculiar essence of a Racinian tragedy was a dénouement related rather than shown in action, a negative quality and one which Racine shared with many another French dramatist. Boothby's admiration of this negative quality is inspired, it appears, not so much by love of Racine as by scorn for the sensationalism in vogue at the moment on the English stage.

I can see in the failure of English adapters and translators to present a single Racinian tragedy intact to English audiences or to English readers little evidence of a clash of the French and the English national genius (Canfield), or of French classicism with English romanticism (Charlanne) or even of a conflict of tradition (Eccles). The features of Racinian tragedy which adapters rejected and those which baffled them are the very features of Racinian tragedy which are departures from French traditions of the tragic genre: the substitution of dramatic irony for the suspense and surprise recommended by most French Aristotelians; psychological naturalism in the portrayal of character,[5] which, combined with Racine's own peculiar variant of the traditional magnanimity of the tragic hero, is the stuff of which Racine's psychological tragedy is made; dialogue which does not directly express the emotion or the motives of the speaker but betrays them rather (a kind of dialogue recommended by La Mesnardière as ideal for "la poésie théâtrale" but an ideal realized only by Racine); the substitution of psychological events for external incidents in the tragic plot and in

---

[5] "La Tragédie de Racine peut être considérée comme la rencontre d'un genre littéraire traditionellement nouri de sublime avec un nouvel esprit naturaliste délibérément hostile à l'idée même du sublime." (Benichou, *op. cit.*, p. 131.)

the drama; the dramatic movement, independent of external events, which is the result of the protagonists' reactions to one another.

Detailed comparison of English adaptations with the originals reveals incomprehension as perhaps the most important cause of the distortion of Racinian psychology to be found in the English versions. This incomprehension is due in some measure in certain adaptations to ignorance of the French language. Distortion of Racine is then to some extent merely an unfortunate accident. Some of the adapters could not read French. But it would hardly be an exaggeration to say that all Racine's imitators, interpreters, or exploiters translated Racinian tragedy without reading it. In reading Racine's dialogue in one scene, they did not have in mind an image of the total array of psychological possibilities suggested in preceding scenes. In reading one speech, they had no image of its psychological relation to a preceding speech. In translating a line, even, they were unaware of its psychological relation to a line preceding it or following it. They lacked the ability to imagine the psychological context of Racinian dialogue, to reconstruct from the clues furnished by the words the sequence of emotions in the dramatic crescendo. They did not perceive clearly the quality of the emotional tension between the speakers and they could not imagine the interplay of emotions implicit in the words spoken. In short, they lacked that kind of dramatic imagination which depends on insight, on psychological penetration.

If this lack of penetration is more than fortuitous and individual, it may conceivably be attributed to the absence of a tradition in England. In France, in the milieu in which Racinian tragedy appeared, a long tradition of psychological curiosity and of a method of psychological investigation had fostered the development of the kind of imagination necessary to the understanding of psychological tragedy and psychological drama. Racine's psychological naturalism was an innovation *in the tragic genre,* but the psychological principles on which he bases his tragic plots, principles which eluded his English translators, were current coin in France. They had been propounded by the *moralistes.* La Rochefoucauld's maxims were the product of a parlor game in the salon of Madame de Sablé and may be considered one manifestation of the psychological curiosity of the age. If the *mondaines* were revolted by "l'âme laide" that La Rochefoucauld attributed to man, they nevertheless understood his theories. The method of psychological in-

SUMMARY AND CONCLUSION

vestigation was that of Racine's personages themselves. Everybody was aware that a man's acts are not motivated by the sentiments which he thinks impel him or which he professes to have. In the literature of the age which reflects actuality most directly, novels and courtesy books, there is evidence that the *mondains* and the *mondaines* cultivated the habit of watching involuntary gesture and facial expression, and of listening for a significant tone of voice in order to penetrate the secret thoughts, feelings, and motives of the people with whom they conversed. Boileau recommended this method of psychological investigation for the comic poet:

> La nature, féconde en bizarres portraits,
> Dans chaque âme est marquée à de différents traits;
> Un geste la découvre, un rien la fait paraître:
> Mais tout esprit n'a pas des yeux pour la connaître.

Before the advent of Racinian tragedy, Molière had introduced into the comic genre psychological drama of the same kind as Racine's. One professor of politeness, the Chevalier de Méré, considers penetration a perquisite of *honnêteté*. Some of his remarks are enlightening. He says:

> Il faut observer que tout parle à sa mode, un nuage espais fait sentir l'orage avant que le tonnerre gronde, et rien ne se passe dans le coeur ni dans l'esprit qu'il n'en aparoisse quelque marque sur le visage ou dans le ton de la voix, ou dans les actions, et quand on s'accoûtume à ce langage, il n'y a rien de si caché ni de si broüillé qu'on ne découvre et qu'on ne desmesle. . . .
> Il faut observer tout ce qui se passe dans le coeur et dans l'esprit des personnes qu'on entretient, et s'accoutumer de bonne heure à connoistre les sentimens et les pensées par des signes presque imperceptibles. Cette connoissance qui se trouve obscure et difficile pour ceux qui n'y sont pas faits, s'éclaircit et se rend aisée à la longue. C'est une science qui s'apprend comme une langue étrangère, où d'abord on ne comprend que peu de chose. Mais quand on l'aime et qu'on l'estudie, on y fait incontinent quelque progrez.

For anyone well versed in this science, Racine's conversations under a chandelier are exciting drama. For those ignorant of this science, Racinian tragedy is so much verbiage. English adapters and translators had not learned the science.

INDEX

INDEX

Achille (Achilles): 83–90, 140–46, 148, 150, 306, 322
Achilles: 82–92, 139–43, 146, 147, 300, 301, 317, 318
Acomat: 70–73, 110, 156, 161, 164, 170, 171, 173, 175, 182, 187, 311
Addison, Joseph: 59, 78, 93, 120 n., 128 n., 132, 133, 218 n., 226 n., 243 n., 274–79
Aeneid: 79
Agamemnon: 83, 84, 87, 90, 140, 144, 146, 148–52, 233, 300, 322
Agrippine (Agrippina): 193–95, 197, 198, 200, 201, 203–206, 208, 209, 333, 335
Alexandre: 263 n., 272 n.
All for Love: 266, 267, 273
Almeria: 59, 61–67, 69, 73, 74, 76, 77, 79, 244, 277
Amurat: 70–74, 156, 161, 164, 170, 171, 173, 176, 177, 179, 311
Andromache: 198, 210, 215, 331, 332; see also Crowne, John
Andromaque: 5, 13, 43, 119–31, 133–38, 183, 254, 261, 266, 305, 314–17, 323, 324, 326, 331, 332; anonymous translation of, 3, 7–11, 91
Andromaque (Andromache): 6 n., 10, 12, 13, 15, 16, 119, 120, 122, 124, 125, 127–32, 134, 135, 138, 183, 278, 287 n., 305, 306, 323, 324
Antigone (Antigona): 186–89, 306
Antiochus: 20–25, 27–56, 326–31
Aricie: 93, 96–99, 102–103 n., 103–105, 107, 113, 115, 259 n., 265 n., 302
Aristotle: 80, 218–19 n., 231, 233, 238, 240, 241, 242 n., 247 n., 250, 257 and n., 258, 266 n., 268 n., 272 n., 275 n., 288–90
Atalide (Atalida): 70–75, 100, 156–82, 253, 254, 287 n., 307–12, 320, 325
Athalie: 254
Aubignac, Abbé Hédelin d': 80 n., 218 n.,
223–25, 226 n., 237 n., 241 n., 255, 263, 283, 284, 295–98, 322
Aureng-Zebe: 293

Barry, Elizabeth: 93, 293, 303
Bajazet: 57–59, 66, 67, 70–75, 97, 99, 100, 102, 111, 117, 118, 154–83, 254, 263, 273, 280, 281, 292, 299, 301, 304, 306–12
Bajazet: 70–75, 156–83, 253, 287 n., 293, 302, 306–12, 320, 325
Belsham, W.: 95 n.
Bénichou, Paul: 260 n., 335 n.
Bérénice: 19, 26–56, 58, 80 n., 243, 254, 257 n., 266, 273, 325–31
Bérénice: 19–25, 27–56, 326–31
Blackmore, Sir Richard: 77, 79, 218 n.
Boileau-Despréaux: 218 n., 224 n., 238–39 n., 255, 268, 274, 275, 282, 284, 337
Boothby, Sir Brooke: 198–210, 332–35
Boyer, Abel: 82–92, 139–43, 146, 147, 299
Britannicus: 192–210, 254, 332–35; Ozell's translation of, 192–98, 206, 333; Boothby's translation of, 198–210, 332–35
Britannicus: 192–96, 199, 200, 204–207, 209, 210, 253, 287 n., 334
Brunetière, Ferdinand: 91, 200, 297
Brunot, Ferdinand: 220, 221
Burrhus: 192–97, 199, 204, 207
Burrows, Dorothy: 267 n.
Bussy-Rabutin, Roger: 255
Byssche, Edward: 226 n., 229, 230, 295

Canfield, Dorothea: 4–6, 32 n., 33 n., 51, 52, 96, 118 n., 119, 121, 136, 137, 154–56, 335
Cato: 95, 305
Charlanne, Louis: 31, 33 n., 81 n., 91, 236, 335
Cheek, Thomas: 82, 91, 92, 299
Cinna: 240, 258 n.

341

INDEX

Clytemnestre: 83, 84 n., 90, 91, 145, 146, 148, 151, 152, 322, 323
Collier, Jeremy: 218 n., 226 n., 227–29
Colloquial style: Racine's, rejected by the English, 9, 54, 55, 87–89, 147, 193, 198, 201, 202, 205, 206, 209, 260, 332, 333; Racine's use of, 18, 54, 55, 87, 89, 91, 146, 147, 193, 198, 201–203, 297, 298; Philips' use of, 118–20, 126
Comparison between the Two Stages, A: 92
Congreve, William: 73–82, 112, 218 n., 227–29, 244, 291–93, 298, 299, 301, 303, 305
Corneille, Pierre: 14 n., 38 n., 80 n., 112, 158, 159, 200, 224 n., 223–35, 240, 246, 248, 251, 253, 255–59, 263, 275, 280, 284, 286–90, 292, 306, 319
Coverley, Sir Roger de: 132, 278
Cratander: 107 n., 112
Crawford, J. P. Wickersham: 57–59
Créon: 187–90, 306
Crowne, John: 3–5, 8, 11–20, 22–25, 261, 266, 331–33
Cymbeline: 80 n., 292

Dacier, André: 218 n., 225 n., 240, 257, 258 n., 259, 268 n., 270 n., 282, 284
D'Aubignac: *see* Aubignac
Dennis, John: 92, 97, 218 n., 220 n., 225–26 n., 247, 268–74, 280, 283, 305
Destruction of Jerusalem, The, Part II: 19
Distrest Mother, The: 6–10, 15, 95, 118–39, 183, 184, 210, 276, 278, 279, 305, 312, 314–17, 323, 324, 332
Dorimant: 132, 184, 185, 190
Drake, James: 245
Drama in English versions: impaired by excision, 15, 16, 50, 121, 122, 168; impaired by interpolation, 33, 45–49, 168, 178-81; replaced by static declamation, 77, 113, 114, 127–29, 144–46, 150–53, 299–301; impaired by stylistic change, 89, 147, 148, 197, 198, 205–10, 321–24, 333, 334; *see also* Racinian drama
Dryden, John: 31, 92, 100 n., 134, 218 n., 219 n., 220 n., 225 n., 229, 240–43, 249, 252, 253, 261–68, 273, 290, 293
Dutton, George B.: 234, 237 n.

Eccles, F. Y.: 32, 33 n., 52, 58, 96, 119, 121, 154–56, 285, 286, 335
Electra: 79, 232, 289, 290

English language, English opinion of: 219, 288
English tragedy, English opinion of: 217, 219 and n., 283, 284, 288
Eriphile: 81, 83–89, 140–47, 149, 150, 254, 300, 306, 317–19
Esther: 80 n., 267, 270
Eteocles: 188–90
Euripides: 95, 96, 98, 99, 102–104, 118, 139, 216, 222, 235, 258, 270, 271, 305

Faguet, Émile: 117, 120, 131 n.
Fatal Legacy, The: 133, 184–91, 306
Filmer, Edward: 245, 246, 293
Fletcher, John: 237, 264
French classical doctrine: as barrier to Racine in England, 81, 286; relation of, to English classical doctrine, 215–20, 230, 233–43, 250–52, 284
French critics: English opinion of, 81, 217, 218, 259, 288; influence on English of, 234, 235, 239–42, 250–53, 288, 294
French dramatists, English opinion of: 27, 217, 219, 288
French language, English opinion of: 217, 219, 281, 282, 288, 298
French tragedy, English opinion of: 217–19, 240, 241, 246, 261, 262, 273, 280, 283, 288

Genest, John: 95
Gildon, Charles: 57, 78, 153 n., 225, 274, 281–84, 295
Gonsalez: 60, 66–68, 76, 187, 244, 245, 293, 306
Gosse, Edmund: 33 n., 58 n., 330
Green, Clarence C.: 238–39 n.
Guenièvre: 38
Hamlet: 63, 79, 245, 273
Heinsius, Daniel: 218 n., 257 n.
Hémon: 185, 186, 188; *see also* Phocias
Héraclius: 80 n., 233, 251, 258 n., 287 n., 290
Hermione: 4, 6 and n., 7, 9 n., 10–12, 17, 18, 121, 124, 125, 127–30, 134, 135, 253, 254, 266 n., 287 n., 293, 315–17, 320, 323, 325, 332
Hippolitus (Seneca): 96
Hippolyte (Hippolytus, Hippolytus): 95–116, 253, 258 n., 259 n., 262, 263, 265, 266, 271, 301–304, 313, 314, 325
Hippolytus (Euripides): 96, 102, 118, 259 n., 270, 271
Horace: 218 n., 257 n., 266 n., 288

342

INDEX

Iago: 246, 294
Iphigenia (Dennis): 273
Iphigenia (Euripides): 259 n.
Iphigenia in Aulis: see Achille; Achilles
Iphigénie: 81–92, 139–54, 254, 270 n., 271, 273, 299, 300, 305, 306, 317–19
Iphigénie (Iphigenia): 83, 84, 86, 88–90, 142–45, 147–51, 258, 259 n., 300, 306, 317–19, 322
Irene: 95, 305
Ismena: 100, 101, 103 n., 112, 113, 301; *see also* Aricie

Jocasta: 186, 187, 189
Johnson, Charles: 82 n., 139–62, 164–72, 174–83, 187, 299–301, 305–13, 317–19, 322, 323, 325, 333
Johnson, Samuel: 62 n., 78 n., 96, 112 n., 264
Juliet: 75
Junie (Junia): 193, 195–97, 199, 203–207, 210, 332, 334

King Lear: 243 n., 248–50, 276, 284, 291, 305

La Bruyère, Jean de: 255
La Mesnardière, Jules de: 80, 221–23, 225, 226 n., 230–34, 236–38, 242, 245, 247, 250, 251, 265, 266 n., 284, 288, 289, 291, 294–98, 335
Lancelot: 38
Lanson, Gustave: 80 n., 287 n.
La Rochefoucauld, François VI, Duc de: 242 n., 279, 309, 311
Le Bidois, G.: 124 n., 190 n., 200, 297
Le Bossu, René: 218–19 n., 224 n., 226 n., 238, 241, 251, 259, 268 n., 284
Lee, Nathaniel: 213
Lemaître, Jules: 108
Longinus: 241, 266 n.
Lycon: 100, 101, 105, 109–11, 116, 182, 187, 188, 303, 304; *see also* Oenone

Macbeth: 66, 273
Manuel: 59–61, 64–68, 73–77, 244
May, Georges: 260 n., 287 n.
Médée: 258 n.
Melodrama: introduced in English versions, 75–76, 83, 84, 108, 110–13, 120, 139, 140, 181, 188–91, 201, 301, 304–306; in English classical theory, 77, 78, 81, 93–95, 102, 233–36, 239, 240, 243–46, 248–51, 260, 276, 286–91, 298,
304, 305; confused with tragedy, 79, 80, 83, 247, 291; in French classical theory, 80, 230–34, 252, 253, 255–59, 290
Menelaus: 83, 150, 151
Méré, Chevalier de: 337
Mistranslation: *see* Paraphrase and mistranslation
Mithridate: 102 n., 254, 266 n.
Molière: 281 n., 337
Mornet, Daniel: 34, 80 n.
Mourning Bride, The: 57–70, 73–83, 112, 150, 182, 187, 189, 227, 244, 273, 276, 284, 291, 292, 298, 299, 301, 303–305

Narcisse (Narcissus): 193–97, 206–10, 332–35
Néron (Nero): 193–201, 203–10, 287 n., 332–35
Nicoll, Allardyce: 6 n., 96, 118 n., 153 n.
Nicomède: 258 n.

Octavie (Octavia): 192, 199, 202, 204, 205, 333
Oedipe: 258 n.
Oedipus: 273, 289
Oenone: 97–99, 103, 104, 109, 110 n., 113, 115, 116, 303, 313
Oldisworth, William: 94
Oldmixon, John: 218 n., 228, 273
Oreste: 4, 6 and n., 7, 9 n., 10, 11, 15, 17, 18, 119 n., 121, 123, 125–27, 130, 131 n., 134, 135, 137, 138, 278, 314–17
Orphan, The: 31, 247, 251
Osmyn: 60, 61, 63–69, 73, 74, 76, 77, 79, 227, 244
Othello: 235, 236, 244, 248, 291
Othello: 294
Otway, Thomas: 19, 26, 28–43, 45–56, 58, 59, 215, 229, 247, 273, 324–31; *see also Titus and Bérénice*
Ozell, John: 192–98, 206

Paraphrase and mistranslation: 11–13, 14, 16, 17, 24, 47, 51, 52, 55, 85, 141, 154, 160, 161, 166, 175, 177, 178, 181, 196–98, 200–201, 204, 207, 331–33
Phaedra: Smith's, 270, 280, 281, 301, 303, 304, 318; Seneca's 303; *see also Phèdre*; Phèdre
Phaedra and Hippolitus: 93–103, 105–18, 120 n., 182, 187, 276, 279, 282, 332
Phèdre: 43, 94–110, 113–17, 198, 238 n., 250, 255, 258, 259 n., 261, 265, 270 n., 276, 281, 299, 301, 304, 305, 312, 313

INDEX

Phèdre: 93, 95, 97–116, 254, 255, 258 n., 265, 271, 287, 299, 301, 302, 304, 313, 314, 317, 325
Phèdre et Hippolyte: 102 n.
Philips, Ambrose: 6–10, 56, 95, 118–39, 183, 184, 200, 210, 226 n., 279, 305, 306, 314–17, 322–24, 332
Phocias: 186, 188, 189
Polyeucte: 258 n.
Polynices: 186, 188, 190
Pompey: 240, 275 n.
Pradon, Jacques: 102 n., 238 n., 265
Preciosity: 34; in themes of *la poésie mourante*, 34–37; in *précieux* metaphor, 35, 36, 40, 50, 77, 199, 326
Prior, Matthew: 95, 112 n.
Pyrrhus: 4, 6 and n., 7, 9 n., 10–12, 15–17, 119, 121, 122, 124, 125, 127–31, 134, 136, 198, 278 and n., 306, 320, 323–25, 332

Racinian characters: realistic motivation of, 17, 21, 22, 35, 38, 48, 103, 104, 115, 116, 126, 138, 142, 158, 164–66, 169, 170, 172, 173, 199, 200, 205, 303, 307, 311, 316; secret motives of, revealed, 17, 22; complexity of, 34, 85, 107, 126, 142, 143, 309, 317; morbid intensity of, 85, 143
Racinian characters in English versions: 327, 328, 333; simplified and conventionalized, 34–43, 56, 85–87, 107, 109–11, 127, 142, 143, 168, 179, 182, 187–89, 293, 302, 303, 305, 306, 318, 319, 326, 327; motivation of, altered, 37, 48, 86, 101, 106, 107, 109, 110, 115, 116, 125–27, 138, 142, 143, 156–74, 183, 199, 200, 204–206, 302–304, 307–13, 316–18
Racinian drama: 121; crescendo of emotion in, 15, 16, 22, 43–45, 77; emotional tension between speakers in, 15, 22; interplay of emotion in, 15, 16, 22, 43, 45; defined, 121, 122, 296, 321, 328; relation of, to style, 296, 321, 323
Racinian genre: considered "irregular" by French critics, 80 n.; anti-heroic, 253, 254; anti-melodramatic, 253, 254; antipodal to English classical ideal, 253, 254, 260, 294; opposed by French classical theorists, 254–59; incidents replaced by psychological events in, 287; classical rules violated in, 287

Racinian style: energy of, 7; importance of verbs in, 7, 89, 123, 203; economy of, 7, 313; irony in, 18, 88, 124; interrogation in, 87, 88, 124, 146–48, 202; metaphor in, 116, 117, 123, 124, 144, 331; concentration and evocativeness of, 123, 124, 203; simile in, 190 and n.; psychological precision of, 195, 196, 203, 313, 314; stychomathia in, 200; symmetrical Alexandrines of, 200; Cornelian manner in, 200, 201; relation of, to drama, 296, 297, 320, 321; dramatic quality of, 296–98; rhetoric of passion in, 297; poetic quality of, 297, 298; *see also* Colloquial style; Style of English versions
Racinian tragic plot: peripeteia in, 104, 113, 121, 173, 174, 301, 302; altered in English versions, 110–12, 312; moral recognition in, 113, 168–70, 302, 310; discovery in, 113, 301; psychological events rather than incidents in, 156, 157, 182, 296; dénouement in, 301, 302
Ralph, James: 219 n., 251 n.
Rapin, René: 215–21, 225, 226 n., 240–42, 253, 255, 259, 268, 284, 288
Realism, psychological (naturalism), rejected by the English: 17, 21, 24, 25, 35, 114–16, 138, 149, 150, 158–61, 164, 166, 167, 169, 170, 196, 260, 279, 288, 303, 307, 308, 311, 312, 316, 317, 320
Richardson, Samuel: 133–36, 138
Robe, Mrs. J.: 184–91, 306
Rodogune: 38 n., 69, 80 n., 233, 234, 253, 258 n., 287 n., 290, 292
Romeo and Juliet: 10, 62, 64, 78
Roscommon: 281, 282
Roxane (Roxana): 70–75, 100, 155–83, 266 n., 287 n., 293, 299, 302, 304, 306–12, 320, 325
Rymer, Thomas: 58, 215, 217–21, 225, 226 n., 230, 234–38, 240–44, 246 n., 247, 248, 251, 261, 264–66, 268 n., 270, 282, 288, 289, 293, 294

Saint-Évremond, Charles de: 13 n., 218 n., 224 n., 239, 256, 263, 268 n.
Seneca: 95, 96, 99, 101–105, 107, 117, 118, 129 n., 191, 222, 224 n., 226 n., 283, 303, 305, 313, 317
Shakespeare, William: 31, 78, 79, 80 n., 100 n., 120 n., 210, 218 n., 225 n., 229, 237, 245, 249, 251, 264–67, 276, 291, 292, 305

INDEX

Smith, Edmund: 93–103, 105–18, 120 n., 188, 189, 210, 276, 279–81, 293, 302–305, 312–14, 318, 332
Sophocles: 79, 216, 232, 235, 289
Spanish Friar, The: 249, 290
Steele, Richard: 81 n., 132, 274, 279, 280, 283
Style: French ideal of, 221–25, 294, 295; French ideal of, rejected by English, 225–27; English ideal of, 227–30, 298; *see also* Racinian style; Style of English versions; Preciosity
Style of English versions: metaphor in, 9, 116, 117, 123, 150, 192, 195, 196, 206, 314; Racinian interrogation rejected in, 18, 87, 88, 124, 125, 146–48, 322–24; irony lost in, 18, 88, 123, 124; hyperbole in, 77, 126, 191; simile in, 86, 117, 127–29, 131, 144–46, 151, 152, 189–91; lavish use of adjectives in, 88–91, 121, 123, 147, 148, 182, 183, 190, 191, 203, 227, 332; visual imagery in, 116, 117, 198; exclamation in, 125, 137; *sententiae* in, 150, 151, 226; conceit in, 182; *see also* Colloquial style; Style; Racinian style
Sultaness, The: 154–62, 164–72, 174–83, 187, 299, 307–13, 324, 333
Summers, Montague: 32 n., 58 n., 78 n.

Tate, Nahun: 243 n., 248, 252, 276, 284, 291, 305
Thébaïde, La: 133, 184–91, 306

Thésée (Theseus): 93, 97, 98, 101–104, 107, 108, 110, 111, 113, 116, 265 n., 301–303
Thierry–Maulnier: 297
Tite et Bérénice: 237 n.
Titus: 19–25, 27–31, 33–47, 49–56, 326–31
Titus and Bérénice: 19, 26, 28–43, 45–56, 215, 325–31; *see also* Otway, Thomas
Titus Andronicus: 79
Tragedy: lost in English versions, 111–13, 116, 117, 160, 169–71, 174, 182, 183, 301–304, 307–14, 316, 320; Racine's sense of, 162, 169–71, 319, 320
Trapp, Joseph: 226 n., 251 n.
Troades: 129 n., 224 n.
Turnell, Martin: 180

Ulysse: 83, 84, 90, 150

Venice Preserved: 31, 273
Venus and Adonis: 100 n.
Victim, The: 82 n., 139–53, 299, 300, 312, 317–19, 322
Villars, l'Abbé de: 257 n.
Virgil: 134, 216

Ward, A. W.: 58 n.
White, Arthur Franklin: 4–6

Zara: 60, 61, 63–69, 73, 74, 76, 77, 79, 228, 244, 293, 299, 303

www.ingramcontent.com/pod-product-compliance
Lightning Source LLC
Chambersburg PA
CBHW020636230426
43665CB00008B/191